Francis Place

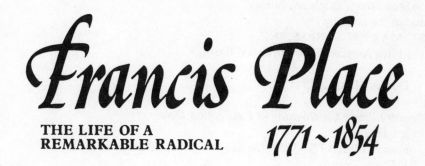

Francis Place
THE LIFE OF A REMARKABLE RADICAL
1771~1854

DUDLEY MILES

THE HARVESTER PRESS · SUSSEX

ST. MARTIN'S PRESS · NEW YORK

First published in Great Britain in 1988 by
THE HARVESTER PRESS LIMITED
16 Ship Street, Brighton, Sussex
and in the USA by
ST. MARTIN'S PRESS, INC.
175 Fifth Avenue, New York, NY 10010

© Dudley Miles, 1988

British Library Cataloguing in Publication Data
Miles, Dudley
    Francis Place 1771–1854: the life of a remarkable radical.
    1. Place, Francis
    I. Title
    362'.92'4   DA536.P7
    ISBN 0-7108-1225-6

Library of Congress Cataloging-in-Publication Data
Miles, Dudley
    Francis Place, 1771–1854: the life of a remarkable
    radical/Dudley Miles.
        p.   cm.
    Bibliography: p.
    Includes index.
    ISBN 0-312-01953-X: $30.00 (est.)
        1. Place, Francis, 1771–1854. 2. Radicals—Great Britain—
    Biography. 3. Birth control—Social aspects—Great Britain—
    History. I. Title.
HN400.R3P576 1988   87-35324
363.9'6'0941—dc19   CIP

Typeset in Times 10/12 by Quality Phototypesetting Ltd, Bristol

Printed in Great Britain by Mackays of Chatham Ltd, Kent

To my Parents,
Robert and Vera Miles
and
Jonathan, Jean, Simon and Angela

Contents

Illustrations

1. Francis Place. Photogravure by Walker and Boutall from a portrait by G.P. Healy in 1843 (From *The Life of Francis Place 1771–1854,* by Graham Wallas, 1898).
2. Twelfth-Day (from *Hone's Every Day Book,* 1825, vol. 1, p. 24).
3. Place to Mrs Place, 24 August 1811 (Add. Mss. 35, 143, f. 201v).
4. Westminster Hustings, 1818, by I.R. Cruikshank (from *The Poll Book, for . . . Westminster,* 1818).
5. *Rump Chronicle,* no. 3, Whig mock newspaper issued during the Westminster Election, 1819 (Add. Mss. 27,842, pt.3, f.593).
6. Election songs for Hobhouse, 1819 (Add. Mss. 27,842, pt.3, f.531v).
7. Caricature of George IV by George Cruikshank (from *The Queen's Matrimonial Ladder,* by William Hone, 1820).
8. Ricardo to Place, 9 September 1821 (Seligman Collection, Columbia University).
9. 'To the Married of Both Sexes' (Place Coll., Set 61, part 2 of 1 vol., p. 43).

Abbreviations

Add. Mss.	British Library, Additional Manuscripts.
Autobiography	*The Autobiography of Francis Place (1771–1854),* edited with an introduction and notes by Mary Thale (Cambridge University Press, Cambridge, 1972).
HO	Public Records Office, Home Office Papers.
LCS	London Corresponding Society.
LCS Papers	*Selections from the Papers of the London Corresponding Society 1792–1799,* edited with an introduction and notes by Mary Thale (Cambridge University Press, Cambridge, 1983).
LMI	London Mechanics' Institute.
LWMA	London Working Men's Association.
MACLA	Metropolitan Anti-Corn Law Association.
MPRA	Metropolitan Parliamentary Reform Association.
NCSU	National Complete Suffrage Union.
NPU	National Political Union.
NUWC	National Union of the Working Classes.
PC	Public Records Office, Privy Council Papers.
PCS	Parliamentary Candidates Society.
Place Coll.	British Library, Place Collection.
SCI	Society for Constitutional Information.
TS	Public Records Office, Treasury Solicitors Papers.
WLLA	West London Lancasterian Association.
WMA	Working Men's Association.

Preface

This book has taken ten years to write, owing to the variety of Place's activities and the quantity of his papers in the British Library. Going through the 290 odd volumes was an arduous but fascinating task.

I should like to thank Professor Albert Goodwin for reading Chapter 3 before publication. I have also received helpful information and advice from the late Professor W.H. Chaloner, Dr John Dinwiddy, Dr Anne-Lise Head-König, Margaret Jackson-Roberts, Dr Dorothy Owen, Dr Alice Prochaska, Betty Shane, E.P. Thompson and Professor E.A. Wrigley. My parents and my brother read the typescript, and their comments have considerably improved it.

I am grateful to the Cambridge University Press for permission to quote from Place's *Autobiography,* edited by Mary Thale.

1   Introduction

Few men have achieved as much as Francis Place without becoming public figures. He was not an MP and he never held any important office. The 'Radical Tailor of Charing Cross' was excluded from polite society — any upper-class hostess would have been horrified if her husband had committed the *faux pas* of inviting a tradesman to dinner. In his own time he was well known to politicians, radicals and trade unionists, but his name was seldom mentioned in newspapers. Yet he played an important role in British history in the early nineteenth century.

The most important of Place's many achievements was the founding of the birth control movement. He was the first man openly to advocate contraception as a means of preventing an excessive growth of population. He wanted to see the standard of living of the working people raised, and he believed that this was impossible without some restraint on the number of births, since otherwise the population would grow too fast, and then a surplus of labour would drive wages down to subsistence level. However, he opposed moral restraint (delayed marriage), which was then the accepted solution to the problem. Happily married with fifteen children (all born before he learnt about birth control) he considered moral restraint neither practicable nor desirable.

In his *Illustrations and Proofs of the Principle of Population,* published in 1822, he urged the use of 'physical means' to prevent a married woman from having too many children, and in the following year he launched the world's first birth control movement by circulating anonymous handbills which briefly explained contraception and justified it on economic and medical grounds. For a short time in 1824–25 his handbills achieved an extensive circulation, but they aroused such opposition that by mid-1826 his campaign was dead. Religious opinion held that, even within marriage, sex was only acceptable for the purpose of procreating children, so the idea of physical means to prevent conception was considered immoral and unnatural, and Place was the only 'respectable' man who dared to face the vicious slander incurred by advocating it. However, pamphlets in its favour were soon published by converts such as Richard Carlile, the leading campaigner for atheism in the 1820s, R.D. Owen, a son of Robert Owen, and Charles Knowlton, an American physician. By the 1830s advocacy of birth control had a place on the political map, and low key propaganda by the circulation of pamphlets continued until the leading freethinkers, Charles Bradlaugh and Annie Besant, were prosecuted in 1877 for reprinting Knowlton's pamphlet. Their acquittal led to an explosion of propaganda for contraception. In the west, overpopulation is no longer considered a danger precisely because Place's solution has been adopted, and it is increasingly recognised that a reversal of the population explosion in the Third World is one of the prerequisites of raising living standards without causing a catastrophic increase in environmental pollution. The movement which owes its origin to Francis Place is now crucial for reasons which he could not have imagined.

However, until recent years the origin of the birth control movement has been outside the scope of 'respectable' history, and Place is best known for securing the legalisation of trade unions in 1824. This was the result of a ten-year campaign of letters to the press, private persuasion of MPs and other influential men, and petitions to Parliament. At first he had little success because the middle and upper classes opposed legalisation, and working men did not believe that it was possible. However, he was no more put off by discouragement than he was by abuse, and by the end of the 1810s had gained important converts among economists, influential MPs and leading newspapers. In 1824 he secured a parliamentary select committee to examine the subject through his leading ally in the House of Commons, Joseph Hume. Behind the scenes, Place managed the committee and drafted the report and consequent parliamentary bill, persuading supporters not to speak in the debates as the bill went through the two Houses, in order to avoid arousing opposition. The result was that the bill passed almost unnoticed. The following year his bill was amended: the position of trade unions was weakened by a vague clause against molestation and a restrictive definition of trade unionism, but working men retained the right to organise and strike.

Place's background made his achievements the more remarkable. The son of a prosperous householder, he experienced desperate poverty as a journeyman breeches-maker in the 1790s. His sufferings and the misery he saw around him made this the formative decade in forging his allegiance and purpose in life. Loyalty to the working classes, and bitter resentment of the contempt shown for them by the upper classes, became dominant in his outlook. For the rest of his life he strove to serve the working people, and would never join any project unless he thought that it would help them. He gained his political education as a member of the London Corresponding Society (LCS), the chief English Jacobin society during the period of the French Revolution. The LCS taught him to believe in manhood suffrage and reinforced the determination he had learnt from books to base his ideas and actions on reason, a principle which led him to reject religion as unproveable.

He also learnt to exercise some control over his hot temper, although he was always a man few dared to cross. An unquenchable self-confidence could sometimes make him pompous and self-important in the face of upper-class snobbery, but it was combined with a talent for business which enabled him to escape from poverty. In the 1790s the fears aroused by the French Revolution made radicalism an unpopular cause, and when it was suppressed by a wave of arrests at the end of the decade, Place dropped out of politics for a few years to start building up a prosperous business as a tailor. In order to succeed he had to adopt the 'Victorian' values of respectability and prudence (which pre-dated Victoria's reign by forty years), but he was always torn between the outlook of the eighteenth century and the nineteenth. In later years, he would point out how gambling and improvidence had brought his father and many of his contemporaries to ruin, yet at the same time he would remember his licentious youth with nostalgia, and secretly look forward to the adoption of free love.

By 1805 his shop was securely established, and in 1807 he played a key role in the election of the radical hero Sir Francis Burdett for the constituency of Westminster. This success led to a revival of the radical movement, and made Westminster its focus for the next decade. Place was the dominant figure in the 'Westminster Committee' in spite of frequent quarrels with his associates. By the late 1810s Place had made enough money to be able to hand over his tailor's shop to his son and concentrate on politics and writing. He had become a close friend of Jeremy Bentham and James Mill, and cooperated with David Ricardo in attempts to disentangle the true state of government finances from the contradictory published accounts. The library over Place's tailor's shop in Charing Cross (now Whitehall) was frequented, he observed, rather in the manner of a coffee shop. It was a radical headquarters, where MPs, middle-class radicals and working men came to exchange advice and information. He provided an alternative civil service for MPs, radicals and lobbyists, doing extensive research, drafting parliamentary bills and advising on parliamentary tactics. His reputation for industry and integrity ensured that he was always overwhelmed with demands for help, and he became an expert on many subjects, ranging from libel law and the restrictions on the press, to government finances, the law on the export of machinery, the law on debt and the restrictions on the hackney carriage trade. Even Tory ministers were willing to listen to his advice, and when Robert Peel reformed the criminal law in the 1820s, he adopted many alterations of detail which Place suggested through his ministerial contacts.

Much of Place's time was taken up in advising working men on setting up trade unions, negotiating with their employers, organising strikes, and seeking legislative changes such as the abolition of the press gang. Place's industry was extraordinary. The addresses and petitions he wrote, and the meetings which he arranged, were legion. Many of the people who called on him each day were looking for help and advice, and he always found it very hard to refuse if he thought that he could do any good. He helped many people privately, whether visiting a man's creditors to persuade them to agree to a compromise, advising a young woman on how to get possession of money which her mother had misappropriated, or arranging for an elderly deranged woman to be admitted to a suitable asylum at the request of her friends. Yet he still found time to write innumerable letters to the press and extremely long narratives of the principal movements which he was involved in, as well as making copies of most of his letters. He was also active in the educational field, and in 1823 played a key role in founding the London Mechanics' Institute, which started the successful nineteenth-century movement for adult education for working men. In 1831–32 Place played an important part in the Reform Bill agitation, and in May 1832 he joined in planning an armed rising when it appeared that the Tories might come to power and emasculate the Bill. In 1835–38 he helped to launch what was to become the Chartist movement, and in 1838 drafted the People's Charter.

A reassessment of Place's career and opinions is long overdue. By the time of his death in 1854 he was almost forgotten, but in 1898 a biography of him appeared by Graham Wallas, a leading Fabian and one of the founders of sociology. Place came to be seen by the Fabians of the early twentieth century as a precursor who used the same methods of research and quiet influence to achieve reforms as they did themselves. There are some 290 volumes of his papers in the British Library, and these have been extensively used by historians, but his reputation has declined since E.P. Thompson attacked him in his *Making of the English Working Class* in 1963. Thompson and other Marxist historians consider Place backward in his thinking because he rejected the socialist ideas which were becoming popular among working people in his lifetime, and opposed the class warfare ideology of the extreme radicals, instead advocating cooperation between the middle and working classes. Historians often accuse him of inflating his own importance and criticising his colleagues unfairly, and he has a low reputation as a writer because of the excessive length of his narratives. The question of how far Place's narratives are reliable is important to historians, because they are a prime source for radical history in the early nineteenth century. This book argues that the reaction against Place has gone much too far, and that most of the criticism of him in recent years is based on misunderstanding of his views and actions.

2 The Sponging-House Keeper's Son

Francis Place was born on 3 November 1771. The London of his childhood was a turbulent city where violence was an accepted part of life and highwaymen were regarded as folk-heroes. Getting drunk was considered an Englishman's national right. The forces of order were very weak, and the main deterrent to crime was brutal punishment of the few criminals who were caught. Hanging days at Tyburn were public spectacles, for which London journeymen were customarily given the day off.

However, the turbulence went with growing prosperity, which accelerated in the second half of the eighteenth century as the country began to be transformed by the Industrial Revolution. This did not greatly affect London directly, but the city benefited by a great increase in trade and financial business. Many contemporaries believed that this prosperity led to idleness and drunkenness among the 'lower orders', but Dorothy George, the leading authority on eighteenth-century London social history, disagreed:

> 'Luxury and extravagance', manifested chiefly in excessive drinking and a passion for gambling, were common to all classes; there is no need to explain them by high wages; temptations to drink and gamble were interwoven with the fabric of society to an astonishing extent, and they did undoubtedly combine with the uncertainties of life and trade to produce that sense of instability, of liability to sudden ruin, which runs through so much of eighteenth-century literature. The 'decayed housekeeper' meets one at every turn in the poor-law records; the debtors' prison and the sponging-house play a large part both in fiction and biography.

In this society Simon Place, Francis's father, appears an archetypal figure. Born in about 1717, he was apprenticed at the age of twelve to a baker in Bury St Edmunds. A few years later he ran away to London after cutting his master's buttocks during a quarrel. In 1746 he married Anna Paling at the Reverend Alexander Keith's notorious May Fair Chapel.[1] This was a fashionable centre for marriages without banns or a bishop's licence, where the Duke of Hamilton was able to marry the beautiful Elizabeth Gunning on impulse at half past twelve at night. Keith was excommunicated in 1742 and committed to prison in 1743, so Simon and Anna Place were married by a curate. The Marriage Act of 1753 put an end to Keith's 'business', and in a pamphlet written to oppose the Act he wrote: 'I have often asked the married pair how long they had been acquainted; . . . the generality did not exceed the acquaintance of a week, some of only a day, half a day, &c.'[2]

In 1747 Anna Place had a daughter, but in about 1760 Simon deserted her, presumably for Francis's mother Mary Gray, who bore him a child in 1762. Francis always assumed that his parents had married, but if they did the marriage was a bigamous one. Either way, Francis was illegitimate. He knew about his father's first marriage, but he does not appear to have attached any importance to it, perhaps because of his incorrect belief that it was a 'Fleet marriage': until 1753 weddings could be validly conducted by clergymen who were undischarged bankrupts in the vicinity of Fleet Prison, but such marriages were not taken very seriously, and sailors and prostitutes would often get married there for a joke. Fleet registers were notoriously unreliable, and they were commonly rejected by the courts as evidence because fraud was suspected.[3]

In the 1760s Simon Place twice built up flourishing bakers' shops and lost them by gambling. Each time he disappeared for several months, leaving Mary to fend for herself. By 1770 their first child had died and Simon had become a bailiff of the Marshalsea Court. He kept a sponging-house – a private debtors' prison – in Vinegar Yard, Brydges Street, next to Drury Lane Playhouse. He would arrest debtors and imprison them in his house; after forty-eight hours they were supposed to be transferred to the Marshalsea Prison, where the conditions were far worse, but they could avoid this by bribery. He made his living by charging exorbitant prices for food, drink and other necessities, and by extorting fees and bribes. The profits were so great that sponging-houses changed hands for large sums. Three of his children were born in the house, Hannah in 1770, Francis in 1771 and George in 1773.

In the eighteenth century the neighbourhood of a theatre was considered a disreputable area, and Drury Lane was particularly notorious. In 1717 it had been the subject of a verse by Gay:

> O may thy virtue guard thee thro' the roads
> Of Drury's mazy courts and dark abodes!
> The harlot's guileful paths who nightly stand
> Where Catherine Street descends into the Strand.

Francis did not have to put up with this threat to his virtue for long, as Simon Place soon moved to another sponging-house in Ship and Anchor Court off the Strand, where his last child Ann was born in 1775.[4]

According to Francis, this house 'was one of the best if not indeed the very best of the sort, and was therefore seldom without an inmate or two of the most respectable or wealthier class of prisoners, if the word wealthy can be

applied to persons confined for sums seldom amounting to fifty pounds . . .'
But they were able to pay for better conditions than prevailed in the
Marshalsea, and to pay the bribes necessary to avoid being transferred there.
The profits enabled Simon Place to live in high style in the middle and late
1770s. He drank with 'the more dissolute sort of barristers, attorneys, and
tradesmen of what were then called the better sort',[5] and kept a horse and
chaise which he used to visit women outside London. His companions
included Jack Broughton and Jack Slack, former boxing champions of
England, and Henry Fielding's blind half-brother, the reforming magistrate
Sir John Fielding.

In 1779 an Act of Parliament stopped most of the abuses of the Marshalsea
Court and thus ruined Simon Place's business. He sold it and bought the lease
of a public house in Arundel Street, in the Strand. He put it into good
condition and fitted up the parlour to a high standard. He took great care over
the quality of his beer and acquired a high reputation for his stout. With these
arrangements, as Francis remarked, he was bound to make money. The early
1780s must have been a time of continued prosperity.

Francis described his father as 'a resolute daring straight forward sort of
man, governed almost wholly by his passions and animal sensations both of
which were very strong, he was careless of reputation excepting in some
particulars in which he seems to have thought he excelled. These were few,
mostly relating to sturdiness and dissoluteness. Drinking, Whoring, Gaming,
Fishing and Fighting . . .' On the other hand, Francis said that all who knew
him placed the utmost reliance on Simon Place's word, and he was always
ready to help anyone in trouble, working with equal perseverance whether his
friend was in the right or wrong: 'With all his follies and vices he was much
respected.' Francis strongly resembled him in appearance and temperament.
As late as 1840 an old man recognised him partly by his resemblance to his
father, who had then been dead forty-seven years.

Simon's treatment of his sons was generally brutal: 'Beating and that too in
excess was with him the all in all in the way of teaching, "a word and a blow
but the blow always first".'[6] Although he was a good swimmer, he forbade his
sons to swim, for reasons which Francis found unaccountable. He used to
send the servant-maid up to the boys' room in the evening for their shoes and
stockings, and if these were wet he would seize the nearest stick and go up to
beat the boys until the stick broke. On one occasion he almost killed Francis:
the servant-maid tried to stop him from beating the boys by pulling back his
coat tails, and his candle was knocked over in the struggle. Hitting out at her in
the dark, he broke the stick across Francis's forehead. These beatings were
always given in a rage which disappeared when the stick broke, and if he was
detained by having to attend to customers he would often forget to thrash the
boys.

However, it seems clear that Francis must have exaggerated his father's
brutality. If Simon had been in the habit of beating his sons in the full force of

a blind rage until the stick broke, then they must have suffered serious injuries at the least, whereas Francis gave a detailed account of the accident which caused the only injury he mentioned. He had a vivid memory and strong passions, and parts of his account of his father seem to have been written from the point of view of his remembered childhood fears. He himself pointed out that his father's ideas about discipline were those of his age:

> He wished, and intended that his children, should be honest, sober, industrious and in every sense of the word respectable and he does not seem ever to have doubted that they would be so. . . . In his opinion coercion was the only way to eradicate faults, and by its terror to prevent their recurrence. These were common notions, and were carried into practice not only by the heads of families and the teachers of youth generally, but by the government itself and every man in authority under it, in the treatment of prisoners and the drilling of soldiers who were publicly beaten by the drill serjeants with a cane.

With fighting as with swimming, Simon Place demanded that his sons 'do as I say, not as I do'. Pugilism was fashionable at this time, and he was a companion of leading boxers and proud of his own proficiency in the sport. Yet he forbade his sons to fight with other boys, fearing that it would lead to acquaintance with boxers. Francis nevertheless said that he himself had been acquainted with most of the leading boxers of the 1780s.[7]

Whereas he gives a vivid picture of his father in his autobiography, he says little about his mother apart from praise of her character and description of the distress she suffered because of her husband's and her children's misconduct. Mary Place appears as a shadowy, idealised figure, with neither her Christian name nor the date of her death mentioned:

> I thought her very handsome and I have heard persons who had known her for many years speak of her as a remarkably handsome woman. She was one of the best women that ever existed. Clean, neat, kind, cheerful, good tempered, warm hearted and always ready to do services to every body, whom it seemed to be possible for her to serve. She was much respected by all who knew her, and greatly beloved by those who knew her best.[8]

Francis was sent to school from the age of four until he was nearly fourteen. However, at his first school up to the age of seven all he learnt was how to read badly, and he said that he fared little better at the next one, which used the usual teaching method of the period, learning by rote. The pupils showed their work to the master in turn, and were beaten on the hand according to the number of errors they made. They called the master 'Savage Jones' on account of the pleasure he seemed to take in beating them. Francis stated that although he received little education, the school had a considerable influence on him. He learnt to be punctual and to do his lessons correctly in order to avoid punishment, and paradoxically he also learnt to prove his courage by accepting challenges to provoke and bear beatings from the master.

Unofficially he was coached in boxing by the bigger boys, and he said that at length he could beat any boy his own size and some much larger.

He was not expected to perform any chores at home, and he played a vigorous part in the London street life of the time. He painted a fascinating picture of it in his autobiography. On Twelfthday, 6 January, pastry cooks' shops used to sell special cakes, and gangs of boys would gather outside, Francis and his group taking their station at a shop in the Strand. Each boy was armed with a hammer and nails, and when passers-by stopped to look at the cakes the boys would nail their clothes to the shops' wooden shutters, causing fury among the victims and raucous merriment among adult on-lookers. Sometimes people would be trapped while they were giving the boys money to buy more nails.

During school holidays Francis went bullock-hunting. In this game youths and boys would frighten the animals as they were being driven through the streets to Smithfield by shouting, whistling and threatening to fight the drovers. If the hunters succeeded in detaching a bullock they would chase it through the streets, hitting it with sticks. When it was partially exhausted it would turn on its tormenters, who would attempt to hit it while the bullock tried to gore them, until it collapsed from exhaustion. Not surprisingly, people were occasionally killed during the game. Francis never saw a hunter receive any injury, but he did see passers-by knocked down, and one or two tossed. Looking back from the 1820s, he said: 'Its cruelty was atrocious, it led to every species of vice and crime, and proves how very low were peoples notions of morality, and how barbarous their dispositions since they could permit such a vile and mischievous pastime to be pursued without interruption for a long series of years.' But he admitted that he was 'exceedingly delighted with this sport'.[9] It was near its end when he took part in it, and when moralists of the early nineteenth century claimed that morals were declining, bullock-hunting was prime evidence for Place's thesis that they had been worse in the past.

He claimed that he excelled his companions in all sports and games, apart from swimming. He could never bear to be beaten, so whenever he was he would practise until he could get his revenge. He did not believe in being modest, and his autobiography displays his vanity at its most extreme. He showed both his early determination to excel and his readiness to boast of his childhood triumphs. An early ability to make money was aided by his proficiency at games. In 'cocks and dumps' boys attempted to knock down lead models of cocks by shying lead counters (dumps) at them. Francis made cocks which projected more at the sides and backs than the usual ones, and were therefore less easily knocked down: 'by this contrivance I for some time won all the cocks and dumps of the boys, 'till they cried me down and then I turned merchant and sold them'.[10] It is remarkable that in his autobiography he boasted of such underhand conduct which would have caused him grief and shame later in life, but he seems to have felt that his behaviour in

childhood should not be judged according to ethical standards because he had
not then been taught the differences between honesty and dishonesty.

At the age of nearly twelve he was moved to his last school. He described the
master, Mr Bowis, as 'a good man, greatly beloved by his pupils'. Francis
attributed the germ of many right notions and much of his ability in reasoning
to the master's advice and care. He thought that this later kept him from
falling too deeply into evil and showed him 'the means of procuring much of
the happiness I have enjoyed, and notwithstanding the adverse circumstances
in which for many years I was placed, I am of opinion, that greater happiness
has upon the whole been enjoyed by but very few men'.

An incident at the school led him to question religion for the first time. Mr
Bowis asked him to expound the account of the miraculous conception in the
first chapter of Matthew, but he was well acquainted with the facts of life
from a popular sex manual called *Aristotle's Compleat Master Piece,* and he
found the miraculous conception hard to credit. 'I could not play the
hypocrite, my master had taught me the value of truth, and to respect myself,
and I could not, at least to him, make up a false statement: I doubted and was
dumb.' He never forgot the embarrassment he suffered. Since his master had
said that grace came from faith, and Francis felt that he did not have faith, he
feared for a time that he was damned. To remove his doubts he read the
Pilgrim's Progress 'and parts of some other equally absurd books, but all
would not do, reason was too strong for superstition, and at length the fiend
was completely vanquished'.[11]

The confidence which enabled him to reject religion as a result of his own
reasoning was partly due to an incident which occurred when he was about
eleven. His father and mother were arguing with a customer when Francis
interrupted to point out a distinction which put an end to the dispute. The
customer's praise for his reasoning had a lifelong effect on him, helping to
convince him of the importance of reason and giving him confidence in his
ability to use it correctly.

However, a belief in reason was to play little part in his life for several years.
'An occurrence', Place wrote, 'which had a considerable effect on me at the
time and no small share of influence on my manners conduct and character
must not be omitted here.' A dozen girls were taught in a separate room, and
as head boy Francis had the duty of checking the girls' sums twice a week. The
master seldom remained until the end, and the smallest girls were always
despatched first. The rest of the anecdote has been cut out of the manuscript,
and the censorious Francis Place Junior commented: 'The Consequence was
bad for both parties giving rise to much licentiousness.'

Although Francis only attended Bowis's school for two years, it had a
crucial effect on him, which was all the more important because his parents
were illiterate and he had learnt little at his previous schools. Bowis provided
better teaching and moral lectures, and he used to invite his older pupils along
to his own room, where he would show them his small collection of books and

encourage them to ask questions about them. This gave Francis a taste for books and knowledge, and he used part of the income from his money-making activities to build up his own library. By the time he finished school he had a fairly large chest of books, and was launched on a course of self-education which continued throughout his life. Another characteristic which was to play a critical role in his life emerged at this time, his hatred of self-display. He refused to take part in breaking-up day exhibitions because of his aversion to such 'degrading' processions.[12]

Simon Place planned to keep his son at school until he was fourteen and then apprentice him to a conveyancer, but in the summer of 1785 Francis announced that he would not agree to the plan. He expected his father to be furious — even to send him to sea as a result — but his father merely asked him what he would like to be instead. He replied that he did not mind, provided that it was a trade. Simon Place immediately went into the parlour of his public house and asked whether anyone would take his son. 'Old Joe France' said that he would, and the next morning Francis was sent on trial for a month to learn 'the art and mystery of Leather Breeches making'.[13] At the end of three weeks he was bound apprentice for seven years, and his father gave his parlour guests a feast on the occasion.

The remarkable aspect of this transaction was not its casualness and speed, since time was left for second thoughts, but the character of the master who was to provide Francis's home. Joe France was then married to his third wife. By his first wife he had three daughters and two sons. His eldest daughter was a common prostitute, the second was kept by the captain of an East India ship, 'in whose absence she used to amuse herself as such women generally do', and the youngest had genteel lodgings where she was visited by gentlemen. His elder son was 'a first rate genteel pickpocket, working at his trade of Leather Breeches making as a blind, he was a gay good looking fellow'. The younger was a thief who was obliged to abscond, and enlisted in a West India Regiment in order to avoid punishment. By his second wife Joe France had two daughters. Place described them as wretched-looking children, probably made so by the ill-usage of their step-mother, who used to get half-tipsy each evening, while her husband 'muddled himself' at the public house.[14] Yet Place wrote that France was not held in contempt by his neighbours and the company he kept. Hitherto, he had paid his way, was supposed to be worth money, and was simple, good-natured and obliging. His story was well known to Simon Place and his friends, yet none of them raised any objection to him acting in *loco parentis* to Francis for the next seven years. The story exhibits Simon's belief that respectability was learnt by discipline and not by example.

Francis was happy to live with the France family in Bell Yard, Temple Bar. As he remarked with retrospective irony, he considered it a much greater state of slavery to attend school, with short hours and frequent holidays, than to work as an apprentice twelve hours a day, six days a week, with three days off at Christmas, Easter and Whitsun. He soon became expert at his trade, and was paid half a man's wage for work beyond that expected of a boy. Joe France was a skilled leather-breeches maker, but he had not kept up with the changing fashions, and his business was declining. He became dependent on Place's help to support his family, a situation which naturally gave the apprentice a powerful position. He refused to accept his master's authority outside his work, knowing that France would not dare to tell Simon Place when his son got into bad company, for fear that the father would blame him for not taking proper care of him, and end the apprenticeship.

Francis said that the six shillings a week he received for extra work, together with a shilling or two from his mother and elder sister, allowed him to become 'a great man for my age'. He associated with about twenty Fleet Street apprentices: 'All of them were older than I was and most of them were "fine men" to some of the prostitutes who walked Fleet Street, spending their money with them in debauchery and occasionally receiving money from them.' Sometimes he spent his evenings at Cock and Hen Clubs, where youths and girls would sit around a long table in a private room in an inn, with a youth at one end and a girl at the other: 'The amusements were drinking – smoaking – swearing – and singing flash songs. The chairs were taken at 8 p.m, and the boys and girls paired off by degrees 'till by 12 o clock none remained.' He would never acknowledge any acquaintance with the girls outside the club room.[15]

These apprentices were all the sons of householders, and they would not have admitted the son of a journeyman to their company, but over half were guilty of crimes, two were hanged at the Old Bailey and others fled the country. Place thought that *The Beggar's Opera* had a 'demoralising effect' on them:

> The success of thieving – the jolly scene of Macheath and the Drury Lane *ladies*, notwithstanding its termination, the exhilaration caused by the songs sung by Polly and Lucy – the gratulations of success between Mr and Mrs Peachum. The careless confidence of the gang of thieves, all receiving the vociferous applause of the audience, and that too – at the time when I was a boy – in proportion to the excess of villainy and the grossness of the performance, not only had a direct effect on me and my companions, confirming us in our immoral and evil courses, but stimulated too many of us to pursue them to a still greater extent.[16]

Francis was also a member of a cutter club, rowing in an eight-oar boat. 'Our club was no better than many others, most of the members either robbed their masters or other persons to supply the means for their extravagance.' Two of the crew were printers, and he often worked all night with them at the end of the month on magazine work, for which they were paid extra. (One of the printers was later transported for robbery, and the other 'was hanged for a murder he did not commit. An attempt was made to set up an *alibi,* but it was said it could not be proved where he was, he being at the time committing a burglary with some of his associates.')

In early 1788 Joe France's difficulties became so great that he decided to 'shoot the moon' (move house surreptitiously) and Place moved with the family to Lambeth. Shortly afterwards, France surrendered himself in an action for debt and became a prisoner within the walls of the King's Bench, while his family survived precariously on the results of Place's efforts in making and selling 'rag-fair' breeches – breeches made from faulty leather and sold to shops. The move brought some change in his way of life, since his new companions were 'not quite so dissolute as those I had left'.[17]

Meanwhile Simon Place was falling into financial difficulties. His troubles started when Anna Place, his 'first' wife, sued him in the Ecclesiastical Court. According to the Libel (statement of her case) submitted to the London Diocesan Consistory Court in May 1785, she had supported herself from the time of her husband's desertion in 1760 until 1783. Finding that her husband was settled in a good public house when she could no longer maintain herself, she 'applied to him to take her home and treat her with conjugal Affection'. He refused. She therefore prayed that 'the said Simon Place be compelled by law to take home and receive the said Anna Place his wife and treat her with Marital Affection and render to her conjugal Rites'.[18] Francis's version, although he admitted that he was unsure of the facts, was that she claimed parish aid as Simon Place's wife. The parish officers advised him to make her a small allowance, but he refused, insisting that she was not his wife, and the resulting inquiries and altercations led to the court case. The case disappeared from the Consistory Court records after May 1786, but Francis said that it ended in his father's excommunication. His legal costs amounted to several hundred pounds, and he gave a supper to commemorate the result.

Simon Place's legal and other expenses had brought him into debt, and since the lease on his public house was coming up for renewal, he planned to pay off his debts by purchasing a new lease and selling it with the goodwill at a profit. The tenant normally had the right of first refusal, and he had been promised it by his landlord and occasional drinking companion, the Duke of Norfolk. But the Duke granted the lease to another man, and Simon was forced to procure a friendly action for debt to be brought against himself. He retired to the Fleet prison, shortly afterwards taking the Rules, which allowed him to lodge in the vicinity of the prison. He threatened to shut up the public house for the remaining two years of the lease, which would have ruined the trade, so the new lessee offered to take over immediately. Francis, then nearly seventeen years old, attended a creditors' meeting to settle the matter. Finding that his father's attorney was doing the business badly, he took over and abused the new lessee, thus gaining the sympathy of the creditors, and obtained a large sum for the goodwill. After paying off most of the debts he carried £340 to his father instead of the expected £200. Simon Place gave him half a crown – the only money he ever gave him.

The story of the end of Francis's apprenticeship has been cut out of the manuscript of his autobiography, but his indentures appear to have been given up as a result of an argument between Joe France and Simon Place in July 1789, when Francis was seventeen years eight months old. The France family lingered on for another year until they went into the workhouse, where the old couple soon died.

Francis now had difficulty in finding employment, and he had two false starts when he thought that employers were trying to take advantage of his inexperience. The first were his elder sister, Hannah, and her husband. Hannah Place had quarrelled with her respectable fiancé and married a journeyman carpenter called Pain. He was a drinker, but a good workman, and the Place family hoped that he would stop drinking and become steady. But his wife, who had only married him to spite her former lover, treated him with contempt. He sought consolation for his disappointment in drinking while she turned to Methodism. Never one to miss an opportunity to point out the dangers in a religious outlook, Place commented: 'She went to chapel, prayed, and sung hymns at home, and was as absurd as he was, she held some office in the religious community to which she belonged, and used to attend meetings when she ought to have been at home.'[19] The Pains suggested that Francis should contract to serve them for three years in order to learn carpentry, but a three weeks' trial convinced him that Pain's offer of eighteen shillings a week was too low. He then obtained work with a leather-breeches maker, but when he asked for payment he was offered less than the journeyman rate. In retaliation he went to a fair instead of finishing some urgently needed breeches, so the master dismissed him. Eventually, he found success with a prosperous breeches maker and tailor called Pike, who was so impressed with him that he soon appointed him foreman in charge of breeches making. His business ability and ambition were already apparent, and at the age of eighteen he was managing fifteen men and earning a guinea and a half a week. Feeling himself now in a responsible position, he gave up the Cock and Hen Club and the Cutter Club, but otherwise spent his evenings in much the same way.

He started an affair with Pike's sister, and on 17 March 1790 she took him to a dance at a neighbouring pastry-cook's shop. Here he met his future wife, an assistant in the shop. The daughter of a coal porter, Elizabeth Chadd was then almost sixteen years old. Francis 'thought her a very fine and handsome person. I danced with her, and fell desperately in love with her. I therefore made it my business to see her again and again. I made enquiries about her and resolved to court her, at first I hardly knew on what terms, but in a little time for a wife.'[20] He needed to stay on good terms with Miss Pike, but he gave up the rest of his old acquaintance and started saving money. Soon afterwards Pike learnt about the affair, and reluctantly decided that his sister would have to marry Francis. But Place, who knew that she was also having an affair with Pike's brother-in-law, refused and was dismissed as a result.

At about this time Simon Place lost the remainder of his money in the State Lottery. Gambling mania centred on the State Lottery in the late eighteenth century, and Francis described the effects in a typically hyperbolic comment: 'Hundreds of thousands of people were totally ruined by it both in body and mind, the evils were complicated and enormous, the degradation among the tradesmen and working people was terrible, their demoralization greater than can now be imagined. It was the cause of every vice that could be practised, of every crime that could be committed, it separated families, it severed husband and wife, it carried devastation all over the Metropolis, and ruined all sorts of people in masses.' He quoted the reminiscences of an old tradesman that people used to sell the clothes off their backs, and respectable women would prostitute themselves, in order to raise money for the Lottery.[21] The Places' disaster was compounded by the fact that Simon was now disabled by gout, and Mary had to take work as a washerwoman.

Meanwhile Francis was again having difficulty in finding employment. Unable to get work at his own trade, he undertook to repair a damaged model frigate, and took it to his future mother-in-law's house to work on it. He did not tell his parents the reason for his absences from their lodgings, and when his brother told them that he had seen Francis with a tall, well-dressed girl, they began to fear that he had attached himself to 'some loose women'. George Place was set to watch his brother, and traced him to the Chadds, whereupon Simon went to enquire about their character, and learnt that it was respectable. The incident shows the horror with which Francis's parents would have learnt of his earlier career. Mary Place then asked Francis about his intentions, and he said that he intended to marry Elizabeth Chadd as soon as he could find permanent employment. He obtained permission to bring her home to meet his parents, and when he did so his father astonished the family by giving up his seat to her, 'and ever afterwards treated her with more consideration and respect than he had ever done any other person'.[22] Simon Place had been considerably subdued by his misfortunes, and he now started to treat his wife with kindness for the first time.

When Francis proposed to Elizabeth Chadd, he told her that he had compared himself with everyone he had met in his trade, and found that he was better qualified to succeed than any of them. With the arrogant confidence which was to play a considerable part in his success, he assured her that he was bound to rise to be a master, even though he did not know how he could get his own business. He said that she did not consent in words, 'but we seemed to understand one another'. He succeeded in getting irregular employment, and the wedding was precipitated when Mrs Chadd turned against it. He admitted that there was some justice in her complaints that they were too young, that he was in a declining trade, and − significantly − that his temper was bad and that he might therefore maltreat his wife. Their quarrels and Mrs Chadd's efforts to break the engagement made Elizabeth uncomfortable at home, so the young couple decided to marry immediately, surreptitiously as she was under age. The marriage took place on 3 March 1791 at Lambeth church. His bride emerges from his account as similar in character to his mother, affectionate, loyal, domestic, with a poor education and no intellectual interests.

Place was then earning only fourteen shillings a week, barely enough to support a wife. The newly married couple took a furnished room at 3s 6d a week over a coal shed − a shop which sold coal. The street was a centre for butchers' shops, with houses which were dark, dirty and full of rats, mice and bugs. Three months later they were able to move to a better room. Francis was still unable to get full-time work, and Elizabeth used to help his mother with her washing, while Francis went for long walks so that his mother would not know that he was half-starved, and offer him food which she could not afford.

> It may be supposed that I led a miserable life but I did not I was very far indeed from being miserable at this time when my wife came home at night, we had always something to talk about, we were pleased to see each other, our reliance on each other was great indeed, we were poor, but we were young, active cheerful, and although my wife at times doubted that we should get on in the world, I had no such misgivings.

They managed to dress better than most people in similar circumstances, and since they were unable to entertain they kept to themselves. As a result their neighbours contemptuously called them '*the* Lady and Gentleman'.[23]

During the winter of 1791−92 a slump in the leather-breeches trade reduced the Places to great distress. When Elizabeth had to retire to her bed in exhaustion, Francis went to his employer and demanded an overdue payment, although he expected to be discharged as a result. Instead, he was given the payment and the materials for an urgently needed pair of breeches. He was told to find another journeyman to share the work, breeches usually being made in halves, but he did the whole of the work himself, an action which aroused deep guilt when he looked back on it: 'My cupidity could not resist the temptation to cheat a fellow workman. . . .This was the only instance in which I ever committed an actual fraud.'[24] This breast-beating over a peccadillo when his wife had collapsed from starvation reflects Place's obsession concerning honesty.

He now started looking for work making stuff-breeches. These were becoming popular at the expense of leather, and Place had gained experience of this branch of the trade during an unprofitable venture making breeches for working men. He was able to obtain sufficient work to earn twenty-six shillings a week. The improvement came at the right time, for Elizabeth had given birth to a daughter. But their hopes were destroyed when the Breeches Makers Benefit Society called a strike of leather-breeches makers in the spring of 1793. Combinations of workmen to defend their wages and conditions were then illegal, and the Benefit Society, ostensibly for the support of sick members and the payment of their burial costs, was really a front for building up a strike fund. Although he was a member, Place was not involved in the strike since he was now a stuff-breeches maker. He only learnt about it when his employers refused him work because the masters had agreed to discharge every leather-breeches maker who made stuff-breeches, in order to prevent them from subsidising the strike.

He went to the Society's club house, where he learnt that seven shillings a week was to be given in strike pay. With a fund of £250 and 250 members, there was only enough money for three weeks. At a meeting of the Society he stood up and pointed out the inadequacy of the sum. He proposed that every member who was willing to 'go on the tramp' should receive a certificate and an advance of seven shillings: according to a custom of the trade any man who brought a certificate to a leather-breeches maker's shop anywhere in the country would be given a night's lodging and a shilling to help him on his way. He also proposed that the rest of the members should be offered two pairs of rag-fair breeches to make a week at a wage of eight shillings. The loss on the breeches would be two and sixpence, a saving compared with the proposed strike pay of seven shillings. Finally, he suggested that an address setting out the reasons for the strike should be printed and circulated. These proposals were all adopted and Place was appointed the manager of a shop to sell the breeches, 'as my knowledge of Rag fair breeches making was well known and duly appreciated'.[25] This strike provides the first example of a pattern which was to recur again and again in Place's life. He was almost always reluctant to become involved in any organisation, but once drawn in he would commit himself to it wholeheartedly and become one of its leaders. On this occasion he paid a heavy price. At the end of May 1793 the strike collapsed and the masters decided that he should never be employed again.

During the three months' strike the Places' child had died of smallpox and their small savings had been exhausted. The six months which followed was the worst period in their life. They were unwilling to enter a pawnshop, and a woman who lived in the same house went for them. When they had surrendered everything but the clothes they stood up in, they survived on credit from their landlady. Elizabeth Place bore her sufferings in an 'exemplary manner', but her husband did not:

> This is the only period of my life on which I look back with shame. . . .My temper was bad, and . . . I used at times to give way to passion and increase her and my own misery. The folly and absurdity of giving way to bad temper was always apparent to me, and I never attempted either to palliate or excuse it to myself, I was indeed ashamed of it, and set about to rectify it, and this I soon did to a considerable extent. . . .Our disagreements were not however frequent and when they did occur the fault was always on my side.[26]

Throughout his life he was constantly trying to keep his temper under control, and often failing.

His natural resilience soon reasserted itself, and he devoted much of his six months' unemployment to studying. Even as an apprentice he had found time to do a considerable amount of reading, and the books he read then included Greek and Roman histories, Fielding's novels, some of Hume's essays, and books on geography, anatomy, surgery, science and the arts. Later he read biographies and books on law. Among the authors he read during his unemployment were Adam Smith and John Locke, but Hume's works proved most influential. He read them two or three times and they 'caused me to turn in upon myself and examine myself in a way which I should not otherwise have done. It was this which laid the solid foundation of my future prosperity, and completed the desire I had always had to acquire knowledge.' As he read, he became convinced that he would one day get into business and succeed in the world, 'by some means or other, not then visible but which must in time be visible'.[27] His wife must have found such optimism infuriating, and she thought he was mad when he talked of being able to retire by the age of forty-five, but thirty years later he triumphantly pointed out that he only just missed his target, since he ceased all active 'interference', as he called it, in business before he was forty-eight.

His mother was also going through a difficult time. Simon Place had become a burden on Mary when he was disabled, so his death in the spring of 1793 produced some mitigation of her poverty, but her peace of mind was destroyed when her younger daughter married a notorious thief and fence, Mat Stimson. Francis was unable to assist his mother while he was unemployed, and in his view her elder daughter robbed her while she was neglected by her other children. After the inevitable quarrels, Francis never spoke to his elder sister again, nor to his brother for some years.

Early in 1794 one of Place's former employers sent for him. He refused to go, fearing a trick because another master had attempted to get him to admit to a combination in order to prosecute him. Finally he allowed his wife to go, and she returned with as much work as she could carry in her apron. The employer had had an attack of conscience over his treatment of Place, and decided to defy the other masters. Elizabeth Place could help her husband with stuff-breeches making, and they set to work sixteen to eighteen hours a day, Sundays included, to recover their pawned possessions. For a month he did not find time even to shave: 'My hair was black and somewhat curled my beard was very thick and my whiskers large, my face somewhat sallow, and upon the whole I must have been a ferocious looking fellow.' Five feet six inches tall, he was thin but muscular.

The rate of work was not one he could maintain indefinitely, and he was probably recalling this period of his life when he wrote forty years later:

> I know not how to describe the sickening aversion which at times steals over the working man, and utterly disables him for a longer or a shorter period from following his usual occupation, and compels him to indulge in *idleness*. I have felt

it, resisted it to the utmost of my power; but have been so completely subdued by it, that spite of very pressing circumstances, I have been obliged to submit, and run away from my work. This is the case with every workman I have ever known . . .

He would go for a run into the country, and then 'return to my vomit'. Soon they were able to relax the pace, made happy by the belief that their sufferings were over.

But once again the Places' hopes were disappointed when Francis was discharged a few months later. He then helped to form several trade clubs of carpenters and plumbers, and as the paid secretary conducted a number of successful strikes.[28] With irregular but highly paid work passed on by journeymen in his own trade, he was able to maintain a precarious prosperity. In April 1794 his daughter Elizabeth was born; she was to be his eldest child to survive.

3 The English Jacobin

The primary issue for radicals throughout Place's life was parliamentary reform. This had first become a major issue during the Civil War, and some republicans went so far as to advocate manhood suffrage. However, the advocates of republicanism and royal absolutism were both defeated in the Glorious Revolution of 1688, after which radical parliamentary reform almost disappeared from the political agenda for eighty years. John Wilkes revived the issue in his riotous campaigns of the 1760s and 1770s, and in 1779 Major John Cartwright, the most indefatigable of the parliamentary reformers, advocated the programme which later became known as the six points of the Charter: universal suffrage (which then meant manhood suffrage), annual elections, the secret ballot, equal numbers of voters in each constituency, the abolition of property qualifications for election to Parliament, and the payment of MPs. The following year the Society for Constitutional Information was founded to publish literature for radical reform.

Meanwhile the Reverend Christopher Wyvill of Yorkshire launched a campaign of the country gentry. The reformers used methods adopted in later campaigns, such as committees to organise correspondence, public meetings and petitions to Parliament. Wyvill had wide support among the Yorkshire gentry and the movement achieved some notable successes in the election of reformers to Parliament, but it was undermined by the Gordon Riots in 1780 – directed against legislation to improve the legal position of Catholics – which strengthened fears about the consequences of democracy, while the extreme London radicals alienated Wyvill's moderate gentry supporters. The Whigs wanted to exploit the agitation to regain office, and they were prepared to press for 'economical' reforms which would limit the Crown's powers of patronage, but they would not support any reform which threatened their own 'rotten boroughs' (constituencies where the election of MPs was controlled by an individual or a small clique). The Whigs' equivocal support for the campaign created a distrust of the party which became traditional among reformers. The coalition in 1783 between the Whig leader, Charles

James Fox, and Lord North, the arch-enemy of reform, further split the movement. At the end of the year the Younger Pitt came to power as a committed supporter, but he was defeated on a reform motion in 1785 and then abandoned the issue. The campaign received little support from the 'lower orders', who had not yet begun to organise politically, although trade unions, dissenting religious groups and debating clubs were beginning to provide working men with political education and experience of organisation.[1]

In 1788 the reformers celebrated the centenary of the Glorious Revolution, and the French Revolution the following year gave them new hope. At first the French Revolution was widely welcomed in Britain. Conservativés saw it as the adoption by the French of the British system of a limited monarchy, while many ecstatic radicals greeted it as the dawn of a new age of liberty and reason. However, this apparent unity did not last long. At a time when radical societies were sending flattering addresses to the French National Assembly, growing conservative doubts crystallised into hostility and fear following the publication of Edmund Burke's *Reflections on the Revolution in France* in 1790. The most notable of many replies was Thomas Paine's *Rights of Man,* the first part of which was published in February 1791. Reformers had long argued that they were only demanding the restoration of lost rights, basing their claim on a mythical manhood suffrage Parliament in Anglo-Saxon England, but Paine rejected constitutional precedent as the 'vanity and presumption of governing beyond the grave', basing his case instead on the theory that men have 'natural rights'. This theory was not new, but he ridiculed hereditary government with a brashness and intransigence never shown before, in terms designed to appeal to labourers and journeymen: 'Placemen, Pensioners, Lords of the bed-chamber, Lords of the kitchen, Lords of the necessary-house, and the Lord knows what besides, can find as many reasons for monarchy as their salaries . . .'.[2] in February 1792, part 2 of the *Rights of Man* was published, with a social chapter which foreshadowed twentieth-century legislation, and by 1793 total sales were claimed (including both parts and abridged editions) of 200,000.

The first reform societies of artisans were formed in Sheffield in late 1791, encouraged by the French Revolution and the *Rights of Man,* and incited by economic distress. In January 1792 a shoemaker, Thomas Hardy, founded the London Corresponding Society – corresponding because it was illegal for a political association to have branches in different towns, and Hardy planned to get round this by corresponding with sympathetic provincial societies. The key difference between the London Corresponding Society (LCS) and the Society for Constitutional Information (SCI) lay in their membership fees, a penny a week against a guinea a year. This allowed the LCS to break through the taboo that politics was not a matter for the 'lower orders', and the breach was one of the principal complaints raised against the society, just as one of the main objections to the *Rights of Man* was that it was

sold in cheap editions. Aristocratic British society was terrified at the success
of revolutionary principles across the Channel, and the LCS's support for
manhood suffrage and annual parliaments, and its sympathy for the French
Revolution, inevitably brought persecution on it as an attempt to destroy the
'Altar and the Throne'.

The SCI and the LCS worked as allies, and under the leadership of the
veteran reformer John Horne Tooke the SCI became the leader of a country-
wide movement. The LCS grew rapidly, claimed 2000 members only six
months after its formation. It adopted an organisation, copied from the
Sheffield societies, of divisions with about thirty members, each of which
elected a delegate to a coordinating General Committee.3 The mood was one
of sturdy egalitarianism, and the divisions were swift to protest if the
Committee dared to decide any important question without referring it to a
referendum. The LCS advocated manhood suffrage on the grounds of
natural rights and utility, and it helped to circulate Paine's works, but it also
used arguments based on the 'Norman Yoke', the belief that the Normans
destroyed a manhood suffrage Parliament. This theory stopped short of
egalitarianism in its implicit acceptance of monarchy and aristocracy.

Place remarked that in 1792 Burke and Paine had made every thinking man
in England a politician, although his autobiography does not suggest that he
was one himself at this time. In April the younger Foxite Whigs formed the
Society of Friends of the People, which aimed to keep alive the reforming
tradition of the Whigs on the one hand, and to counter the Paineite
propaganda of the radicals ('Horne Tooke's people') on the other. The
loyalists were also turning politicians. The Paris massacres of royalists in
September and the Fraternal Edict in November, which offered support to
peoples who wanted to overthrow their rulers, coincided with congratulatory
addresses from British reform societies to the French. The LCS address
congratulated the French on their success in arms and declared: 'Frenchmen,
you are already free, and Britons are preparing to become so.' The result was a
loyalist backlash in Britain, and many old supporters of reform were
alienated. The best known of the 'Church and King' societies, the
'Association for Preserving Liberty and Property against Republicans and
Levellers', was formed in November with government support. It issued
pamphlets attacking the LCS, which replied with an address which admitted
espousing the 'Rights of Man, Liberty and Equality', but repudiated the
slogans 'No King and No Parliament'.4

In 1793 the main pressure was on Scottish reformers, who did not have the
protection of independent juries. After heavy sentences on reformers early in
the year, a British Convention was held in November in Edinburgh, and
several English societies sent delegates, challenging the Scottish Bench to treat
Englishmen as it had treated Scots. The challenge was accepted. The LCS
delegates, Joseph Gerrald and Maurice Margarot, were among those arrested
in December, and their farcical trials ended in sentences of fourteen years'

transportation. When Gerrald urged that Jesus Christ had been a reformer, Lord Braxfield, the notorious presiding judge, said 'muckle he made o'that, *he* was hanget'.

Early in 1794 the LCS and the SCI agreed on their reply: a second British Convention of reformers from all over the country. The LCS set up a secret committee to organise it, but their preparations were halted by the arrest of their leading members and the suspension of habeas corpus in May. The government claimed that the Convention was a revolutionary attempt to usurp Parliament and take over its powers, and Parliamentary Secret Committees set up to examine the evidence for treason produced alarmist reports. The SCI became inactive after the arrests and the LCS suffered many defections − deserters were commonly referred to as 'panic stricken'. During the summer and autumn the society operated under great difficulties, infiltrated by spies to the highest level, and weakened by further arrests and lack of money. But the government was also in trouble. Its law officers could show that some small-scale arming had taken place,[5] but they could not find proof of a revolutionary conspiracy.

Ministers did not feel able to bring lesser charges of sedition after the alarm they had created, so they finally decided to bring charges of high treason against twelve men, who became known as the 'twelve apostles'. In November and December Thomas Hardy, John Horne Tooke and John Thelwall, the principal radical lecturer and orator of the 1790s, were successively acquitted by London juries, and the remaining prosecutions were abandoned. The verdicts caused jubilation among reformers and probably prevented an English 'Terror' − Charles Grey, leader of the Friends of the People and future Whig Prime Minister, believed that the acquittals saved his life. They became a potent symbol for reformers until Chartist times, and annual dinners were held to celebrate them until the 1840s.[6] The evidence given in the trials by government spies showed that the reform societies had been thoroughly infiltrated, creating paranoia among the radicals about spies. The result was that a number of genuine reformers came under suspicion, including Place in the 1810s.

* * *

Place probably went through a short anti-radical phase in late 1793 or early 1794, as he was later reported to have said in the LCS General Committee that he had once been a Loyal Briton. The Society of Loyal Britons was formed in October 1793 as a would-be successor to the effective but short-lived Association for Preserving Liberty and Property. His brief period of loyalism may have reflected bitterness at the failure of his fellow journeymen to help him when he was suffering for his role in their strike, as well as his determination to rise in the world.[7]

On 28 April 1794 he sat in his landlord's room while his wife was giving birth, and he passed his time by reading a copy of Paine's deistical *Age of*

Reason which he found there. He was so delighted with the book that he sought an acquaintance with its owner, a member of the LCS, who persuaded him to join the society in June. In his autobiography the decision comes as a surprise, since he does not seem to have taken any interest in politics previously. His own explanation was that the arrests in May

> frightened away many of the members of the society, and they withdrew from it.
> Several persons among whom I was one considered it meritorious to join the society now that its founder and secretary was persecuted; those who did so were men who possessed something decided and energetic in their characters and they became very active members.[8]

His decision to join may have been a gesture against the tyranny of authority, and it is probable that he only became seriously committed to the society's political doctrines after he joined, just as he had been drawn into the breeches makers' strike by circumstances, but once he was involved he rapidly became a committed and energetic activist.

Place's autobiography is often the only source for important episodes in his life, so the question of how far it is reliable is important. He was generally accurate, but he sometimes made minor errors over dates, and he was liable to persuade himself that the view that he took in retrospect was the one he had taken at the time – as he acknowledged and warned his readers. Both these biases especially affect his account of his role in the LCS, because he wrote it thirty years later, whereas accounts of later events were generally written soon afterwards. Two drafts of the chapter on the LCS survive, and the second one is the least reliable of all his writings, since he presented himself as more pessimistic about the prospects for reform and less willing to support an activist policy than he showed himself in the franker first draft. This bias was unconscious – he stated that he preserved the first draft because it contained information about the LCS which was not to be found elsewhere, and he would not have done so if he had intended to mislead in the second draft.[9]

He said that he was soon elected to the General Committee, and he became a member of one of the committees set up to assist the defence in the treason trials from October to December 1794:

> I used to attend daily at the Old Bailey from noon 'till night. Go to work when I came home, and again in the morning early 'till noon, and thus I contrived to do as much as an ordinary days work. I was very active and useful in directing others, and was well pleased to see the esteem in which I was held by those with whom I acted who were clever men in circumstances very superior to mine.[10]

He also used to visit men confined in Newgate for seditious libel and other political crimes.

After the trials, Thomas Hardy, who was greatly affected by the death of his wife following an attack on their home by a loyalist mob, dropped out of active politics. The SCI disappeared, leaving the LCS at the head of the parliamentary reform movement, but at first it was too preoccupied with paying its debts and too torn by dissension to assert its new role. Arguments over the constitution of the society became entangled with charges of spying against a leading member, John Bone, and the principal antagonists on each side seceded to form separate societies.[11]

The constitution of the LCS was a continual subject for dispute. Place wrote that he was 'one of a committee which drew up a new constitution on a comprehensive scale for the society, assimilating its organisation as much as possible to what we conceived to be the best form for governing the Nation. It was printed by the Society . . . and is, I am still of opinion; a striking proof of the talents and judgment of the men who were selected to draw it up.' This must be a mistake, since the report he refers to was printed before he joined the society. Its proposals were rejected by the members on the grounds that they would make the divisions cyphers and the government of the society monarchical, and the society never made any major changes to the regulations printed in May 1792, apart from those forced on it by the 'Two Acts' of 1795.[12] Each division elected a delegate to the General Committee on a quarterly basis. The Committee, which met weekly, referred major questions to the divisions and dealt with minor ones itself. The topics discussed included publications and meetings to spread the society's views, correspondence with other societies, finance, the establishment of new divisions and the encouragement of sluggish ones. There was also an Executive Committee composed of six members elected monthly, and a secretary and assistant secretary elected quarterly. Delegates and officers were liable to be superseded if they neglected their duties, and the right was frequently exercised.

Whether it was this system or a similar one which Place regarded as a model for the government of the country, he clearly believed in an extreme form of direct democracy. Some members were even more extreme, using arguments derived from William Godwin's utilitarian anarchism to reject the idea of a constitution altogether. According to a letter from the Executive Committee to the divisions in April 1795, the anti-constitutionalists argued that 'the only means of securing social happiness is by the general diffusion of knowledge, and this being effected, all regard to constitutional or legal rules would become unnecessary'. They also argued that since every case is unique, no rules could ever cover every possible situation, and nothing should be done to fetter the society from adopting the best solution in every case. Their opponents replied that constitutional regulations 'are to be considered as beacons rather than fetters', and that *ad hoc* rules adopted in an emergency would be the offspring of passion rather than reason.[13] Place was a great admirer of Godwin's *Enquiry Concerning Political Justice,* but he was also a great believer in keeping to rules, so he must have been among the anti-Godwinians in the LCS.

Each division of the LCS met weekly, Place's in a private house in Covent Garden. The first hour was devoted to political education, and Place described the procedure:

> The chairman, (each man was chairman in rotation,) read from some book a chapter or part of a chapter, which as many as could read the chapter at their homes the book passing from one to the other had done and at the next meeting a portion of the chapter was again read and the persons present were invited to make remarks thereon. As many as chose did so, but without rising. Then another portion was read and a second invitation was given − then the remainder was read and a third invitation was given when they who had not before spoken were expected to say something. Then there was a general discussion. No one was permitted to speak more than once during the reading. The same rule was observed in the general discussion, no one could speak a second time until every one who chose had spoken once, then any one might speak again, and so on till the subject was exhausted − these were very important meetings, and the best results to the parties followed.

This description brings out two aspects of the LCS which Place valued: political education and the teaching of self-discipline. But it also exhibits his tendency to 'sanitise' the society. He also said that eating, drinking and smoking were forbidden in divisions and committees, but some divisions met in public houses, and were chased from house to house by magistrates who threatened the publicans' licences. Publicans used to offer the use of their premises − presumably they were willing to risk the magistrates' wrath because of the extra business which a division brought.

In May 1795 the constitutional issue was settled when the members decided in a referendum to keep the existing regulations.[14] The society was becoming more united, and provincial correspondence, which had almost lapsed, was reviving. More cautious after its tribulations, the LCS dismissed Paine from its publications and emphasised traditional constitutional arguments. When other societies asked for literature they were sent a letter written by the Duke of Richmond in 1783, which advocated manhood suffrage together with a restoration of the rights of the monarchy, and a report by the aristocratic Society of Friends of the People on patronage in parliamentary elections. But this was a matter of tactics rather than principle − on at least one occasion General Committee minutes were dated in French revolutionary style.

The society declared that its chief aim was 'the Diffusion by means of cheap publications of such Knowledge as may tend to awaken the Public Mind to the necessity of Universal Suffrage & Annual Parliaments', but the members' growing confidence was shown when they voted in a referendum to hold a public meeting, the first since the arrests of May 1794, in spite of fears that it would give the government a pretext for a renewed suspension of habeas corpus. Place was one of the most assiduous in selling tickets for it − he sold seventy-four at sixpence each.[15] The meeting was held on 29 June in St George's Fields, and estimates of the attendance ranged from over 7000 in a hostile newspaper report to 100,000 by the chairman, the surgeon and orator

John Gale Jones. It agreed Addresses to the Nation — grandiloquent in parts — and to the King, and it heard a fiery speech from Jones, but it dispersed peaceably. 'This meeting', Place observed, 'was necessary to counteract the reports industriously and generally spread that the Society existed only in name. It was also necessary in consequence of two of the divisions having seceded and formed separate societies, which tended much to embarrass many persons.' As a result, 'A very large accession of members was obtained and the communication with the country considerably increased.' The number of members reported present at the weekly meetings of the divisions rose from 485 on 2 July to 1842 on 3 September.[16]

By July Place was sometimes acting as chairman of the General Committee.[17] 'It may easily be supposed', he wrote,

> that among so many persons, of various dispositions no small portion of whom were eager to make speeches, and impatient of control, that the office of Chairman was not an ordinary one, and that but few of the members were qualified to fill it. The forms of the House of Commons were as nearly as possible observed; . . . and as the arrangement was strictly conformable to the Constitution of the society, I never permitted any deviation, from the course laid down. It was soon perceived that this method accelerated the business . . .

At one meeting an unsuccessful vote of censure was moved against him as chairman for delaying business by reading motions not signed and seconded — perhaps it was intended as a gibe at his meticulousness. A chairman was elected for each meeting, but in the autumn a referendum decided that he should be elected for three months instead. On 3 September Place was chosen: 'It was the post of honour and was eagerly desired by several others as well as by me.'[18] The remark shows that he did not then feel the aversion to recognition and honour which he displayed in later life.

1795 was a difficult year for Pitt's Government. The war with France was going badly and economic distress caused widespread food riots and general discontent with the Ministry. A gardener was charged before a London magistrate with seditious words because he cried 'peas and beans, and good *Republican* measure', and sold his goods so fast that his rival was injured in business. 'The state of irritation which the circumstances of the time produced', Place wrote, 'drove the people into clubs and associations to obtain Peace, Reform and Cheap bread. Those who associated were fully persuaded that by causing as great a ferment as possible the government would be overawed and concede what they had requested.' In the second half of the year the LCS reached the peak of its membership and influence, and in early September the members voted for another public meeting by 488 votes to 346.[19]

In the first draft of his autobiography Place said that he and his allies opposed the meeting on two grounds:

First that it would be used by Ministers as an instrument to create a fresh alarm, and thereby enable them to recover the power and influence they had lost, whereas if no excuse to create an alarm was furnished them, their power and influence would continue to decline and that this might lead to Reform; the Second objection was the state of the societies funds, which on account of the expense; made the meeting inexpedient.[20]

The opponents proposed instead a national campaign of petitioning for reform, which would, they argued, help to weaken the power of Ministers without giving them an excuse for creating a fresh alarm. In the second draft he said that he had no expectation that Ministers would be compelled to grant reform, and urged the society to proceed as quietly and privately as possible. Here he was almost certainly deceiving himself, presenting himself as more pessimistic and quietist than he really was.[21]

E.P. Thompson has argued that he was advocating a policy of acting as the auxiliary of middle-class reformers, against activists who urged that the artisan reformers should build bridges with the tumultuous poor. Gwyn Williams, on the other hand, suggested that Place favoured a retreat by the artisan reformers out of the political arena into their own 'Common Wealth of Reason'.[22] Place's franker first draft implies that his differences with the activists were merely tactical. Both sides aimed to mobilise support from below in order to create a crisis which would bring down the Government and force the Foxites to introduce radical reform. The question was how far an aggressive policy of agitation could be carried without enabling the Government to rally support for a policy of repression. Over the June 1795 public meeting the activists were proved right, as it helped to revive the movement without bringing repression. But it sowed the seed for the society's downfall, by encouraging it to hold meetings which were to prove disastrous, and ensuring that the LCS would be constantly split by arguments between supporters and opponents of public meetings.

The society claimed an attendance of over 150,000 — doubtless an exaggeration — at its meeting on 26 October 1795 in a field near Copenhagen House. The meeting agreed a militant Address to the Nation which warned that *'his Majesty should consider the sacred obligations he is bound to fulfil, and the duties he ought to discharge: he should recollect, that when he ceases to consult the interests and happiness of the People, he will cease to be respected; and that Justice is a debt which the Nation hath a right to demand from the Throne!'* It also, Place complained, 'contained an absurd declaration that *"if ever the British nation should loudly demand strong and decisive measures, we boldly answer — 'we have lives!' and are ready to devote them, either separately or collectively, for the salvation of our country.'"*[23]

Three days later the King was met by a hostile crowd when he went to open Parliament. Place, who was present, wrote: 'When the State Carriage came into the Park at St James's the crowd which was immense, Hissed and groaned and called out "No Pitt – No War – Peace Peace – Bread Bread".' A pane of glass in the carriage was broken and the King was alleged to have cried out as he reached the House of Lords: 'My Lords, I, I, I've been shot at.' The Government later admitted that the pane had been broken by a pebble, but it blamed the trouble on the 'inflammatory discourses' and 'subversive proceedings' at the Copenhagen House meeting and introduced two bills against treason and sedition. Place, an inveterate conspiracy theorist so far as Ministers' motives were concerned, shared a wide suspicion that the incident had been engineered in order to give an excuse for repression. All sections of the opposition, including the Foxites, united in a fierce campaign against the bills, and Place gave 'all the assistance in my power'.

On 12 November the LCS held a public meeting against the bills. Place thought that it was probably the largest ever assembled in London, although he admitted that the claim of an attendance of over 300,000 must have been an exaggeration. 'More order than was observed at this meeting', he asserted, 'was never observed at any meeting.' The resolutions and petitions, less violent than those passed at the October meeting, 'were principally composed by Citizen John Thelwall and may even now [1824] be read with approbation. The meeting produced a considerable effect among the people, as well in London as in the country, but', he commented ironically, 'none at all on the majorities in the two houses of parliament.' He was involved in finding a site for another public meeting on 7 December:

> It was with the greatest difficulty any place could be procured and much time which could be exceedingly ill spared from our ordinary occupations was consumed in waiting on different persons, to obtain permission to occupy one of their fields. All the active men on the committees were industrious men, very few of them were masters and many of them had families wholly maintained by the work of their hands, to such persons loss of time was not only a great pecuniary evil, but also [resulted] in the discomfort neglect of business occasioned at home. These circumstances reduced the number of those on whom the burthen fell to a small number. It may be doubted by those who are friendly to the people that it was wise in any man to make such sacrifices as the condition in which the society was placed demanded.[24]

Many years later Place remarked that his wife disliked conversation on public matters, and this passage contains a rare hint that she resented the sacrifices which his involvement in politics required.

The 'Two Acts' received the Royal Assent on 18 December. By the first it became High Treason to 'imagine, invent, devise, or intend' the death or wounding of the King, or depriving him of his Crown or any of his dominions, by any writing or overt act. 'Nothing need be said of this barbarous bloodthirsty act', Place commented bitterly, 'the time will come when people will be filled with pity for those who could submit to such a law.'[25] The second

Act banned meetings of over fifty people without previous notice to a magistrate, who was given wide powers, including that of dispersing legally convened meetings.

The Two Acts achieved their object, and thereafter the LCS and the other reform societies steadily declined. The reformers had been grossly overoptimistic, and working men daring to interfere in politics for the first time were easily discouraged when the Government refused to be intimidated by their campaign. To a considerable extent Place had shared their hopes, and he was doubtless recalling his frustration and disappointment when he wrote:

> Never within the memory of man were ministers placed in such untoward circumstances as were Pitt, Dundas, Windham and Grenville at the opening of the session, never before did any administration, so pertinaciously cling to power and hold it as it were in despite of circumstances. These men however not only held it but by a bold and dextrous line of conduct, increased it to an extent, greater than had ever been exercised by any of their predecessors, since the King came to the throne . . .26

'No sooner had the bills received the Royal assent', Place observed, 'than the reformers generally conceived it not only dangerous but also useless to continue to exert themselves any longer. The fears of some and the machinations of others reduced the numbers of the members in every one of the Divisions, and caused several of them to abandon the society altogether.' An address dated 31 December called on the members not to forget the pledges they had made to maintain and uphold the society. It had some effect, but the numbers present in their division fell from 1096 in February 1796 to 188 in December. Place and others tried hard to prevent this decline, and he remarked that he had to visit as many as three divisions in one evening and urge them on to a greater state of activity. In order to keep General Committee meetings below the new legal limit of fifty, an intermediate tier of District Committees was introduced, but these proved troublesome. 'As they had no legislative powers', Place wrote, the members 'had nothing to do but report to one another, this was unentertaining tiresome and monotonous. The consequence was that the district committees were but badly attended and many divisions got the reports from other delegates or remained in ignorance of what was going on, these things could not fail to produce dissensions and to drive away some of the best of the members.'27

The societies outside London were also in decay, and in February the LCS sent two leading members, John Binns and John Gale Jones, as deputies to Portsmouth and Rochester at the request of local societies. These missions were successful, so the following month the society sent Jones and Binns on a tour of northern towns, but they only got as far as Birmingham. On 18 March the Executive Committee heard that they had been arrested there and decided to send Place to Birmingham to help them — it was the first time that he travelled more than thirty miles from London. James Powell, a spy on the

General Committee, reported to the Government the receipt of a letter from Place four days later: 'He had some difficulty in obtaining an interview with them & when he did two constables were always present. He stated they were visited by the most respectable citizens of Birmingham . . . & their dungeon had absolutely become a political debating Room.'[28] In the end Jones was convicted but not sentenced and Binns acquitted. Place paid heavily for his help to them. His journey to Birmingham alarmed his female employer and so Place ceased to go to her for work, reducing him again to poverty.

Place had supported the decision to send out deputies, showing that he was not opposed to a wide agitation. The proposal to send deputies round the country had originally been approved at the October 1795 public meeting but, he observed, 'the change which had taken place rendered the sending of deputies not only unnecessary but actually absurd. It happened however that we cajoled ourselves and each other with delusive expectations which proves us to have been very silly people.'[29]

'Another absurdity', Place wrote, 'was the setting up a magazine.' *The Moral and Political Magazine of the London Corresponding Society* was published monthly between July 1796 and May 1797, and instead of paying a penny a week for dues, members paid fourpence halfpenny a month and received the Magazine: 'a better contrivance to prevent the society pay its debts could hardly have been devised'. The Magazine was much praised in letters from country societies, but it proved such a financial drain that by the end of the year the LCS had borrowed £170 to cover its losses from a fund established to pay for the defence of Jones and Binns. Place claimed that he opposed the Magazine from the start, but this is unlikely. On 5 May he was elected assistant secretary to replace John Bone, who had resigned in protest at the Magazine, which he feared would damage his own paper, *The Politician*. Place thus accepted personal responsibility (jointly with the secretary, John Ashley) for paying for the paper for the Magazine, which is hardly the conduct of an opponent of the proposal. He said that he accepted the post because business was getting into arrears, and he also accepted the remuneration of £3 2s 6d per quarter: 'Although the secretary and assistant secretary were hired servants and were most badly paid I took the money with great reluctance, had I not been miserably poor I should have refused it, as it was, it gave me great pain at times, when I reflected that I had taken money for my services.'[30]

Towards the end of 1796 Place joined Ashley and others in trying to persuade the society to give up the Magazine and cut down on expenses in order to pay the debts: 'we knew that the very name of debt was enough to drive many members away and to prevent others from joining it'.[31] He said that their opponents argued that a public meeting would produce an influx of members and money, while he and his allies believed that it would ruin the society. Ashley and Place also had a personal reason for opposing the Magazine: they feared that they would have to make good their personal

liability for the cost of the paper for it. On 30 November the Executive
Committee received a letter from Place stating that he would no longer be
answerable for the paper. According to Powell's reports the General and
Executive Committees were rent with personal quarrels, and Ashley gave
notice of his resignation as secretary when his right to vote on literary matters
in the Executive was questioned. On 29 December there was an argument in
the General Committee after Ashley and Place refused to deliver up the stock
of society publications, retaining them as security for the debts for which they
were liable. Ashley was accused of making a property of the Magazine by
advertisements on the covers, of injuring the society by keeping back the
accounts, and of including in the accounts charges which were 'extraordinary
and extravagant'.[32] The Committee resolved, by the chairman's casting vote,
to allow Ashley and Place to keep the stock, but several delegates promptly
walked out, declaring that they would not attend the Committee or take the
Magazine while it was in Ashley's hands. Place resigned as assistant secretary
soon afterwards.[33]

In March 1797 the LCS finally decided in favour of a public meeting, after a
long period of argument. Place said that he and Ashley then resigned from the
General Committee, and concentrated their efforts on making up the
deficiency in the fund for the defence of the deputies: 'As John Binns was the
friend of both of us, as Jones was a very old acquaintance of Ashleys and
rather an intimate acquaintance of mine, and as both of us had concurred in
sending them to Birmingham, we were in every respect bound to render them
all the assistance in our power and we did so, as well in the Society as in
private.'[34] The money was subscribed a second time, and Place allowed his
membership to lapse at the end of June.

*   *   *

Place seems to have contemplated solving his financial difficulties by
becoming a bookseller and publisher. A pamphlet published in about October
1795 includes him in a list of vendors. Its title is a play on Burke's phrase
'swinish multitude': *A Political Dictionary for the Guinea-Less Pigs, or a
Glossary of Emphatical Words Made Use of by that Jewel of a Man Deep
Will. In his Administration, and his Plans for Yoking and putting Rings in the
Snouts of those Grumbling Swine, who raise such Horrid Grunting, when
Tyrannical Winds Blow High.*[35] A year later Place decided to publish a cheap
edition of the *Age of Reason*. He was sure that he could dispose of 2000 copies
through the LCS, and he was in good credit with a papermaker because of his
transactions on behalf of the society. He chose a poor bookbinder called
Thomas Williams to get the work printed, and the profit was to be divided
between them, but when Williams found the venture profitable he cut Place
out and started printing a larger edition. Early in 1797 Williams learnt that
William Wilberforce's 'Society for carrying into effect His Majesty's

Proclamation against Vice and Immorality' (better known, Place observed, as the Vice Society) was prosecuting him for publishing a seditious and blasphemous libel. He promptly went to Place, greatly alarmed, and told him 'WE are prosecuted for the Age of Reason'. 'WE', Place retorted, 'no Tom, not WE – how can WE be prosecuted. YOU as soon as YOU found that money could be made by the sale of the book took care to exclude ME from any participation. . . . YOU must therefore change your note and sing I, not We.'

Thomas Erskine, who had been the principal defence counsel in the 1794 treason trials, was approached to act for Williams. Erskine was the author of a declaration by the Society of Friends of Freedom of the Press against societies bringing libel prosecutions, but to Place's fury he had already agreed to act for the Vice Society. Place was so bitter that he devoted an appendix in his autobiography to an attack on Erskine's conduct. Williams was tried and convicted in June 1797, but he was released on bail until February 1798, when he was committed to prison pending sentencing in April. Erskine then wrote to the Vice Society to request them to show their 'charity and Christian forebearance' by asking the judge to consider the time served as Williams' sentence, and when they refused, he returned the fee and withdrew from the case. Place claimed the credit for the decision, stating that he had made use of private information to harass Erskine, and that he had succeeded in operating on his fear of public censure. Erskine complained in court in February that his conduct had been 'arraigned in the public prints as an attack on the liberty of the press'. Williams was sentenced to a year's hard labour in the Middlesex House of Correction.[36]

Place's use of the LCS to sell the *Age of Reason* gave ammunition to enemies of the society who accused it of espousing infidelity, and in 1800 W.H. Reid, a former radical, claimed that the LCS had officially sanctioned Williams' edition. Reid was clearly well informed, but the details of his account suggest that he confused religious controversy in the society in 1795 with the circulation of the *Age of Reason* in 1796. On 17 September 1795 a motion was brought before the General Committee 'that there are in the Society Atheists, Deists & other blasphemous Persons who go about propagating the most horrible Doctrines, contrary to every Principle of Liberty, & which frighten all good Christians from the Society. They likewise make use of the most diabolical expressions such as calling the Deity "Mr Humbug", "Damning the Bible", Blasting all Christians & declaring the Society will never do any good until they are without them.' The motion was 'passed to the order of the day with contempt', and its supporters seceded to form The Friends of Religious and Civil Liberty, which prohibited members who did not believe in Scripture. In a letter to a Birmingham society a month later the chastened LCS warned 'our associated friends to avoid themes of religious opinion . . .'.[37] Although Place said that nearly all the leading members were deists or atheists, he insisted that a rule that religion should not be discussed in society meetings was strictly observed. The evidence confirms his claim (except in 1795), but the successful circulation of the *Age of Reason* through the LCS supports the view that many radicals turned to free thought when hopes of political reform faded after the Two Acts.

*   *   *

In 1795 Place had moved to Fisher Street, Holborn,[38] partly in order to be near a 'good shop of work', and partly because the lodging was only two doors away from the shoeshop kept by his close friend, the secretary of the LCS, John Ashley. Ashley had spent several months in gaol during the suspension of habeas corpus in 1794, although he was never charged, and Place probably became acquainted with him when he visited the prisoners in Newgate. Very little is known of Ashley's political views, but he appears to have been an efficient organiser in the same mould as Place. According to Place, 'He was less scrupulous than I was and consequently had more customers among the members of the society and was much better off than I was. He was a serious thinking man of rather an imposing appearance. . . . He was a man of undoubted courage on all trying occasions, was honest and sincere. He was much attached to me and I to him.'[39]

In September 1796 Ashley moved to a house in High Holborn, and he persuaded Place to rent his second floor. Place agreed to pay the high rent of sixteen guineas a year on Ashley's assurance that he would find him orders to help him pay it. But Ashley was unable to do much for Place, and a few months later he got into trouble himself. He started an affair with a lodger in his house, whom Place described as 'a fine tall handsome woman named Lambert, she had been in high keeping and well versed in intrigues, she was about thirty-three years of age. Ashley had all his life long been a sedate sober steady man, and was as simple with respect to what relates to such women as a child. As it sometimes happens to such women she fell desperately in love with Ashley and he fell as desperately in love with her.' His wife was twelve years older than him, 'a short, square built, large boned, ill made woman, her manners were vulgar, . . . in her temper she was a very devil and had in her frequent fits of utterly unfounded jealousy been a perfect fury. . . . Ashley soon became ashamed of his folly, yet was unable to extricate himself.'[40] His wife would not let him attend to his business, and she constantly drove him back to Mrs Lambert for solace.

To escape ruin he decided in September 1797 to leave both women and go to Paris. 'Attempting to go to France was at this time Treason', Place wrote. 'But there was no great difficulty in going to Helvoetslays by means of smuggling vessels.'

> Ashley had urged me very strongly to go to France with him, he had no doubt of obtaining assistance from persons whom he knew there and he said we could make common cause until each of us could get business or employment of some kind to

maintain ourselves separately, that my wife should share any money that might be got in from his book debts, that she might live with my mother and do something towards getting a living for herself and her two children until I could send for her. I was miserably poor at this time and was all but resolved to go, but when the probabilities came to be calculated and discussed with my wife, I gave up all thoughts of going to France.[41]

This is the only example of Place saying that he had been influenced over an important decision by his wife.

When Ashley left he was under attack again in the LCS, and since he got much of his business from the members this may have been an additional motive for his flight. He was accused of failing to pay money owed to a papermaker for the Magazine and concealing their legal proceedings against him to recover the debt, thus involving the society in legal expenses. There were calls for him to be expelled from the society and to repay the legal expenses. Place indignantly denied an allegation by a Parliamentary Secret Committee that Ashley became the representative of the LCS in Paris, and the circumstances of his flight make the allegation implausible, but Ashley's conduct in Paris might have given credence to the idea. In memoranda to the French Government in 1798, he gave a greatly exaggerated account of the influence of the society and the support a French invasion would receive. His motive is suggested by his plea for 'some present succour'. He stayed in France for the rest of his life and prospered in later years.[42]

* * *

In early 1797 government weakness gave hope of a change of ministry, and the naval mutinies at Spithead and the Nore in April and May severely shook public confidence. LCS strength recovered, and on 25 May 518 members were reported present in the divisions. But in the second half of the year hopes of rousing the nation against the Government died. The public meeting which had provoked Place's resignation from the LCS was finally held on 31 July, but it had hardly got started before it was dispersed by the Middlesex magistrates, who arrested some of the men on the platforms. They were subsequently released without being charged. Soon afterwards a score of members resigned in protest at the meeting and the society's decline resumed. Reactions among reformers to this further disappointment varied. The LCS took a more friendly attitude towards the Foxites, encouraged by their help with the defence in John Binns' trial for the mission to Birmingham, but some leading members began to turn to conspiracy in desperation. The two approaches were not incompatible – Binns supported both of them.

In January 1798 Father James O'Coigley arrived in London from Ireland. Place 'saw him three or four times, and liked him much, he was a good looking man of remarkably mild manners, kind and benevolent'. Place knew that he was a member of the revolutionary Society of United Irishmen, but not that he was on his way to France as a delegate of the society. A month later Binns was trying to find transport for him when both men were arrested and charged with High Treason. O'Coigley was convicted and executed, while Binns was acquitted and went into hiding before a lesser charge could be preferred.[43]

Place said that Benjamin Binns, a man 'of much meaner understanding' than his brother,[44] and Thomas Evans, the secretary of the LCS but 'a sort of absurd fanatic', then attempted to form a Society of United Englishmen on the Irish model, led on in Place's opinion by spies: 'The object of this association was to promote a revolution, a more ridiculous project was never entered by the imaginations of men out of Bedlam. I attended two or three meetings when some half dozen were present, and pointed out to them the extreme folly of their proceedings. They did not however desist, and I am fully persuaded that this was owing to emissaries who were sent among them'. Place denied an allegation by the Parliamentary Committee of Secrecy that there were forty divisions of United Englishmen in London, and said that he did not believe that a single division existed. He was among many people invited to a meeting on 18 April to form the society, and he proposed sending for Binns, Evans and 'a foolish fellow their coadjutor named James Powell' (who was never suspected of being a spy), and threatening to inform the Government about the project if they did not drop it. But other opponents objected to the idea, and Colonel Despard (who was to be executed in 1803 for plotting a rebellion) argued that it would appear dishonourable. It was proposed instead to go to the meeting and expose the mischievous tendency of the society.[45] Place luckily or wisely refused to go – the meeting ended in the arrest of those present.

Meanwhile the General Committee of the LCS had been discussing what attitude the society should take to a bill to establish local volunteer corps to resist a French invasion. At a General Committee meeting on 6 April, Thomas Evans bitterly criticised the destruction of liberty in France and the treachery and tyranny shown by the French Government towards conquered nations. He proposed – no doubt with ulterior motives – that the society should offer itself as a military corps to the Government to resist a French invasion. His opinions on France met with general approval, but his proposal was scouted, on the grounds that it was bound to be rejected and if accepted would put the members under the control of men they did not trust. On 19 April the Committee had just agreed on the necessity of publicly declaring the society's opposition to a French invasion when the Bow Street Runners entered and arrested the delegates.[46]

The two groups were committed to gaol by the Privy Council under a renewed suspension of habeas corpus. Place said that he immediately called a meeting of half a dozen members and ex-members of the LCS, and suggested that a subscription should be raised for the relief of the prisoners' families. No one else could be persuaded to act as secretary in the prevailing climate of fear, so Place took on the task himself, identifying the subscribers by codes rather than names in the committee book. He persuaded the gentleman reformer, William Frend, to form another committee among his own friends, and he sought the help of the Horne Tooke circle for a campaign against the arrests. But there was little that they could do – no newspaper would publish a statement from the prisoners which Place took to every editor in London. He was able to pass on to the prisoners an assurance from Tooke that free legal help would be provided, but this proved superfluous since the prisoners were never charged.[47]

The spy, James Powell, had been arrested at the United Englishmen meeting, but he 'escaped' and came to Place for help:

> It occurred to me that the safest place in which Powell could be put was my apartments. It never would I concluded be supposed for an instant, that he would seek concealment with a person so liable to be apprehended himself, as I was, and that unless therefore they came to seize me, they would never look for any one else in my lodgings.

Place then went to Richard Ford, a magistrate at the Treasury, to ask him whether the Government intended to provide for the prisoners' families. Ford 'good naturedly said I might think myself well off that I was not also sent to gaol, and asked me if I was not afraid to come to him'. Place retorted that 'Ministers wanted a new alarm so they seized men indiscriminately and had succeeded, and as no purpose could now be answered I knew very well they would let me alone.' The conference 'convinced Powell that he was safe, as he thought it very unlikely they would molest me, and would not suspect him of taking refuge with me'. In fact, the arrests probably resulted from a report from Powell to Ford, and Ford's amusement during the interview may have been due to the knowledge that Place was helping the Government by concealing Powell – perhaps thus saving Place himself from arrest. Place arranged Powell's passage to Hamburg, and sent him to Harwich, but Powell went to Yarmouth, possibly as part of a plan to get his passage paid by both sides.[48] Place's conduct showed a disregard for danger which contrasts with his extreme care in later life not to lay himself open to prosecution.

At first the subscription for the prisoners went well, and their wives used to call on Place to collect their weekly allowance, but trouble occurred when they came to Elizabeth Place's room and refused to leave, apparently because she showed resentment at her husband handing out larger sums than he earned himself. He turned them out, drawing a protest at his behaviour from their husbands. Place replied that he was not conscious of having done wrong, and that he could say no more because it related to matters between man and wife. The incident left a residue of ill-will, and a further clash occurred in the autumn when the prisoners demanded the distribution of the accumulated surplus in a lump sum. Place persuaded the subscription committees to refuse, because he believed that compliance would put an end to the funds and reduce the families to want. He resigned as secretary of the committees when he went into business in April 1799, and the fund ran out in mid-1800, after which the Government provided for the families until the prisoners were released in 1801.

In April 1798 the LCS had not declined back to the low point of December 1796, but the arrests effectively extinguished it, although it issued a printed statement in June 1798, and according to spy reports it continued an underground existence into 1799.[49] It was finally proscribed by name under the Corresponding Societies Act of 1799.

*   *   *

'All the leading members of the London Corresponding society were republicans', Place wrote in the first draft of his autobiography, 'that is, they were all friendly to representative Government'.[50]

> A great majority of the members were also republicans, but they were generally convinced that a republic could be advantageously produced in this country by slow degrees only, it was quite a common saying that 'a republic produced by our vices could not be permanent', that no change which was not the consequence of conviction of its utility could be useful. There were some, however, that believed a Reform of Parliament would be obtained and that it was compatible with what they called the constitution, others again believed that a reform would be obtained and that a house of Commons really chosen by the people, would in time have all the power and set aside the King and Lords. Others expected that a reform would be obtained which would at once convert the Government into a republic. Some were of opinion that no reform would ever be obtained, but that Ministers would on some occasion drive the thing to extremities and the whole system of government would break up, that it was therefore the wisest way to point out to the people, the advantages of representative government, and with this view the report of the Committee of Constitution was made and printed. I was one among the number who embraced the last named opinion. A very few were for using violence, for putting an end to the government by any means foreign or domestic, these were always few and had no weight in the society.

This account leaves out the Godwinian group and it underplays the strength of the violent faction at the end of the society's life, but it does make clear how revolutionary the society was, and it is easy to see how frightening it must have seemed to many contemporaries in the hierarchical world of the 1790s. Even in the second draft Place hardly presented himself as a moderate, writing that he believed that 'the Government would be carried on, the abuses continually increasing "until corruption had exhausted the means of corrupting" when an explosion would be caused, and a representative Government spring out of the Chaos . . . .'[51] It is remarkable that he was still optimistic enough in the 1820s to believe that a representative government would 'spring out of the Chaos'.

It seems clear that Place was not an opponent of revolution, only of attempts at revolution which were doomed to failure, as he was to show in

1810 and again in 1832. The hopes of the United Englishmen of recruiting him, his expectation of being arrested and his willingness to smuggle Powell to France, suggest that he was close to the revolutionary group; so do his account of meeting and liking the United Irishman O'Coigley, his earlier willingness to emigrate to revolutionary France and his familiarity with the means of travelling there illegally. His quarrel with the revolutionaries was tactical, not one of principle, and since they had only turned to conspiracy in desperation at the decline of radicalism, he was justified in dismissing their plans as insane. As another leading member of the LCS, Alexander Galloway, told him thirty years later: 'You and myself and 10,000 others did 30 years ago understand every political and theological truth, as well as we now know them and yet if we had spoken out and demonstrated these truths to the mass of the people, they would have assisted and applauded a Pitt . . . in hanging, drawing and quartering us.'[52]

By the spring of 1798 revolutionary societies of United Irishmen and United Englishmen were organising in England.[53] A number of leading members of the LCS had turned to conspiracy, but it is still unclear whether an organisation of the United Englishmen had got off the ground in London, and the case for implicating the LCS is even weaker. The quality of the Government's intelligence on the LCS had seriously declined since 1794, when they had a number of spies whose reports could be cross-checked. In early 1798 Ministers were primarily dependent on the untrustworthy James Powell.[54] The LCS papers seized when the General Committee was arrested on 19 April suggest that the organisation and preoccupations of the society were much the same as when Place had been active, and according to the contemporary account by the chairman, Richard Hodgson, the General Committee was united in its disillusionment with developments in France and its determination to resist a French invasion. The situation was complicated by the Irish dimension. Dr Elliott has argued that the United Englishmen, numerically insignificant in itself, should be seen as an aspect of the attempt to raise a rebellion in Ireland, rather than as a movement in its own right. The Irish element in the LCS was strong, and men who dismissed an English rebellion as doomed to failure may well have been prepared to assist an Irish revolt with French assistance. None of the United men appears to have attended the LCS discussions on the attitude the society should take to a French invasion, apart from Thomas Evans.[55] By this time the supporters and opponents of revolution were beginning to separate out between the United movement and the LCS, a trend which was reversed after the arrests of late April.[56]

Place played down the support for insurrection in the LCS, and some historians have argued that the LCS was not the moderate body which he portrayed, but in fact he did not really portray it as moderate. He regarded radical parliamentary reform as unarguably just and reasonable, and cited the aristocrats and gentlemen who had supported it in the 1780s as proof of its respectability. But upper-class men urging reform in the quiet 1780s were a very different matter from artisans claiming the right to interfere in politics for the first time just when the French revolutionaries had offered their help to any people wishing to overthrow their rulers. Place's account presented the aim of subverting the established order of society as a modest and respectable one. His attitude to the French Revolution was probably the one he was to express in 1814, that it had caused great cruelties, but the harm was temporary, whereas the good it did was permanent.[57]

The London Corresponding Society was a remarkable organisation. Its members showed an extraordinary degree of courage and persistence in keeping it alive for seven years in the face of severe persecution, which (except in 1795) had the support of the loyalist mass of the people. In 1841 Place compared the Chartist movement unfavourably with the LCS, whose leaders had been wise enough to regard political education in favour of their views as the society's main object. He pointed out with some justice that the society's discretion had ensured that it could never be prosecuted with any chance of success.[58] It was frequently marred by in-fighting and splits, but in the long run it showed a tolerant spirit towards defectors, and often managed to draw them back into the fold. The constant preoccupation with rules could become tedious, but it reflected the attention to detail which was one of the society's strengths. The leaders did not make it easy for members to drop out, and Place was one of those who gave up many evenings to urge slack divisions on to greater activity.

Place displayed in later life a fanatical loyalty to the society and he formed a romanticised view of it. He always intended to write its history, but never did. He considered it 'the very best school for good teaching which probably ever existed', and he explained how it transformed men's lives:

> the moral effects of the society were very great indeed, it induced men to read books, instead of spending their time at public houses, it induced them to love their own homes, it taught them to think, to respect themselves, and to desire to educate their children. It taught them the great moral lesson to 'bear and forbear'. The discussions in the divisions, and in the sunday afternoon reading and debating associations held in their own rooms, opened to them views to which they had been blind. They were compelled by those discussions to find reasons for their opinions, and to tolerate the opinions of others. In fact it gave a new stimulus to a large mass of men who had hitherto been but too justly considered, as incapable of any but the very grossest pursuits, and sensual enjoyments. It elevated them in society.[59]

In 1822 he met twenty-four former delegates at the annual dinner to celebrate the victory of the 1794 treason trials. All of them were flourishing men, and he considered them a sample of those who had benefited from membership. By this time his enthusiasm for collecting materials for the history of the LCS, and his failure to get down to writing it, were already notorious, and John Thelwall declared at the dinner that 'there was one man who would deserve to be damned, if he did not write the history of the London Corresponding Society'. Place claimed that the society 'was a great moral cause of the improvement which has since taken place among the *People*'.[60] The desire to prove this was one motive for his research into the history of morals, although his hostility to religion led him to ignore the contribution of religious movements to the improvement.

The LCS gave Place a feeling of liberation and a new egalitarian sense of his own worth. His experience as chairman of the General Committee from September 1795 to February 1796 and assistant secretary from May 1796 to early 1797 gave him training in methods of political organisation and agitation. By the end of the 1790s his basic political ideas were set: parliamentary reform was the crucial issue, and he retained throughout his life his belief in manhood suffrage and annual elections, although he became increasingly doubtful of the desirability of introducing it without educating the people first.

The book which Place always recommended to working men – he urged it on the founders of the London Working Men's Association in 1836 – was Godwin's *Enquiry Concerning Political Justice*.[61] In the 1790s radicals made use of the traditional 'Norman Yoke' belief that they were reclaiming lost rights, the Paineite natural rights theory that they were claiming what belonged to them as men, and utilitarian arguments that parliamentary reform would increase social happiness – often all three in conjunction. Place is never likely to have had much sympathy with traditionalist arguments, and Godwin persuaded him that 'the active rights of man . . . are all of them superseded and rendered null by the superior claims of justice'.[62] *Political Justice* was critically important in forming Place's outlook, teaching him some of his key attitudes and ideas and confirming others: his utilitarianism, his desire to see the scope of government reduced to the smallest possible extent, his preference for gradual over sudden change, his belief that a man's character is formed wholly by his circumstances, his conviction that truth must triumph over error, and his obsessive concern with honesty and frankness. But he had to wait until he became acquainted with Bentham and James Mill in the 1810s before he found a satisfactory strategy for applying utilitarian theory to the development of specific policies.

By contrast the development of his ideas on economics had not even begun, and he later confessed that there were few 'erroneous notions' of the working people which he had not once accepted.[63] The LCS saw parliamentary reform as the panacea which would cure all ills. It owed much of its strength to economic distress, but apart from blaming distress on the high taxes caused by parliamentary corruption and the war with France, it generally confined itself to arguments for political liberty and equality, and its ideas on economics were virtually non-existent. 'In their ideas of equality', a handbill of 1795 declared, the members of the LCS 'have never included (nor, till the associations of alarmists broached the frantic notion, could they ever have conceived that so wild and detestable a sentiment could have entered the brain of man) as the equalization of property, or the invasion of personal rights and possessions.'[64] But some members did advocate the equalisation of property in land, including Place. Thomas Spence, the advocate of municipal ownership of land, came to London in November 1792. He opened a bookstall in Chancery Lane and Place, who loved bookshops and bookstalls, soon became acquainted with him. Spence was a leading member of the LCS before the 1794 arrests, and he was held for several months during the suspension of habeas corpus. He continued to advocate 'Spence's Plan', in spite of great poverty, and harassment and imprisonment by the Government, until his death in 1814. Place later collected materials for a memoir of him — the only memoir among the many books he planned — and described him as 'one of that class of extraordinary men from whom the greatest changes in society have proceeded. Had he lived in times propitious to his views, it is probable he would have been of considerable consequence.' In 1839 Place expressed 'my hope and belief that the time will come when men will be sufficiently wise to agree that all the land shall belong to all the people, and that too upon the plan or some such plan as Mr Spence has promulgated, by which the people shall be the sole landlord and receive all the rent'.[65]

*　　*　　*

Personal friendships formed through the LCS were important to Place. John Binns, the son of a Dublin ironmonger, joined the LCS at the end of 1794. Place described him as 'a very well informed man, on many subjects, but inexperienced, very desirous of increasing his stock of knowledge, but at times volatile as most Irishmen are'.[66] He used to come as early as he could from his job as a plumber's labourer to read with Place, who would carry on with his work — when he had work — so that both men obtained knowledge at the same time. Binns was lucky to escape execution for his part in promoting a French invasion of Ireland.

Place also met a number of educated men. John Fenwick was a leading member of the LCS in 1796–97, one of the few gentlemen to play an active role in the society after the treason trials. Place described him as 'one of my benefactors. He taught me much of what I was desirous of knowing in literature, so far as conversation and an occasional reference book, with grammatical observations and directions, went. He was a remarkable man, bred a gentleman, and brought up a scholar.' He was a close friend of Godwin and Charles Lamb, and featured as Ralph Bigod Esq. in Lamb's 'Two Races of Men'. He was notorious for drunkenness, and Lamb referred to him as one of the 'friendly harpies' who forced him to consider forming a 'diabolical resolution' of banning liquor from his house. Fenwick died an alcoholic in great poverty. Place described Colonel Despard as '*a man whom I always esteemed* as much as one man could esteem another, a man of whose mildness, and kindness, and goodness towards everyone I had very many opportunities of knowing'. He often used to visit Place, while William Frend gave him great help with his mathematical and astronomical studies. Colonel Bosville, a rich reformer who dressed like a courtier of George II, would have been willing to set Place up in business, but Place's 'absurd' notions of independence led him to refuse: 'This was sad folly, and I have often when I have thought of it been ashamed of my self.'[67]

In 1827 Place recalled that he had had to work at his trade even when talking to visitors:

> Very few therefore of those whose circumstances were more affluent than my own visited me. It was a mark of respect, and as it regarded me, & of my importance also, that, any man who was well off in the world, and well instructed, condescended to visit me at all. I lived on the second floor, in a room in which many of the concerns of the family were carried on by my lately deceased, and most dearly beloved wife, without assistance from any one, and notwithstanding the peculiar care she bestowed upon the place and the children, and herself; as to neatness and propriety, it was not a place which many persons would choose to frequent. I was however visited by some remarkable men, . . . and those visits were very advantageous to me in intellectual and moral points of view.[68]

These contacts ceased when he retired from politics between 1799 and 1806 in order to concentrate on building up his business. His temporary retirement was well timed: at the height of the reaction he had no strategy, and there must have seemed little that he could usefully do to promote the radical cause.

4   The Tailor of Charing Cross

It is commonly believed that Francis Place was brought up in poverty, but his own account shows that this is untrue. His father's life witnessed extreme fluctuations of fortune, but Francis's childhood and youth occurred during a period of prosperity. According to his own ideas Simon Place did everything possible to provide for his son's physical and moral welfare, and he showed the sincerity of his intentions by sending him to school from the age of four to fourteen. Although the standard was low until the last two years, this reflected the poor education then available to the children of tradesmen. (Forty years later, Francis attempted to establish a secondary school partly because of the difficulty he encountered in finding good schools for his own children.) It would be misleading to describe his background as working class. The key social distinction in the eighteenth century was between gentlemen and the 'lower orders', but finer gradations of class were important. Francis was the son of a prosperous householder, and as a youth he mixed with apprentices who would not have accepted the company of the son of a journeyman.

He encountered difficulties because of two misfortunes: his father's ruin, and the fact that he was himself in a declining trade. But he regarded the setback as temporary, and it was natural for him to make the position of a master his goal. In his autobiography he described the fates of a number of prosperous tradesmen, friends of his father, who wasted their money and ended their lives in desperate poverty, some of them selling a niece or a ward into prostitution on the way down. These examples made a strong impression on him, and it is probably no coincidence that he changed his way of life at the time of his father's final ruin. He could no longer hope for his help in setting up in business, and falling in love with Elizabeth Chadd helped him to break completely with his past in favour of industrious sobriety.

Simon Place's ability to rise time and again from the total collapse of his fortunes shows that he must have been a man of considerable character. Francis inherited his business acumen and perseverance, as well as his hot temper. However, Simon never talked to his sons except to command or upbraid them, and this may well have benefited Francis. It opened him to the

44

influence of his schoolmaster, Mr Bowis, as a father figure, while his sympathy for his mother predisposed him to see the dangers in Simon's way of life. Indeed, Francis's life can be seen as a violent and successful attempt to repress and redirect the passions which had destroyed so many of his father's generation.

Francis's career helps to explain the psychological value of what is now considered the most unattractive of 'Victorian' virtues, respectability. The streak of humourlessness and priggishness in his character – although less evident in social intercourse than in his writings – helped him to resist being drawn into the criminal way of life of his apprentice companions, and to abandon his 'dissolute' way of life without apparent regret when he met Elizabeth Chadd. His earlier refusal publicly to acknowledge the girls he knew in the Cock and Hen clubs appears hypocritical, but it reflects his unwillingness to surrender wholly to the temptations of eighteenth-century London. As he commented on his later determination to dress well even at the worst times, no working man was wholly lost while he had sufficient self-respect to keep up appearances. The way that the Places dressed was a symbol of their determination to succeed.

By the time Place wrote his autobiography in the 1820s, what later became known as 'Victorian' morality was already dominant.[1] He was convinced that it represented a great advance on the standards of the eighteenth century, but he could not wholly detach himself from his past, and his own attitude was ambivalent, as he himself recognised. Respectability meant to him the growth of higher standards of self-discipline, self-respect and honesty, the decline of drunkenness and the spread of education. He would cite the greater chastity among unmarried girls as a proof of the improvement in morals in his lifetime. But the cruelty shown towards women who were 'unchaste', and the double standards applied to men and women, caused him great distress; and he would recall that the girls of his youth, who had not been chaste, had afterwards made good wives. Each of the Fleet Street apprentices had his own sweetheart, the daughter of a tradesman. (Place's was the daughter of a hairdresser and wig-maker – he was 'very fond' of her, but she married a young man of property and went to the East Indies.) He said that the girls usually turned out better than the boys, 'in as much as in other respects they were not like them dissolute. I could name several of them now living long since married to young men who were as well acquainted with them before marriage as afterwards, and I never knew any one of them who made a bad wife.'[2] The conflict in his outlook is also seen in the nostalgia with which he described such games as bullock hunting; and when revisiting fairs which he had known in his childhood, he would comment on the increased sobriety as a proof of the improvement in manners and morals, but at the same time complain how dull it all was compared with the lewd kissing and tumbling games of his youth.[3]

When the leading radical hostess, Mrs Grote, read Place's autobiography, she remarked that his history had 'relation to little other than *rogues* and *rips*'. He had been brought up in a society where cheating and dishonesty were hardly regarded as faults, and his own father had made a living out of legalised blackmail as a sponging-house keeper. A popular song in praise of thieving had the chorus line, 'then who would work and not go a thieving', and tradesmen would join in singing it.[4] Honesty became necessary to his self-respect and reputation, but since his ideas were formed by an intellectual process, through reading and his schoolmaster's lectures, he applied them rigidly. But even his rigidity brought a reward in the unquestioned faith placed in his integrity by friends and opponents from the 1820s onwards.

Place emphasised how much he owed to his schoolmaster, Mr Bowis. 'My temperament was sanguine, my temper violent and impetuous', Place observed, 'his good instructions enabled me to regulate both to a considerable extent as I grew up'. Confidence in himself, and especially in whatever he believed to be true, perseverance under difficulties and reliance on honest industry, were all features of his character for which he gave much credit to Bowis's teaching. Even when he mixed with the Fleet Street apprentices he disliked getting drunk, probably because he knew that losing his temper could lead to serious trouble with such companions. In later life his attempts to control his temper, and his passionate belief in honesty and frankness, found expression in a brusque manner and an outspoken readiness to criticise which made him many enemies. Remarking in 1817 that he had given notice that he would not receive callers after 3 p.m., he observed that his 'character for abruptness' would secure him from much intrusion.[5]

His awareness of the strength of the passionate and irrational elements in his own character probably played a part in his almost fanatical insistence on forming his views according to reason rather than emotion. His confidence in reason – as well as in his own ability to reason correctly – was doubtless encouraged by the incident in his childhood when he was praised by one of his father's customers for settling an argument. This insistence on following through the consequences of his own reasoning, and on accepting the conclusions however unpleasant they appeared, frequently put him at odds with radical associates – and with 'respectable' opinion.

His method of operation in politics, almost always behind the scenes, was determined by his aversion to self-display, which led him to avoid publicity. He was suspicious of a desire for public reputation because of the temptation it held out for a man to compromise his independence of mind and support 'vulgar errors' for the sake of popularity. In the 1800s and 1810s fear of damaging publicity for his business and a charge that he was a government spy helped to make his aversion to publicity a fixed habit of mind – one which he encouraged because he was aware that it greatly enhanced his political influence. Few well-known public men would have been willing to cooperate openly with a tailor. They would work with Place because they knew he would stay in the background and allow them to take the credit for what he achieved, and thus enhance their own public reputations. Place made sure that his own claims were recorded in his voluminous papers.

Self-confidence was another critically important element in his character. It enabled him to survive the desperate poverty he suffered in the 1790s and to seize every chance to rise to prosperity as a tradesman when most men in his situation would have despaired. In politics he was always ready to defend an unpopular opinion and take a courageous stand. He admitted that vanity was his weakness, and it produced the self-importance which mars his autobiography, but after 1830 this largely disappeared. A capacity for hard work and logical thinking, and an insatiable desire for knowledge on all practical matters, were equally important. They enabled him to build up a library of information which made him a one-man alternative civil service for the radicals, and to provide sound advice on the drafting of legislation and political tactics. His energy and self-confidence made him willing to take the lead when the going got rough, and this greatly enhanced his influence. His efficiency guaranteed his success in business, and often led men who disagreed with him politically to seek his cooperation on specific matters.

His interests outside politics were mainly practical, and in 1804 he showed his versatility by inventing an improved musket lock. He showed a wood and metal model to Captain Drewry of the Army Agents and

in a few days a tall good looking swaggering soldier like gentleman marched into the shop and seating himself on the end of the counter, with an air of supercilious dignity said to me.

Oh you have improved the musket Lock, so Mr Drewry tells me?
Place: Yes I have made a very simple lock which is secure at half cock.
Officer: Eh! Have you made it of cloth?
Place: Yes. And that's more than you could do.
Officer: Well then let me see it?
Place: Yes, if you will tell me who you are?
Officer: Why then my name is Bloomfield.
Place: The son of [Colonel] Bloomfield?
Officer: Yes.
Place: Well then I am glad to see you for as your father is a scientific man and has busied himself in such matters, I shall also conclude that his son is a clever fellow and understands a gun lock when he sees one.

I then gave him the lock, he took it in both his hands and instantly sprang off the counter, exclaiming 'By God, here it is, done by a tailor, my father and I have all our lives long been trying at it, and have failed and now it is done by a tailor.' We were now pretty well on a level and very sociable.[6]

After many delays Place was offered £10,000 for the lock, but payment was never made, due to the incompetence of the Board of Ordnance. Place believed that £100,000 could have been saved by the adoption of his invention.

His determination to establish his financial independence ensured that his

life in the twenty years after 1790 would be extremely laborious, and it seems
extraordinary that he never saw the sea until the Christmas of 1809, when he
was thirty-eight years old – especially since shipbuilding and rigging had
been a favourite subject since childhood. His first sight of the sea was quite
unexpected, coming when he was travelling in Essex on business: 'My
sensations were very remarkable. I was so extremely elated with the sight that I
was scarcely conscious that my own body had any gravity. It seemed as if I
could leap from the chaise to the ocean. I was at the moment more exhilarated
than I ever had before been or ever have been since.'

The early 1810s were the quietest period of his life, because his business was
securely established and he had temporarily retired from politics. He used to
take holidays in the autumn, long walking trips with tradesmen friends
exploring the south of England. His letters to his wife show that he took great
pleasure in scenery and architecture, and in spite of his opposition to religion
and the aristocracy he enjoyed visiting churches and great houses. These
letters display a side of his personality which is not shown by the rest of his
papers, warning her not to call him an old fool for getting a gift of a piece of a
mummy or he would not show it to her, and telling her about his habit of
breaking into song as he travelled – 'I rather think it is hereditary on my
mothers side'. With his tradesmen friends he was in no danger of being
patronised, so he was at ease, and could even display a somewhat heavy sense
of humour. On one occasion he arrived at an inn to learn that a friend was
staying there. The friend did not know that Place had left London, and Place
sent him a letter which purported to display a supernatural knowledge of what
he was doing.[7]

Place's normal serious-mindedness is displayed in his comments on two
barristers he knew: 'Blackburn so far as I could make him out is in most things
right minded; but he is one of those who drives me away, he puns, and jokes
and jibes in the midst of the most serious matters, and this always silences me.
I know some who like him and dislike his friend Joshua Evans. "Blackburn
they say is lively, Evans is a proser." I like his prosings, there is always
something sound in them, always something to learn from him on every
subject to which his attention has been turned. Blackburn by his fooleries will
neither allow me to reason, not to hear him reason . . . .'[8]

If humour is rare in his papers, it is equally so in his correspondents. By far
the wittiest was the radical publisher, William Hone. In 1824 he poked fun at
Place's habit of starting letters abruptly with 'Hone', and complained of the
awkwardness of knowing how to reply: 'All *this* comes of not being able to get
over plain "Place" – and I think I hear *him* saying "Why *what* is the fool
about? did you ever *hear* such a fool? He is *drunk*!" "*No,* I am *not* drunk!"
"Why then you are as great a *fool* as you *were*!" "*Very* likely." Why I *say,*
what the *L's* the matter with you?" "Oh I'm only a little merry or so." "*So*!
Go and *sew* below along with Frank's men – you're *drunk*!" ' Hone

explained that he had seen no one for a fortnight, having been ill with cholera, so he decided to 'disport me' on paper.[9]

Place's character and outlook disposed him to radicalism. In an age when judges held that christianity was the law of the land, and the Church of England was a pillar of the state, Place's atheism predisposed him against the established order. His belief in reason made him a natural ally of Paine and Godwin against Burke, who held that reason should be subordinated to tradition, because this embodied the collective wisdom of history. With his aggressive self-confidence, Place was not likely to be content with a social system which cast him as an inferior, while resentment of his father's tyranny, typical as Francis pointed out of the behaviour of anyone in a position of power, probably contributed to his general suspicion of authority.

In the 1790s Place's outlook became fixed. He learnt the passionate sympathy with the sufferings of the poor, and the bitter resentment against upper-class contempt and ill-treatment, which became (together with his belief in reason) the dominating forces of his life. His life-long loyalty to the working people was the result of his own observations and sufferings:

> I saw amongst them, much merit − much patient suffering − wonderful endurance − industry − care and desire to be and to appear respectable. I saw also the oppression of the laws as well as of most of their employers, and that also which in its immediate effect is even more intolerable, the contumely with which all who thought themselves above them treated them. I not only saw all this but I felt it also, and I resolved never to abandon the working people and I never will.[10]

The roots of Place's radicalism lay in the desperate poverty he knew. This gave him a sympathy and identification with the sufferings of the poor which never left him. It also allowed him to see for himself the courage and patience with which many working people faced up to poverty, and the sacrifices they made to help each other. His background helped him when he later set out to examine the way of life of working people as a social investigator. His period of poverty taught him what upper-class contemporaries were ignorant of, while his prosperous childhood gave him the detachment to see and record what those with working-class backgrounds took for granted.

*   *   *

By 1796 Place was trying to find customers of his own, as a first step towards setting up his own business. He had put off this decision for fear of injuring others and ruining himself by contracting debts which he could not repay, but his doubts were allayed by reading Godwin's *Political Justice*. The first edition has a sub-heading: 'Virtue the road to prosperity and success in the world', under which Godwin argued that the financial advantages of a good name to a tradesman would outweigh the profits which he could make by trickery.[11] *Political Justice* convinced Place that he could turn other people to account without dishonesty, and that 'the ordinary tricks of tradesmen' were

not necessary for success. In order to persuade mercers and drapers to give
him credit, he used to make part of his small purchases at one shop, and then
carry them under his arm to another to buy the remainder. Shopkeepers
would then offer him credit in the hope of gaining the whole of his custom,
and by repaying within the period allowed, he gained a reputation for
punctuality and integrity with three mercers and two woollen drapers. He
could therefore expect any amount of credit when he started his own shop.

In January 1796 Elizabeth Place gave birth to another daughter, Annie.
Francis now had two children to provide for, but two months later he lost his
'shop of work' as a result of his journey to Birmingham to help the LCS
deputies. The Places were thus reduced to poverty again, but Francis
nevertheless decided to work in future solely for his own customers, against
the opposition of his wife, who was humiliated by seeing her children
sometimes fed by Ashley, and urged Francis to seek journey work. He insisted
that there was no hope in that way of becoming a master tradesman, and thus
being 'able to maintain my family respectably'.[12] Their few good clothes were
taken great care of so that they could make a respectable appearance outside
the house, and they were generally considered as flourishing people who
wanted for nothing.

After Ashley fled to France in September 1797, Place moved to a similar
lodging nearby. He managed to get more customers, but he found that since
he was obliged to give credit, the more he increased his business the more he
got into debt. Suffering what would now be called cash-flow problems, he
found that he could not take too many orders, or he would have been unable
to pay for his materials on time, and would thus have injured his chances of
getting credit when he took a shop.

He decided that as he was certain to succeed once he got into business, he
would give his children the best possible education, and in order to be able to
help them he decided to learn French. He found four other students to share
the cost, all members of the LCS, but their teacher proved unsatisfactory. He
taught by rote, and refused to give explanations: 'His notion was the old one,
that unless the learner did everything for himself, he did nothing, and he was
therefore a bad teacher.' The students later managed to find an emigrant
priest who proved a much better teacher, and Place started reading Helvétius,
Rousseau and Voltaire.

In March 1798, with another child on the way (Francis Junior was born in
June), Place took one of his fellow students, Richard Wild, as a lodger to help
pay the rent: 'he was abstemious and remarkably industrious, he was of a
sedate reserved and somewhat suspicious disposition and therefore not a very
amiable man'.[13] He was a tailor, and in March 1799 Place proposed that they
go into partnership and take a tailor's shop. Wild agreed, but they had a hard
task raising the £84 demanded for the lease of the shop they chose at 29
Charing Cross, and as well as collecting the debts due to them, they had to
borrow from friends. (Place exaggerated when he later said that he had

received help from no one in setting up in business.) They had only 1s 10d between them when they moved in on 8 April, but Place's care to build a reputation with mercers and drapers allowed them to make a good display with goods bought on credit. In order to preserve the impression of meaning to do business in a good style, they concealed the poverty of their furniture by smuggling it in at night.

Soon after he moved Place was faced with a family problem. On 8 May his brother-in-law, Mat Stimson, was convicted of highway robbery. Stimson was sentenced to death, but he was a great favourite with his fellow thieves and the turnkeys in Newgate, who attempted to procure him a pardon. They secured the help of some influential City men, and Place heard that a pardon was looked on as certain. He thought that Stimson would inevitably be hanged the next time he was caught, so he went to the Treasury magistrate, Richard Ford, told him about the plot, and urged him to have Stimson transported as the only way to prevent further mischief and save him from the gallows. Place's intervention was successful, but it became known to the thieves, who made threats that he was 'to be done for', alarming his mother and wife. To put an end to their fears he borrowed a pair of pistols and went along to the thieves' club night:

> I soon made myself known to them all, avowed that I had been the cause of Mat's being transported, insisted that I had done him service, and saved his life. Much noisy disputing followed, and I adverting to their threats 'to do for me', told them there was not a man among them who dared attack me. They one and all disclaimed any such intention, but some of them abused me as unfeeling and unnatural in getting my own sisters husband transported. I shortly defended myself and left them in by no means bad temper with me.[14]

The incident displays both his courage and his determination to act on his own notion of duty, even when it went against traditional ideas. After Stimson was transported, Place's sister married an old suitor. Place had always been fond of her, and he hoped that she would now do well, but she fell into a state of melancholy apathy. Her husband took to drinking and she died in miserable poverty. Her daughter by her first marriage was brought up by Stimson's sister, who was married to a man who dyed stolen property for thieves and fences, but the child did well and married a man of property.

Place and Wild frequently worked from 6 a.m. until midnight and Place gave up all connection with politics. 'No one was either neglected or disappointed', he claimed, 'a thing very unusual at that time.' By Christmas 1800 they had thirty-two tailors and three or four leather-breeches makers working for them. 'No such rapid increase of business had ever been known. We had before us, the prospect of one of the largest businesses in London, and a certainty as we thought – of making a rapid fortune.' Place's remarkable ability to make money was one source of the later suspicions that he was a spy, since outsiders thought that he could not have done it unless he had some secret source of finance.[15] However, the efficiency which he displayed throughout his life made his success in business inevitable, and the low standard of service then given by tradesmen made his task easier, since customers found a tailor who kept his promises a welcome change.

But he still had one more disappointment in store. In September 1800 Wild married a former prostitute, and at Christmas Place learnt that he was planning to take over the whole business with the aid of a loan from her former lover. When the partnership was dissolved, all the property would be assigned to the creditors, from whom Wild could purchase the business. Place would receive nothing until the debts had been collected and the creditors paid, and the profits would probably be swallowed up in lawyers' fees. He would have little prospect of ever getting back into business. He tried to conceal what had happened from his wife until he had spoken to his attorney, but he was so upset that he could not keep quiet. When he told her:

> The effect as I had anticipated was terrible, neither tongue nor pen can describe her anguish. She saw nothing before her but destruction there were the three children and another coming. She was sure we should all be turned into the street, industry was of no use to us, integrity would not serve us, honesty would be of no avail, we had worked harder, and done more than any body else, and now we were to suffer more than any body else, I made no attempt to soothe her, I knew it would be useless and my feelings were too much in accord with hers to permit me to do much, more than participate with her, it was undoubtedly the bitterest day of my life. She dreaded the horrid poverty she now saw before her and she felt the more acutely, since she had thought that her troubles and difficulties were ended, and that abundance and happiness was before us. I was the more affected as I did not see my way before me.[16]

He swiftly recovered from his despair. Indeed, the crisis brought out his latent pugnacity, and he threatened to thrash both Wild and their principal creditor for insolence towards him. The partners' attorney condemned Wild's conduct and procured offers of loans totalling £500 for Place, who was finally offered over £1600. He was delighted, reasonably regarding such offers, when he had no security to give, as a tribute to the good opinion he had earned by his conduct as a tradesman. Wild outbid him for the business, but Place was able to set up on his own. On 8 April he moved into a former brothel at 16 Charing Cross, which was to be his home for the next thirty-two years. It was known as the Royal Bagnio, and Place thought that it had probably once been the Palace brothel. Eventually Wild failed in business, and Place forgave him, even contributing to subscriptions to save him and his wife from the workhouse.

For the next five years, Place continued to devote himself wholly to establishing his business securely. Curiously, the 'Radical Tailor of Charing Cross' never thought it worthwhile to learn the skills of a tailor:

> I knew I could procure competent persons for these purposes, and that the most profitable part for me to follow was dancing attendance on silly people, to make

myself acceptable to coxcombs, . . . I knew well that to enable me to make money I must consent to submit to much indignity, and insolence, to tyranny and injustice. I had no choice between doing this and being a beggar, and I was resolved not to be a beggar. . . . I can imagine nothing except being a footman or a common soldier as more degrading than being either a barber or a tailor.

Commenting on Place's remarks in the 1890s, Graham Wallas could understand his bitterness: 'Men are still apt to look upon their tailor as in some sense a menial servant. But eighty or ninety years ago the humiliations of the position were such as a proud man could hardly endure.' To make money as a tailor, Place observed, a man 'should be either a philosopher or a mean cringing slave whose feelings had never been excited to the pitch of manhood'.[17]

In practice, his character was far too passionate for him to be able to suffer the degradation with philosophical detachment, and hatred of the aristocracy was always an important factor in his political outlook. When he returned to political activity in Westminster in 1807, he declared hyperbolically: 'so inveterate was the hatred produced by my conduct on the opposers of the people that nearly one and all of my customers left me, and that my losses in consequence amounted to many hundreds if not thousands of pounds'. Even more dangerous was for his customers to learn that he read books, and he carefully concealed it. Once, when his foreman incautiously showed a customer Place's library, he lost a large quantity of business from him and his friends.

Had these persons been told that I never read a book, that I was ignorant of everything but my business, that I sotted in a public house, they would not have made the least objection to me. I should have been a 'fellow' beneath them, and they would have patronised me; but, — to accumulate books and to be supposed to know something of their contents, to seek for friends, too, among literary and scientific men, was putting myself on an equality with themselves, if not indeed assuming a superiority; was an abominable offence in a tailor . . .[18]

His willingness to put up with such treatment paid rich dividends. In 1815 he made profits of £2500.[19] The following year Francis Place Junior returned from the continent, where he had completed his education in Paris and Dresden. He joined his father's shop, and in 1817 Place handed it over to him and retired from business.

In the same year Elizabeth Place had the last of her fifteen children, eight of whom survived to adulthood — ironically her husband wrote in 1822 that 'children are very little like to die if properly attended to'. The two eldest daughters worked as governesses until they married in 1818. Elizabeth married William Bridges Adams, the son of William Adams, a friend and ally of Place in Westminster politics. Annie was taken up by James Mill, who told her when she married John Miers that she must bring up her children well from the moment that Tristram Shandy began his story – at the time of his own conception – or she would hear of it 'in her deepest ears'. Both couples went to South America to make their fortunes, and Place smuggled 100 tons of machinery out to them (the export of some types of machinery was then illegal), but they failed in their enterprise and Place's losses reduced his income by nearly £300 a year. Elizabeth Adams died in Chile, and when her widower returned to England in 1826 he made advances to one of her younger sisters, but Place objected because he considered Adams 'half crazy'. Adams went on to gain some fame as an inventor and writer. His writings were admired by John Stuart Mill, and he became one of the *Monthly Repository* circle of the Unitarian minister, William Johnson Fox. John Miers stayed in South America longer, but Place lamented that 'nothing ever goes right with this painstaking persevering excellent and clever man'.[20]

By the 1810s Elizabeth Place was becoming increasingly fretful. She could read but not write, and she felt her inferiority in education to her elder children. She probably also felt her importance to her husband to be less once he was securely established financially and acquiring intellectual friends. She disliked conversation on non-domestic matters, and she would cause disputes by treating general remarks as personal imputations, with the result, according to her husband, that the elder children treated her with less respect than they ought to have: 'she sometimes told them', Place said, 'that if she and I were alone, or if none but the youngest were with us, we should never hear a word spoken in anger by the other'. Annie chose to remain a governess rather than return home, apparently because she did not get on with her mother, while Francis Junior protested to his father about his mother's constant unreasonable complaints about him. Elizabeth Place's favourite child was her eldest daughter and namesake, and on at least one issue she took her mother's side. 'I . . . have no doubt', Place told James Mill in 1815, that the younger children 'would be infinitely more to my mind could I bestow a certain portion of time every day on them, notwithstanding the difficulty there is of convincing, I might have said the impossibility of convincing the grown females that I know at all what I am about'.[21]

Place disliked heavy drinking and large dinners where, he said, a man had to show off or be voted a bore. He hardly ever attended the public dinners which played an important part in keeping up party spirit among the radicals. He relied mainly on his family circle for relaxation, and he would seldom visit or receive his friends in the evening. His old LCS friend Alexander Galloway once gibed: 'I am afraid after all that you have great faith *"of going to Heaven"* and seeing all your friends there as you have been most niggardly in giving them any of your social time here.'[22] 'My greatest pleasure', Place told John Miers shortly after his wife's death,

> was to have her as my *companion,* my delight was to see her and hear her voice, and
> as you well know I should have been happy to have spent more time with her than I

did, had she at all times been willing to accept attentions . . .. The only relaxation I really either coveted or courted was her society. This was my solace, my recompense, and [had] she been fortunately able to appreciate this correctly and fully, we must have been the happiest of human beings. A man may be the friend of another man, a *woman* alone can be his *companion*.

But he admitted: 'I do not pretend to say that on all occasions I was as calm and acted as judiciously as I ought to have been and done.' In a letter to James Mill, he sent the women's compliments to Mrs Mill: 'she is their favourite acquaintance, the more so as she poor woman as well as my wife "has a grumpy husband who bites her nose off".'[23]

Elizabeth Place died on 19 October 1827, and he was so distressed that he was unable to attend her funeral: 'all that was in my power was hiding myself in a barn to indulge my sorrow'. Time did not relieve his anguish, and at the end of three months he had lost nearly twenty pounds in weight. With his belief in reason he naturally tried to overcome his distress by reasoning, but he failed. 'I confess my weakness to a considerable extent', he told Miers, 'and only wish I was what no one ever was, strong at all points, at all times and under all circumstances.'[24] He came to the conclusion that the only solution was to seek a female friend, and within six months of his wife's death he was courting an actress at Covent Garden, Mrs Louisa Simeon Chatterley, to the horror of his children.

Born in 1797, Mrs Chatterley was younger than Place's two eldest daughters. In 1813 or 1814 she had married the actor William Simmonds Chatterley, who died of drink in 1822. Soon afterwards she became involved in a scandal due to her friendship with a banker's clerk called Christmas. In 1823 Christmas's wife was imprisoned on a suit from Mrs Chatterley, who felt that she was in danger on account of Mrs Christmas's jealousy. It was said that Mrs Chatterley and Christmas took a house together, occupying separate quarters. Following a letter from Mrs Christmas to her husband's employers, pointing out that he was living above his income, he was found to be speculating with their money – he had gambled £968,000, but lost only £7000 of it. In September 1825 he was transported for fourteen years, and eight months later Mrs Chatterley began to appear in Place's diary, when she sought his advice about her business affairs. Apparently some of her own money was still in Christmas's hands, and on 20 October 1826 Place and his wife walked to Mrs Chatterley's house in Brompton Square in order to see a letter from him.

After his wife's death Place found solace in Mrs Chatterley's company, but when he realised that she expected an offer of marriage he decided against it for the sake of his family. He told her so, and she said that they had better not see each other for six months, but it was only three days before he sought another interview. Their friendship was resumed and they were married on 13 February 1830. At first the marriage went well. Place encouraged her to continue her acting career – she was said to give the best portrait of a

Frenchwoman on the English stage – but her contract with Covent Garden was terminated soon afterwards. The radical MP, Colonel Perronet Thompson, once called on Place to find him sewing a rather attractive pair of white ducks for which his wife appeared to be waiting at the top of the stairs – Thompson surmised that it was intended for a part in a play.[25] She does not appear to have agreed with him politically – Joseph Parkes, who opposed Place's intransigent anti-Whig line in the 1830s, sometimes ended his letters with best wishes to 'Mrs (Whig) Place'.

Place had always taken an interest in the stage, although he only visited the theatre intermittently due to dissatisfaction with the quality of the acting. Reading Restoration comedies in 1826 for his history of manners, he observed that he had spent much time to little purpose: 'Piddling among books even in this way is however trifling a real source of great enjoyment, which never fails, which never surfeits, and never makes a man worse, while it seldom fails to make him better . . .' He now became a financial 'oracle' to his wife's theatrical friends, and when the playwright James Kenney wrote to borrow £5 Place noted that this made the total lent £125. In 1834 he told the radical MP and popular novelist, E.L. Bulwer, that the drama was 'a matter of much more general importance than any public man besides yourself appears to think it is'. Place generally insisted that the theatre reflected rather than formed public opinion, but in his own case he gave evidence to the contrary concerning the *Beggar's Opera*.[26]

In 1832 Place's income was reduced from £1100 to £400 a year by the incompetence of his attorney, who persuaded him to lend money on the security of land to which the borrower had no title. His wife readily accepted the necessary economies, and they moved to her house in Brompton Square in early 1833. Explaining his feelings about his two wives to Mrs Grote in 1836, he said:

> If ever I were to wish for a heaven, it would be that I might meet [Elizabeth] again there. Does it seem strange to you that I should say so, having as I have a most amiable woman for my wife now, one whose temper is of the very best, one who suits me in every particular, one who is as happy with me as a woman can well be; if it does I can hardly explain it unless you are willing to call my feelings by the name of love. . . . I love my present wife dearly, but there is something about me in relation to my first wife, the wife of my youth, who grew up with me, and went through all sorts of privations and difficulties with me . . .

According to a newspaper article on Place in 1837: 'To this hour, he never speaks of the participator in his youthful life without a softening of the voice, and a glistening of the eye . . ..'[27]

5 The Revival of Radicalism: Westminster 1807–1812

The election of Sir Francis Burdett for the constituency of Westminster in 1807 provided the impetus for the revival of radicalism over the next decade. Before the Reform Act of 1832 the qualifications for voting and the number of voters varied greatly in different constituencies, and the prestige of a constituency depended on the size and 'respectability' of its electorate. Westminster had the great advantage that Parliament met within its boundaries, and it had 15,000–18,000 electors under its 'scot and lot' (ratepayer) franchise, so it was one of the most important constituencies in the country. Like almost all constituencies it returned two MPs, and Charles James Fox, the immensely popular leader of the Whigs, was one of its two members from 1780 until his death in 1806.

As there was no secret ballot the scope for bribery and corruption was very large, and in 1788 the Whigs and Tories were said to have spent £40,000 each on a famous by-election. The efforts of the Whigs to raise popular disaffection as a counterweight to the power of the Crown, the appeals by both parties to the 'Independent Electors', and the sheer excitement of elections with their mob violence and flood of literature, helped to raise popular interest in politics in the late eighteenth century. At the same time, the contrast between the pious protestations of the Whigs and Tories and their free use of corruption, violence and intimidation strengthened anti-party feeling. Thus when the parliamentary parties agreed to share the constituency and avoid a contest after the fantastic expense of the 1788 by-election, they opened the way to an independent candidate. John Horne Tooke stood in the 1790 and 1796 General Elections, and although he was defeated, the recent history of the constituency, as well as the effects of the French Revolution, ensured that he would achieve a respectable poll. Tooke's campaign in 1790 was the beginning of the 'Independent Electors' as a separate force in Westminster which rejected control by the aristocratic parties.[1]

In the period 1800–5 interest in reform in the country was at its lowest ebb, although in the General Election of 1802 a reformer again achieved a respectable poll in Westminster, while Sir Francis Burdett, Horne Tooke's disciple and close friend, won Middlesex with Whig support. Burdett had gained great popularity in London by his parliamentary battle to improve the conditions of the political prisoners held without trial in the 'Bastille' – Cold Bath Fields prison – but his election was also aided by his great wealth, and his campaign was probably as corrupt as his opponent's. The House of Commons ordered a new election on the ground that his majority had been gained by invalid votes, and in the by-election in 1804 he was returned by one vote, but the Sheriff overturned his victory on a technicality concerning the time of the close of poll. These contests helped to keep radicalism alive during the dark days of Pitt's repression.[2]

In February 1806, Fox led the Whigs into a coalition Government with Lord Grenville's dissident Tory faction. At first the radicals had high hopes of the new administration, but they were rapidly disillusioned. As Place put it, the Whigs had condemned 'the system' of Pitt for years, and almost incited the people to revolt, but their good teaching went with promises which they did not keep; when they took office with the worst of the Tories (the Grenvillites), and carried on the system which they had condemned root and branch, they increased the number who distrusted both parties, laying the foundations for the success of the radicals in Westminster.[3]

In 1805 Place had begun to relax his sole concentration on business: 'I permitted several respectable and well judging men to come and gossip with me occasionally' – this was the kind of remark which earned him a reputation for being irritatingly consequential. His new friends were tradesmen-electors and great admirers of Fox, but like many others they were shocked by the coalition. The growing dissatisfaction was encouraged by William Cobbett, who commenced a long series of letters to the 'Electors of Westminster' in his *Weekly Political Register* on 9 August 1806 with a quotation from Rousseau's *Social Contract:* 'The English are free only forty days, once in seven years; and, the use, which they then make of their freedom, shows that they deserve to be enslaved all the rest of their lives.' Cobbett accused the electors of selling their freedom and violating a sacred trust: 'To hear some persons talk of an election for Westminster, a stranger to the state of things would believe, that the electors were the bondsmen, or, at best, the mere menial servants of a few great families.'[4]

In September, Fox died and the Grenvillite Duke of Northumberland put forward his son Lord Percy in the consequent by-election. Many electors took great offence at this since it appeared to confirm the view of Westminster as the private fief of great families. Sheridan, the playwright and Foxite Government Minister, had long expected to succeed Fox. (He was already an MP for an obscure constituency, but election in Fox's place would have raised his prestige.) With the reformers' support he got his friends to call a public meeting to put him forward. But Lord Grenville had already alienated Northumberland by failing to consult him over the formation of the coalition, and the Government forced Sheridan to withdraw for fear of losing the support of the Duke's group of half a dozen MPs.[5] At the public meeting Sheridan urged acceptance of Lord Percy, but the audience of electors angrily refused and appointed a committee to find another candidate. According to the reformers, the Whigs then nominated each other as members and delayed matters until it was too late to find an opponent for Lord Percy. Burdett and the left-wing Whig Samuel Whitbread were approached to stand, but both had already pledged themselves to Percy, who was elected unopposed. The reformers' anger was greatly increased when the Duke of Northumberland's liverymen distributed free food and beer to a crowd outside his door. When opponents tipped the beer into the gutter, some of the mob tried to retrieve it, and Place complained bitterly that 'to see these people representing as it was said the electors of Westminster, was certainly the lowest possible state of degradation.'

Seeing the anger of his tradesmen neighbours, Place

suggested the propriety of looking out for a proper person to represent Westminster, to open a subscription when such a person was found, and to persevere until he or someone else should be returned free from all expense to him. My mind was made up, to watch circumstances to take advantage of them and never to desist until Westminster had by returning one member in the way proposed shown its power and importance, driven away the factions as far as was possible and made the way clear to return both its members by the sole exertion of the Electors.

He enlarged his acquaintance among the electors in order to urge this course, but without success. 'At this time Cobbetts Register was in high repute,' Place observed,

and his remarks on passing subjects were eagerly looked for. In several letters addressed to the electors of Westminster he clearly pointed out their duty to them, and in his fourth letter he ably commented on the conduct of the Whigs, and reproached the electors with meanness and ignorance, the letter was much read and was very useful, it produced shame in many and a desire to do something on another occasion, but it did not remove from them the notion which long practice had confirmed that a contested election could only be carried by money, money in immense sums, and this prevented me from expecting any extraordinary exertions would be made by the electors for themselves at the expected general election.[6]

In October 1806 Parliament was dissolved and Lord Percy retired. Once again only one candidate stood in Westminster for each of the parliamentary parties, Sheridan for the Whigs and Lord Hood for the Tories, but James Paull stood as an independent. Paull was reputed to have made a fortune in India, and he had returned to England in 1804 in order to try to impeach Marquis Wellesley for misconduct as Governor-General of India. The Whigs took him up in order to embarrass the Government, but when they came to office they told him to 'lay on his oars'. He refused, and was therefore execrated by Whigs and Tories alike. His candidacy had the support of

Burdett, who nominated him on the hustings and eulogised him, of Cobbett, who came up to London to campaign for him, and of the veteran reformer, Major Cartwright. 'Paull had shown much courage', Place wrote, 'much tact and great perseverance.' But unlike other radicals Place did not actively support him, probably because he was not known to be a parliamentary reformer.

The election commenced with nomination on the hustings, and a vote by a show of hands, after which the candidate who lost the vote demanded a poll of the electors. The polls stayed open for fifteen days, and the electors voted in public. They could either vote for two candidates or plump (cast a single vote) for one candidate. Thus the scope for corruption and intimidation − and tactical voting − at the end of a close contest was immense. Paull led in the early days, but Sheridan and Hood then 'combined their interests' − each asking their own supporters to vote for both candidates. Hood finally came top with 5478 votes, Sheridan was also elected with 4758, and Paull received 4482. Meanwhile, Burdett was standing again in Middlesex. He was an immensely wealthy man, but the elections of 1802 and 1804, together with election petitions in the House of Commons, were rumoured to have cost him over £100,000. By 1806 even his wealth was coming under strain, and he refused to pay any more. Opposed now by the Whigs, he was easily defeated. The contests in Westminster and Middlesex, fought between the radicals and the Whigs as a single campaign, completed the breach between them.

Place thought that the Westminster election did much to unmask the Whigs by forcing them into an open coalition with the Tories:

> it had also considerable effect in convincing many of the electors that they were of more consequence in an election than they had conceived, and might in a vast many cases interfere without injury to themselves in any way. . . . It laid the foundation of the subsequent emancipation of the electors from the control of the two factions to which they had long submitted, and relieved them from the effects of the infamous bribery, corruption and perjury to which a large portion of them had been subjected.[7]

About the middle of the election Place had plumped for Paull, and when he heard that Paull's committee had no regular plan of proceeding he wrote one and sent it to them. The lack of organisation cost Paull the election, because it made it too easy for fictitious votes to be cast for his rivals. On the day the election ended, Place attended a dinner for the friends of Mr Paull − the traditional phrase for the supporters of a candidate − at which it was agreed to open a subscription for a petition to the House of Commons against Sheridan's election. Soon afterwards Paull called on Place to thank him for his plan, and in January 1807 he sought his help in preparing evidence to support the petition, complaining that the committee appointed for the task was neglecting it. Place soon found that Sheridan had received many fictitious votes, and he gave Paull considerable assistance. He several times advised him to give up, because the cost of fighting a petition in the House of Commons would ruin him, until Paull silenced him by declaring that he would not abandon it if he had to eat bread and water in Newgate for the rest of his life. In fact Paull was already ruined, but obstinacy was the principal feature of his character, and Cobbett later wrote that 'what our man wanted in point of talent and knowledge, he amply made up for in *industry* and *pluck*. He was a man of diminutive size; but what there was of him was good. He was game, every inch of him; a real game cock.'[8]

On 6 April, Place met two members of the petition committee, who told him that Paull had taken the management of the petition out of the committee's hands and spent the subscription as he pleased, and this was why they had failed to act. They also said that Paull had been unable to pay the expenses of the elections, estimated at £6000, and that his attorneys had appropriated £1000 contributed by Burdett for the election petition to cover money Paull owed them. Paull's cause can hardly have been helped by the fact that the spy James Powell was the manager for the attorneys – Cobbett described him in his *Register* as a man 'whose heart, I am convinced, is as pure as his manners are amiable and his talents are bright.' Burdett and Cobbett were also urging Paull to drop the petition, but his persistence helped the reformers' cause by keeping alive anger over the election and creating new grievances over the Commons' treatment of the petition. Cobbett continued his exhortations to the electors: 'To stifle *your* voice, is now [our enemies] great object; because, they clearly perceive, that, from you, either of freedom or slavery, the whole nation will, finally, take the example. In the hands of the free and independent electors of Westminster is deposited the political destiny of England . . ..'[9]

On Sunday 26 April 1807 the King dismissed the coalition Government and called a General Election, because Ministers refused to guarantee that they would not bring forward proposals for the removal of Catholic disabilities. Place immediately called a meeting of his new associates, including three former members of the LCS, William Adams, George Puller and John Ridley. The meeting agreed that they could carry on an election for Burdett and Paull at a comparatively small expense by an active canvass and a systematic mode of proceeding, and Place was deputed to find out from Paull whether Burdett was willing to stand.

Over the next few days the group heard from Paull of daily changes in Burdett's sentiments, and they became increasingly suspicious about Paull's truthfulness. When a newspaper advertisement appeared on Wednesday 29 April announcing Burdett's determination not to be a candidate for any seat, on the ground that to do so would only be aiding a delusion, Adams and Place were deputed to go to Burdett and find out the truth. They looked for him first at Colonel Bosville's house, where they learnt that Paull had lied when he said that he dined there with Burdett on the previous day. They went on to Burdett's house in Wimbledon, and Adams introduced Place to the baronet. Burdett insisted that he had always refused to be a candidate, and had refused to play any part in the election beyond nominating Paull on the hustings. He also complained that Paull had advertised a public dinner on the following Friday with him in the chair without his consent. Pressed to become a candidate, Burdett refused, but when he was asked whether he would accept the seat if he was elected without his interference, he replied: 'certainly, this is the right way − electors ought to seek representatives, not candidates electors. If I should be elected for Westminster − Middlesex, or even Old Sarum, I must and should obey the call and do the duty of a faithful steward but I will neither spend a guinea nor do anything whatever to contribute to such an election.'[10]

At a meeting with his associates that evening Place urged that they should write to Paull to say that he had deceived them by gross falsehoods and was unworthy of assistance, but all the others disagreed, arguing that Paull had no one else to rely on until the public dinner on Friday. If they abandoned him before then, they would be using him badly and would take away all chance from the electors of having a choice in the election. A motion was passed unanimously resolving to put forward Burdett and Paull jointly, with the intention of withdrawing quietly once a committee was appointed at the dinner. As chairman Place had not voted, and he refused to sign the motion, but after a long argument he finally gave way at 1 a.m.

> I was very uneasy at what I had done, I could not think the proceeding was honest, I was sure it was very foolish. It was one of the few acts committed by me at a mature age of which I have never ceased to be ashamed as often as any circumstance has recalled it to my recollection. I have generally had resolution enough to do what I thought was right at the time and had obtained a character for uncomplying obstinacy; yet I never hesitated to yield to others when I could not convince in matters of small moment, or on indifferent subjects, reserving my obstinacy for occasions which seemed to me to include an abandonment of some principle or likely to do more harm than good to others, or to make me think meanly of myself. In the present instance my compliance included all these considerations, and yet I suffered myself to be persuaded to do what I at the moment believed to be incorrect. It was certainly an example of weakness of the worst sort . . .[11]

The following morning Place's associates had second thoughts, and Paull was told that the motion was cancelled. But he insisted on carrying on, explaining Burdett's refusal to attend the dinner by an advertisement which stated that Paull would take the chair because motions were to be put which concerned the baronet. To Burdett this was the last straw, because it implied that he had dissembled in his advertisement declining to be a candidate, and he sent his brother to the dinner to read out a letter complaining about the use Paull was making of his name. Place, who felt that this was treating Paull with unnecessary cruelty, unsuccessfully attempted to dissuade the envoy from reading it out. Paull passed off the letter as the result of a misunderstanding, eulogised Burdett and got motions passed to nominate himself and Burdett for Westminster. But Place and his colleagues were determined to withdraw, and Paull could not find active supporters to replace them. At that point he must have realised that his position was desperate.

That evening he set off to challenge Burdett to a duel. Place was later told that he had been encouraged to think that a challenge would extract an apology which would serve him in the election, because Burdett had apologised when challenged by Samuel Whitbread in the previous year. But Burdett did accept, and in the event he was wounded in the leg and Paull in the thigh. The quarrel and duel aroused enormous public interest, and were followed by a vituperative pamphlet war between Horne Tooke and Paull.

The quarrel was caused by confusion as much as by Paull's dishonesty. He knew that he had been cheated out of victory in 1806, and he was fanatically determined to get justice, even at the cost of his own ruin. He needed Burdett as his fellow candidate in order to pay the expenses of the election. But Burdett had resolved on retrenchment, faced with the prospect of having to sell part of his estates after the expense of the Middlesex contests. He was willing to accept a seat if he could be elected without trouble and expense, but he was determined not to accept the financial obligations of declaring himself a candidate. Since neither man was likely to spell out his position, confusion and allegations of treachery were almost inevitable. Place and his associates were caught between their recognition of how much Westminster owed Paull for his stand, their unwillingness to work for a man they could not trust, and their fear of being accused of treachery if they abandoned him. Paull committed suicide the following year.[12]

On Saturday 2 May the little group of reformers had met before the duel became public knowledge, and agreed to send Place and Adams to advise Burdett to withdraw his name from all further association with Paull, lest he should be drawn in for the expenses of the election. The deputation arrived to hear news of the duel. Paradoxically, it was the duel which allowed the group to reverse their decision to withdraw from the election, and thus made the reformers' victory possible. Although Burdett had refused to be a candidate, and was now being held incommunicado by his doctor, this did not prevent him being put forward because under electoral law a man could be elected without his knowledge or consent. Place revived his proposal to attempt to return a parliamentary reformer free of expense to him: 'Burdett being popular and his situation being such as to command sympathy and commiseration, offered an opportunity for putting my notions to the test, which was not to be lost.' Far more important, although Place did not mention it, was that popular denunciation of Paull for endangering Burdett's life meant that complaints of treachery and desertion by Paull were no longer such a threat.

'It seemed to me to be a matter of great importance', Place wrote:

Independently of the election of Burdett, I thought it would be a demonstration of power and independence in the people which could scarcely fail to produce good effects, every where . . . . I proposed that we should set about it immediately, I offered to abandon my business wholly and devote my time to the election. I said I entertained no doubt of success if half a dozen active intelligent men would do as I had proposed to do. Several present agreed to give up a considerable portion of their time, and Brooks and Powell to give up theirs wholly. I agreed to take the management on myself. Summonses were immediately issued for a meeting of some thirty persons who had been active either in the late Westminster election for Mr Paull or in Middlesex for Sir Francis Burdett.[13]

In the evening twenty men met and agreed to run Burdett and carry on until their money ran out, and notice was sent to the newspapers of a public meeting on Monday 4 May at the Crown and Anchor tavern.

Paull's chief supporter sent professional rioters − men paid to make riots at sales of goods under execution − to disrupt the meeting, and this was, Place observed, done with much care and judgement: 'As soon therefore as we entered the room one of these men attached himself to each of us, and never left us. When any one of us attempted to address the audience the man who had been planted for the purpose bawled out, Paull! Paull!! Paull!!! and all the others joined in the cry, . . . I know of no word so well calculated to confound an audience as the open sound Paull.'[14] A motion to propose Paull with Burdett was carried by acclamation without anyone being allowed to speak against it, and Burdett's supporters retired to a private room which they had booked against the eventuality. Here they agreed a resolution which showed impatience at Burdett's attitude: in refusing to stand for Parliament at this critical juncture, he could not have reflected that duty increases with difficulty, and it would be to the immortal honour of Westminster and a glorious example to the electors of the United Kingdom to return him free of every sacrifice and expense. A committee was appointed which contained several former members of the LCS: Place, John Richter, an accountant, Paul Lemaitre, a watchcase maker, John Ridley, a bootmaker, William Adams and George Puller, curriers − and James Powell, government spy. The list shows the enormous contribution the LCS had made in forming a generation of radical activists. 'We were all of us obscure persons', Place wrote, 'not one man of note among us, not one in any way known to the Electors generally, as insignificant a set of persons as could well have been collected together to undertake so important a public matter as a Westminster Election, against, Wealth − and Rank and Name and Influence.'[15]

The poll opened only three days later, on Thursday 7 May. The principal managers of the campaign were Samuel Brooks, the treasurer, Place and his two lieutenants, John Richter and Paul Lemaitre. 'Mr Brooks was a remarkably ignorant man', Place observed,

but a clever man of detail in business. He was generally imbecile but on particular occasions he was quite the reverse. On the present occasion he not only stood firmly by me but he volunteered to pay all the expenses of the election for monday if subscriptions were not raised. He was a man of figures punctual precise and indefatigable, a most useful man for us in our situation.[16]

A glassmaker, Brooks was to become the public figurehead of the Westminster Committee. Richter and Lemaitre had both been detained without trial on political charges in the 1790s. Lemaitre was one of the most experienced election workers on the committee. He had worked for Horne Tooke in 1796, for Burdett in Middlesex in 1802 and 1804, and in 1806 he had laboured to bring some order to Paull's chaotic campaign.

The committee had its headquarters in a gin shop called the Britannia Coffee House, and Place had his own room there. He would arrive by 7 a.m., always finding Brooks already there, and leave after 11 p.m. 'A great deal was done but we were never in a bustle, we kept the whole matter in perfect order.'[17] The committee set out with only £84, although they soon received £100 from Horne Tooke. They dispensed with inspectors on the hustings at 2–5 guineas a day, counsel on the hustings at 10–20 guineas, canvassers at 1–5 guineas, and an attorney who usually received large sums, replacing them with volunteers. Anything involving expense could only be ordered by a subcommittee appointed for the purpose or by the treasurer with the permission of the general committee, and orders could only be given on a printed form containing prices and quantities or named services, and signed by those authorised and countersigned by the treasurer. Accounts were paid immediately the bill was received, and no credit was taken.

The confusion in the reformers' camp had left very little time to organise support, and Place remarked that when the poll opened 'some of my coadjutors were exceedingly depressed, we had scarcely any money, nobody had joined us and we appeared as forlorn as the Whigs and Tories had predicted we should be. Some among us who had borne abuse very well, could not bear being laughed at, and the ridicule which was cast upon us almost disabled them from acting.' At the close of the first day's poll Lord Cochrane, a naval hero and independent radical, had 112 votes and Elliott, a rich Tory brewer, 99. Burdett only had 78, although all of the committee who had votes had used them. 'This indicated uncommon apathy nothing like it had ever before been known, the electors by the small number who came forward to poll seemed to say, they had no interest in the issue.'[18] The committee struggled on until Saturday, by which time Cochrane had 476 votes, Elliott 407 and Burdett 309. Sheridan and Paull, who had now joined the contest, had 87 and 45 respectively. But by this time the prospect for the reformers was looking more hopeful; money was coming in and there were signs of greater interest among the electors. On Sunday, Place went canvassing for the first and only time in his life for about two and a half hours in some back lanes and courts. The committee divided into parties and went round Burdett's chief Middlesex supporters to ask them to bring their friends for a procession to the poll on Monday. Place believed that this procession decided the election; the number did not exceed 250, but from the noise people thought half Westminster was coming, and enthusiasm was raised to a high pitch from which it never subsided.

One of the committee's bills[19] read:

Nelson's Last Signal

ENGLAND EXPECTS EVERY MAN TO DO HIS DUTY

ELLIOTT to brew our **Beer**

SHERIDAN to write our **Plays**

COCHRANE to fight our **Enemies**

BUT

BURDETT

To Guard our **CONSTITUTION!!**

At the end of the fifteen-day poll on 23 May, Burdett had 5134 votes, Cochrane was also elected with 3708. Sheridan had 2646, Elliott 2137 and Paull 269. Burdett must have involuntarily received several hundred false votes, because towards the end of the contest Cochrane and Burdett's supporters took away their inspectors, and Sheridan hired people to poll over a thousand false votes in order to make a respectable showing. Many of these must have been shared with Burdett.[20] The committee had no contact with Burdett between the duel and the end of the election. Indeed, the baronet was kept in isolation by his doctor, and knew nothing of the election until 15 May, by which time he was well on his way to victory.[21]

The confusion in the radical camp made the success all the more remarkable. A key problem was the lack of communication between the tradesmen election organisers and the gentlemen of the Burdett-Tooke circle – only thirty years later a reader of Place's memoir found it extraordinary that the committee should have tolerated it. But the parliamentary parties were also in some disarray. The Whigs were probably unenthusiastic about Sheridan, who was by this time considered a follower of the Prince of Wales rather than a Whig,[22] and only after polling had started did it become clear that Sheridan would stand and the sitting Tory MP, Lord Hood, would not.

This probably helped to make the election relatively peaceful, since the party candidates did not have the time and money to organise the usual corruption and bludgeon men. The effect was not only to make the reformers' task easier, but to allow them to turn on its head the usual charge of anti-reformers that since popular elections commonly caused disorder, reform would enormously increase it. The peace was due even more to the reformers' own example of honesty, economy, frequent appeals for order and the avoidance of the usual insults by their hustings spokesmen. 'Purity of Election' was not just a slogan to them, but expressed their passionate desire to change the morals as well as the results of Westminster elections. The victory only cost them £790, and it was important both because it showed that a major seat could be captured without massive expenditure, and because for the first time the radicals won against Whig opposition. The resulting prestige made Westminster the capital of radicalism until the late 1810s, and the Committee succeeded in controlling the constituency, apart from occasional failures to carry the second seat, for the next sixty years.

Place has been accused of making exaggerated claims for his role in the victory, but he made no such claims. His most important contribution was to propose that Burdett should be put forward without his consent after the duel, on the basis of his own declaration that he would not stand, but would serve if elected. This was a logical development of the position taken by earlier reform candidates – Horne Tooke had declared that he would neither spend his own money nor canvass for votes – but it was the first time that the reformers succeeded in combining economy and efficiency and the first time that they ran a man who had not agreed to stand as a candidate. The element of chance in the origins of the Westminster Committee is shown by the fact that until the duel the reformers only considered running Burdett and Paull as candidates. Their decision to go ahead without Burdett's consent – or even his knowledge – allowed them to claim the victory for the electors rather than the victor, and thus provided the basis for the Committee's informal but important political role. Its claim to independence was widely disbelieved, especially by upper-class contemporaries who were unable to accept that a group of mere tradesmen could have succeeded in anything so important as a Westminster election without Burdett's money and guidance, and it was often compromised by its dependence on the baronet's personal popularity. But as a committee of the electors the Westminster men were able to play an independent political role to a degree which would have been impossible if they had emerged from the election merely as Burdett's committee. The principle that electors chose representatives, rather than candidates seeking support, gave the electors a new sense of their own importance, thus helping to break down deference for rank and wealth, a principal object of Place throughout his political career.

The platform on which the Committee fought the election – barring placemen from the Commons, repeal of the Septennial Act (which extended the maximum period between elections to seven years) and the disenfranchisement of rotten boroughs — was Burdett's Middlesex programme of 1806, but the Westminster radicals' political outlook was very different. Burdett was a romantic traditionalist, part-radical and part-Tory. He may have been involved in the Despard conspiracy in 1802, but by the middle of the decade he was becoming more moderate. Accused of being an enemy of the King and constitution during the 1806 Middlesex election, he replied that he objected to usurpation on the rights of kings as well as on those of the people. His role in the revival of radicalism was critical and many years later Place said: 'He was made the centre round which the reformers congregated, and but for him there would have been no congregating no good teaching, but a retrogradation towards ignorance. From 1797 to 1820 he was our only parliament man.'[23] The Westminster reformers paid lip-service to 'restoring the constitution', but most of them were democrats at heart, who had learnt in the corresponding societies of the 1790s to believe in manhood suffrage and look forward to the abolition of the monarchy and the aristocracy.

They relied for their support on the more prosperous shopkeepers and craftsmen who had gained the coveted status of 'householder', and who formed three-quarters of the electorate. The Committee claimed in their report on the election (written by Place and Richter) that their views on corruption and reform were those of the people 'who had most reason to think upon the subject, — the middle classes of society'.[24] The Westminster Committee was not a formal body with an identifiable membership, but a name used for a loosely-knit group who would take the lead in forming *ad hoc* committees to arrange public meetings, draft petitions, raise subscriptions and fight elections. Its members were more commonly known as the Burdettites, or later by Cobbett's insulting nickname of the 'Rump'. From the beginning, established reformers looked on them with suspicion as a self-appointed clique. Horne Tooke was said to have advised Burdett to cut them as often as possible, fearing that they would try to dictate to him, and Burdett was thought to be disposed to follow the advice. As a result, the members of the Committee were reluctant to approach him, even in emergencies. Major Cartwright did work with them from the early years, but his plans for public meetings and dinners were often seen as impractical or badly timed, and his presence among them caused constant controversy.

The Committee tried hard not to lay itself open to charges of dictation, and Place described how they would arrange a public meeting: 'we met at first a small number of persons and conversed on the subject of the meeting. I generally took notes and from these drew up the necessary resolutions petitions &c. I then met Richter, and he and I finally arranged the matter for the previous meeting. Richter was always too idle to prepare anything for himself.'[25] The formal 'previous meeting' was summoned by a circular note from Samuel Brooks to the leading men in the seven parishes, who were requested to bring as many others as could be induced to attend. The objects, Place said, were to obtain money and to get the concurrence of as many as possible, thus ensuring unanimity and making the matters to be brought forward as much as possible the deliberate act of the electors.

*   *   *

One of Place's principal concerns was to keep down the cost of elections. Even apart from principle, he knew that the parliamentary 'factions' were bound to win a contest of money. One aspect concerned the extortionate charges imposed on candidates by the High Bailiff of Westminster for conducting elections, and Place masterminded a long, and partially successful, campaign against him in Parliament and the courts. In 1827 he remarked with pride that the High Bailiff 'has since said that I was "a damned scoundrel and had ruined him". I am not at all angry with him for saying this. He must have been sorely vexed.'[26]

In 1807 Burdett had promised to refer any demand from the High Bailiff to the Committee, but in April 1808 the members learned by accident that the High Bailiff had commenced an action against Burdett, who had failed to inform them about it. They urged Burdett's counsel to argue that the Dean and Chapter of Westminster, who had sold the High Bailiff his office for £3000, were liable to conduct the election at their own expense, and further that Burdett had not been a candidate, since the Committee had acted entirely without his authority and without communicating with him, and that he could not therefore be liable. But the counsel refused to put these arguments, although Place and others attended the court in person to demand to be allowed to give evidence, and a reduced amount of £117 was awarded against Burdett. Place believed that the defence had been deliberately sabotaged by Horne Tooke, who had objected to making elections too cheap 'lest every blackguard should become a candidate'. Place angrily demanded that the Committee expose Burdett by publishing a narrative of the case, but his 'pusillanimous' colleagues wisely refused − the issue was hardly important enough to justify a break with the hero of radicalism − upon which Place made the first of his many announcements of his withdrawal from Westminster politics. Recounting the episode, he declared that he never knew Horne Tooke, but he knew a great deal about him from people who had acted with him, and 'I never believed he was an honest man'. Horne Tooke enjoyed equivocation and enticing others into scrapes, characteristics not likely to appeal to Place.[27] He was several times invited to the famous Sunday dinners Tooke held for leading reformers, but he never accepted. One member of the Committee, Samuel Miller, did attend the dinners, and he seems to have been regarded by his colleagues with some suspicion as a result. Horne Tooke died in 1812.

Place was now getting to know many leading radicals. He had known Major Cartwright during the 1790s, and their acquaintance was renewed after the 1807 election. The author of the six points of the future Charter, Cartwright had campaigned indefatigably since the 1770s for manhood suffrage and annual elections. 'When he was in town', Place wrote,

> he used frequently to sup with me, eating some raisins he brought in his pocket and drinking weak Gin and water, he was cheerful, agreeable, and full of curious anecdote. He was however in political matters exceedingly troublesome and sometimes as exceedingly absurd. He had read but little or to little purpose, and knew nothing of general principles, he entertained a vague and absurd notion of the political arrangements of the Anglo Saxons, and sincerely believed that these semi-barbarians were not only a polished people, but that their 'two fold Polity', arms bearing and representation were universal and perfect . . .. he did not advocate universal suffrage in the election of members of parliament, annual parliaments and voting by ballot, all good in themselves, and deserving to be at all times advocated simply on the advantages they would be of to the people, but because they had been practised at some remote period . . .

The charge that Cartwright knew nothing of general principles is unjust, since he also used natural rights arguments, but to Place 'general principles' meant utilitarianism.

Cartwright's niece wrote: 'To have passed a single day without devoting the greater part of it to writing, would have been in his laborious life, a very remarkable and almost unprecedented occurrence.' Place emphasised both his incessant activity and his good intentions: 'That he most religiously intended to benefit his own country and to extend the benefit to the whole world cannot be doubted by anyone who knew him.' But he was, Place complained, quite unable to conceive that any measure he proposed could be either wrong or badly timed. 'When therefore he came among us in Westminster, his conduct led to almost interminable disputes, and there again as I was continually called upon either by the Old Gentleman or by others to interfere kept me much more actively employed in political transactions than I intended to be. Many were his propositions to hold public meetings which I had to combat.'[28] In late 1808 Cartwright sent Burdett a plan of reform which he proposed should be adopted by a conference of delegates from all over the country. Burdett sent it on to Place, who did not even read it – he said that the plan would have filled a volume and would never have been agreed by delegates. He nevertheless joined the Committee of Friends of Parliamentary Reform in Middlesex, established by Cartwright to help advance his scheme, and he helped Cartwright to organise a reform dinner on 1 May 1809 with stewards from all over the country. It proved a great success, reflecting the revival in the parliamentary reform movement which the victory in Westminster had sparked. Cartwright's indefatigability often achieved useful results, even if not the ones he hoped for, and Place frequently praised his efforts, but the trouble he caused led Place to underestimate Cartwright's overall contribution to the reform movement.

In 1809 another issue helped to keep Place involved in politics. In the House of Commons on 27 January, Colonel Wardle accused the Duke of York, the King's second son, of using his position as Commander-in-Chief of the Army to sell commissions through his mistress. Wardle was introduced to Place by fellow MPs, and frequently came to him for advice and reassurance. Place described him as a weak and timid man, who would never have brought the charges if he had known the trouble and worry he would have trying to substantiate them. Indeed, Place believed that his support saved Wardle from committing suicide. The House of Commons refused to appoint a committee to investigate the charges, but the Duke was forced to resign, and the campaign thus served its purpose, from the radicals' point of view, by bringing discredit on the Royal Family and the Commons. Afterwards, Wardle was rumoured to be in financial difficulties, and a subscription was started to relieve him as a victim of government persecution. A leading role in launching it was played by Philip Mallet, described by Place as

> a very extraordinary man, one who had he lived would have made a figure in society. He was a scholar a gentleman, a man of extensive knowledge and singularly blessed with an enlarged understanding, a noble spirit and great courage. A close friendship was rapidly growing up between us when ill health compelled him to withdraw from all public matters, and in about a year from that period he died exceedingly regretted by everybody who knew him. I was equally proud of him as an acquaintance and of myself at finding that such a man should desire my friendship.

The comment shows that Place was not above taking pride in friendship with a gentleman on the very rare occasions that he found one who did not condescend to him as a tradesman. The subscription for Wardle was collected by Samuel Brooks, who raised £4000, but he was 'in some respects very weak, and was more hurt than could well be imagined' when he heard that Wardle had said that he had detained money in his own hands in order to advance his business.[29]

The 'O.P.' (old price) riots in 1809 showed that the members of the Westminster Committee were not above encouraging violence at times. In September 1808 the Covent Garden Play House had burnt down, and when it reopened after rebuilding a year later the prices were raised. This caused angry protests, especially since the Covent Garden and Drury Lane theatres had patents which gave them a monopoly in London. When the audience demonstrated in favour of the 'Old Prices' after the first performance in the new building, the management made the mistake of calling in magistrates to read the Riot Act, and thus provoked a long and violent campaign for the 'O.P.' The next morning James Powell called on Place to concert opposition. Powell cut the letters O.P. from a card as a badge of the protesters, and Place improved on this by cutting O.P. in a hearthstone to make a mould. He commented that the newly-cast letters in lead or pewter looked bright and distinctive on a black hat.

The riots continued for three months, and Place often attended the theatre
– whether to observe the riots or take part in them he did not say. They
alienated some supporters of reform, but the Old Prices were finally restored.
Demonstrations still continued on subsidiary issues, and a final agreement
between the theatre managers and the supporters of the O.P. was agreed at
Place's house on 23 December. He was offered free admission as thanks for
his help, but he refused such an offer which would have compromised his
independence.[30]

1810 was a disastrous year for Place. A charge of spying for the
Government poisoned his life for a decade, and he quarrelled with the two
leading figures in radical politics, Burdett and Cobbett. He had known
Cobbett since the 1807 election: 'We were what is called good friends, and he
seemed to have more than common respect for me.'[31] On 1 July 1809 Cobbett
published an article attacking the flogging of militia men, and this brought a
prosecution for criminal libel. He frequently consulted Place about his
defence, and on 22 December Place attended a meeting with Lord Cochrane
and others to decide tactics. Cobbett wanted to conduct his own defence, but a
barrister quoted the lawyer's saying that 'he who defended his own cause had
a fool for a client'. Place did not know what to advise; he doubted whether
Cobbett would be able to put up an effective defence, but he knew that no
barrister would defend him properly for fear of offending the Chief Justice,
who was to preside over the trial. Then Cobbett took him aside and explained
that he planned to base his defence on complimentary letters written since the
libel by eminent men such as Castlereagh, and Place agreed that he would be
wise to dispense with a barrister's services. A libel trial was biased against the
defendant because it was tried by special jurymen, who were favourable to the
prosecution, and Place thought up a plan to get a fairer jury by going to the
Crown Office when the master was away and persuading the clerk to let
Cobbett pick half the names. The clerk agreed, but when it came to the point
Cobbett was in a state of panic about the trial, and his bluster so annoyed the
clerk that he withdrew his consent. The master then picked a jury who could
be relied on to give a verdict of guilty.

Place was furious at Cobbett's conduct, but he nevertheless agreed to
attend the trial, much to his regret. Cobbett put up a disastrous defence, and
at times had the whole court laughing at him. Place wrote: 'I was thoroughly
ashamed of him and ashamed of myself for being seen with him, and when he
concluded his speech without producing any one of the letters, I was
astounded.'[32] Cobbett was sentenced to two years in gaol and a thousand
pounds fine, and when he called on Place a few days later Place inevitably told
him what he thought of his conduct in the plainest terms. Cobbett tried to
compromise with his prosecutors by offering to give up his *Register,* but the
offer was refused. Place declined to visit Cobbett in gaol, and the quarrel was
never made up.

Place complained with good reason about Cobbett's cowardice, his lies and contradictions, his wild abuse and his insane egotism, but he could not help admiring his brilliant writing in the service of reform, and he admitted that 'upon the whole he was an useful leader'. Twenty-one years later he explained his attitude in a letter to Cobbett about a case that they were both interested in:

> You have so heartily done justice in this case, that now as at other times I cannot but forgive you your iniquities.
>   John Horne Tooke in one of his letters to Junius says – 'Personal emnity is a feeling fit only for the Devil'. I have no such feeling towards any man living, and never had, you on the contrary make the Devil's feeling your own and preach revenge as a virtue, and so because I affronted you, now just twenty-one years ago, you have been solacing yourself occasionally ever since in abusing, and scolding at me, and I dare say you have *'damned my eyes'* pretty well before you have read this much of this letter. Well never mind, words break no bones, so scold away if it gives you pleasure to the end of the chapter.

Place regarded revenge as the 'very worst passion of human Nature', perhaps as a defence against allowing his hot temper to lead him into vengefulness.[33]

The train of events which were to lead to a quarrel between Place and Burdett started in February 1810, when John Gale Jones advertised a debate at the 'British Forum' on the question: 'Which was the greatest outrage on public feeling, Mr Yorke's enforcement of the standing order to exclude strangers from the House of Commons or Mr Windham's recent attack on the liberty of the press.' A motion by Yorke had excluded the public from the House of Commons debate on the Walcheren expedition (an attempt to seize the mouth of the Scheldt which proved a fiasco) and Windham had violently attacked the press in the House. Yorke brought Gale Jones' advertisement before the House as a breach of privilege, and Gale Jones was summoned to attend at the bar of the House. Place knew that Gale Jones would be committed to gaol, and he decided to do what he could to oppose an 'illegal and pernicious exercise of power'. Gale Jones 'was always a poor emaciated crazy looking creature, possessed of considerable talents but as devoid of judgement as any man could well be'. Place summoned him and urged him to make no submission to the House, since it would not save him from gaol, and a defiant stand would make it possible to raise a substantial subscription for him. Gale Jones promised to follow the advice, but according to Place he had previously shown a lack of personal courage, and in the event he apologised to the House, being nevertheless committed to prison on the ground of the fiction that he had obstructed its proceedings. Place, showing the intolerance which marked his conduct during the 1800s and 1810s, refused to do anything further for him since he had shown himself to be a 'dastard'.[34]

Burdett then brought forward a motion in the House of Commons to free Gale Jones, condemning the imprisonment as an illegal and unconstitutional violation of the personal liberty of the subject, and fiercely attacking the conduct of the House. He revised his speech as a letter to his constituents in

Cobbett's *Register,* and on 5 April the House debated whether Burdett was guilty of breach of privilege for this publication. Place, who considered the speech 'an honour to Burdett', analysed the speeches of his opponents, the 'pretended friends of liberty', who defended the right of the House to imprison a man for breach of privilege. Place's *bête noire* was William Wilberforce, 'fiend like as he looks':[35]

> Wilberforce, who with singular powers of speech which he generally used as a Jesuit against the people of England, said 'Parliament had no right to give up the privileges of the people of England of which the right claimed by the house was undoubtedly one' — the right of being imprisoned by ones own representatives.[36]

After debating all night, the House of Commons voted on the morning of Friday 6 April to commit Burdett to the Tower by 190 votes to 152. Burdett replied by denying the legality of the Speaker's warrant, and declaring that he would obey nothing but force. Large crowds gathered outside the Tower, where water was let into the ditch and some guns were taken down from the ramparts and placed within the Tower. Thousands more collected outside Burdett's house in Piccadilly, including a number of men and boys who pelted those who did not pull off their hats as they passed. Always ready to put the worst interpretation on the authorities' conduct, Place said that this could have been stopped by half a dozen constables, but it suited the Ministers and magistrates to let it go on until an excuse was found to read the Riot Act and bring in troops.

In the afternoon the Horse Guards were ordered into action:

> It was their common practice to ride upon the foot pavement and drive the people before them, pressing on them in such a way as to cause great terror, frequently doing some of them injury and compelling them to injure one another, striking those who could not get out of their way fast enough with the flat of their swords. . . . The mob as it was called was by no means a rabble, only, people of all ranks were in the crowd . . .

Returning home from a meeting of electors at 11 p.m., Place found the houses partially illuminated: 'There was a solemn stillness, and a gloom half visible which produced on me as upon enquiry I afterwards found it had on others, that peculiar sort of feeling which has been represented, as being felt by soldiers waiting for the dawn of day to commence a battle.'[37]

On the following day, Saturday the 7th, Burdett wrote to the Sheriffs of Middlesex demanding their protection against the Speaker's illegal warrant by *posse comitatus,* householders called out by the Sheriffs to aid in enforcing the law. The situation was extremely confused, with the Government unsure whether the Speaker's warrant gave them authority to break down Burdett's front door. Both the Sheriffs and Bow Street magistrates, the latter acting under the authority of the Government, claimed the right to give orders to the soldiers outside the baronet's house. One of the two Sheriffs, Alderman Wood, was a reformer, but he was unsure of his powers. On Sunday, however, he agreed to call out the *posse comitatus* on Monday morning, and then to demand the withdrawal of the troops. The reformers' object was to gain time. The crowds were said to be greater than at the time of the Gordon Riots, and part of the army to be more disposed to join them than to fight them. The alarm had become so great that the Ministers would have been in an extremely difficult position if they had had to meet Parliament on Monday afternoon with Burdett still at large, and Place thought that the House of Commons would have had to withdraw the warrant to prevent worse trouble. He also hoped that the use of the *posse comitatus* would show that order could be kept without troops, and thus make it more difficult for the Government to use them in future.

Place spent Sunday helping to make arrangements for using the *posse comitatus*. He was to take charge of the volunteer householders at the Gloucester Coffee House until the Sheriff arrived. At 11.30 p.m. Jones Burdett, Sir Francis's brother, called on Place and told him that the baronet wanted to see him immediately. He expected his house to be forced and Jones Burdett was going to fetch Lord Cochrane, who had contrived an effectual mode of defence. Place went to Burdett's house, and found him with Roger O'Connor, who claimed the title of King of Ireland, and Hanbury Tracy, a Whig MP. Burdett, Place wrote, went over the ground and declared

> that he was resolved not to be taken, and was content to risk his life in any way we might think best. He asked me if I could not find some men of courage who were qualified to take a lead in directing others. I said I could easily find some twenty such men, who might be depended upon for judgement, courage and perseverance, and from whom at a crisis much might be expected.

There was a general conversation while they waited for Cochrane, and it appeared that there was no plan beyond the immediate defence of the house:

> at length I said 'Well, it will be easy enough to clear the Hall of constables and soldiers, to drive them into the street or destroy them, but are you prepared to take the next step, and go on?' This produced instant conviction of the folly of attempting anything. It was all at once, and by all, agreed, that nothing should be done in this way, but that as the Sheriff had consented to avail himself of the civil power . . . the matter should be left to him . . .. Sir Francis at length addressing himself particularly to me, asked what I would advise him to do. I said 'go to bed and sleep soundly. Government will never consent to bear the obloquy of breaking into your house in the night to drag you from your bed, and tomorrow morning we shall see a very different state of things.'

On Monday morning, Place was at the Gloucester Coffee House at the appointed time of 9 a.m., but Alderman Wood had little taste for a confrontation with the army and the Ministry. He was still on his way when he heard that Burdett had been arrested, taken while reading Magna Carta to his son. The events of the day were to cast a long shadow. According to Place, Wood was often reproached for his conduct, and the desire to remove the stain on his reputation was a principal motive for taking the lead in the Queen Caroline affair in 1820.[38]

'I did not then, I do not now disapprove of Sir Francis Burdett's notions', Place wrote in 1827,

> Had circumstances been such as to promise an effectual resistance, not only at the House of Sir Francis but anywhere else, had there been anything like a sufficient body organised to have assured the soldiers that power enough existed to protect them, . . . I should have concurred in resisting the usurped power of the House and the conduct of Ministers. Had matters stood thus, there would have been a fair chance, in the then disposition of men, and of no small portion of the army that a sufficient effort at the outset would have given them confidence and that many and perhaps nearly all the troops in London would have revolted. But there was no organisation no arms, and to have resisted under such circumstances would have been madness.[39]

As in 1798, Place would have supported a revolution if he had thought success probable. The reformers' helplessness in such a favourable situation was the result of the atomisation of the movement of the 1790s following Pitt's repression, which prevented effective radical organsation.[40] Most radicals accepted that the war against Napoleon was a battle against tyranny, and the movement could no longer be accused of treasonable sympathy for the French Republic. At a moment of crisis it could command far wider support than in the 1790s, but disillusionment with the high hopes of the French Revolution had lost the cause the dedication and fervour which kept the corresponding societies going through hard times. Until the Reform Bill period political societies more formal than the Westminster Committee were almost always to prove ineffective or short-lived.

Burdett was later to claim that Place had promised to fill his house with men on the Monday morning to beat out the soldiers, and had instead betrayed him, but he clearly did not blame him at first, since he promptly summoned him to the Tower to discuss the situation. 'I had not sought to obtain the confidence of Sir Francis, but I was pleased to find I possessed it. Like most such confidences however, when reposed by a man in a superior station, in a man in an inferior station of life, it did not last long.' On 17 April, a Westminster public meeting was held to protest at the action of the Commons in depriving the constituency of one of its representatives. The well-drafted resolutions, written by Place and Richter, emphasised the demand for parliamentary reform. The petition to the House of Commons was deliberately made as offensive as possible, while using 'no word called unparliamentary', with the aim of causing an argument in the House which would be reported in the newspapers. A petition was useless so far as the

House was concerned, Place observed, but it provided the best vehicle to address the public. He thought that this meeting was probably the largest ever held in Westminster – a claim made for a remarkable number of meetings. Many other meetings were held around the country to protest at Burdett's imprisonment, including a Middlesex one for which Place and Richter drafted the petition. According to Place: 'Sir Francis Burdett was now at the Zenith of his popularity, and few men ever were so popular as he was.'[41]

The reformers decided to hold a procession for Burdett on his release, which would take place when Parliament was prorogued on 21 June. As usual, everyone was in favour except Place, but he agreed to assist in arranging it. Burdett's consent was obtained by Place and Major Cartwright, who were then considered the men in whom Burdett had most confidence. The whole work of organising the procession devolved on Place as John Richter, the only other efficient member of the committee, was unwell: 'my coadjutors knowing my habits of business, and calculating on the certainty of my attention now that I was fairly entered into it, left it almost wholly to me'.[42]

These preparations were interrupted when Place was summoned to attend a coroner's jury. During the night of 30 May 1810, the Duke of Cumberland roused his household with cries for help. The Duke was found to be seriously wounded in the head, and he said that he had just fought off an unknown assailant, who had attacked him in his bedroom with a sword. In his distress the Duke called for his Italian valet, Joseph Sellis, but Sellis was found in his room with his throat cut. The Duke was the most hated of George III's sons, and when the news broke in the morning the radicals immediately assumed that he must have murdered his valet. They looked forward to a great scandal, and when Place became foreman of the jury at the coroner's inquest on Sellis's death, they must have thought that their highest hopes were going to be realised. Almost all the jury were prejudiced against the Duke, and Place got the inquest off to a good start by using his legal knowledge to insist that reporters must be allowed to attend.

But the jury unanimously concluded that Sellis had attacked the Duke and then committed suicide. Sellis's reason never emerged, although it was rumoured that the Duke had made advances to his wife. When a verdict was brought in of *felo de se* (suicide), the radicals were furious, and Place was summoned by Burdett to the Tower to defend himself against charges by Colonel Wardle that he had been bribed by the Government. Wardle seems to have been an example of the many men Place succeeded in alienating by showing his contempt even while he was helping them.[43]

Place assumed that he had satisfied Burdett, and carried on with organising the procession. It soon became clear that the attendance would be vast, with people coming from Scotland and Ireland to see the show, and Place made elaborate preparations to prevent disorder. Those in general command on horseback were to have a white wand with a gilt top as a sign of authority, and those in subordinate command a plain white wand. The night before the procession James Powell, the secretary of the organising committee, claimed that his pocket had been picked and the committee minutes and arrangements stolen. But the plan proceeded smoothly, and on the day all London seemed to be in the streets, many of the houses were decorated and views along the route commanded high prices. 'Almost every decently dressed person had a blue cockade in his hat. The ladies wore blue bonnets — blue feathers — and blue necklaces made of very large beads manufactured for the purpose . . .. the day was remarkably fine, all was happiness — hilarity and good humour.' The crowd was estimated at half a million.[44]

But when Parliament was prorogued at 3.30 p.m. Burdett evaded the procession and left the Tower by boat, to the horror of the organisers, who feared catastrophic riots if the crowds believed that they had been betrayed by their hero. Place did not know what to do, but William Adams, the captain of the procession, took charge. In order to appease the crowds he spread a story that Burdett had been forced to leave by boat, and then led the procession with the triumphal car empty, as the only hope of persuading the crowds to disperse quietly. John Gale Jones joined the procession in a cart with his name written in chalk on the sides, causing considerable amusement and releasing the tension, and the day passed without trouble.

Burdett's behaviour was never satisfactorily explained. Henry Hunt told Place in 1815 that Burdett had persuaded himself that Place might have arranged with the Government to have him shot, and this receives some support from the version of events which William Frend passed on to his daughter. He told her that he and Jones Burdett were alarmed at the size of the crowds, and they persuaded Sir Francis that his conspicuous place in the procession would expose him to the danger of well-aimed shots, and thus endanger the peace. Since Jones Burdett and Frend appear to have shared the suspicions of Place at this time, the version tallies with Hunt's story, but it also brings out that the decision was an impulsive one, without any real thought for the consequences. If Burdett had withdrawn his consent to the procession beforehand, his decision would have been justifiable, but the danger of allowing a crowd of half a million to gather and then betraying its expectations must have been greater than the danger that a hypothetical shot would lead to disorder.[45]

Place was naturally furious with Burdett, who 'had deliberately placed the metropolis in the utmost danger, he had risked a massacre of the people in the most wanton and inexcusable manner. . . . Were I to say what I can hardly help saying I might be accused as I was at the time of rashness, and yet it does seem, more honest, than rash, to say what ought to be said of such conduct as that.' At a meeting of the reformers a few days later, 'I said very freely what I thought of his conduct'. According to Henry Hunt, he called Burdett a 'd——d coward and paltroon'. Everyone apart from Place and three or four others agreed to pass the matter over, but he declared 'that after the conduct of Sir Francis I was utterly unable to place confidence in him, or trust to him on any emergency'. He announced that he would cease all public interference in political matters, apart from helping to pay off the debt incurred. Burdett lost some of his popularity, although he retained enough to make a challenge to his parliamentary seat impossible, and his resistance to the Speaker's warrant greatly enhanced his reputation outside London.[46] Place's violent reaction was understandable, especially since Burdett had created what was perhaps the only situation in Place's life which he was completely unable to cope with, but in the long run he was to realise that a refusal to work with Burdett could only harm the cause of reform.

*   *   *

For the next two years Place played no part in politics. Cartwright and Burdett attempted to build an alliance with Whig supporters of reform, but by May 1811 this had broken down in the face of the opposition of the Whig leadership, and in 1812 the radicals again entered a General Election opposing both the parliamentary parties.

Shortly before the election Place sent Brooks a plan for conducting it, together with a letter which said that he would not leave his house on election business, but that he would give any help he could at home. On 19 September, John Richter wrote to him on behalf of the leading members of the Committee, asking his advice on election tactics: 'I . . . have no doubt that tho' you will not publicly act you will privately advise; which by the bye is the least you can do and is also absolutely necessary to prevent things going wrong.' In reply Place agreed with Richter that 'the persons who interfere to manage the next election' – he objected to Richter's use of the name 'Westminster Committee' – ought to try to return two members free from expense and personal trouble; that Lord Cochrane was open to objection as second candidate because of his health and his profession of naval officer, which made him liable to be sent overseas; that William Roscoe, the former MP for Liverpool and author of reform pamphlets, was the best alternative, and Walter Fawkes, an active parliamentary reformer and former MP for Yorkshire, was the second best. But Place argued that Cochrane should be chosen if a contest could thus be avoided, since this would not only ensure success and save money, but make the result known in time to encourage reformers in other seats:

> Your questions have so often occupied my thoughts that I find no difficulty in answering them – the answers must however be considered as implying a conduct in those who may manage the Election which omits no matter of detail in the previous arrangement or in the conduct thereof – which has no subterfuge – more depends on these points than those less conversant with the management of bodies of men than myself can well appreciate.
>
> You know my opinion of the persons with whom you must act if you go into the business, and you are not ignorant that I consider the electors as themselves very little worthy – and without any sound political knowledge – those your immediate

associates have no doubt the best intentions − and are in their political views and actions independent and honourable − but they will do nothing where there is no noise which they mistake at times for the voice of the *people* − neither do they understand how the mischief is either produced or prevented by the thousand little quiet things which happen continually.[47]

The arrogance and intolerance are typical, although equally typical is that Place said nothing which he could not have justified. His experience of 'the management of bodies of men' stood him in good stead, but they never persuaded him − in spite of some soul searching − that tact was anything other than dishonesty.

The Committee soon found that it was badly split, with Cochrane, Roscoe and Fawkes all having supporters, and some wanting to run Burdett alone. Letters were sent to Roscoe and Fawkes asking whether they were willing to be nominated. On 27 September Place wrote an anguished letter to Richter urging that, as politicians, the Committee had to accept Cochrane and take the credit for electing him if they were to preserve their importance, but questioning whether they could support him as honest men in view of their doubts about him. The following day, with Roscoe having refused and no answer from Fawkes, his doubts were borne out when a meeting of 72 voted narrowly for Fawkes, who had been considered as second candidate in 1807.[48] Cochrane promptly replied by announcing his candidacy, and soon afterwards the Committee received Fawkes's refusal. After Cochrane had called on Place and discussed the objections to him, he wrote to Brooks justifying himself and affirming his commitment to parliamentary reform, on which he was considered suspect. This gave the Committee an excuse to change their minds, and Burdett and Cochrane were adopted at a public meeting and elected unopposed.

The successful outcome confirmed the Committee's growing importance and confidence − it was significant that Burdett had not attempted to interfere in the choice of second candidate − and some members tried to set up a formal constituency association. Place did not like the idea, because he did not believe that there was enough enthusiasm to make it viable, but he agreed to draw up a plan. His scheme bore a close resemblance to the LCS, with a democratic organisation based on the parishes and a central general committee. Contemporary suspicion of any body which might interfere with the 'free' choice of the electors and the amount of work it would have required led to its rejection at the public meeting held to launch it.

Members of the Westminster Committee also attempted to help reformers in other seats. Place wrote to a Coventry reformer explaining his plan for managing an election, and he drafted an address to the freeholders of Staffordshire on behalf of Mr (later Sir Charles) Wolseley. But the radicals' strength had seriously declined since 1810. In 1811−12 the Luddite disturbances had frightened many of the middle classes away from reform, while better war news helped to dampen public discontent. Radical candidates in Southwark and the City of London were defeated, and Middlesex was not even contested. The election also encouraged the growing differences among reformers. Henry Hunt, who was to become the Committee's bitterest critic, later complained that he had not received its support in his fight at Bristol, while Cartwright was disappointed not to be considered for Westminster and he tried to make trouble at the public selection meeting. At the same time, Henry Brougham, the ablest figure in the Whig ranks, began to look for a radical seat. He was turned down for Middlesex and hankered after Westminster, telling Leigh Hunt that it was a seat to aspire to since 'in truth it is the summit of popular ambition – and it is a really important situation and may enable a man to do infinite good'.[49]

*   *   *

Any chance that Place would return to active involvement in the Westminster Committee was destroyed when Samuel Brooks began to raise a subscription for the radical weekly, the *Independent Whig,* at the same time as it was bringing charges against Place over the Sellis affair. From August 1812 the *Whig* began printing anonymous letters which posed questions about the affair, many of which could have been answered by reference to its own report of the inquest. On 8 November it claimed that Place had been hired by the Treasury to suborn the jury, and in addition he was accused of having betrayed Colonel Despard, who had been executed on a charge of High Treason in 1803. This charge especially upset Place because Despard had been one of his heroes.

He intended to bring a charge of slander against the editor of the *Whig,* but he dropped the idea when the Duke of Cumberland brought a charge of criminal libel. This only fuelled suspicions, because truth was not a defence against the charge, so the accusations against Place were renewed. The *Independent Whig* was run by extortioners, and Place believed that their plan was to force the Duke to buy their silence.[50] The grievance against Place seems to have been personal. One of the *Whig*'s writers was John 'Jew' King, a notorious moneylender who had clashed with Place when he tried to cultivate the leaders of the LCS,[51] and another was Thomas Evans, who had been barred from Place's house when he used money Place lent him for a dishonest purpose.

Many people urged Place to refute the calumnies, but he argued that it would be absurd to notice anonymous charges, since the writer would only reply with more insinuations. However his old friend John Bone did reply, partly because he had also come under suspicion. A former secretary of the LCS and political detainee, Bone had suffered insinuations ever since 1795, when charges that he was a spy had caused a split in the society. In November 1812 he addressed a printed letter to 'a member of Mr White's committee', probably Samuel Brooks, who had taken the lead in raising a subscription for

White, the editor of the *Whig*. In the slander against the Duke of Cumberland, Bone said,

> it could not escape the discernment of many persons, that two of your own Friends were the victims *in petto*. When I say *two of your Friends,* I by no means speak in the terms called for by the occasion. – I ought to say two of your *oldest* – your *honestest* – your *steadiest,* and your *best* Friends. . . . Of that individual, therefore, whom Mr White has chosen to stigmatise under the *libeller's slang* of a 'certain Juror', and of myself; I have no hesitation in saying, that no two men can be found in this kingdom, to whom the cause of Liberty owes more, than to us. It has not been our way to count either our losses or our gains. . . . It should be remembered, that our services were given when it was less genteel and fashionable to be patriotic than at present. If that individual would allow me to answer any of the wicked and shameful slanders that have been circulated against him, I am afraid few of you gentlemen would be found free from the reproach of having by your silence lent an improper degree of countenance to Mr W's treacherous conduct; but he, without a due regard to himself, in my opinion, has resolved to treat the calumniators and their calumnies alike with indignant contempt.[52]

Although Place refused to answer the charges, he did attempt to persuade Brooks to drop his countenance of White or demand proof of his charges, but Brooks only replied that he did not enter into the matter on either side. In January 1813 Place sent him a final appeal : 'When I consider the good you are continually doing, when I consider that you are one of two men who amongst all whom I know I have selected in the event of my death, as the most certain of all men to be depended upon for honourable and disinterested assistance in the concerns of my family I cannot give you up without an attempt to convince you of your error.'[53] Brooks reacted by arranging a meeting to discuss the matter, but when Place refused to attend, Brooks again said that he would not enter into the matter. Place tried hard to be philosophical about the charges, arguing that they were inevitable because most men would rather believe such a scandal about the Duke than take the trouble of investigating the facts. He claimed that the slanders caused him no distress, in which he deluded himself, and they accentuated the aggressive self-righteousness which characterised his attitude during the 1810s. The perpetual quarrels among the radicals frequently led to charges of spying, and the story about Place would probably have died but for its revival by the *Independent Whig*.

In 1811 a parliamentary bill had been brought forward making candidates for Westminster liable for the High Bailiff's election expenses. Place succeeded through a sympathetic MP in getting a parliamentary select committee on the High Bailiff's claim, but the only witnesses were supporters of the claim and the bill passed. During the election the reformers made sure, on Place's advice, that nothing was done which identified Burdett and Cochrane as candidates, so that they could not be sued under the Act. But Place's quarrel with Brooks at the end of 1812 prevented him from interfering when the High Bailiff brought an action to recover his costs for Lord

Cochrane's election, and the High Bailiff was awarded £225 plus costs. Place then wrote a long and angry letter to another member of the committee, together with a case for counsel which he had drafted. This was used to brief Henry Brougham to defend Burdett's case and the High Bailiff was non-suited – Burdett's failure to interfere on this occasion is another indication of the committee's rising prestige. The High Bailiff then sought compensation for his losses from Parliament, but Place managed to prevent this by writing to MPs denying that he had a fair claim. This put a stop to it until 1818, when another attempt to vote the High Bailiff compensation was dropped after being opposed by MPs Place had briefed. He attributed his success to the unwillingness of the High Bailiff and his friends to have a full enquiry which would have exposed the corrupt nature of the claim. The story provides a sample of the energy and efficiency which made the Westminster reformers feel that they could not do without Place however much they resented his hectoring.[54]

6 Schools for All

Political education had been a central concern of the members of the LCS, who held the general radical belief that if truth was stated with sufficient clarity then it must be believed. Place, like many other radicals, held a purely environmentalist view of the formation of character, believing 'that the generality of children are organised so nearly alike that they may by proper management, be made pretty nearly equally wise and virtuous, and that it is the want of wisdom in their teachers which prevents their being so, taking the word teachers in a large sense.' He considered his friend Edward Wakefield's belief in 'innate propensities' an excuse for not attempting to remove his children's faults.[1] Thus it was natural that reformers should see universal education as a guarantee that the people would learn to understand and accept the truths of the radical creed, and in the 1800s radicals had become interested in children's education.

The principal obstacle to universal education was that the poor could not afford to pay school fees, and Joseph Lancaster's 'monitorial' system of setting older children to teach younger ones provided a possible solution to the problem. Place took a close interest in Lancaster's school from 1804, when he became a subscriber at half a guinea a month. At this time he seems to have been almost alone among the radicals in seeing the potential of the plan to provide education at a price which the poor could afford. Lancaster's enthusiasm and inventiveness as a teacher persuaded many to respond to his appeals for help and attracted royal patronage, but he was very extravagant, and in 1808 he was on the verge of bankruptcy. He was rescued by a rich dentist, Joseph Fox, but by 1810 even Fox and his friends could not keep up with Lancaster's debts, and support for him was institutionalised in the Royal Lancasterian Association, which contained a curious amalgam of Royal Dukes, reformers, Quakers and dissenters. Effective control lay in the hands of five trustees who had advanced a total of £5600, headed by Fox, a Baptist, and William Allen, a Quaker philanthropist. Although its committee included Anglicans, the Association was generally regarded as an organisation of dissenters, and in 1811 the Church party founded its rival

'National Society for the Education of the Poor in the Principles of the Established Church'.

By this time Place had become personally acquainted with Lancaster, who was involved in constant quarrels with the trustees over money. In June 1813 Place and John Bone agreed to try to help him, and they proposed to Fox that they should address the trustees on Lancaster's behalf. Fox welcomed the offer, but Lancaster's unreasonable demands ensured the failure of the negotiations. He appealed to the Dukes of Kent and Sussex for support, and they asked Joseph Hume to look into his affairs. The result was the crucial introduction of Place to Hume, who was to be his main parliamentary ally. Place disliked him at first, considering him selfish, and subservient to his royal friends, but he soon found that he was diligent.

In November 1813 Lancaster was pensioned off and the Royal Lancasterian Association was reconstituted as the British and Foreign School Society. 'I had done so much for the ease and comfort of the Trustees', Place observed, 'and had shown such an aptitude for business that I was earnestly requested to lend my assistance in the committee of which I was considered a member.' John Bone refused to join the new society because of the coldness of three of the trustees towards him: 'It was well known that he was poor, and notwithstanding his integrity which was as perfect as any mans could be, it was impossible for him to be accepted on the same footing as I was by the three Trustees I being reputed rich.' To the end of his life, Place urged young reformers to try to make some money before they set out on a political career, because then they would command far more respect and could be much more useful.[2]

Place threw himself into the work in a spirit of enthusiasm and optimism, but difficulties soon appeared. His main concern was to introduce a proper system of financial checks and cut out unnecessary expenditure, believing that this would allow the work of the Society to be enormously expanded. Economy would also have made the Society less dependent on charity, and thus less vulnerable to a diminution of interest among the charitable. But he soon found an obstacle in Fox, who was the secretary of the Society and had an almost unlimited control over the funds. At first they were friends and Fox sometimes went to Place for consolation in his periodic fits of depression, but when he realised that Place was determined to prevent him acting without the control of the committee he became his enemy. Lancaster was doing his best to sow dissension, and he turned against Place in March 1814, when a subcommittee including Place found him guilty of indecent behaviour with his apprentice teachers. Lancaster wrote a letter of resignation to the committee accusing it of being perverted to infidel purposes, and taking leave of those 'who do profess what are called Infidel opinions and boast of having been leaders and founders of the London Corresponding Society'. Many members now heard for the first time that Place was an unbeliever, 'and being very sanctified, serious persons were horrified at the information'. Fox

insisted that the charges should be investigated at a meeting at Kensington
Palace, in the presence of the Royal patrons of the Society, the Dukes of Kent
and Sussex.

Place stated that he got on well with the Royal Dukes, who valued his
businesslike methods, a fact which seems to have given him more pleasure
than was consonant with his republican principles: 'Much of the business
done at the Palace was under my direction, few liked to propose anything in
the Presence of the Dukes, and whenever anyone did it was generally with a
circumlocutory introduction, in which the words Royal Highness was
frequently repeated, I on the contrary never once used these words, never
found it necessary to use them, and yet I was always well received by the
Dukes, and made so free with on some occasions by the Duke of Sussex as to
make us both look somewhat ridiculous.'³ On this occasion his opponents
were disconcerted that he dared to turn up, and since the Dukes were on his
side, the investigation never got off the ground.

Place had some success in persuading the committee that money was being
spent wastefully – on one occasion he forced Fox to admit that two boys sent
to Edinburgh as schoolmasters had cost the Society over £500 each. He also
had influential supporters, notably Henry Brougham and Joseph Hume, but
Brougham never gave the help he promised and Hume 'despaired and was
inefficient'. The committee was dominated by Fox and William Allen, and
Place was inhibited by the knowledge that they had kept the Lancasterian
movement alive for years at a very heavy cost to themselves. Place never tired
of praising Allen's good heart, but he complained that he was led on by the
'exceedingly artful' Fox. According to Place, 'Fox could hardly be said to be
sane, and when excited by religious feelings was decidely insane. . . . The
notions, he himself formed, he succeeded in persuading himself were
ordinances of God, and as he thus made his own personal purposes holy,
every means was fair, for their accomplishment.'⁴ Fox had a history of
insanity.

In January 1815 the committee agreed to take up a plan Place put forward
for organising education in London south of the Thames, and he secured
unanimous agreement that the expensive boarding-school for training
teachers should become a day school. However, Allen and Fox persisted in
nominating boarders, and when Place objected Allen declared that he would
withdraw if the matter was persisted in – he and others had supported the
Institution in times of difficulty at great expense and trouble, and now other
gentlemen who had not shared the trouble came forward, and he hoped their
arrangements would be more successful. Fox also said that he would resign,
and since their resignations would have wrecked the Society Place ceased to
attend. Soon afterwards Fox dropped his name from the committee. Place
said that he could have destroyed Fox by exposing his maladministration to
the subscribers, but this would also have wrecked the Society. Place had
visited most of the Lancasterian and rival National schools in London, and he

had been impressed by the superiority of the Lancasterian ones. The British and Foreign School Society went on to play an important role in the development of elementary education in Britain in the nineteenth century.

* * *

Place's quarrel with his Westminster Committee colleagues led him to concentrate increasingly on popular education, and in 1813 he had helped to found the West London Lancasterian Association (WLLA). This was Edward Wakefield's plan to introduce universal primary education in West London using Lancasterian methods. Wakefield was a gentleman farmer and author of a political and statistical survey of Ireland, and in 1812 he met Place at the offices of the printer John McCreery. In the same year Wakefield introduced Place to James Mill, and Mill introduced Place to Bentham.[5] In 1813 Wakefield, Place and Mill took up the WLLA. Fox's generosity to Lancaster made him appear an ideal ally in launching it, so they sought his help, and when the WLLA was launched in June he became its secretary. The proposal attracted strong support from the Westminster men, and many of them joined the committee, which also contained a religious group led by Fox and Allen, and Benthamites such as James Mill and Wakefield, while Whig magnates such as Lord Holland and the Duke of Bedford became trustees. Wakefield pioneered enquiries into the extent of education in parts of Westminster, and the results were incorporated into evidence given to the House of Commons Select Committee on Education in 1816.[6]

Fox expected the same control over the WLLA as he had over the British and Foreign. He told Place: 'Confidence has been placed in Mr Allen and me in our other quarter and we have acted as the occasion demanded.' When he discovered that the rest of the committee would not allow him to act as a dictator, he did all he could to make trouble. Religion provided a ready means of causing dissension. The British and Foreign had a rule that the Bible was to be the only book for reading lessons, but the WLLA adopted a rule drafted by James Mill and agreed by Fox that the Bible was to be the only religious book to be read, intending to teach other subjects as well, such as geography and mechanics. 'As far as the observations of my friends and as far as my own extended', Place wrote, 'we concurred in believing that this teaching of Geography would produce the effects we had witnessed in others – namely a desire for information, which of all things operates to keep working men from their bane, *the public house*.'[7] The belief that drinking was a prime obstacle to working class improvement was shared by moderate and extreme radicals.

When Fox failed to gain control, he demanded that the WLLA adopt the British and Foreign rule, and he and his allies caused altercations which drove away supporters and funds. The 'saints', Place complained, 'had no particular wish to elevate the people, they had another motive, namely a reversionary interest in heaven, a blind, mysterious, ill comprehended something they could not define even to themselves, which was to be

promoted and obtained . . . by low cunning — intrigue, and persecution.'
Place himself was sometimes guilty of sowing dissension among the different
religious factions: 'Never in my life did I see malice, and the most unqualified
rancour exhibited, as these base passions were exhibited in the committee. On
some occasions when for the purpose of seeing the saints fully exhibit
themselves I prompted the parties who were opposed to each other, (for I
never would be a party in their disputes), these passions were pushed to an
almost inconceivable extent.'[8] The committee had great difficulty in finding a
site for a school, and for some time Fox blocked a proposal that they should
take over a disused British and Foreign one.

Another cause of dispute was the question of whether the schools should
charge fees. The religious educationalists were generally opposed, whereas
Place and his allies were in favour of small fees. They wanted schools which
would cater to all classes, but if fees were not charged, then the schools would
be regarded as second-class charity ones for the poor, and middle-class
parents would not send their children to them. Mill was the author of a
pamphlet with a famous title, *Schools for All,* while Wakefield objected to the
terms ' "Poor" or "lower orders" which are hateful upon principle and
detrimental if our plans are to be extended to "schools for all" in which ranks
or castes are not to be thought of.'[9] The radicals also thought that a small fee
would make poor parents set a much greater value on the education provided
without proving a deterrent.

The delays caused by these dissensions roused criticisms from some of the
subscribers, and in May 1814 Joseph Fletcher, a brewer who had failed in
business, came to Place to say that two of the WLLA's principal supporters,
Burdett and Lord Stanhope, were dissatisfied that a school had not yet been
built, and at the committee's extravagance. Fletcher, who had gained
Burdett's confidence, put forward two plans, one for a machine to grind corn
which the boys in the schools could operate and pay the running expenses,
which Place rejected as useless, and the other for building a school cheaply,
which the committee rejected as absurd. Lord Stanhope was easily satisfied
that his complaints were groundless, but Burdett was a different matter.
Fletcher presented a demand signed by the baronet for four men to be placed
on the committee, including Fletcher himself, Thomas Evans and Arthur
Thistlewood, a gambler and *qui tam* informer (one who informs for reward),
who was later to be executed for his part in the Cato Street conspiracy. Evans
and Thistlewood had been involved in the slander against Place in the
Independent Whig. According to Fletcher, Burdett demanded that '*Francis
Place* and *John Richter* might be expelled the committee. Place being a spy
employed by the government to ruin the Institution and Richter being his
tool.' Sir Francis would not pay the £1000 he had promised unless Place was
expelled.[10]

Up to this time a number of the rumours about Place had circulated behind
his back, but now he heard various stories about the accusations made against

him. On 1 July he heard from James Mill that Burdett had told him and Bentham the previous year that he was a spy, and cited as evidence that when he was resisting the Speaker's warrant, Place had promised to fill his house with people to beat out the soldiers but had instead betrayed him. Another member of the committee told Place that Brooks had refused to give the WLLA a list of active reformers in Westminster for fear that Place would use it against the popular interest in an election. Place concluded that his continued presence on the committee would do more harm than good: 'I have considered most seriously, your objections to my withdrawing', he wrote to Mill on 8 July, 'I will not say that I could divest myself of all prejudice, and suffer no partial feelings to obtrude, neither will I say that I possess the wisdom to enable me to decide on the very best line of conduct, but I can safely say, I have subjected myself to a severe examination — I have done my best — and I shall resign.' In his letter of resignation he angrily condemned those who had destroyed his usefulness, naming Burdett as the chief of them: they were 'base and malignant persons whom I despise'.[11]

On 14 July a delegation of Wakefield, Brooks and Sturch, a leading Westminster reformer, saw Burdett and justified the committee's refusal to accept the men he had nominated. Burdett appeared to regret having been led so far by Fletcher and told Wakefield that he was well disposed towards Place, a statement Place flatly refused to believe. He declined to attend the committee meeting held on 18 July to discuss his resignation, because he feared that he would give the members an excuse for treating him unjustly by failing to show Burdett the respect they would expect. At the meeting Fletcher and Evans were severely handled by Henry Brougham, but they refused to give any evidence for their allegations. Burdett opposed a motion regretting Place's resignation after hearing the abuse in his letter, saying, so Place was told, that 'I was angry enough at having my character assailed, but that I did not hesitate to speak freely and plainly enough of the character of others and he could not after all that had passed consent to express regret.' The motion was defeated 8–7, but another thanking Place for his services was passed 8–0.[12]

The failure of Place's accusers to substantiate their charges seems to have scotched the rumours, at least among his Westminster associates. Mill remarked in a letter to him that every one of the committee apart from Burdett said that he disbelieved the tale, and soon afterward William Adams came to Place in hopes of a reconciliation with Sir Francis. Place demanded that he repudiate the story that he had promised to fill his house with people to beat out the soldiers, a condition that he knew Burdett would reject, and the reconciliation had to wait until 1819. The charges also brought an awkwardly worded tribute from Mill: 'You had no occasion for this declaration to satisfy you respecting my opinion of you, to which I should have been far from alluding, had it not been for the malignity with which I see your character is pursued, and which makes it my duty to declare on all occasions that I have met with few men in my whole life of whom I think so highly.'[13]

Burdett's role in the affair is difficult to disentangle. It is probable that he had convinced himself that Place had promised to fill his house with people – in later years Place would take for granted that any contradiction in Burdett's statements was to be attributed to his bad memory. His carelessness is also likely to have made him inclined to accept inventions by Place's enemies without checking whether there was any evidence for them, an inclination doubtless encouraged by Place's own charge of cowardice against him over the procession from the Tower. Place made enemies by his readiness to show men that he held them in contempt, but he was far from being the only man who suffered from false accusations – continuing paranoia about the Government's use of spies ensured that other men such as John Bone and Major Cartwright's secretary, Thomas Cleary, were also objects of suspicion.

After Place's resignation Fox took advantage of the confusion to resign as secretary of the WLLA, on the ground that the schools were intended to be used for infidel purposes. The committee were also dispirited by a report from Place and Sturch which showed that the cost per pupil in the British and Foreign schools was much higher than claimed, thus undermining hopes that the WLLA would be able to provide education at a low price. The WLLA dragged on for two more years, and it only succeeded in founding one school. At times Place considered returning to the committee, only rejecting the idea because he did not think that he would find efficient colleagues. It seems likely that by the time of his resignation the dissensions raised by Fox had already ruined the Association's chances of raising the enormous funds which would have been required for any serious attempt to carry out such an ambitious scheme. Place had resigned in a rage, but he stayed out because he saw no hope of success. In 1816 the British and Foreign proposed that the WLLA should become one of its auxiliary societies, but the Association rejected the condition that the Bible should be the only reading book, and preferred to dissolve itself. In the same year Place testified to the Parliamentary Select Committee on Education on the inaccuracy of the estimates of the costs of the British and Foreign schools, but also on the superiority of the education they provided compared with the National Society ones.[14]

*　　*　　*

The last of Place's three abortive efforts in the field of education in the 1810s was the Chrestomathic school, Bentham's term for a Lancasterian secondary school. This was Place's own idea, inspired by the difficulty he found in providing his sons with a good education at a reasonable cost. He also hoped that it could be an evening school for adults and apprentices. In November 1833 he wrote:

> That nothing can be of so much importance to mankind as a system of education which shall lay the foundation of great intellectual knowledge – and which may be communicated to all, or nearly all the people, seems to me so self evident a

proposition, that any attempt to prove it would be as absurd as an attempt to prove on a bright summers day that the Sun shone.

It was a thorough conviction of this great truth which led me to seek for the cooperation of some of my friends in an attempt to introduce a mode of teaching which I then thought and still think, must have set an example which from its cheapness and goodness would have been generally adopted. Had it been set, as it ought to have been, I cannot doubt for a moment that by this time it would have produced so great a change for the better in the whole of the community from the richest to the poorest, that instead of the bitter complaints we are continually compelled to hear from almost every rank in life, of the evils which oppress them, we should have put an end to many of these evils, have lessened others and had a prospect before us of unheard of happiness.[15]

Place's remarks illustrate both his tendency to invest projects which failed to get off the ground with grandiose retrospective merits, and the almost unlimited belief of radicals in the power of education.

In February 1814 some members of the WLLA formed a separate association to launch the Chrestomathic school, and Bentham offered the garden of his London house as a site. The project also persuaded him to set out his views on education in his *Chrestomathia,* which was published in the summer of 1815. Place, Mill and Wakefield worked hard to make the project a reality, and it received powerful support from David Ricardo. In 1817 he almost purchased a site for the school in Leicester Square, pulling out at the last minute because the ownership of the site was uncertain. But Place's involvement prevented the participation of Burdett in the crucial early stages, and Bentham's support proved a double-edged sword. His offer of the garden of his London house for the school had increasingly stringent conditions attached to it, until the promoters finally had to reject the offer. They never raised enough to pay a commercial price for a site and build a school, and in 1821 they dropped the project and returned the subscriptions.[16]

*   *   *

In the 1810s Place's efforts to improve children's education had brought him only frustration, but in the 1820s he found a more fruitful field in adult education. He played a key role in launching the London Mechanics' Institute, and its success encouraged a movement which led to a network of mechanics' institutes all over the country.[17] He also helped to found London University, although his aid was restricted by prejudice against him due to snobbery and his views on religion, by his inability to purchase a share due to South American losses, and by Brougham's jealousy.

Educational standards were higher in Scotland than England, and in the early nineteenth century the leading centre for education for working men was the Andersonian Institution in Glasgow. In the early 1800s the professor of natural philosophy at the Institution, George Birkbeck, gave highly successful lectures for mechanics, and other lecturers carried on his work after he moved to London in 1804.[18] However, in July 1823 a group of mechanics broke away after a dispute in order to form their own institute. By this time increasing interest among artisans had made the time ripe for founding similar institutes in England, and it was clear that they would have to be under the mechanics' own control in order to gain their allegiance.

In September 1823 Joseph Robertson, joint editor of the newly founded *Mechanics' Magazine,* conceived the idea of an institute in London similar to the Glasgow one. His co-editor was Place's close friend, Thomas Hodgskin, a half-pay naval lieutenant whose socialist economic theories influenced Karl Marx. Hodgskin naturally took the idea of a mechanics' institute to Place, who welcomed the proposal – he was already thinking along the same lines as a result of discussions with Dr Ure, Birkbeck's successor at the Andersonian. Place said that Hodgskin gave the impression that Robertson was a new acquaintance, but it later came out that he had known him in Glasgow – Robertson had left the city 'disreputably', and this was why Hodgskin concealed the earlier acquaintance.

The editors drew up an address which was corrected by Place and published in the *Mechanics' Magazine.* It proposed an institute to acquaint mechanics with the sciences of chemistry, mechanical philosophy and the creation and distribution of wealth, and warned that workmen who went to the pot-house every evening joined in their own degradation. Mechanics were urged to follow the Glasgow example and form their own institute, depending on themselves, not charity for money.

From the start, Place disagreed with Robertson and Hodgskin over finance. He said that they knew little of London mechanics, and they had not calculated the expenses of the establishment they were proposing. He was convinced from experience that it would be impossible to obtain enough money from the artisans, but when he failed to persuade his colleagues he decided to attempt to carry out their programme. With great difficulty he found out the addresses of many secretaries and leading men in trade clubs and benefit societies, and he went round them day by day. Many welcomed the project and promised support. He also sent copies of the address to every club and house of call (a public house where the men of a trade would meet and to which employers would send for hands) which he could discover, and thus helped to make it better known. With success, his horizons expanded, and he decided that schools could be established for many useful purposes if only money could be found to build a centre. Remembering his own struggles to educate himself he wanted mechanics to have the best of everything, and he laid detailed plans before Hodgskin and Robertson for a large house with a lecture room for 1000, a laboratory, a museum, a workshop, books, schools and furniture. He persuaded them that the assistance of donors would be required, and that far from them controlling the institute it would be impossible to get them to attend when required. The mechanics would thus be able to run the institute as they pleased.

There were further reasons for optimism. The publication of the address had raised the circulation of the *Mechanics' Magazine,* and Birkbeck had offered his assistance, which was to prove crucial to the institute's success. A meeting to plan the London Mechanics' Institute was attended by fifty people, including Brougham, Birkbeck and leading engineering employers. It was agreed to launch a subscription at a public meeting on 15 November, and a general committee was appointed. Place, Robertson and Hodgskin became members of a subcommittee appointed to draw up a set of rules. As usual, the work was left to Place, and with his normal thoroughness he went round the London literary and scientific institutes, getting copies of their original and current rules and finding out from their secretaries and older members what problems had arisen. The result was a complex set of rules, designed to guard against every loophole for confusion and mischief making, and these were amended and approved in the subcommittee. At this stage everyone was elated and confident, almost all the newspapers recommended the institute and the leaders were confident of raising £10,000.

But Robertson and Hodgskin were becoming increasingly uneasy at the domination of middle-class figures such as Birkbeck and Place, and before the general committee met they privately went round the artisan members of the committee and warned that an institute built with charitable donations would make the donors the masters and the men their dependants. The men's suspicions were easily roused, Place observed, because they had so often been betrayed by upper-class collaborators. At the committee they supported Robertson and Hodgskin in an attack on a motion to ask for donations. Place angrily pointed out that they had supported donations in the *Magazine* and in the subcommittee, and he accused Robertson of treachery for secretly undermining what he publicly supported, but the motion had to be withdrawn. Robertson then opposed Place's rules – which he had also supported in the subcommittee – but he was so offensive that the artisans became alarmed that Birkbeck and other leading men would withdraw, so Place was able to get the rules examined. After several hours of wrangling over two days they were adopted after amendment, and Place and his allies were able to proceed.

Robertson's group was soon discredited, but he and Hodgskin were joint secretaries of the committee, and they continued to cause trouble until elections were held on 15 December, when their chief ally was voted off the committee and a paid secretary was appointed in their place. Hodgskin had never been personally offensive, and he soon changed sides and became a close ally of Birkbeck, but Robertson continued to snipe at the London Mechanics' Institute in the *Mechanics' Magazine.*

There was some justice in the secretaries' criticisms, as Place was later to recognise implicitly. Lecturers sometimes assumed too high a level of knowledge in their students, the secretary's hours were set during the day when the mechanics were at work, and clerks soon formed a high proportion of the membership. But the problems were largely the result of the equivocation of Roberston and Hodgskin. If they had stuck to the idea of a small-scale institution which did not require heavy expenditure they would have received Place's support, as others did with similar projects. By supporting donations and then turning round and opposing them they caused dissension which prevented enough being raised while enthusiasm was high. Although Burdett gave £1000, a large loan from Birkbeck was necessary to allow building to go ahead, and the LMI was always short of money and returning to the donors for more, a situation which made real control by the artisan members impossible.

Both sides in the argument agreed that the LMI should be run by its members, and the rules provided that two-thirds of the committee must be artisans, so Robertson was able to make great capital out of the election of Francis Place Junior as an artisan member. He was put on the wrong list by accident, which was not discovered until after nominations had closed. Against his father's advice, he was persuaded to allow his nomination to go ahead, and he devoted considerable effort to sorting out the accounts, which were in confusion because Robertson and Hodgskin had destroyed all the papers in their hands and failed to account for the money they had raised. In spite of its early problems, the LMI proved highly successful. Ironically, it eventually became Birkbeck College of London University.

Place himself was not consistent on the issue of how far the working people should accept middle-class leadership. He welcomed the artisans' increasing unwillingness to accept control from above, and in 1834 he alienated the Society for the Diffusion of Useful Knowledge by publishing correspondence with them in which he criticised their scheme for opening a mechanics' library under their control. He was sure that it could not succeed, and he welcomed the fact as a proof of the improvement among the better sort of working people, who could no longer be led like children.[19] But he was ready to accept middle-class leadership in the establishment of mechanics' institutes, because he knew that without it they could not get off the ground. He also showed intolerance by objecting to Hodgskin being allowed to give lectures at the LMI on political economy because of his socialist views.

Projectors of new institutes often turned to Place for help, and he played an important part in founding the City and Western institutes for clerks, while his eldest son served on the committee of the Western. Place also helped institutes at Spital Fields, Borough, Mile End, Westminster, Rotherhithe, Horslydown, Bermondsey, Southwark, Plymouth and Manchester. His extensive contacts enabled him to be extremely helpful in getting aid from upper-class sympathisers of donations of money and books, and Burdett normally referred requests for help to him for his advice. Place wrote articles for such journals as the *Trades' Newspaper* urging working men to join institutes.[20]

*   *   *

In about 1822 the poet Thomas Campbell started advocating the establishment of a university in London. He urged the project on Place, who rejected it at first because the failure of the Chrestomathic school had convinced him that it would not be possible to raise enough money. But the success of the LMI changed his mind – indeed he later claimed that the establishment of London University was mainly due to the LMI[21] – and from June 1824 he helped Campbell to bring the scheme to the attention of influential men. By January 1825 Campbell had received enough encouragement to persuade him to put forward his idea in a letter published in *The Times*. This cited his friend Place anonymously as an example of the advantages of education in raising a man from poverty and ignorance, with an exaggerated account of his acquirements. When Joseph Hume read the letter he came to Place and promised to get subscribers for £100,000 if Place and Campbell would draw up a prospectus, and this was done by Campbell.

After this the project passed into the hands of upper-class men capable of raising the capital required, and Brougham pushed Campbell and Place out in order to claim all the credit of the project for himself, much to Campbell's distress. The University Council launched a joint stock company, but their efforts to sell £100 shares suffered a setback at the start because the stock exchange crash of 1825–26 discredited this type of company. Place persuaded the Council to sell shares by sending delegations round prospective contributors, and he devoted much time to organising and taking part in these efforts.[22] Although he was never formally connected with the University he seems to have had some influence, and he was sometimes canvassed for support by candidates for professorships. In 1830 he complained bitterly when a Church of England school was established under the auspices of the University, and he succeeded in getting the terms of the connection amended.

Brougham objected violently to his interference, drawing the curious remark from Place that 'Brougham has not perhaps much reason to respect me, I have as little personally to respect him.' He qualified this by saying, 'I do respect him, not as a politician, not as a legislator, but as a man diligently and zealously employed in promoting the greatest of all possible services to his country, the education of his fellow citizens, and this *his* charity covers a multitude of sins.' On another occasion Place complained that Brougham had tried to rob him of his share in the credit of founding the LMI in revenge for articles which he wrongly supposed Place had written in the *Westminster Review*. Place attacked Brougham's readiness to garble accounts and play tricks on his friends to serve his own purposes, but again he concluded 'there is not a man living who has a stronger desire to have the people instructed than Mr Brougham, nor one who has exerted him more than he has, to promote that object' – on another occasion he put Brougham's contribution second to Birkbeck's. Brougham in turn complained of Place's dictatorial style – to Place's puzzlement! – but he would call on him to talk over his latest project, consult his library and indulge in political gossip. At a preparatory meeting for the LMI he had come up to Place and said: 'This matter will go on well I see. You are always to be found where there are proceedings to be taken for the good of the people. Your presence is a guarantee that the society will go on well.'[23] Personally and politically Place and Brougham often clashed, but each was compelled to admire the other's energy and efficiency, especially in the educational field, and they found each other too useful to stay on bad terms for long.

*   *   *

Place's Godwinian suspicion of government led him to oppose state education until 1835. In that year James Simpson put forward a plan to the Select Committee on Irish Education for free and universal compulsory education, with government funding for the building of schools. Running costs would be paid by a parish or district rate set by local elected education boards, which would supervise the schools. Place was converted by Simpson's evidence. He at last faced up to the impossibility of paying for universal education by charity and fees, and became an advocate of Simpson's plan for publicly financed education.[24]

7 The Benthamite

Place lived in London all his life and hardly ever left it on political business, but from the early 1810s he started building up provincial contacts. In 1812 he was given information about the organisation of the Luddites, but he gave contradictory accounts of the use he made of it. He believed that 'King Ludd' was Gravenor Henson, the organiser of the United Committee of Framework Knitters, and in 1828 he said that he had persuaded Henson to approach George Rose, the Vice-President of the Board of Trade. The two men had a meeting, as a result of which the disorders stopped. According to another account, he 'suggested to the minister for the home department the plan which I thought advisable for the Government to pursue. I showed what was the organisation but named no one. This I have reason to believe led to the suppression of the bad conduct of the parties. Had I known the particulars earlier there would probably have been no mischief. The result was an intimacy with some of the leaders . . .'[1] Place's claim that he was responsible for the suppression of Luddism is implausible; although his writings are permeated with hyperbole, such inflation of his own importance is rare.

Unlike more peripatetic reformers such as Cartwright and Hunt, Place only succeeded in building up limited contacts with provincial reformers in the 1810s. More important was his growing contact with Members of Parliament and the Utilitarian circle. James Mill, a respected philosopher in his own right, was principally responsible for carrying the ideas of the reclusive Jeremy Bentham to the wider world. In the late 1810s Mill started building up the influential school of young and able Utilitarian thinkers, a role which was taken over in the mid-1820s by his son, John Stuart. In the early 1810s, James Mill used to dine with Bentham once a week, and in 1812–13 he would call on Place on the way for an hour's talk. When Mill moved away from London in 1813 they used to exchange long letters, Place's keeping Mill up to date with political and educational affairs in the capital, while Mill would give advice on such topics as the need for Place to control his temper. They would also discuss politics and philosophy and exchange accounts of their family and financial situation. By 1814 Place was welcoming Mill's description of Bentham as 'the first philosopher in Existence'.[2]

At first Place treated Mill as a mentor, but he gradually became less deferential. When he criticised Ricardo's views on rent and the Sinking Fund, Mill warned: 'Don't meddle with Ricardo. It is not easy to find him in the wrong I can assure you. I have often thought I had found him in the wrong but I have always eventually come over to his opinion.'[3] Place does not seem to have become a close friend of Bentham until the autumn of 1817, when he spent two months with Bentham and Mill in Somerset. The invitation, Mill told Ricardo, was a reward for managing very well some business for Bentham, who was so impressed with Place that during the stay he altered his will to make him his literary executor. Bentham later replaced him with the merchant and linguist, John Bowring, but this did not lead to any breach between Place and Bentham. In 1826 Place observed that Bentham's friends regret

> that he should be so much as he is under the control and management of Bowring, but this seems at present to be unavoidable. Bowring gives much of his time to him . . . and for this Bentham undoubtedly owes something to Bowring. Bowring also panders him, is his toad eater, and can therefore command him, and as something of the sort is necessary to Mr Benthams comfort, to deprive him of Bowring without substituting someone in his stead would if it could be done, make him unhappy.

A few months later Place remarked that he did not mention visits by Bentham in his diary because they entered each other's houses as freely as their own.

Like Bentham's other admirers, Place complained about his abstruse style, arguing that it cut him off from much of his potential readership, although he doubtless resented Cobbett's description of Bentham's *Catechism on Parliamentary Reform* as 'not only *bombast,* but *quaint bombast,* and puzzling and tedious beyond mortal endurance'.[4] Bentham's style was one reason, apart from the chaotic state of his manuscripts, why Place and others had to edit his works for publication.[5] After his death Place remembered him as 'my twenty years friend, my good master from whom I learned I know not how much as it spread in so many directions. He was my constant excellent venerable preceptor, of whom I think every day of my life whose death I continually lament, whose memory I revere, and whose absence I deplore, on every account and more especially as he has left a void not likely to be filled, a void to me personally which makes me at times very uncomfortable.'

Bentham had a remarkable capacity to explore exhaustively and systematically any notion which he took seriously, and Place's main debt to him was a logical method of analysing legislation, of developing proposals for reform, and of drafting laws carefully designed to achieve his object. Place's thought nevertheless always retained a Godwinian cast. He had learnt from Godwin his optimism about progress, and he was always far more sceptical than Bentham about the power of government and law to do positive good, seeing instead the main engine of improvement in education and social and economic evolution. Place's enormous efforts to reform the law were almost wholly directed towards reducing its power over people's lives. He did follow Bentham in his belief that men rarely knew their own motives, deceiving themselves by only attending to arguments which served their own interests. Place was not always consistent in following this view, sometimes condemning men for dishonesty when his own logic would suggest that they were deluding themselves. He sided with Bentham against Godwin in arguing that men always follow their own interests, although these could include the self-approbation produced by benevolence, but he parted from both philosophers in taking a more cynical − or realistic − view of human nature.[6]

* * *

The contempt that Place suffered as a tailor probably helped to produce the sympathetic attitude he displayed towards unpopular groups such as Jews. Although he was opposed to slavery and denied that blacks were intellectually inferior to whites, he played no part in the anti-slavery movement, which was dominated by the evangelical 'saints' whom he loathed and who would not have accepted his assistance. His hard-headedness could lead him into attitudes which appear abhorrent. Believing that insanity was hereditary, he thought that it was wrong to release cured lunatics from asylums in case they had children, and believing also that it was impossible to prevent ill-treatment by keepers in an asylum, he argued that it would really be kinder to kill lunatics. At the same time he thought that since they were kept alive they ought to be better treated. In 1813−15 he devoted considerable effort to trying to improve their conditions, in conjunction with Wakefield. He supported an abortive project to build a London Lunatic Asylum, helped to block a parliamentary bill which was designed to benefit the College of Physicians rather than patients, and toured county lunatic asylums with Wakefield to collect evidence for a Parliamentary Select Committee.[7] Radicals were moving increasingly from exclusive concentration on parliamentary reform to work for the reform of specific abuses, in cooperation with MPs and philanthropists such as the Quakers. Radicals also increasingly emphasised the need for research to find the best remedy for abuses and problems. Place was to prove the most diligent and successful of them all.

The first major legislative change which he helped to bring about was the repeal of the Statute of Apprentices, an Elizabethan law which required journeymen to have served a seven-year apprenticeship. By the early nineteenth century it was largely inoperative due to the dominance of *laissez-faire* opinion, and an artisan campaign to enforce it provoked a counter-campaign to abolish it. The two leading figures in the campaign for repeal were both former members of the LCS and friends of Place, John Richter, then a sugar refiner and secretary to the committee of manufacturers which organised support for repeal, and Alexander Galloway, who owned a large engineering business. The repeal was carried in 1814 against wide artisan opposition, but it was an issue where the self-interest of men such as Galloway and Richter coincided with their egalitarian beliefs, since apprenticeship operated to preserve the position of a privileged section of the working people at the expense of the unskilled and men who wished to change trades because their own were declining. It was also the type of issue on which Place and his allies could hope to exert influence, because their belief in commercial freedom coincided with parliamentary orthodoxy.[8]

Place's chief parliamentary ally in the middle and late 1810s was Henry Grey Bennet, a Whig MP of the 'Mountain' group – named after the extreme left-wing party during the French Revolution – whom Place described as 'an active useful man in unmasking abuses, and promoting good objects, he was also friendly to reform'.[9] Place would raise matters which he wanted brought up in Parliament, advise on tactics, supply facts and arguments for Bennet's speeches, and help to edit parliamentary reports and see them through the press. In 1815 he helped to find evidence for the Select Committee on Mendicity in the Metropolis, and over the next three years Place and Bennet worked together on committees on the police. Place was a hard taskmaster. By 1819 Bennet had turned 'sulky', and Place said: 'I told Bennet from the first that I should wear him out, and that he would be obliged either to shun me or lead a dogs life with his party . . . he has done so – but next session he will come again and as he certainly means well I shall be pleased to see him.'[10] The quarrel seems to have been made up, but Bennet was never an important ally of Place thereafter because he was no longer active in the House of Commons.

These activities were largely an apprenticeship for Place's more important role in the 1820s, but as early as 1815 he seems to have aroused a respect bordering on fear among MPs he came into contact with. Describing his examination before the Mendicity Committee he told Mill: 'I was treated with marked attention and a hollow politeness beyond anything I expected, Bennet had alarmed them. . . . I told them of their ignorance and of their absurd legislation. . . . I told them of the calumnies that had been related to them respecting the morals and manners of the journeymen and I refuted them.' He also defended the refusal of journeymen to work for less than full wages:

> Let us suppose, there were 40,000 men unemployed and 40,000 employed, all the work required is at the time done by 40,000 and there is no demand for any more – if the 40,000 men unemployed were so unwise as to undersell the others, they might displace them, but these in their turn would be displaced, and they would soon be reduced to the situation to which *you* have reduced the agricultural labourer, they would all be paupers, and being so in this large city they, would loose all the independence and self respect they now possess, . . . they would become vicious and beastly, and full of crimes of all sorts, cruel, vindictive and miserable beyond all example, and the whole nation would feel the sad consequences. Gentlemen need not be alarmed, there can be no reason for concealment, you not they are ignorant

of these things; they know them well, understand them thoroughly, and act most wisely, no danger can therefore arise from their seeing in print what they already know.

His evidence was not printed on the ground that it was irrelevant.[11] His comments show his continuing attachment to traditional artisan economic doctrines – he was soon to become convinced that it was impossible for any group of workmen to maintain their wages if they were double the number of men required.

His general policy was to work with any MP who was willing to cooperate with him on a specific issue, and he followed a similar policy with the press. He often bitterly criticised the leading Whig paper, the *Morning Chronicle*, but it published his letters and articles on 'safe' subjects such as government finances. He was able to write on a wider scope of subjects in reform journals, and those he contributed to included Leigh and John Hunt's *Examiner* and *Yellow Dwarf*, John Wade's Benthamite *Gorgon* and Thomas Wooler's more extreme *Black Dwarf*. He spent much of his time on research, and in 1817 he was studying parliamentary history in order to prove the radical claim that annual parliaments and manhood suffrage were ancient practices. 'It is a laborious job', he told Thomas Hodgskin,

but from being a lazy fellow lying in bed till 8 or 9 in the morning, I have risen at 6. . . . You will justly remark, . . . why should the customs of a rude age govern us now, what we ought to desire is that we should adopt such an arrangement as may be in accordance with our improved state of knowledge – and this would be conclusive if numbers were not led more by authority than by reason; when Lords Grey & Holland, and others in high stations assert roundly that the custom was – so and so – and, misapplying the word *Right*, tell us that the people have no *right* to certain things . . . it becomes necessary for some one to stop the mouths of such preachers by showing them they are teaching false doctrine . . .

The result was an article in the *Westminster Review* in 1827, which set out the reformist view of parliamentary history. He gave up the claim that there had once been universal suffrage, and put forward a detailed but unconvincing case that parliaments had been summoned annually in the Middle Ages.[12]

In 1834 Place wrote:

When I lived at Charing Cross a considerable number of persons from the poorest of the Hand Loom Weavers to now and then a Lord of Parliament used to call upon me.

My library was a room built by me up two pairs of stairs in what was formerly a back house lighted by a large sky light, warmed in the winter in part by heated air, and made as to temperature as comfortable as it was quiet. My library was a sort of gossiping shop for such persons as were in any way engaged in public matters having the benefit of the people for their object, and it was well frequented. . . . Here was undertaken generally by me and sometimes by Mr Hume the superintendence of many small and two or three considerable publications.

A tract would be paid for by putting it up over the fireplace with a notice inviting contributions, and callers would read it and put down a sovereign if they approved of it. Place's books were ordered and indexed so that he could lay his hands immediately on any paper he wanted. With his library 'as open and nearly as much frequented as a tavern', he was in a strong position to influence MPs in favour of the legislative changes he advocated.[13]

The launching of the *Westminster Review* by the Benthamites in 1824 gave him a chance to write at greater length than in a newspaper, and it published two articles by him, a refutation of French claims that they could have held Egypt after Bonaparte's invasion of 1798, and the article on parliamentary history. Other articles were attributed to him, giving him a spurious reputation as a leading contributor around 1830, but he does not appear to have contributed again, although the editor, Bowring, asked him for further articles. The Mills refused to contribute to the journal after quarrelling with Bowring and Bentham over the way it was conducted, and Place tried to reconcile the 'refractory and unreasonable deserters'. He succeeded in persuading James Mill to write his influential article in favour of the secret ballot for the *Westminster* in 1830.[14] Place's reputation as a writer was higher in his own day than it is with historians, who judge him mainly by his narratives, in which his tendency to verbosity had free rein. He wrote far better when he was restricted for space, and he was constantly in demand to draft petitions and addresses for meetings, while his letters and articles sometimes helped to sell radical newspapers. In some of his shorter writings his reasoning is confused, probably because he was working under pressure of time and failed to revise his first draft, but most exhibit clear arguments and an intransigent style designed to appeal to artisan readers. He was careful to avoid the condescension and tactlessness which made the publications of Brougham's Society for the Diffusion of Useful Knowledge unpopular.

* * *

Place never made any secret of his irreligion, and he was always ready to help with freethinking propaganda, but after his narrow escape over the *Age of Reason* in 1797 he never again risked prosecution. In December 1810 he offered to contribute to the *Freethinking Christian Magazine,* but he warned the proprietors that he would accept no personal responsibility for his contributions, and sent them a pamphlet on the *Age of Reason* trial in order to warn them of the dangers that they were running. In 1834 he told his friend Samuel Harrison that he could do anything he liked with remarks Place had sent him on religion 'excepting printing them *with my name* to them, this too you might do but that the superstitionists would take away their custom from my son at Charing Cross and I am not at liberty to do him so great an evil'. Although he called himself an atheist, he was really an agnostic, since he did not believe that the existence of a deity had been disproved, only denying the claims of the 'superstitionists' to have proved the reality of God. He was extremely hostile to the Church of England. 'If it wasn't for this cursed Established Church', he said in 1828, 'we would have excellent schools for the people everywhere.' Like most nineteenth-century freethinkers he was extremely interested in religion, and was regarded by his friends as an authority on the Bible. He had a great respect for the Unitarian minister W.J. Fox — he described him as 'our friend at the head of our club' — and in 1835 he helped Fox draft lectures on morality.[15]

Place was also ready to help journalists who were persecuted for attacking religion. In 1817 he helped William Hone with his defence on blasphemy charges for publishing parodies of the Catechism, Litany and Creed, and in 1819 he offered similar help to Richard Carlile, who refused because he was set on conducting his defence alone. Carlile was convicted for republishing the *Age of Reason,* and from prison he continued to publish his weekly *Republican,* the first journal devoted to attacking religion. His shopmen were constantly arrested, but they were replaced by strangers who responded to public advertisements. He remained in prison for years, refusing all offers of conditional release, until finally in 1825 the Government gave up and released him unconditionally. His determination made nonsense of the laws against blasphemy, and weakened the restrictions on the press introduced in the 'Six Acts' of 1819. Place was a principal influence behind Carlile's move from deism to atheism, and the *Republican* carried a number of articles by him. His 'St Paul the Apostle, and William Campion', which compared the persecution of St Paul with that of one of Carlile's shopmen, was reprinted as a pamphlet. He also edited Bentham's *Not Paul, but Jesus* for publication. This argued that Paul destroyed the spirit of Jesus.[16]

*   *   *

Place wrote that James Mill, 'would help the mass, but he could not help the individual; no not even himself, or his own'.[17] This could not be said of Place himself, who found it very hard to resist a plea for help, and devoted much of his time to advising and aiding people who were in trouble. He frequently arbitrated in financial disputes, including those between Bentham and James Mill, and helped people who were in difficulties by going round their creditors and persuading them to agree to an accommodation. James Mill and Thomas Hodgskin were among those whom he helped with loans, which were not always repaid.[18] Mill himself was not very helpful on such matters. In 1829 Mrs Sarah Austin, wife of the jurist John Austin, asked Place to help a Piedmontese friend called Prandi who was in financial difficulties — she asked him not to mention her name lest she was accused of indelicacy for trying to help a man. Place was unable to help because of his South American losses, and he rejected as futile her suggestion that Mill might recommend Prandi to a benefactor: 'I may tell you that on subjects relating to money I never speak to Mill.' When a treasurer was required for a fund to help a reformer such as Thomas Hardy who had fallen on hard times, Place was a natural choice. In 1818 he ruefully quoted Sir Francis Burdett's remark that politics was 'a rather costly profession'. He made the remark in a letter seeking help in setting up in business Thomas Evans Junior, the son of one of the chief propagators of the story that Place was a spy.[19]

After 1820 Burdett often used to pass begging letters to him, asking him to deal with them as he saw fit and add donations to his 'account'. Replying to a letter from Place in 1832 he said: 'you know my ideas so well upon subjects of this sort that I need say nothing now – but with Bentham yield to a derivative judgement & beg you therefore to contribute for me & let me know the amount'. A request in 1827 was slightly unusual: 'I am going to ask you to take a little trouble, but reckoning on your desire to do good make no apology; & as you are a great walker, you will think still less of it.' He asked Place to go and see a butcher in Marylebone who was said to have taken in a family of deserted children, although he had eight children of his own. If this was true and 'no humbug' then Place was to give him a letter and £100. Place confirmed the story with the butcher's neighbours and learnt that the father of the deserted children owed him £1500. When he handed over the letter, Place told Burdett, the butcher 'wiped his eyes, & as soon as he was able requested me to read it. I did so after a pause, I could not help being greatly affected, &, spite of all I could do, the man & woman's agitation & tears made me wipe my eyes'. A man with eight children, 'who had lost the whole earnings of an industrious careful life; to take in the 6 children of the man, by whom he had been defrauded of his all, is, I think, unique, "is virtue", & I never in my life felt more of what is called "heart-felt satisfaction" than I have felt this day in the execution of your request.' Even political opponents paid tribute to Place's private generosity, and when the moderate radical, Colonel Leslie Grove Jones, broke their political connection in 1832 he told him: 'Personally, I feel as warm to you as ever I did, attached to you by the many kind acts you have done for me. . . . Your private life has been dedicated to friendly actions and generous assistance in every way you could command towards objects of misfortune and misery.' Displaying a typical contradiction between hard-headedness in principle and kindness in practice, Place disapproved of charity on principle: 'all charities multiply claimants, and this is reason enough for their abolition'.[20]

In a good cause he was even capable of using 'courtier-like' language. Thaddeus Connellan taught the poor in Ireland to write in their own language, and he had translated and published extracts from the Bible and other books. Place had known him since the late 1810s, and often examined poor Irish he had qualified as teachers. In 1839 he sought government support for Connellan, and drawing a brief for Brougham to show to the Lord Privy Seal in 1839, Place wrote that Connellan's teaching helped to make the Irish 'better subjects'. The sentiment contrasted with his oft-stated view that the attempt by Britain to hold down Ireland was doomed to failure, and that the best thing to do was to withdraw and leave the Irish to fight it out among themselves, after which progress towards civilisation would become possible. The previous year he had tried to obtain the help of Lord Melbourne's secretary, Tom Young, in selling Audubon's bird books. If Audubon was properly known, Place said, he would be supported by 'the men of wealth and taste with which this country abounds', and he thought that Melbourne ought to advise the Queen to become a patroness.[21]

His most sustained effort to help an individual brought only disillusionment. When Godwin sought his acquaintance in 1810, and his help with his financial troubles, Place was naturally delighted. Together with two other admirers of Godwin, he started full of enthusiasm and optimism:

> I had been engaged in several similar concerns, had been serviceable in all of them, and singularly successful in some of them. I had been instrumental not only in saving several families from absolute ruin but I had succeeded in reestablishing others in such a way as to enable them to flourish. I did not always, escape, harmless from these interferences, in the affairs of others, I occasionally lost money and in some cases rather large sums.

But Godwin was not the man he had been in the 1790s. Although he lived simply his affairs were so disorganised that he was always on the verge of ruin, and he begged widely, persistently and plausibly to keep his head above water. Place and his two allies hoped to put Godwin's publishing business on a sound footing, but they found that the accounts on which they had based their calculations were false, although whether this was due to dishonesty or muddle is uncertain. By November 1812 Place was becoming distressed at the extent of the securities he had given for Godwin's loans. Told that he was a 'firm man' for refusing a further request, he replied: 'I told you I would lessen the number and amount of the securities I had given for the convenience of others, and yet within four days I entered into another. . . . There are no secrets whatever between me and my wife, except in relation to these securities, but, of these I cannot tell her, she would never more be happy. This makes me resort to subterfuge, compels me to accuse myself and to feel that I am debased. Say then, where is my firmness?' The securities he had given for Godwin and others were almost as large as his net worth, and he feared that if he were to die his wife and children might not be provided for – a fear which he dared not share with his wife, who never fully recovered from the terror she suffered as a result of Wild's betrayal in 1800. Godwin replied to Place's letter disingenuously, declaring himself highly gratified by Place's 'frank and cordial' communication, and urging again his request for the further security.

Their friendship ended in a bitter exchange of letters in September 1814, with Place accusing Godwin of dishonesty, while deeply regretting that he had allowed himself to be talked into conniving at it, and Godwin querulously asserting his integrity and twisting phrases in Place's letters to accuse him of being mercenary. 'Mr Godwin had however many good points', Place wrote in the calmer light of hindsight, 'and no man could keep company with him without being benefited.' But the distress he suffered by having constantly to resist Godwin's demands outweighed the benefits, and he rejected further overtures. His losses amounted to £365.[22]

* * *

'You are a useful, independent honest citizen, but a lazy one in some respects', Place told his friend, George Rogers, in 1832, 'you get hold of things by intuition, or inspiration or both and reading and plodding is not so necessary to you as it is to me, who am obliged to work hard for whatever I get.' One thing Place never lacked was a willingness to work hard, and his lifelong passion for self-education carried him far. In an estimation of his attainments written mainly in 1825, he wrote that he could read French with ease, and law Latin, law French and Saxon sufficiently for his legal and antiquarian studies. He had a good knowledge of machinery and had assisted in simplifying more than one complicated machine; shipbuilding and rigging had been a favourite subject since childhood. In science he had some knowledge of chemistry, geology, natural history, mathematics and astronomy, and his studies in anatomy included attending dissections; his knowledge of geography was very competent. Metaphysics he considered the 'master science; without it, I suspect, no man ever was a good moral or political reasoner'. He said that it had taught him to reason clearly and caused him to subject himself at times to rigid examination, which taught him almost all he knew of himself. His acquaintance with Ricardo from 1817 led him to make a close study of political economy, and he believed that he understood it as well as almost anyone, a claim which is justified by the evidence. His greatest expertise was in law and jurisprudence – even opponents such as Peel were ready to listen to his advice on the drafting of parliamentary bills. He prided himself most of all on his ability to influence and lead men.[23]

One of his main assets in exercising this influence was his reputation for integrity and judgement in money matters, and anyone with a project such as a new radical newspaper or a joint stock company to supply London with purer water would come to him for advice and help. He was extremely careful to protect his reputation, and his refusal to support projects which he considered financially unsound killed a number of radical publishing plans and brought resentment from their supporters.

The question of how happy a life Place had is difficult to answer, not least because he naturally gave a different impression depending on his mood. He often boasted that he had never wanted for friends, but he was also capable of saying that 'in my estimation of a man as a friend, I have *not one*'. His reputation for unsociability and the laboriousness of his immense researches and writings suggest a dull life, but the well-frequented library over his shop cannot have been a dull place. The atmosphere in the rest of the house was not always serious: remarking on the Quakers' disapproval of music and dancing he observed that when parties of young folks were dancing, singing and playing at his house, one Quaker would find excuses to stay and watch. When Place used to visit the Benthamite MP, Colonel Perronet Thompson, in the 1830s, he would thrill Thompson's children with a demonstration of how he had planned to fight off the press gang if they had tried to take him in the 1790s, dancing around the room making thrusts with an imaginary knife.[24]

Place's papers suggest an aggressive and difficult personality, but Gustave D'Eichtal, visiting England in 1828, found him ' a very likeable man, and also much esteemed, full of the wisdom of experience and possessing a fund of knowledge'. Mrs Grote told Place: 'I never quit your *personal* society without a certain measure of exhilaration, and encouragement – your *written* society on the contrary, casts me into a slough of distaste and dislike towards the *species*.'[25] Part of the reason for this was that his manuscripts were devoted to political transactions which were constantly arousing his ire, whereas in social intercourse he tried to avoid thinking of things which would inflame his temper. John Stuart Mill said that his father had scarcely any belief in pleasure, but Place was far too passionate in character to adopt this outlook. He was as capable of intense pleasure as he was of anger, and he derived deep pleasure from his home life, from the success of his projects, from praise from men he respected, and from the occasional tributes he received for his efforts from working men.

He never lost his Godwinian belief in progress, which was encouraged by his own success in life, and he derived great pleasure from contemplating the improvement in morals and manners of the working people in his lifetime. But his passionate sympathy with misfortune was always in danger of degenerating into cynicism and misanthropy when he observed the callousness which people displayed towards each other in ordinary life. This sometimes led him to say that he wished he could exterminate life by turning the atmosphere to poisonous gas or putting out the sun, and it made him doubtful whether progress could ever make life really worth living. In 1840, he remarked that the future was bound to produce great miseries at times: 'such is however the fate of our race, on its march towards a better state of things, a state after all scarcely worthy of being envied even when it has arrived at its best. Changes of seasons – Malaria — Epidemic and ordinary diseases, – waywardness of disposition – grasping – greedy – ill conditioned – eccentric & somewhat crazy people – and "the thousand ills that man is heir to", will never permit more than a distant approximation towards a really happy state of mankind.'[26] Optimism and pessimism were constantly at war in his outlook, each uppermost in turn, depending on his mood and his experiences at the time. His frequent claim that few men had enjoyed greater happiness is unsustainable, and at times his determination to be cheerful seems to have been a strategy to prevent himself becoming misanthropic in face of the constant evidence he found of the folly and dishonesty of mankind.

In 1826 the artist William Tijou persuaded him to sit for a portrait. Several of his friends admired the result, but he felt that it showed a man infirm of purpose:

> I know my own want of firmness on some occasions, I am pretty conscious of my own misgivings but I do not feel that compared with others, . . . I am a man infirm of purpose. . . . I am not aware that I ever in my life shirked a responsibility, or when the time came for acting ever held back, on the contrary when it became necessary to do things, I generally took a lead however disagreeable and unpromising affairs appeared, and have not on any occasion that I know of been reproached with want of courage or energy by my coadjutors. In cases which I have thought of moment, when others have been daunted, or have deserted I have never felt dismay but on the contrary, these have been the occasions in which I have always had the strongest desire to act, and in which I have acted with the most confidence in myself and the most energy.

His wife disliked the portrait, saying that it was 'milk and water', calculated to give a stranger a notion of mildness and amiability which did not belong to him. The portrait was taken in the dress he wore at home, a loose double-breasted mixed baize coat and waistcoat, with buttons up to the neck. People would often comment on the remarkable difference between this and the black which he wore in the street, and his wife persuaded him to sit again in black. He thought that the second portrait was a sour likeness, but his friends thought that its expression was much more characteristic except when he was unusually cheerful. Everyone thought that both portraits were excellent likenesses, but they scarcely resembled each other.[27]

Place generally showed himself well aware of the weaknesses in his character, although he occasionally displayed a surprising blindness to the effect he had on others. Vanity, he declared, 'is my soft place', although James Mill saw a contradiction. When Place got out of an embarrassing remark — implying that Mill's head looked weak — by saying that modesty had prevented him from making himself clear, Mill seized on it: 'I am . . . to understand from your own lips that you have a thing about you called *modesty* which is very apt to restrain your tongue and your pen — when did *you* begin to set up for a *modest* man? However after all the boasting you make of the opposite quality, I have seen some specimens of modesty and even of bashfulness about you which showed me it had a pretty strong root in your nature.' Place warned Thomas Hodgskin against self-depreciation because people would take him at his word and set him below his true worth, but sometimes Place feared that he himself went too far the other way. In 1826 Hodgskin's German wife worried him when she criticised the conceit of Goethe in his Memoirs in thinking that all he did was interesting — Place concluded that he was just as bad and decided to give up his diary. The next day: 'the devil of vanity having routed all the other spirits here am I continuing the diary'.[28]

James Mill was less tolerant of another of Place's faults. When Place was driven to distraction by Wakefield's weakness in dealing with his son, Mill told him: 'You must treat Wakefield on this subject a little gently who chiefly fails through an infirmity of your own of blabbing out whatever visions form themselves in his brain.' Place replied that he knew that

> the mode I have pursued is frequently obnoxious to many persons, and its consequences, or rather the inferences of the generality of observers, make some of them shun me and cause others (I mean those commonly called good men) to act cautiously, which . . . is the natural result of what they observe in me. I have many times examined myself, and reasoned thus, what shall I gain or lose in usefulness . . . by more of policy, or in other words hypocrisy, shall I respect myself more, shall I increase or diminish the actual respect which my children have for me, and I have as often determined not to change. I have, and do still, and probably always shall, say and do indiscreet things, others . . . escape being called upon to be useful, as but for their cautious character they would be, the difficulty is to attain what I am certain I shall never attain; that point between the two which is really the most useful. I have always contemplated the probability of being released from business, and I have been afraid of too much caution, as tending to produce cold heartedness. It would be damnable to have little employment and no feeling. But I am not averse from advice, nor unwilling to learn, or so weak as not to bear being told of my infirmities, so you are not to be mealy mouthed in your observations, you know I am not so with those I would serve, and for once at least you may excuse yourself for following a bad example.[29]

Like his mentor, Godwin, Place carried his belief in the duty of complete frankness to the point where it sometimes became counterproductive.

His friend George Ensor once declared that he did not 'rave like Place', who always had difficulty in controlling his temper. 'You and I are both fiery fellows and easily moved by our feelings', Place told Mrs Grote after an argument in 1837, 'I do endeavour to command mine but my reward then out they will burst.'[30] His temper was at its worst in the 1810s, a result of the degradation which he had to put up with at the hands of his customers, the slander against him over Sellis, and his wife's querulousness. The last factor was especially important because he relied almost exclusively on his domestic circle for relaxation. His outspoken criticism of conduct which did not meet his standards made enemies and caused arguments, and he was sometimes ready to quarrel with allies because he could not get his way on points of detail. After 1820 he only quarrelled when he had serious grounds for doing so, and other men were more willing to put up with the outspokenness of a leading figure in the radical movement than they had been to overlook the insults of a 'consequential tailor' in the 1800s and 1810s.

From an early age he insistently asserted his own dignity and integrity, a defence against upper class disdain, and in the 1820s his successes led him into the consequential self-importance which is, unfortunately, strongest in his autobiography. After 1830 this largely disappears, partly because he had now gained a secure position of respect, and probably also due to the influence of his second wife — his family's bitterness against her has disguised the fact that Elizabeth Place was very difficult during the last twenty years of her life, whereas his second marriage was a happy one for the first twelve years.

Place was never quite sure how seriously to take himself. In 1819 he observed: 'I hate the collector and retailer of anecdotes of his friends or of those he acts with, and I hold him to be a *rascal* who keeps any account of his own immediate and private intercourse with other men.' By this standard he was often a *rascal* himself, and when Mill complained about the gossip in his letters, he retorted: 'I am sorry for you my friend, and should grieve no little I assure you if I were not fully persuaded your affliction was only temporary, for I am as fond of gossiping as an old woman, and think you are pretty much in the same situation yourself.' Discussing a book on philology, Place remarked that the author 'is coarse — vulgar, abusive, and sometimes almost a savage, but he appears to be a thinking — independent minded man, in many points I think he resembles me, and as he must be a curious fellow, I shall go and see him'.[31]

8   The Battle with the Whigs: Westminster 1814–1830

In February 1814 a group of speculators perpetrated a famous hoax on the Stock Exchange, when men dressed as British officers rode into London and announced a great victory over the French. Government stocks rose and the speculators made a quick killing. Cochrane benefited from the plot, probably innocently, but he was charged with involvement. Manoeuvring soon started for the seat which would become vacant if he was convicted and expelled from the Commons. The most likely Westminster Committee candidate was Henry Brougham. A leading supporter of the anti-slave trade and popular education movements, he had been an effective Whig opponent of the Government in Parliament in 1810–12. In 1812 he received Burdettite support in an unsuccessful election campaign for Liverpool, and in the same year he made clear his interest in Westminster, moving towards radicalism and praising the example of the Westminster electors in the *Edinburgh Review*.[1]

However, Brougham was one of Cochrane's counsel in the fraud trial, and the Committee were unwilling to move until the proceedings ended for fear of prejudicing his trial. On 29 May Place wrote to Brooks, warning him of the dangers of delay. Place urged that whoever the Committee took up – and he supposed that it would be Brougham – they must get a declaration in writing in favour of annual elections and a suffrage of every man subject to direct taxation: 'The man who will not sign such a declaration shall not have my vote.' He thought that this would palsy all opposition. But he also said that he would not interfere in an election, declaring that he cared little who was elected: 'I know that "corruption must continue until it has exhausted the means of corrupting" – and we may as well attempt to arrest the course of nature as it.'[2] This was the standard justification of any radical justifying quietism. Place claimed to have argued it in the 1790s, and it was put forward by the Sheffield reformers as an argument against holding public meetings in the summer of 1797. Burdett had used it as his excuse for refusing to stand in 1807. Place still maintained the view in the 1820s, and the implication that tyranny could only be ended by revolution provides a strange contrast with the gradualist measures he advocated in practice. However, he feared that if there was a revolution before the people were ready for it, the result would be disastrous. Practicable reforms, especially the extension of popular education, gave the best hope of averting this danger.

A public meeting on 8 June agreed that a candidate for Westminster must subscribe to the three principles laid out by Burdett in Parliament in 1809: the two specified by Place and a fair distribution of seats. The following day Cochrane was convicted, and Major Cartwright promptly announced his willingness to be elected. Brougham was considered suspect on the all-important subject of parliamentary reform, and Place initially welcomed the Major's announcement. Told by an emissary that Cartwright feared opposition from him, Place declared: 'I would do more for him than for any other person', although he repeated that he would play no active part in the election.³ But Place soon withdrew his support. Cartwright, complaining that Brougham had criticised the reformers in an anonymous article, praised himself for putting his name to his works, but he made the extraordinary error of making his remarks in an anonymous pamphlet, thus discrediting himself in the eyes of potential supporters. Place had already come to admire Brougham's talents as a result of their contacts in the popular education movement, and his claims were strongly pressed by their mutual friend James Mill, so Place was ready to switch his support when he heard that Brougham was willing to declare for the three principles. At his suggestion Brougham made his declaration at a parliamentary reform dinner of the Livery of London on 23 June, and when Place found newspaper reports of the speech unsatisfactory he cut out two of them and sent them to Brooks with a request that they be laid before the Committee, who might send them to Brougham for correction. This was done and the following day Mill brought Place a copy of the speech in Brougham's own hand with the required declaration.

Cartwright still had influential supporters, but the danger of a contest was averted when a wave of public feeling in favour of Cochrane's innocence led to him being re-elected unopposed. Thus a split among the Westminster reformers was again narrowly averted. Place's influential role behind the scenes provides a remarkable contrast with the situation at the same time in the WLLA, where the trouble over allegations that he was a spy was coming to a head. His letter to Brooks urging the Committee to get a correct account of Brougham's speech came only a week before he learnt that Brooks had refused to give the names of the Committee's supporters to the WLLA for fear that Place would misuse the information. However, by this time only Burdett really believed that Place might be a spy.

According to a later memoir, at the end of 1814 Place was freed from all connection with politics, and cooperation with his Westminster Committee colleagues was at an end.⁴ He still had some contact with Major Cartwright, who wanted to 'stand well' with him, because of his influence in the choice of a Westminster candidate. Place stated that he was ready to cooperate with anyone to increase the knowledge of the commonalty, but he did not intend to become involved in politics beyond writing in newspapers and privately discussing and advising: 'Such events however occurred as no one anticipated. The country became agitated from one end to the other, men of every rank in life became interested in public proceedings, and it was not possible for me wholly to refrain from taking part occasionally.'[5] The end of the war with France brought unemployment and falling prices, and Parliament sought to protect the landed interest by restricting the importation of corn. Place joined in the fierce resistance, but the Corn Law was passed in the spring of 1815.[6]

Major Cartwright had already undertaken tours of the Luddite areas in order to try to divert the discontent to peaceful pressure for parliamentary reform, and the general distress helped him to extend his campaign over much of the country. Together with his assistant, Thomas Cleary, he carried on an extensive provincial correspondence under the auspices of the London 'Hampden Club', an association of propertied men who supported parliamentary reform. It was Cartwright and Cleary, Place observed, 'who gave the tone to many places and revived the dormant desire for reform'.[7] In December 1815 Place began to work closely with Cartwright again when he agreed to help him with a plan for delivering lectures on reform. He was now in the remarkable position that he had broken with his Westminster Committee colleagues, and yet he was being courted by Cartwright and Brougham for the sake of his electoral influence.

Henry Brougham had returned to Parliament in July 1815, when the Whigs found a seat for him after losing their ablest House of Commons spokesman by Samuel Whitbread's suicide. In the autumn Brougham planned his assault on the Tory Government in the 1816 session, and he consulted Place in order to keep his options open in Westminster. Brougham's programme included demands for retrenchment and the removal of income tax, and reform proposals concerning the slave trade, prisons, commutations of tythes, education of the 'lower orders', and the freedom of the press. Place approved of the plans, apart from the attack on income tax, which he objected to partly on the ground that it was financially unsound and partly because its removal would only benefit the better-off, whereas the taxes to replace it would be levied on the poor. In putting forward the latter argument he was siding with Hunt and Cobbett against the great majority of reformers. Brougham secured promises of support for his programme from Burdett, Bennet and others, and Place remarked hopefully in a letter to Mill that if they 'would pull cordially together, be incessant in attacking the enemy I have no doubt, that in a year or two a great sensation would be felt all over the country'. But he had his doubts about Brougham: 'I do not know enough of him to make up my mind fully on his character. In political affairs I always fear for those who are not in all things republicans from principle. I think a man who is not so cannot know enough of himself to be able to trust to himself in all times and in all seasons.'[8]

By this standard the proportion of trustworthy men throughout British history has been very low.

Place's hopes were soon disappointed. Brougham attempted to keep on good terms with the Westminster reformers, but he was also trying to establish himself as the leader of the Whigs in the Commons. He hoped to build a Whig-radical alliance, but this was impossible at a time when the radicals were becoming more extreme and most Whig MPs were suspicious of parliamentary reform. The party was, moreover, allied with the conservative Grenvillites, who were violently opposed to reform, and Brougham wanted to maintain the alliance. The result was that he fell between two stools, frightening the Whigs with an occasional radical speech and disillusioning the radicals by a generally conservative stance. On 23 February 1816 he attended a Westminster public meeting against the income tax in order to make himself better known to the electors, but he lost ground when he and his Whig friends walked off the platform when they were attacked by Henry Hunt, instead of staying to reply. On 23 March he delighted the reformers and dismayed his own party by a violent attack on the Prince Regent in the House of Commons. Place promptly sent Brougham a congratulatory letter which shocked him when he read it again in 1829. The excessive praise he had bestowed on the speech showed, he thought, how much 'our feelings, when excited and countenanced by those with whom we associate mislead our judgements and benumb our understandings. It now seems matter of surprise that I should have written such a letter, which had so totally escaped my recollection, that if told I had done so I should have doubted if not denied it, until it had been shown to me.'[9] The anxiety of reformers such as Place to draw Brougham over to the reform camp could involve them in embarrassment, but the benefits if they had succeeded in gaining a leader of such ability and prestige made the risk worthwhile.

In May Brougham again lost ground. On the 8th he declared that: 'With one or two exceptions, our Constitution was never in a better state than now',[10] and on the 23rd he cried off the Westminster reformers' annual dinner at the last moment when he heard that Hunt had turned up. He also greatly annoyed the radicals by his support for the Corn Law and for a grant of £60,000 a year for Princess Charlotte, the Prince Regent's daughter. When Bennet wrote to Place on Brougham's behalf in October asking about his chances in Westminster, Place replied that he would have no chance.

In the second half of 1816 public distress and agitation increased, and Place was drawn into a greater involvement in politics. On 29 July he helped to organise a radical protest at a public meeting at the City of London Tavern to raise subscriptions for the relief of distress, which was attended by royal dukes. He told Mill:

> many years have passed since I witnessed anything so exhilarating. I went with Robert Owen, who promised as we went along not to subscribe at the Tavern, but

his vanity could not hold out . . .

I saw Cochrane before the business commenced and cautioned him against impetuosity, and feeling, and promised to stand by him, if any attempt was made to use him ill, as I fully expected would be the case, I told him to talk as he would fight, to be calm and not to fire his broadsides until the smoke had cleared away and he could see his object, . . . he took the advice and fought his battle in admirable stile.

Cochrane stated the causes of distress, and when he ended with the enormous load of taxes 'a shout of approbation burst from all parts of the room like a clap of thunder, it was more than sympathetic, it was a shock from an immense voltaic battery. . . .Upon the whole the sensation or rather the agitation this meeting has caused exceeds anything of the kind I ever witnessed.'[11]

The following month a public meeting was called by the recently formed Westminster 'Committee of Public Safety' to consider what should be done in the gloomy state of the country. Place went along to the well-attended meeting with resolutions in his pocket, somewhat to his later puzzlement in view of his determination not to interfere publicly in politics. Only two of the 31 members of the Committee turned up, and Place found himself playing a leading part. First he read resolutions drafted by Cartwright which were, he told Mill, 'very long – very prosing – very full of good points, but very irrelevant'. They were coldly received, so Place then read out his own resolutions:

1. That the Knowledge, the Talent, the Ingenuity, the Industry, the Capital and the moral conduct of the people of this country, ought to have secured to them, the full enjoyment of liberty, and an abundance of everything useful to mankind.

2. That all these invaluable characteristics of our people have by a corrupt House of Commons which does not represent them, been perverted or forcibly applied to abridge their own liberties and to destroy the liberties of other nations.

3. That the conduct of this corrupt House of Commons has long and extensively inflicted evils on other nations which is now brought home to the people of this Country in the most frightful shape.

4. That the means used by this corrupt House of Commons against the liberties of mankind have exhausted our resources in unnecessary, long continued, and unusually bloody wars, injured our trade, and manufactures, closed our mines, ruined our agriculture – pauperised and starved the people.

5. That the course pursued by this corrupt House of Commons has at length brought us into a situation in which palliatives are worse than useless, in which one peaceful remedy alone remains – namely – such a reform in the Commons House of Parliament, as shall make it not a sham representation of the people – but as it ought to be, as our ancestors

intended it should be – and as but for the basest of their sons it would be – a real representation of the people.

6. That unless the people will now do 'their easy duty', and reform the house of commons, they may have to reproach themselves with not having prevented a violent revolution, or with having suffered a cruel military despotism to be established upon the ruins of their liberties.

7. That to avert these evils, – to restore the liberties of their country – and to possess those comforts which of right belong to them; it is necessary that the people should assemble in Counties, Cities, Boroughs, Towns, Villages and Parishes and insist on a radical reform in their own house, in the House of the commons of the whole people of the United Kingdom.

'Each of them was received, as the Players have it with unbounded applause', Place told Mill proudly, 'and at the conclusion with 3 distinct peals.' He considered himself a poor orator, but he then made one of his very rare public speeches, 'with which I was not at all satisfied, altho' I saw it producing effect'. It was agreed that Place's resolutions should be put to a formal Westminster public meeting in Palace Yard. 'The meeting being thus agreeably terminated and the business put fairly on its legs, I withdrew from all further interference.' The Palace Yard meeting in September adopted his resolutions. His withdrawal brought criticism on him. 'I had objected to become active among men who invariably left me to do all the business', he told Mill, 'and when I had done it found fault not with the business, but with me, that when they could do without me I was a spy, and when they could not do without me I was a fine fellow, that among such persons I should be careful how I again committed myself.'[12]

Cartwright had arranged the Westminster meeting, and he now turned to the moribund Hampden Club for a wider effort. He persuaded the president, Burdett, to summon a meeting of delegates from around the country in January 1817 to agree on a plan for parliamentary reform. The summons, together with lectures, meetings and petitions organised by Cartwright and Cleary caused, Place observed, 'a remarkable sensation which had spread widely and in several direction'.[13] For a short period in the autumn of 1816 there was unity among the reformers, but it was soon destroyed. Henry Hunt, seeking to build a reputation in London, accepted an invitation from the revolutionary Spenceans to speak at a public meeting on 15 November at Spa Fields. This was attended by a large crowd of working people and dispersed peaceably, but at a further meeting on 2 December two of the leading Spenceans, Arthur Thistlewood and Watson Junior, persuaded a section of the crowd to attempt to provoke an insurrection by marching on the Bank of England. The mob was easily dispersed, but the incident angered less extreme reformers by giving the Government an excuse for claiming that all reformers were revolutionaries and introducing repressive measures.

By the middle of January 1817 the riot and provincial unrest had killed any hope that the country would come forward for reform. Burdett's enthusiasm was dampened, and he became suspicious of Hunt and strongly resentful of his demands that he present an insulting address voted at the Spa Fields meeting to the Prince Regent. When the delegates met in January 1817 Burdett ignored the meeting he had summoned. Hunt and the northern delegates rejected the pleas of Cobbett and Cartwright for household suffrage, but since they knew that Burdett would be unwilling to introduce a parliamentary bill for universal suffrage, they agreed to leave him to bring forward his own bill. Burdett further angered the reformers by failing to present the petitions brought to London and by parliamentary inactivity.

Place showed his sympathy with the complaints by inserting Cobbett's bitter comments in his memoir:

It is very notorious, that the Reformers looked up to Sir Francis Burdett as the man who was to be the great advocate of their cause *in Parliament.* Indeed, the calls, which he had been making upon *the People,* for so many years, to *come forward in a body,* naturally led to the universal opinion, that he would be transported with joy, when he found, that they had actually come forward in far greater numbers and with demonstrations of greater knowledge, zeal and resolution than he ever could have anticipated. Strange to say, the reverse was the fact, and that in the precise degree, that he perceived the People to wax warm, he appeared to wax cold; and to see nothing but obstacles in the pursuit of that, to the full accomplishment of which he had always declared, that nothing but the hearty and unanimous good will of the people was wanting. . . . People were surprised that *no Meeting took place in Westminster.* What! Palace Yard, which had been the very focus of Reform, and which had been sending forth its burning rays so long, NOW, when all the rest of the nation was in a blaze, to become dead and cold as a horse-pond.[14]

When Parliament met at the end of January both parties attacked the reformers as dangerous revolutionaries, and Place replied in an advertising address for a new weekly periodical, *Hone's Reformists' Register.* Place praised the public meetings which had been held and the unanimity of the people, and he declared his faith in 'the blaze of intellect – the glorious light of knowledge. . . . To war against *mind* is to ensure defeat. A man cannot be made to unlearn that which he knows; . . . "KNOWLEDGE IS POWER".' But improvement was not to be found among 'our *hereditary* guardians', who supported all government measures and opposed public meetings.

They would have all *quiet* – quiet as death. They prove, as a wise man once said of them, that 'in knowledge they are a hundred years behind the state of society in which they live'. . . . It is to the MIDDLE class *now* as at *other* times, in this country, the salvation of all that ought to be dear to Englishmen must be confided . . .

This uncritical faith in the middle classes was soon to be killed by their failure to support such projects as the Chrestomathic school, but Place never lost his belief that the working people were powerless to effect any good in the political field without their cooperation.

The second issue of Hone's *Register* was also written by Place, and headed 'Universal Suffrage and Annual Parliaments *against* Mr Brougham and the Whigs'. He waxed sarcastic about a claim by James Perry, the editor of the *Morning Chronicle,* that universal suffrage would be the ruin of the country:

> Only think what an *enormity* it would be to allow those 'who have nothing to do with the laws but to obey them' − the 'scum and dregs of society, the swinish multitude', to have a vote! − of what service are *they* to the state? − *they* pay no taxes, *they* fight none of our battles, . . . *they* sow no corn. . . . No, no Mr PERRY, the RICH do all these things with *their own* hands; and, praised be their benevolence, they clothe the naked and feed the hungry . . .[15]

In the House of Commons on 14 February, Brougham savagely attacked the reformers and Lord Cochrane, who was now their only parliamentary champion. Place retaliated by publishing the speech Brougham had delivered during the 1814 Westminster election, in which he declared for annual elections and household suffrage. Place had it printed in a *Register Extraordinary* and he gave Cochrane the original in Brougham's own hand to read in the House of Commons. The result was a sensation, especially since Brougham was now denouncing annual parliaments in the most violent terms. At the same time parliamentary secret committees produced reports which grossly exaggerated the threat of revolution, Parliament passed repressive Acts which suspended habeas corpus and restricted freedom of speech, and Cobbett fled to America. The Whigs put up some limited opposition, but Place blamed them for the extent of the measures, arguing that their violent denigration of the reformers early in the session had encouraged the Government to go further than it had originally intended. Once the crisis was over and the legislation passed Place again retired from politics.

Burdett had seemed closer to the Whigs than to the radicals at the start of the session, but he gradually moved back as the Government's repressive intentions became clearer. In spite of all the bitterness there was even a *rapprochement* between the Whigs and the radicals in the spring, and in early May it was rumoured that Brougham would again declare for annual parliaments.[16] He did not, although he attended the Westminster reformers' annual dinner on 23 May, and made a speech praising their efforts. Burdett's move back towards the radicals was encouraged by revelations in July that the government spy Oliver had acted as an *agent provocateur,* with the result that there was a small-scale armed rising at Pentridge near Nottingham. Burdett was particularly annoyed because Oliver had sometimes claimed to be speaking in his name.

The mid-1810s saw a growing split between the extreme reformers led by Cobbett, Hunt and Cartwright, and moderates such as the members of the

Westminster Committee. The extremists accused the Committee of reneging on reform, and historians have generally accepted their charges that the Westminster reformers retreated from 'agitation unlimited', but their reasons were personal rather than political. Place disapproved of the delegates' meeting of January 1817 as giving a handle for repression, and he regarded Henry Hunt as dangerous and turbulent, but he said that Cobbett did more good than harm – naturally he disliked his abuse of the Westminster Committee – and he referred approvingly to Cartwright's agitation in his memoir of the period. The Committee was less active than before partly because the members were embarrasssed by Burdett's inconsistent conduct, and partly because without Place they lacked energy. Place complained that he was involved in heavy expenses and considerable work whenever he took part, because very few electors would subscribe or help with organisation, although they would attend public meetings and incur losses in order to vote for radical candidates. Other members of the Committee were doubtless reluctant to be too active for the same reasons. Burdett's conduct split the reformers between those who turned against him, led by Cobbett and Hunt, and those who sympathised with the complaints against him but still considered him irreplaceable as a parliamentary spokesman. Place was one of the latter.

*   *   *

In February 1818 a group of upper-class parliamentary reformers formed the Rota Club, which was to contribute a new element to the Westminster Committee in the three elections of 1818, 1819 and 1820. The members included Burdett, Douglas Kinnaird, a banker and supporter of universal suffrage, John Cam Hobhouse, who had returned from staying with Byron in Italy in order to look for a parliamentary seat, Henry Bickersteth, an able barrister, and Scrope Davies, a wit and dandy. Byron also became a member, although he lived in Italy. The club met fortnightly while Parliament was sitting and devised plans of reform, framed motions to be moved in the Commons and drew up addresses for parliamentary candidates. Bentham had become a convert to parliamentary reform by 1809, but he did not publish his opinion until 1817, when his *Plan of Parliamentary Reform* appeared. This advocated the full radical programme including female suffrage, but Bentham incurred some ridicule by also urging that criminals and lunatics should have the vote. The work was nevertheless greatly admired by the radicals, and in early 1818 Henry Bickersteth and Place brought Bentham and Burdett together. Burdett's genuine admiration for Bentham was doubtless a factor in his conversion to manhood suffrage, but the main reason was to protect his electoral position in the forthcoming General Election in the face of damaging charges by Cobbett and Hunt that he had reneged on reform. In June Burdett moved resolutions in the House of Commons in favour of manhood suffrage and annual elections, but only Cochrane supported him.

Bentham, the Rota Club and Place all had a hand in drawing up the resolutions.[17]

Meanwhile, Cochrane had decided to accept the command of the Chilean navy in their war of independence against Spain, and when he publicly announced his intention at the annual Westminster dinner on 23 May, manoeuvring was already under way over the candidate to replace him. Henry Hunt announced his candidacy at the dinner, but he was silenced by the hisses of the company. He had Cobbett's support, but as a demagogue associated with the revolutionary Spenceans and a vitriolic critic of the Westminster Committee, he was equally unacceptable to the electors and to the Committee.

Cartwright's anxious claim to be considered was far more embarrassing to reject. All reformers including Place recognised his enormous contribution to the movement, but his reputation was far higher in the country than in Westminster. He was unacceptable to the electors because of his old age, poor health, weak voice, old-fashioned ideas and dullness and verbosity as an orator. Place also complained that he was obstinate — the pot calling the kettle black — a poor strategist and given to fatuous overoptimism. Even his supporters admitted that he would make a poor MP, but urged that he deserved the honour as a reward for his past services, an argument which Place rejected on principle.[18] Since no one was willing to criticise Cartwright publicly, his opponents objected to him solely on the grounds of his old age and poor health, laying themselves open to the accusation that they were manoeuvring to block his claim with frivolous and hypocritical excuses. Burdett laid himself especially open by the implausible claim that he had not supported Cartwright because he did not think he wanted to be elected. Even Place was driven to a rare act of hypocrisy, protesting in a letter to a supporter of Cartwright (which was not sent): 'Of his merits, only one opinion can be entertained by either of us, and as to personal respect, no one can have more than I have . . . . were he not in the opinion of the electors as I believe he is unqualified from age no doubt could be entertained that he would be the man for whom all the friends of freedom should join their exertions.'[19]

Burdett played a far more active role in choosing his fellow candidate than he had in the past — probably pushed into it by his Rota Club friends — and in a letter to Samuel Brooks he named three men as acceptable choices: Walter Fawkes and two Rota Club members, Kinnaird and Hobhouse. But Fawkes was a non-runner because he had long made clear that he was unwilling to be elected, and Kinnaird was preferred to Hobhouse because he had already declared his support for annual elections and universal suffrage. Hobhouse was willing to declare, but the Committee's experience with Brougham had made them wary of conversions for electoral purposes. Place was apparently dissatisfied with the choice of such a little-known figure as Kinnaird, and he asked Bennet to sound out Lord Folkestone, who was widely respected as a reformer and an opponent of repression. He had recently told Place privately that he supported annual elections and universal suffrage, but family pressure made it difficult for him to declare his opinion publicly, and he replied that he could not give up the borough he already sat for. Bennet suggested Sir Samuel Romilly. He was a leading legal reformer, and Place had met and admired him during his stay with Bentham the previous year, but he replied that Romilly would stand no chance because he had refused to declare in favour of parliamentary reform when he was sounded out for Middlesex in 1811. This was to prove an unfortunate prediction.[20]

The Westminster reformers followed their usual procedure in preparing for an election, and Samuel Brooks circulated an invitation to 200-300 electors to attend a meeting on 1 June and bring their friends, but only twenty attended, including Place and James Mill. They agreed to summon a public meeting on 4 June at the Crown and Anchor Tavern to select two candidates, and Place announced that after that he would neither sit on any committee, nor attend any meeting outside his own house. Cartwright was then proposed, with Samuel Brooks seconding, and Place countered with Douglas Kinnaird. Place insisted that Cartwright could not be carried, and was confident enough to suggest that each side should select thirty electors who had plumped for Burdett in 1807, who would be asked whether they would vote for Cartwright, the result to decide his eligibility, but this was not adopted. The meeting voted for Kinnaird by 17 votes to 2. Place does not explain how such an unknown figure as Kinnaird acquired such strong support in the leading reform constituency.[21] The decision was not taken in obedience to Burdett's diktat: Brooks was singled out by Cobbett and Place whenever they complained of the Committee's subservience to Burdett, yet he supported Cartwright,[22] while Place was still not on speaking terms with the baronet and would not have supported Kinnaird unless he was independently convinced that he was the best choice. The explanation lies in the lack of any viable alternative. Following Burdett's declaration for universal suffrage, the same commitment was considered a prerequisite for his running mate, but he also had to be a gentleman to have any hope of being elected. Men with these qualifications were very hard to find.

At the public meeting on 4 June the Westminster reformers were joined for the first time by their upper-class allies, Hobhouse and Scrope Davies of the Rota Club, together with Joseph Hume, who was about to commence his long and fruitful alliance with Place. Place wanted Kinnaird to attend in order that he could be introduced to the electors, but his colleagues apparently insisted on sticking to the principle that the electors were seeking a representative rather than a candidate seeking votes. When Place discovered that Cartwright's supporters intended to propose him, he had Cartwright's nomination added to the order of business, but the meeting was disrupted by Hunt and his allies, and after vainly trying to restore order for two hours the organisers withdrew to another room booked against the contigency. Hunt's interference destroyed any chance of unity among Burdett's supporters, since a vote at a public meeting was the only verdict which might have been accepted by the losing side, and the private meeting broke up in recrimination. Separate committees were then formed for Kinnaird and Cartwright.

At first Kinnaird's supporters were confident and on 5 June Hobhouse wrote to Byron in hopeful terms, but the split among the reformers naturally encouraged the 'factions', and the Whigs put up Sir Samuel Romilly, whose reputation as a legal reformer was great enough to attract support from the radicals' own ranks. The Tories threw their support behind Romilly and started their own candidate, Sir Murray Maxwell, in the hope of driving out Burdett. The campaign for Burdett and Kinnaird soon ran into trouble, and the large committee which had been appointed proved inefficient. Place gave help in his own house, but he resisted increasingly desperate appeals to come to the committee rooms and take charge.[23] The committee made a serious mistake by recommending Kinnaird to the electors as a personal friend of Burdett, thus giving colour to Cobbett's charge that the Rump had turned Westminster into Burdett's private property. The error was compounded by keeping Kinnaird out of the campaign. This was done partly on principle and partly to avoid the High Bailiff's charges, but since Kinnaird was unknown to the electors it was a great disadvantage. Moreover most of the London radical press opposed him. *Sherwin's Political Register* supported Hunt, Wooler's *Black Dwarf* and even the Bethamite *Gorgon* backed Cartwright, while only Leigh Hunt's *Examiner* supported Kinnaird.

Cartwright's and Kinnaird's supporters held several unsuccessful meetings in order to try to agree on a second candidate, and by the eve of polling on 17 June the fears had become so great that Kinnaird wrote to the committee offering to withdraw. On the same day Place wrote angrily to Brooks denouncing talk of abandoning Kinnaird after accepting nearly £400 from his friends, a policy 'as *cowardly* as *dishonest*'. He also complained that 'notwithstanding, I have done much more than I promised, . . . I am again to be, talked of as having behaved ill, altho I have done ten times as much as those who choose to propagate calumnies'.[24]

The committee struggled on for the first three days of polling, at the end of which Romilly had 1270 votes, Maxwell 1241, Burdett 484, Kinnaird 63, Hunt 33 and Cartwright 30. Kinnaird and Cartwright were then withdrawn on Saturday the 20th and their committees united. On Sunday, Place finally surrendered to the desperate pleas of the reformers to come and take charge, and in the next two days Burdett received 1687 votes. At the end of the fifteen-day contest Romilly headed the poll with 5339 votes, Burdett was also elected with 5238, the Tory Maxwell received 4808 and Hunt 84. The result was a great boost to Whig morale nationally, yet it confirmed the Whig weakness shown in Sheridan's performance in 1807. Burdett received 2308 plumpers and Maxwell 2204. Romilly only received 453, but he headed the poll because many reformers and Tories gave him their second vote in order to try to keep each other out. In the light of the figures it is remarkable that Hobhouse and

Place independently concluded in restrospect that Kinnaird could have been carried if he had been kept on the poll at the beginning of the second week. The claim is not wholly implausible because Burdett's large gain at this stage was not due only to Kinnaird's withdrawal (and Place's entry into the campaign). The reformers generally did badly at the end of the week because men who held official positions were most active at this time while tradesmen concentrated on business. Both the 1807 and 1818 contests started badly for the reformers partly because the polls commenced on a Thursday.[25]

Kinnaird spoke on the hustings after his withdrawal, and his oratory in the turbulent atmosphere won high praise. Scrope Davies, Hobhouse said, 'makes the Committee laugh and discomposes the staid intelligent ironmongers and curriers of our party. Captain Maxwell's face is daily covered with saliva from the patriot mob. Scrope says it reminds him of *Spithead!!*'[26] Henry Hunt stayed in the contest to the end, although he soon lost the support of the hustings crowd, and the later stages were enlivened by a bitter running argument between him and Major Cartwright's secretary, Thomas Cleary. It started when Hunt read out on the hustings a private letter by Cleary, written soon after the Pentridge rising of 1817. Cleary told Hunt that Cartwright was unwilling to raise a subscription for the rebels, and reflecting on the damage that the rising had done to the cause of reform, Cleary said that he would willingly hang the leader of the rebellion himself. But the later revelation that the rising had been fomented by the spy Oliver brought sympathy for the rebels, so Hunt was able to quote this remark against Cleary and (because Cleary had joined Burdett's committee following Cartwright's withdrawal) against the 'Rump'. Towards the end of the election Hunt read out another private letter from Cleary, who replied by reading out a letter which Place had given him, sent by Cobbett in 1808 to his agent to warn the reformers against Hunt. He urged them 'not to mix with men of *bad character*. There is one Hunt, the Bristol man — beware of him! He rides about the country with a whore, the wife of another man, having deserted his own.'

Cobbett denounced the letter as a forgery, but he was eventually forced to admit that it was genuine. The row dragged on for over two years, ending with actions against Cobbett by Cleary, who was awarded 40s, and against Hunt by John Wright, the recipient of Cobbett's warning, who was awarded £1000. Place gave evidence for Wright, and he was so angry about Cobbett's misrepresentation of it in his *Register* that he consulted Brougham about the possibility of legal action,[27] but apart from this Place got off surprisingly lightly, and Cobbett rejected an attempt by Cleary to pass responsibility for the supposed fake to Place. The abuse by Hunt and Cobbett reached new heights. Hunt claimed that Cleary was kept by his mistress, and he called Thomas Wooler (for taking Cleary's side in the *Black Dwarf*) 'such a profligate drunken wretch . . . that there is scarcely a *Brothel* or a *Stew* in the Metropolis that does not stink with his debaucheries'. Cobbett meanwhile moved from detailed criticism of Burdett, and insinuations that Brooks had profited from his position, to wild accusations of corruption against the Rump and exultation that he had almost brought about a Tory victory over Burdett.[28] Place has rightly been accused of being overcritical towards his colleagues in his narratives, but his abuse did not begin to compare with the insults and lies routinely employed in public by Hunt and Cobbett, who have not been subject to the same criticism by historians. Indeed, the radical scene was marked by constant quarrels, and Place was far less inclined to indulge in public abuse than many other reformers.

The final result on 4 July showed that Burdett had lost some of his popularity. He received 100 more votes than in the great 1807 contest, but his performance is more accurately shown by the decline since 1807 from 60 to 51 per cent in the proportion of voters who gave him one of their votes or a plumper. He had many active supporters, with a general committee of 130 in theory, and at least some parish committees, but the chaotic state of the general committee was one factor in Burdett's poor early showing. The finances suggest some decline in the electors' zeal since 1807. The expenses were £1200 compared with £790 in 1807, and receipts were £830, out of which friends of Kinnaird contributed nearly half. The election was followed by the chairing of Burdett through the streets, Place as usual alone opposing it. Hobhouse declared that it was 'the finest sight I ever saw, it beat the Champ de Mai hollow. It is supposed that so large and orderly a crowd were never before assembled in London.'[29]

On 11 July Major Cartwright issued a bitter *Address . . . to the Electors of Westminster,* which accused the Rump of having endangered Burdett's seat by a 'desperate intrigue' for a 'paltry personal preference'. But moves were soon under way for a reconciliation, and Kinnaird was invited to chair a public dinner for the Major. Place approved of the idea, and Burdett was present at the dinner on 25 August, although Cartwright was too ill to attend.[30] Meanwhile the Westminster Committee had accepted an offer from Place to draw up a plan for the next election.

When Sir Samuel Romilly committed suicide on 2 November following the death of his wife, Place showed the insensitive side of his nature, expressing his 'regret that Romilly should have been so weak a man'. (When his own wife died in 1827 he was shocked to discover that he was equally capable of weakness.) Immediately he heard he wrote an outline of a handbill for Kinnaird in the election to replace Romilly, and during the day Maxwell's friends started to canvass. Place's dictatorial instincts now took charge, and he decided to make sure that there was no repetition of the chaos during the General Election. He expected to carry out his election plan 'with a high hand', and the next morning he wrote a bill for Kinnaird and sent it to the printers. Bentham called and approved of the bill, and Place then took it to Bickersteth, whom he described as 'a very intimate friend of Burdett and a very clever good, clear headed, courageous man'. By this time he had got to know Hobhouse well enough to form a high opinion of his abilities, and he agreed with Bickersteth that 'Mr Hobhouse was the man most likely to fulfil the wishes of the people', but they could not drop Kinnaird after he had been successfully brought before the electors, and Bickersteth approved of the bill. They also agreed that a meeting should be called for Kinnaird, and that his friends and the electors should be approached for contributions. Place returned home to find Hobhouse and others urging that the reformers should wait to see what the Whigs did, and he immediately sent the printer an order for 6000 bills 'as I saw nothing but mawkish drivelling notions prevailing among these people'.[31]

He sent some of the bills to friendly public houses, others to thirty active reformers with letters saying that they would probably distribute the bills if they approved of them. At first everything went well. He heard that the bills were enthusiastically received and the printer's house was beset for copies. A meeting was called on 5 November to consider the best means of returning Kinnaird. Here Place had his first setback. He wanted to keep up the momentum by drafting a letter to Burdett asking him to chair a public meeting for Kinnaird, circulating copies of the letter for signature by the electors, starting a subscription and opening a campaign office. But the traditions of the Westminster Committee required a public meeting first to select a 'fit and proper person' to represent Westminster, and this was agreed against Place's violent objections that such a meeting would be disrupted by the Huntites, and that the subscription would have to be delayed until Kinnaird was officially endorsed, by which time the enthusiasm of the electors would have subsided. Place promptly walked out, declaring that he would not stir unless £1000 was raised: those who prevented it being raised his way were bound to raise it in their own.

The argument reflected a fundamental weakness in the Westminster Committee's procedure. The choice of a candidate at a public meeting was supposed to ensure unity and to counter claims that the Committee dictated to the electors, but it was open to rivals to prevent a choice being made by making a riot, and then the informal structure of the Committee provided no procedure for coming to a decision. Some of the objectors to Place's proposal did favour other candidates. Two days later Samuel Miller Junior, Place's closest ally at this stage, wrote to tell him that some reformers were determined to put up Cartwright, while others favoured Hobhouse or Michael Bruce, another Rota Club radical: 'Kinnaird is by some thought inadequate. . . . Here is consistency with a vengeance. Kinnaird having been tried and found equal to all that could be required, is now, after having been taken up and fairly placed before the Public to be rejected, and his friends proposed before him.'[32]

The Whigs were saying that they would accept Hobhouse but not Kinnaird, and on 10 November Kinnaird called on Place in a sulky mood and said that he would not accept nomination. He also remarked 'significantly' that

Hobhouse would make a good representative, and condemned the proposal for a public selection meeting as insane. Since Hobhouse had said that Kinnaird was insisting on such a meeting, Place suspected double-dealing by Hobhouse. Two days later, Bickersteth relieved his mind by assuring him that Kinnaird had written to Hobhouse saying that he would only accept nomination at a public selection meeting. By this time the reformers had decided to settle on Kinnaird, and Place decided to ignore his remarks as an exhibition of vanity which had probably passed. When Place was asked to draw up resolutions for Kinnaird for the public meeting on 17 November he agreed, but on the 15th the reformers were forced to think again when they heard that Kinnaird had definitely refused – possibly because he had lost the confidence of his Rota Club friends by his equivocation. Place now switched his support to Hobhouse, who was accepted at a private meeting on the 16th. Place refused to attend in protest at the decision to hold a public selection meeting rather than a public meeting in support of a candidate previously chosen, and he later said in his draft of the reformers' account of the election that he had taken no part in the choice of the candidate, but Hobhouse insisted on the deletion of the statement as untrue in spirit in view of Place's private advocacy.[33]

Place attended the public meeting predicting chaos. But although Burdett had great difficulty in controlling the meeting, the turbulence was principally caused by the audience's unwillingness to hear Hunt and his supporters, who proposed Cobbett. Cartwright's friends failed to put him forward, but Lord John Russell was proposed by a group of Whigs. Hobhouse made an able and energetic speech, thus ending the tradition that the nominee was not a candidate after the disastrous result of keeping Kinnaird out of the General Election campaign. Hobhouse was chosen by an immense majority, and even Hunt declared his acceptance of the decision, although he soon changed his mind. Place exulted over 'the miserable and contemptible state of poor lousy whiggery',[34] and he agreed to join the small managing committee. The election was not due until February 1819, and for the next three months he devoted himself to the campaign.

Hobhouse was a curious mixture of opportunism and sanctimoniousness, but he also possessed considerable talents and a strong desire to be useful, which appealed to Place. He was friendly with leading Whig families such as the Hollands and the Russells, and if he had been wealthy enough to purchase a seat he would doubtless have become a Whig of the liberal 'Mountain' group. He did consider borrowing the money required, reassuring his Tory father that he would pay off the debt by marrying a fortune, and once in Parliament would 'do something which will render future expense unnecessary, for being . . . *in the seditious line,* I have little doubt of a free seat for the future'.[35] His active support for Burdett and Kinnaird during the General Election led to cooler relations with the Whigs, and he wrote one of the most abusive bills. (As one of Byron's friends, he had a grudge against

Romilly, who had advised Lady Byron while retained by her husband.) After Romilly's death Hobhouse was torn between loyalty to his friend Kinnaird and his desire to encourage signs of Whig approval of his own candidacy. Once he was selected he could devote himself to the difficult task of keeping both sides happy. He made a good start at the selection meeting, where he managed the remarkable feat of saying nothing to offend the Whigs and yet winning Place's praise: 'Hobhouse made a speech full of energy, and good matter professed himself an open friend of parl reform, to its utmost extent – said he held himself bound to answer questions, to receive instructions, &c &c.'[36]

Sir Murray Maxwell had announced his candidacy for the Tories on 16 November, so Hobhouse fought an active campaign, frequently addressing parish meetings and dinners, with the result that Maxwell retired on 11 January. Place's election plan had been put into effect and his organising genius given free rein. The results, he boasted to his friend Ensor, were

> a large committee in each of the parishes – a general public meeting in each of the parishes – a complete canvass of the whole of the City and Liberty by the Parish Committees and books in as fine a state as perhaps it is possible to make them, a public dinner also in each of the Parishes and on Monday week next another public general meeting of the whole body of the electors, to whom a report will be made, it then [to] be printed and extensively circulated. You must know that we never before dared to call a public meeting in the parishes, never had a proper parish committee, and no system of regular canvassing. The General Committee now consists of upwards of 330 persons and the subscription amounts to £1,800. This is a *New View of Society*, all this has been done very quietly and [at] a comparatively very small expense, and the long period from 3 November to the present moment has been so well occupied that the enthusiasm of the people which was roused at the beginning has never subsided, the Minister has been fairly driven of the ground, and all the contrivances of the dirty, sneaking Whigs, have ended in nothing . . .[37]

This letter was written in the calm before the storm. The chief agitators for a Whig candidacy were two of the party's most liberal MPs, Bennet and Brougham. Bennet's reasons are uncertain, but Place was unaware of his role, and he reacted with hurt puzzlement when Bennet steered through Parliament a bill reintroducing the right of the High Bailiff to charge candidates for his expenses. Brougham was doubtless intent on revenge for the insults he had received from the Westminster Committee. However, Hobhouse had supporters among the Whigs, notably Edward Ellice, the brother-in-law of the Whig leader, Lord Grey. Ellice told Grey that Hobhouse was 'as good a Whig as I am', and that £2000 in the radicals' hands would go as far as £20,000 for any Whig candidate, a remark that the radicals would have seized on with glee as proof of how far their enemies relied on bribery and corruption to match their unbought votes. Burdett helped by making a speech praising the Whigs in December, and the Whig leaders agreed not to oppose Hobhouse, but they condemned the radical reformers at a Fox Club dinner in Newcastle on 31 December. After Grey had abused them, his son-in-law, Lambton, scornfully dismissed them as 'brawling, ignorant, but mischievous quacks', who associated with 'the lowest of the rabble'.[38]

Place replied in a Report to the Electors on the progress of the campaign, which condemned the Whigs as a faction and Grey as an apostate. Place and his associates had learned about Hobhouse's manoeuvres with the Whigs, and the report was intended to force him to repudiate his implicit alliance with them, and to ensure that the party would not be able to claim the credit for his return. After Burdett's speech in December, all their efforts for reform were in danger of resulting in the return of two Whigs. Hobhouse naturally opposed the report. As he told Lambton, he felt that it would induce the Whigs 'not only to draw the sword, but throw away the scabbard'. On 18 January the report was approved by a special meeting of the managing committee attended by Bickersteth and James Mill, and a meeting of the general committee 120 strong unanimously agreed to submit it to a public meeting of the electors on 9 February. But some members had second thoughts, and a few days later the managing committee received a deputation from two of the parish committees, which protested that the report might bring forth a Whig candidate and endanger Hobhouse's election. The delegation was persuaded by the argument that Hobhouse's return was of secondary importance compared with the cause of parliamentary reform, and that for the sake of the cause it was necessary for the reformers to stand alone and fight all their enemies, even if this resulted in defeat.[39]

At the public meeting Place's report was adopted and ordered to be printed, although the audience grew impatient at its length and refused to hear the whole of it. Hobhouse offered further provocation to the Whigs by declaring that he was one of the 'extravagant' reformers who had just been condemned in the Whig *Edinburgh Review,* but he was no more specific than before on what plan he would adopt. He received an almost unanimous vote of support in spite of opposition from Hunt and Cartwright's supporters. The report was circulated to 21 country newspapers, three Scottish and two Irish ones. It was the attack on Lord Grey, even more than the general one on the Whigs, which provoked the party to put up a candidate. The speeches by Grey and Lambton at the Newcastle Fox dinner might have been thought to justify the reformers' hostility, but the Whigs' high aristocratic notion of honour required them to vindicate their leader's character, and George Lamb, the brother of the future Prime Minister, was persuaded to 'rough it'. He was chosen, Lambton told Grey, because he was 'not of sufficient consequence in the Party to make his failure a party disgrace'.[40]

The success of the reformers' campaign was a main cause of their problems. By forcing the Tory out of the field they ensured that any Whig candidate could expect the votes of all anti-reformers, and thus made a decision to contest the election viable. Cartwright's supporters had also been encouraged to put forward his claim for recognition of his past services, arguing that the need for a strong and active candidate had disappeared. Cobbett had publicly threatened to stop calling Cartwright 'our leader' unless he broke with Burdett, and the Major complied in an *Address to the Electors of Westminster* on 4 February. He accused the Westminster Committee of being a secret cabal which had plotted to exclude him, and attacked Burdett for praising the Whigs and looking forward to their adoption of household suffrage and triennial elections. Annual elections, he claimed, were our right under the law of God. Did Burdett think that he and his Whig friends knew better than God?[41]

The equivocation of Hobhouse and Burdett now induced the more intransigent reformers to back Cartwright as a candidate, but Place and the Westminster Committee refused to break with Hobhouse. They knew that Cartwright could only get a derisory vote, and if they backed him they would destroy the cause of reform in Westminster. Place was almost always dissatisfied with the MPs for Westminster, but in his view what mattered was the example which Westminster set of independence of aristocratic control and the rejection of the politics of deference. In comparison with this the character of the men elected was less important. One factor in the choice of a Rota Club candidate which Place did not mention was money. The reformers spent far less than the £5000 normal for Whig and Tory candidates in Westminster, but out of £1780 received by the end of the year, £1700 had been contributed by friends and relatives of Hobhouse, including £1000 by Burdett and £100 by Kinnaird.

At the nomination of the candidates on 13 February, Hobhouse received a great majority over Lamb and Cartwright in the show of hands, but his speech contained a tortuous declaration on reform which proved a serious liability. He said he considered that security against misgovernment might be obtained with a suffrage far short of universal, and the extension of suffrage was of third-rate importance compared with uniform qualifications for voting and electorates of equal size; every Parliament was too long which could be shorter and he saw no objection to annual parliaments but no necessity for them. This declaration was seized on with glee by his opponents. Lamb's committee offered £1000 to anyone who could explain it, while the Tory *New Times* claimed that his principles would allow him to vote for a further restriction of the suffrage and decennial parliaments. Lamb said that he stood on Sir Samuel Romilly's principles, which was safe enough since he had never enunciated any. Lamb received strong support from the Tories and later from the extreme democrats, when they found that Cartwright's cause was hopeless. Faced with such an unholy alliance, Hobhouse did surprisingly well. He and Burdett, both good orators, spoke daily from the hustings and held the support of the crowd throughout.

Lamb soon appealed to the extreme democrats by declaring for household suffrage and triennial parliaments, and Hobhouse replied by announcing his support for annual parliaments and a suffrage more extensive than householders. He came to sound more and more radical as the battle become hotter. The Whig strategy was to present Lamb as the *real* liberty candidate, and the support of the extreme radicals made the claim plausible. Burdett and Hobhouse had difficulty in showing that they stood for distinct and more radical principles. Hobhouse's solution was to say that he stood for the paramount importance of parliamentary reform and to attack Whig apostasy on it with increasing bitterness. He remained a Whig at heart, as he showed when he declared on the hustings that 'my principles have been those of the Whigs of 1798 in contradistinction to the Whigs of 1819'. This was apparently his real view; before the election he had told Lambton: 'My views on reform are similar to those of the Society of the Friends of the People — uniformity of suffrage and possibly triennial elections.'[42] He was far more radical than most of the party, but no more than some men who were happy to call themselves Whigs.

The polling started on a Monday, which helped him since the radicals did better earlier in the week, and for the first three days he held the lead; thereafter he sometimes outpolled Lamb in the daily total but he was always behind overall, finishing with 3861 votes to 4465 for Lamb and 38 for Cartwright. During the election Place spent all his waking hours in the committee room, and although he tried to stay in the background his role became well known. The Whigs published a mock newspaper, *The Rump Chronicle*, which celebrated Lamb's victory with a squib which referred to Hobhouse's father, Sir Benjamin, who had changed his party in order to accept office under the Tories:

> To gain a place by purchas'd seat
>   Was Ben, the Patriot's case;
> Jack chang'd the plan, and Jack is beat, —
>   He'll gain no seat by *Place*.[43]

The daily speeches from the hustings, together with a stream of lampoons, skits and songs — the Whig ones far wittier than the radical ones — produced a high level of popular excitement.[44] Lady Caroline Lamb, George Lamb's sister-in-law and Byron's ex-lover, joined in enthusiastically, following the famous example of the Duchess of Devonshire, who gave a butcher a kiss in exchange for a Whig vote in the Westminster election of 1784. In the later stages the 1819 election was marked by considerable violence, caused by bludgeon men hired to get the Whig spokesmen a hearing on the hustings, and after the close of polling the Whig committee room, the offices of the *Morning Chronicle* and the houses of several leading Whigs were wrecked. Two of the victims successfully sued Burdett and Place for the damage to their houses, but this was only a propaganda ploy since they were really suing the local government for compensation, and they could select any two householders as nominal defendants. Counsel for Burdett and Place argued that the riot had been caused by Whig bludgeon men who were dissatisfied with their low pay, but they were not allowed to bring evidence on the point because they could not prove that the victims were members of Lamb's committee.

A key factor in Lamb's victory was the employment by his committee of rate-collectors as inspectors, who would disallow any voter for Hobhouse who was not up-to-date with the payment of his Poor Rates. The reformers could not afford the heavy expense of hiring rate-collectors, and the injustice was compounded by an arbitrary decision of the High Bailiff not to allow householders to pay when they came to vote. Voters for Lamb would not be challenged, and Hobhouse later claimed that this alone accounted for his defeat. These factors, together with the pressure which had been exerted by the Government and the aristocracy on tenants, employees and tradesmen allowed the reformers to claim a moral victory, telling the electors in a handbill: 'your coalesced Enemies, the WHIGS, the TORIES, and the ANARCHISTS have barely succeeded in obtaining the return of a Member. They have obtained NO Triumph!' Hobhouse wrote in a memoir that 'defeat, instead of discouraging my Westminster friends, made them more zealous; and the usual demonstration – a public dinner at the usual place, the Crown and Anchor in the Strand – helped to keep us alive'. Place was especially pleased because he thought that the election had raised Burdett to 'his proper situation' in public opinion, and separated 'the whigs who are not reformers from those who are reformers'.[45] The election had also seen the end of the long breach between him and Burdett, when the baronet came up to him in the committee room and started talking to him as if they had been friends all along, and Place responded in kind.

Place's conduct in the election has been criticised by historians, who have said that his handbill for Kinnaird the day after Romilly's death showed bad taste. However, he was slower off the mark than the Tories, and the only contemporary complaint raised on that score was by the Whigs, who were playing for time until they could find a candidate of their own. His action was seen at the time as dictatorial, although he was following the usual practice in putting forward a particular candidate. Only the Westminster Committee used to seek the approval of a public selection meeting, and by this time the procedure had broken down. Place would have preferred Hobhouse, but Kinnaird was the popular choice after his success on the hustings in the General Election, so Place tried to put sufficient momentum behind his selection to prevent rivals causing a split. When his colleagues insisted on a public selection meeting he showed pointless stubbornness in refusing to accept the decision.

In 1826 Place set out his own view of the election:

In 1818 Mr Hobhouse made common cause with the Whigs, and in the original draft of his address to the electors, he said he should endeavour to tread in the steps of that illustrious man the late Charles James Fox, he had a sort of compromise with

Lambton, Ferguson and others and was to have been the Whig candidate, he had in fact committed himself to them, but this would not do for us, and was one of the reasons which induced me to draw up the report which produced George Lamb and lost us the election. Had that report not been written Westminster would have had two avowed Whig members, for Burdett would have concurred with Hobhouse. The consequence of this would have been that in 1820, Hobhouse would have been ousted by a ministerial candidate, and Westminster would have again been divided between the two factions, to the exclusion of all interference of the people. As it is Burdett and Hobhouse are little if any better than mere drawling Whigs but the influence of the people in their own affairs was assisted and maintained in 1820, and the fear of the reformers still remains. [46]

The Tories would almost certainly have won a straight fight with the Whigs. Out of Lamb's 4465 voters, 2763 had voted for the Tory Maxwell in 1818 and 1073 had given him plumpers.

After the election Hobhouse clearly thought that it was necessary to keep on good terms with Place if he was to realise his parliamentary ambitions, and this was easier to achieve because his bitterness over Whig conduct during the election had driven him further towards radicalism. Over the next year they kept up a close correspondence and cooperated in a pamphlet war against Lord Erskine, once the hero of the 1794 treason trials but now a conservative Whig. In March 1819 Erskine issued *A Short Defence of the Whigs from the Imputations Attempted to be cast upon them during the late Election for Westminster,* which defended the conduct of the Whigs and argued that their retreat from reform was necessary since the violence of the reformers had made its achievement impracticable. Place replied anonymously with *A Reply to Lord Erskine* by 'an elector of Westminster', in which he declared that the charge, as Erskine had formulated it, that the 'Whigs are a corrupt and profligate faction . . . shall be fully proved'. He accepted that there were many men in both parliamentary parties whose private characters were exemplary: 'the only matter for surprise is, that such men should be found acting in their respective parties as if wisdom, honour, and honesty, formed no ingredients in their characters'. He claimed that his report had prevented the Whigs from claiming the merit for an unopposed return of Hobhouse, and that the contest had enabled a large portion of the people to see through Whig pretensions. A reformer in the House of Commons was of small importance compared with the chance an election afforded 'of unmasking and exposing the people's enemies, and thus rendering them comparatively harmless: thus teaching them to depend on themselves'. [47] He also gave the usual comparison between the Whig declarations for reform in the 1790s and their crimes and apostasies since then, and he particularly attacked Lord Grey. The reformers' habit of singling out Grey infuriated the Whigs, but as Place pointed out, he had no right to complain, because in the 1790s he had used the same tactic of quoting Pitt's early declarations in favour of reform. Place kept a 'black book' of radical remarks by men who had later apostasised. Erskine replied with *A Letter . . . to 'An Elector of Westminster'*, which gave a disingenuous defence of Whig conduct.

Hobhouse replied to this pamphlet, urged on by Place and working in close collaboration with him, which was published anonymously as *A Defence of the People*. This displayed his literary ability, his populist aspirations (he intended to entitle it a defence 'by one of the rabble', but the publisher objected), and the fact that his hostility to the Whigs was less extreme than Place's. In August, Henry Hunt addressed a public meeting of 60,000 in St Peter's Fields in Manchester, and mounted yeomanry, sent in by the magistrates to arrest Hunt, killed eleven people and wounded four hundred. Some Whigs joined in the angry denunciations of the 'Peterloo massacre'. Place decided not to publish another reply to Erskine which he had prepared, lest he gave the Whigs an excuse for staying away from the protest meeting being organised in Westminster, but in the event they did not attend. In October Erskine's *Defence of the Whigs* was reissued with a new preface, and Hobhouse replied with *A Trifling Mistake*. The radicals, and many non-radicals, were bitterly indignant at the Government's defence of the conduct of the Manchester magistrates, and Hobhouse ended his pamphlet with a diatribe against Parliament and the Government. One passage, written or altered by Place, led to Hobhouse's commitment to Newgate by the House of Commons:

> What prevents the people from walking down to the House, and pulling out the members by the ears, locking up their doors and flinging the key into the Thames? Is it any majesty which hedges in the members of that assembly? Do we love them? Not at all, – we have an instinctive horror and disgust at the very abstract idea of a borough-monger. . . . Their true practical protectors then, the real efficient anti-Reformers, are to be found at the Horse Guards, and the Knightsbridge barracks . . .[48]

In January 1820 George III died. The law required a General Election when a monarch died, and circumstances favoured the electoral prospects of the Westminster Committee. The repressive Six Acts of December 1819, which aimed to suppress agitation, increased the Government's unpopularity; while the exposure of a plot by Arthur Thistlewood and a few associates to assassinate the Cabinet, which became known as the 'Cato Street conspiracy' from the place where the conspirators were arrested, frightened the extreme radical press which had been sniping at the Committee. Henry Hunt, the chief troublemaker, was in prison for his part in Peterloo, and Cobbett had returned from America looking for a reconciliation with Burdett. Hobhouse and Burdett were both in a position to command sympathy. Hobhouse had been gaoled by a vote of the House of Commons for *A Trifling Mistake* in December without being tried or even heard in his own defence (the latter because an officious friend had urged in the House that he should be spared the trouble of appearing), and only the dissolution of Parliament on the

King's death saved him from several months' imprisonment. Burdett was convicted in the middle of the election for a savage attack on the Government's conduct over Peterloo. Furthermore, the reformers had secured a court decision which prevented the High Bailiff from refusing the votes of electors who were in arrears with their rates, but who offered to pay when they voted. Lamb had alienated the Government by acting as a member of the regular opposition, and many Whigs, realising that they faced almost certain defeat, were reluctant to embark on the expense of a contest. Place was sounded out and promised not to crow over the Whigs if they withdrew, and Lamb himself had doubts, but finally he decided to stand.

This time Place had things all his own way. A private meeting on 11 February resolved to run Burdett and Hobhouse, and the decision was endorsed by the General Committee of the 1819 election. Over 300 were invited, but entry was restricted to those who produced the letter of invitation. At the nomination on the hustings the show of hands was almost unanimous for the two reformers, who built up a lead of almost 900 during the first week. After this Lamb received some help from the Government, and he ended with 4436 votes, almost identical with his 1819 figure. Hobhouse gained a thousand to end with 4882, and Burdett headed the poll with 5327.

Place said that during the election he was in the committee room 'from 7 in the morning every day to midnight. . .where my presence seemed so absolutely necessary that I was unable to take a single meal at home, or even so much time as was required to read half a column of a Newspaper'. A letter he received from the radical publisher William Hone in the middle of the election suggests that his efforts to rouse radical fervour extended to organising social events:

> Friend Place
> Here is a *Parody* for the good old Cause. . . . Now knowing you not to be *very* musical I think it possible, though barely possible, that you may not know the Air. If Mr Roundthwaite or any other member of the Committee with music in his soul will hum it to you I incline to believe that you will find it calculated to tell well in a good Glee room.[49]

When the election ended on 25 March, the candidates evaded the usual chairing, so the crowd took the horses from the carriage of Hobhouse's sisters and paid the homage to them.

For the next ten years Lamb showed a dislike of Place, who assumed that he held him in contempt, but in 1830 he heard that Lamb had complained that he had been pelted with mud during the 1820 election at Place's instigation. Place indignantly denied it, but he discovered that it was true. Some electors had come into the committee room and made a nuisance of themselves complaining about offensive remarks by Lamb on the hustings, and to get rid of them he told them to go and pelt him. He did not learn that they had taken him at his word until he heard of Lamb's complaint. Lamb's grievance was assuaged by an explanation and a joke, and in the early 1830s he would often consult Place as an emissary of the Home Secretary, his brother, Lord Melbourne.[50]

* * *

The extremely high standard of dedication which Place expected made it inevitable that Hobhouse would fail to meet his standards. He thought that Hobhouse was influenced by Burdett, who regarded attention to the details of legislation as beneath a gentleman. In 1821 Burdett remarked in a letter to Place from his country house that 'Mr Hobhouse is here, you will say perhaps seduced by me, enjoying himself much.' In the 1822 session Hobhouse assiduously supported Hume's campaign of dividing on every possible occasion on the finance bill, but he soon tired of such hard work for no visible result. He denied Place's charge that he was lazy: 'I can work hard enough when there is anything to do. But the Den [the House of Commons] is a damper to industry.'[51] Place regarded him as good-natured and well-meaning as well as talented, but he was constantly infuriated by his lack of application and the ease with which he was discouraged by difficulties. In 1826 he observed: 'If this man would but learn how to work he would make a figure.' Place would write Hobhouse long letters warning him that he was jeopardising his seat by his inattention to his constituents, and Hobhouse would reply complaining how discouraging it was for a man to do his best and find that he gave no satisfaction. He also indulged in moralising and displayed jealousy of the reputation earned by the slow witted but industrious Joseph Hume.[52]

Another cause of dissension was the drift of both Westminster MPs towards the Whigs. In 1822 Place reacted indignantly to a suggestion that the date of the annual dinner to celebrate the 1807 victory should be changed to suit Whigs who wished to attend. He declared that he would like very much to have them there, but he was against any compromise to attract them. He was even more indignant – and with better reason – when it was decided not to drink to radical reform because Hobhouse thought that it would offend the Whigs. 'Puller, Puller', he protested to an ally, 'what but *Radical Reform* was it that caused you and I to take so much trouble, to lose so much time and spend so much money.'[53] The dinner was nevertheless held with an impressive contingent of liberal Whigs.

Place often worked with Hobhouse in the 1820s. In January 1825 he turned his attention to the current mania for gaming in joint-stock companies : 'the course I pursued and the efforts I made principally in conjunction with Mr Hobhouse checked some of those fraudulent gaming speculations, and saved the property of thousands of persons from destruction'.[54] In the same year he worked with Hobhouse and the leaders of the cotton workers to secure an Act of Parliament to restrict children's hours in cotton factories. Place said that he drafted the Act, but it was amended to meet the objections of the masters.

A dinner of Manchester cotton spinners to celebrate the passage of the bill toasted Place as 'the poor man's friend'. Although a number of successful prosecutions were brought, in general the Act did not prove effective. Hobhouse brought in a further Act in 1831, but in 1832 Place was still working to stop the 'horrid cruelty practised on these poor helpless children'. Although largely ineffectual, the Acts provided the basis for the successful development of factory legislation.[55]

In the less frenetic 1820s Place was able to keep to his perennially stated determination not to go out of his house on election business, but he nevertheless managed the Westminster campaign in the 1826 General Election behind the scenes. Burdett and Hobhouse were greatly embarrassed when a resolution of the election committee, drafted by Place, referred to the defeat of the 'factions' in 1807, complaining that their Whig friends would accuse them of using one language to their face and another behind their backs. Their draft replies deprecated the insult, but when Place pointed out that such a repudiation would cause the committee to disband and invite a contest they hastily backed down. 'As for the embarrassment of Sir Francis and Mr Hobhouse', Place observed with malicious satisfaction, 'they have brought it upon themselves, and deserve all the trouble and all the vexation it may occasion them.' The MPs were also worried by the discovery that almost all the efficient workers had either died or dropped out, the consequence of the disappearance of the generation of activists educated in the struggles of the 1790s. According to Place, Hobhouse was almost reduced to panic by a rumour that Canning was going to stand, but in the event it came to nothing and the sitting members were re-elected unopposed.[56]

The three elections of 1818–20 proved a severe strain on the reformers' finances, and although Place contributed £130 towards settling the debt, it was not finally cleared until 1827. 'I have again to do the disagreeable', he told Burdett, 'no one else will do it', asking him to pay the balance of £108. Part of this was for the 1819 action against the High Bailiff, part for the 1826 election, which seems to have been the first in which the candidates paid part of the expenses. Place wrote to Hobhouse that the Committee had had seven elections since 1807, three public chairings, six court actions, over thirty public meetings, twenty-four public dinners, three House of Commons petitions and sundry publications for a total expenditure of under £10,000, less than the expenses of the Whig and Tory candidates in 1818.[57]

Hobhouse's anxiety to preserve his position in his constituency delayed his drift to the Whigs, and when Canning's moderate Tory administration was formed in 1827 he refused to join Burdett and the main body of the Whigs in crossing to the ministerial side of the House. However, by this time the Westminster MPs had long rejoined the Whig social centres, such as Holland House and Brooks Club, and Place complained of their emasculating influence on men who entered the House of Commons with the best intentions. In his diary Hobhouse made the same point. Reformers strongly disapproved of the practice of granting pensions to public men and their families, and in May 1828 Hobhouse voted against a pension for Canning's family, but he did not speak against it. 'This debate', he wrote,

> furnished me with another proof of the utter impracticability of speaking all the truth in Parliament. There is always some private reason, some fear of offending delicate tastes, or of maintaining unpopular propositions, which silences men even of the most independent and disinterested character. This will fetter public men so long as they take pleasure, not to say pride, in associating with the members of a fashionable club, or being the well received guests of some great house, the headquarters of some great party. Yet how this is to be avoided by those who have lived together at school and at college, and the gatherings of social life, I do not know. If you avail yourself of the knowledge which such intimacies impart you are looked on as a traitor and a spy. If you enter into all the schemes of a clique, you become a mere tool, and lose the representative character altogether.

On the other hand, Hobhouse did secure significant reforms. As well as the Factory Acts, in 1831 he pushed through the Select Vestries Act (under great pressure from Place and other constituents), which enabled parish reformers to abolish unelected and corrupt select vestries and introduce democratic local government in a number of metropolitan parishes.[58] The generally low opinion of Hobhouse was as much a result of the unrealistically high expectations formed when he entered Parliament as of his own failings.

The death of George IV in June 1830 brought a General Election, and it was clear that Joseph Hume's Scottish seat was in danger. Some Westminster reformers suggested that he should be nominated for the constituency, alarming Hobhouse who knew that Hume was the one man who could beat him. He therefore suggested to Burdett and Place that Hume should stand in Middlesex. Place welcomed the scheme on the ground that if Hume was elected for Westminster, someone even less efficient than Hobhouse would be elected for Middlesex. Hobhouse also approached the Whigs for support. They, like Hobhouse and Burdett, hated Hume because he too often showed up their moderation by going beyond them, but they were nevertheless open to persuasion because they would lose prestige if they opposed him and were defeated – better to put him forward and take the credit for his victory.

Place's part was carefully concealed from the Whigs, who would have refused to cooperate if they had known that he was involved. Hume almost ruined the plan by vacillating over whether to accept, frightened about the costs he might be involved in. Hobhouse told Place that when Hume wanted to decline, Brougham kept encouraging him, saying

> it must be done, and handsomely – no rabble election – no 'Westminster thing' – and then he asked querulously – "Place has nothing to do with it, eh! ["] when Hume at once in the most off hand manner, and without any change of countenance said NO. I never in all my life, said Hobhouse, heard any man tell a lie on the spur of the occasion with so good a face.

'Yet', Place observed, Hobhouse 'was himself an adept in this way'. Hume finally wrote two letters accepting and rejecting, leaving it to his friends which to adopt. They chose the one accepting, and Hume was elected without opposition after a campaign directed by the radical MP Henry Warburton, Place and Hobhouse. In his diary Hobhouse claimed credit for the victory, because he recommended the project to Burdett and Place, an indication of Place's influence in electoral matters beyond Westminster. Burdett and Hobhouse were re-elected without opposition.[59]

                                       *   *   *

There is no justification for the accusations by Cobbett and Hunt that the Westminster Committee became a 'Rump', a clique which abandoned its democratic principles. Indeed, the apathy of the electors meant that it was always in the position of seeking as many people as possible to share the work and expense of organisation. The Committee tried hard to remain democratic. It consulted as widely as possible by open meetings of radical supporters, and submitted its candidates for endorsement at public meetings. This was a main cause of the debacle in 1818. Cobbett had some influence in Westminster, but it was only a negative one to reduce the popularity of Burdett and the Committee. Since the candidates endorsed by Cobbett and Hunt always received derisory votes, it was they who were trying to dictate to the electors by forcing unpopular extremists on them. The charge of subservience to Burdett has more substance, but as Place was forced to recognise, any break between Burdett and the Committee would have destroyed the reform cause in Westminster.

The members of the Committee were more radical than their supporters, and in 1818–20 it had more identifiable former members of the LCS than in 1807. Among the supporters of Kinnaird in 1818 were Place, John Ridley, William Adams, Thomas Hardy and Paul Lemaitre; Alexander Galloway and Place's old partner, Richard Wild, supported Cartwright, and when he was withdrawn they joined the united committee for Burdett. Later in the year John Richter, John Thelwall and William Hone supported Hobhouse. John Gale Jones, on the other hand, was a leading supporter of Henry Hunt.[60] In the years after 1807 the Committee played a key part in reviving the cause of reform. The decline of its influence in the late 1810s was inevitable because radicalism had become too powerful to be the property of a single constituency.

The importance of Place's role is attested by the great desire of aspiring candidates to be on good terms with him, and in 1817 Romilly wrote that his influence was so great as almost to determine the choice of member.[61] The Sellis affair, and his own hot temper and his unwillingness to conceal his opinion of those he despised, frequently put him at odds with his associates, but he was almost always on the winning side on key issues such as the choice of candidates, and his organising genius and tactical sense were important assets of the Westminster Committee.

9 Founding the Birth Control Movement

The desire to control human fertility goes back to prehistory, and methods of preventing conception, of varying effectiveness, have been widely found in primitive societies. The use of *coitus interruptus* and the vaginal sponge for medical reasons are authorised in Hebrew texts going back to the first century AD. But Place's *Illustrations and Proofs of the Principle of Population*, published in 1822,[1] was the first book to put the social and economic case for contraception, and it was his persistent propaganda during the 1820s which launched the world's first birth control movement. In 1823–26 he circulated anonymous leaflets which gave advice on contraceptive techniques, and in the 1820s and 1830s he took every opportunity to put over his case by articles and letters in the press. In private, he was constantly trying to convert his friends and acquaintances to the cause.

At that time the very idea of physical means to prevent conception was considered unspeakably wicked and obscene. Even the Reverend Thomas Malthus was accused of blasphemy for questioning that God sends food for every child which is born, and Place knew when he started his campaign that he would be subject to savage attack. Of all the vilification he suffered, that on account of his birth control activities was by far the most virulent. In 1826 the *Bull Dog*, a short-lived journal established principally to attack the proponents of birth control, accused him of a

> *most foul and devilish attempt, at corrupting the youth of both sexes in this country: an attempt at making no less than* CATAMITES *of the male portion of the youth,* and of the *females,* PROSTITUTES.

Among its many fabrications about Place's private life were that he was the 'bosom friend' of a jeweller called Armstrong, who 'was compelled to cut and run for practices abhorrent to human nature'; and that he turned an illegitimate child of his from his door with the words *'if I provide for this I shall have half-a-dozen more come upon me'*. It also called him 'Eunuch Place'![2] Place was willing to bring such abuse on himself because he was

convinced by Malthus's *Essay on Population* that the proclivity of mankind
to multiply its numbers tended to produce overpopulation, and thus
starvation, but he considered that Malthus's remedy of delayed marriage was
both impracticable and undesirable. In his view contraception provided the
only way out of this dilemma.

*   *   *

The early history of the birth control movement is obscure, since almost all its
supporters tried to keep their involvement secret. Place gave his version of its
origin in an anonymous letter published by the *Black Dwarf* on 1 October
1823:

> You, I am sure, will give that truly benevolent man, Mr Robert Owen, credit for
> good intentions, whatever opinion you may entertain of me, as an unknown
> correspondent. I will therefore relate an anecdote respecting him. It was objected to
> his plan that the number of children which would be produced in his communities
> would be so great, and the deaths from vices, misery, and bad management, so few,
> that the period of doubling the number of people would be very short, and that
> consequently in no very long period his whole plan would become abortive. Mr
> Owen felt the force of this objection, and sought the means of averting the
> consequences. He heard of the small number of children in French families
> compared with English families. He knew from authentic sources that the peasantry
> in the South of France limited the number of their progeny. He knew that while our
> unfortunate countrymen were reduced to pauperism, and to six shillings a week
> wages, the peasants in the South of France received 2s 6d a day, which in their fine
> climate, and with their abstemious habits, enabled them to live in the most
> comfortable manner. He knew that these people were cleanly, simple and well
> provided with every thing desirable in abundance, and he knew also that they
> married young. Mr Owen resolved to ascertain the means by which this desirable
> state was produced and maintained. He went to France, discovered the means
> which prevents too rapid a population, and he brought back with him several pieces
> of spunge, two of which he gave to his friend who had been the cause of this enquiry.
> Mr Owen no longer feared a too rapid increase of the people in his communities; he
> saw at once what to him was most desirable, the means of marrying all his people at
> an early age, and limiting their progeny to any desirable extent. Ask him, and he will
> acknowledge what is here asserted.[3]

Owen did not acknowledge the truth of Place's story. Indeed, he did not hear
of it for some years as he was in the United States, but in the *Morning
Chronicle* for 8 October 1827 he flatly denied any connection with the
introduction of birth control.[4]

Owen seemed an unlikely pioneer of birth control, because he was an anti-
Malthusian, and Place's account of the origin of the birth control movement
has generally been rejected. Owen's visit to France took place in 1818, and
historians have argued that Bentham advocated contraception in the 1790s,
twenty years before Place said that Owen discovered it. This suggestion was
originally put forward by Norman Himes, who published the first academic
history of birth control in 1936. Himes pointed to a 'riddle' about a sponge by

Bentham in 1797, which he interpreted as advocating the use of a sponge as a barrier contraceptive. In 1969, J.R. Poynter pointed out that the riddle really referred to a plan which Bentham was putting forward to solve the problem of rising poor rates, but Poynter stated that Bentham advocated birth control in a passage written in Latin in his 'Manual of Political Economy' of 1795. However, comparison with Bentham's writings on sex in the mid-1810s suggests that the passage was a defence of homosexuality, and the evidence that Bentham advocated birth control in the 1790s does not stand up to examination. In order to discover whether contraception could have been unknown to the Malthusians until the late 1810s, as Place's story implies, it is necessary to consider the history of attempts to solve the Malthusian dilemma.[5]

Contraception was not unknown in England in the seventeenth and eighteenth centuries, so it would seem surprising if the advocates of limiting population were unaware of such an obvious means of achieving their objective. But at this time the condom was associated with prostitution and 'illicit' sex, *coitus interruptus* was ranked with such folk remedies as sneezing during intercourse, and the sponge was almost unknown. The only method of limiting births in significant use appears to have been abortion, a conclusion supported by Place, who conducted the first serious (but very limited) investigation into the extent of attempts to limit births. Around 1820, he found that abortion was used 'to a considerable extent' by the wives and sweethearts of London journeymen, especially before marriage, but contraception was unknown.[6]

The pioneers in raising the problem of population appear to have been equally ignorant of the possibility of contraception. In 1786 the Reverend Joseph Townsend, a forerunner of Malthus, argued that an excessive growth of population could only be prevented by the starvation of the surplus people, and he advocated the limitation of the poor rates. In the *Essay on Population* in 1798, Malthus professed not to understand obscure remarks by Condorcet, which may have referred to birth control, supposing that he referred 'either to a promiscuous concubinage, which would prevent breeding, or to something else as unnatural'. In 1801, Godwin accepted the principle of Malthusianism, even though Malthus had developed the theory in order to prove the impracticability of Godwin's rationalist utopia. Godwin argued that Malthus was correct but irrelevant – the wisdom to restrain the number of people was merely one of the necessary conditions for the realisation of his utopia – and he refused to accept the despairing conclusion of Malthus's first edition, which saw no solution to the problem. Godwin considered infanticide, abortion and legal restrictions on the age of childbearing, but concluded that in the ideal society he advocated people would voluntarily delay marrying until it was prudent to do so. He thus anticipated Malthus's own eventual solution. In comments written in the mid-1810s (but not published until 1931), Bentham argued that the legalisation of infanticide and of homosexual intercourse would help to solve the population problem. As late as January 1818 Place, by then a close friend of James Mill, Bentham and Owen, wrote that since control by delayed marriage was at a great distance, only 'Vice and Misery' could keep the population down at all.[7] Thus it appears that the Malthusians had no knowledge of contraception until the late 1810s, when Place said that Owen imported the sponge. Furthermore, remarks by Malthus and Ricardo provide independent support for Place's story by implying that Owen accepted the reality of the Malthusian dilemma.

Malthus's remarks were in the fifth edition of the *Essay on Population,* published in 1817. He argued that the natural check to early marriages is the difficulty of supporting a large family, but that this depends on the laws of property,

> and in a state of equality and community of property could only be replaced by some artifical regulation of a very different stamp, and a much more unnatural character. Of this Mr Owen is fully sensible, and has in consequence taxed his ingenuity to the utmost to invent some mode, by which the difficulties arising from the progress of population could be got rid of, in the state of society to which he looks forward. His absolute inability to suggest any mode of accomplishing this object that is not unnatural, immoral, or cruel in a high degree, together with the same want of success in every other person, ancient or modern, who has made a similar attempt, seem to show that the argument against systems of equality founded on the principle of population does not admit of a plausible answer, even in theory.

Ricardo implied Owen's acceptance of the Malthusian theory in 1821, when he described contraception as 'one of Owens preventives to an excessive population'. Malthus, Ricardo and Place were close friends of Owen in the 1810s, and he used to have long discussions with them about his ideas (Place helped to prepare Owen's *New View of Society* for the press), so they cannot have been mistaken about his views on the question.[8] At some stage Owen did accept that the danger of overpopulation was real, and both Malthus and Ricardo implied that he proposed more than one solution.

However, the obvious conclusion, that Owen brought over the sponge as a convert to Malthusianism and then denied it later, raises problems. The main one is that Owen's visit to France, which was made in the summer of 1818, appears to be too late. Malthus's statement that Owen was 'fully sensible' of the danger of excessive breeding was published in 1817, so his temporary conversion must have occurred before then, but he had changed his mind by July 1817 when he declared in a letter to *The Times* that any such fear was a chimera. Furthermore, before Owen visited France, James Mill as well as Malthus published comments which are regarded as verdicts on birth control. Mill's comments were in an article he wrote on the topic 'Colony', published in the *Supplement to the Encyclopaedia Britannica,* in February 1818:

> What are the best means of checking the progress of population . . . it is not now

the place to inquire. . . . It has, till this time, been miserably evaded by all those who
have meddled with the subject. . . . And yet, if the superstitions of the nursery were
discarded, and the principle of utility kept steadily in view, a solution might not be
very difficult to be found; and the means of drying up one of the most copious
sources of human evil . . . might be seen to be neither doubtful nor difficult to be
applied.[9]

When the idea of birth control had become familiar in the 1820s, Malthus's
and Mill's comments were regarded as verdicts on contraception, but this may
not have been the original intention of the writers. Malthus may have been
criticising Owen's support for other ideas, such as those discussed by Godwin.
Mill's reference to 'the superstitions of the nursery' does not suggest that he
had contraception in mind, but what he meant is far from clear − indeed, he
seems far more open to the accusation of having 'miserably evaded' the issue
than Malthus.

Although it is clear that there was a time when Owen accepted
Malthusianism, and a time when he advocated birth control, this does not
necessarily mean that he advocated neo-Malthusianism (the late nineteenth-
century term for the theory that birth control provided the solution to the
Malthusian dilemma). Place stated that Owen was a secret advocate of free
love,[10] and this may have been why he acceded to the request of his friend
(almost certainly Place himself) to find out how the peasants in the south of
France restricted the size of their families. This would explain the apparent
contradiction of Owen searching out the solution to Malthusianism after he
had repudiated it, and it would not be surprising if Place wrongly conflated
the two. Owen does not appear to have taken any interest in birth control after
1818.[11]

A probable history of the introduction of birth control to Britain can thus
be outlined. Rumours of a technique used in France to prevent unwanted
births were circulating by 1818, and when Place heard them he tried to find
out details. Shortly before visiting France in the summer of 1818, Robert
Owen was planning to stay with Place in London, and such a stay would have
provided an ideal opportunity to persuade Owen to seek out the
information.[12] Owen brought back several pieces of sponge from France, two
of which he gave to Place, who then started to advocate birth control in
private conversation among the Utilitarians. Supported by James Mill, Place
got a number of converts, but none was willing to incur the opprobrium which
would inevitably follow a public avowal.

*   *   *

It may be no coincidence that Place sought information about birth control
shortly after the publication of Ricardo's *Principles of Political Economy* in
1817. Place wrote in 1833 that his attention had been called to the *Essay on
Population* soon after the publication of the first edition in 1798, 'and I have
ever since been a careful observer of and a diligent enquirer into the habits and

circumstances of the working people, and especially in regard to the consequences of population amongst them'. In October 1814, he demanded of James Mill: 'when will the wholesome truth be acknowledged, that population is constantly pressing against the limits of production?' But he was still ready to take a sympathetic interest in the ideas of Robert Owen, and he remained attached to traditional radical economic doctrines. When he wrote an advertising bill to launch *Hone's Reformists' Register* in January 1817, he declared that Ministers 'have reduced the mass of the nation to a state of poverty – of dependence – of starvation, . . . who, but for their conduct, would have been living as became men – independent-minded men – on their own *earnings*'. Place himself pointed out the significance of the passage thirteen years later, saying that James Mill and Bentham then approved it, but now believed, like himself, that the condition of the working people was due almost wholly to their numbers increasing too rapidly.13

In September 1817 Place told Ricardo:

> I have been studying your incomparable book which must I think become *the Book*. Mill risked nothing when he said he was ready to defend it against all the world, this might be done by one who was not possessed of half his knowledge and talents. I have pushed the reasonings to the utmost to discover erroneous conclusions, but have arrived at none. I have analysed whatever appeared ambiguous or was in opposition to my prejudices but have found nothing to condemn as an ambiguity.
> The most curious part of the enquiry was perhaps that in reasoning on those parts which were most in opposition to my notions, I constantly found I was reasoning in a circle, and I always came at last to the very point where I had started, being compelled to adopt your conclusions to make the same inferences.

His reading of Ricardo drove him, very reluctantly, to conclude that in the long run wages were controlled solely by the supply and demand for labour. This meant that such measures as a reduction of taxes would only benefit the people temporarily, because the higher standard of living would produce a growing population, and thus a growing supply of labour, until competition drove wages back to subsistence level. This made a solution to the Malthusian dilemma appear far more urgent – indeed, a precondition of social and political reforms producing an improvement in the condition of the people in the long run. In the 1810s Malthusianism had come under increasing attack because of the comfort it gave to supporters of entrenched privilege, who no longer had to rely on outdated concepts of natural hierarchy, but could instead make use of the rational argument that poverty was due to 'the reckless over-breeding of the poor' – unequal distribution of property, corruption and excessive taxation were not to blame. This implication was to prove the decisive obstacle to the Benthamites' efforts to convert the working classes to Malthusianism. In 1843 the Huddersfield Chartist, Lawrence Pitkethly, told Place: 'My mind revolts from a calm reflection of a subject out of which has arisen the infernal new poor law.'14 Place's commitment to forming his views by reasoning did not allow him to reject Malthusianism because it led to conclusions which he disliked, and he never hesitated to point out the implication that the salvation of the poor lay in their own hands. This view was utterly unacceptable to working-class radicals, who refused to examine a theory which denied that poverty was caused by economic inequality and 'blamed the victim'.

Place's acceptance of Ricardo's doctrine made the inadequacy of Malthus's solution to the dilemma appear far more important. In January 1818 George Ensor told him that he had written a book refuting Malthus. Place replied:

> I do not know exactly what you mean, . . . his propositions assumed at random may be easily refuted, they were assumed for the purpose of illustration, and are necessarily incorrect, much too of his reasoning may be refuted, but I do not expect to see what I call the principle disproved – namely that in all old settled countries, the population presses against starvation, and is kept from increasing with the rapidity, which but for the want of produce it would increase. . . . No doubt a somewhat better mode of producing, accumulating and enjoying might be devised, but the time when this will be understood and acted upon is I fear very distant. . . . It is not of much consequence whether England contains 12 or 15 million of bipeds, . . . but of much importance it is that they should be well instructed, and well governed, and made comfortable, but these desirable purposes can only be accomplished by restraining their increase, but between you and I, this restraining from moral causes is at a great distance, the Messrs Vice and Misery, of Malthus is the only firm that can keep them down at all, . . . and thus we come round again to the point we set out from moral restraint, which has served so well in the instance of you & I – and Mill, and Wakefield – mustering among us no less I believe than 36 children . . . rare fellows we to teach moral restraint.[15]

One primary motive for Place in advocating contraception was that preaching moral restraint would have meant urging others to do what he doubted whether he could have done himself. He almost certainly took up birth control later in the year when Owen returned from France with samples of the contraceptive sponge, and for the next three years he advocated it in private.

Meanwhile Godwin had turned against Malthusianism, and he launched a bitter attack on it in his *Of Population*. His arguments were not impressive, and when his book was published in November 1820 the initial reaction of the Malthusians was to ignore it. But they soon found that this was a mistake. Probably due to Godwin's reputation, his book was welcomed by critics of Malthus as a decisive reply, and by the end of January 1821 Place had decided to write an answer to it. His decision to include references to 'physical checks' in the *Illustrations and Proofs of the Principle of Population* was taken, he said, 'with the concurrence of friends who were themselves afraid to encounter the certain obloquy of such allusions'.[16] He had completed it by April, but after this he seems to have abandoned the idea of publication until August.

He then showed the manuscript to Mill, who told Ricardo unenthusiastically: 'There is in it pertinent matter, sufficient to establish the conclusions though not always displayed to the best advantage.' Place then sent the manuscript to Ricardo, in the hope of a recommendation to a publisher. He reacted more enthusiastically, especially to Place's proof that the population of the United States doubled every 25 years, even if the effect of immigration was excluded. It is remarkable that Place succeeded in doing this although at this time he did not understand the difference between geometric and arithmetic progressions – the error was corrected before publication, and in later years Place would often show the power of population to multiply by tracing the effects of a doubling of population every 25 years from a date in the Middle Ages. Ricardo also welcomed Place's defence of the working people against aristocratic slander, although he complained that Place had exaggerated the slander and unjustly accused Malthus of sanctioning it. Ricardo told Malthus : 'Nothing that I have ever seen from Place's pen ever appeared to me to have half the merits of this Reply – he meets Godwin on all his grounds and everywhere triumphantly answers him.' To Mill he wrote, 'I am much more impressed than ever I was before with an idea of his talents, – he has shewn more of patient investigation in this work than I ever knew him to shew before.'[17] This is perhaps the only case of anyone calling Place's industry into question, and it comes as a shock to anyone who has grappled with the vast mine of the Place papers, although one reason for the size of the mine is that he was much better at embarking on literary projects than completing them.

Malthus, Mill and Ricardo were anxious that Place's work should be published, but in spite of Ricardo's recommendation Place had difficulty in finding a publisher. *Illustrations and Proofs of the Principle of Population* was finally issued in February 1822, too late for success. Critical reviews of Godwin's book in the *Quarterly* and *Edinburgh Reviews* (the latter by Malthus) and the passage of time had already destroyed its reputation. Place thoroughly refuted Godwin, but a refutation of a discredited work was superfluous, and the only sections of the book which were interesting were those in which he gave his own views. Out of 500 copies printed only 227 were sold, and almost all the rest were returned to Place to give away.[18]

In *Illustrations and Proofs* Place advocated birth control in unambiguous terms, but he did not explain contraceptive methods. He denied that his recommendation would increase promiscuity, arguing that the most effectual mode of diminishing indiscriminate intercourse was marriage, and if 'precautionary means' were adopted, then the supply of labour would be kept below demand, wages would rise and all could marry; poor rates would soon be reduced and might even be abolished, while prostitution would be much reduced and rendered 'less pernicious, even to those females, the most degraded and unfortunate of all human beings'. He saw much cause for hope that moral restraint would increase and physical means of prevention would be adopted.[19] At this stage he was still adopting an intermediate position, laying the main stress on contraception but ready to advocate delayed marriage as well, before moving to the view that moral restraint was actually undesirable.

Illustrations and Proofs also gave Place the chance to make his differences with Malthus clear. He had already complained of Malthus's 'calumny against the working man' in notes he made on the *Essay on Population* in 1819, reacting with savage fury to

> a blundering argument about convincing a starving man to consider his starvation in the light of a fit of sickness which he was obliged to endure, and *if* he had any coarse food given him by the *higher* orders to receive it not of Right but as a favour, very thankfully.
>
> This the author thinks would be his own feeling. Now I who have been a poor man and have seen some starvation, know that I could never have reasoned thus, had my starvation proceeded a little further I should and that too without reference to any consideration of the Poor Laws have helped myself to food. And if no other means of obtaining it short of knocking out the brains of the Author existed I should not have hesitated on the question about which of us should live . . .
>
> The Higher Orders may please themselves with the doctrine here laid down by the author they may persuade themselves that the poor will in time be convinced of their justice, and they may punish those in their power meanwhile for not believing, but the ill used starved people will never act upon them, I hope they never will, why should not the deaths be reciprocal why not the poor man who is idle from necessity, if he must die, take an idle rich one along with him?[20]

In *Illustrations and Proofs* he repeated this criticism in more moderate terms, complaining that such passages 'impeded the progress of information, respecting the principle of population among the people'. Malthus castigated the working man for

> 'idleness and improvidence'. Idle he is not, improvident he generally is, to some extent, and it can hardly be otherwise. He must spend an odd sixpence or a shilling now and then, although he had certainly better save it. But as to idleness – all the work is done that is desired to be done; and there he stands, ready and willing to be engaged to do the hardest, the most disgusting, and the most destructive kind of work.
>
> He is not, however, dissolute. Some men are idle, some are dissolute, but the number of these among the working people in this country is very small; and it is quite time that those who wish to see the people wise, virtuous, and happy, should acquire correct notions on this important subject, and cease to calumniate and libel the working man. Such men as Mr Malthus, have not had the opportunity of judging correctly of the working people. . . . He can know but little of the shifts continually made to preserve a decent appearance. Of the privations endured, of the pains and sorrows which the working people suffer in private, of the truly wonderful efforts long continued, even in the most hopeless circumstances, which vast numbers of them make 'to keep their heads above water'.

He argued that the working people were no more dissolute than other classes proportionally, but the dissolute working people were continually open to observation and the character of the whole class judged by them, whereas the virtuous ones were seldom seen.

> I at least may make some pretensions to better information. A hired workman myself for several years, enjoying the confidence of large bodies of workmen, an active promoter and conductor of trade-societies during those years, and an encourager of them to the present hour, I have had opportunities of *seeing* and *feeling,* and knowing most intimately, the characters and habits, the virtues and vices, the pleasures and pains, the joys and sorrows, of large masses of the population.

He was convinced that there had been a great improvement in the morals and health of the working people during his lifetime. Godwin's new pessimism in foreseeing a decline in population

> had totally eradicated his old hypothesis of the perpetual tendency of mankind towards perfection.
> I however shall not give up this doctrine quite so easily. It was Mr Godwin who first led me to the contemplation of the progress of human intellect in its march towards happiness, and I am neither to be made to doubt of the improved state of mankind, at the present moment, compared with former periods, nor of the still higher state at which they will arrive.[21]

In the summer of 1823 Place embarked on his campaign to spread birth control information by circulating leaflets of practical instruction anonymously. Their authorship is not certainly known, but probably Place followed his usual practice of making a first draft, and then showing it to a number of people who would suggest amendments. Clergymen who had testified to a parliamentary committee about the rise in pauperism in their parishes received packages of handbills headed 'To the Married of Both Sexes', which contained instructions concerning the use of the sponge together with a brief justification of contraception on economic and medical grounds.[22] He told one clergyman that there appeared to have been a great increase of people in his parish in the last twenty years, and all added to the number of paupers:

> A truly lamentable circumstance. If you will have the goodness to examine into the causes, and to think of the consequences of this terrible state of society, you will not fail to discover that no Legislative enactment can cure or even mitigate the evil, but that on the contrary, all such enactments must as they have hitherto done, continually increase it, – that every Legislative and *Parochial* interference must inevitably still further degrade the people, that the more they are degraded, the less provident they will become, and that as their provident care diminishes so their numbers will increase, until wretchedness and crime, ignorance and brutality shall make England a place not fit to live in. In order to do my part towards preventing such tremendous evils, – towards restoring a more prosperous and happier state of

1. Francis Place. Photogravure by Walker and Boutall from a portrait by
   G. P. Healy in 1843 (from *The Life of Francis Place 1771-1854*,
   Graham Wallas, 1898).

2. Twelfth-Day (from *Hone's Every Day Book*, 1825, vol. 1, p. 24).

N°14   Dunstable — 6 o clock — P.M   235
              Friday Sept. 24. 1813

There, accuse me again if you dare — say I do not pay
the little attentions so dear to women — you did not expect
a letter — but you see how true it is —— that —
———— "thou art present,"
"wheresoe're I go." ———— we breakfasted and at a
quarter past 7 AM set out on our travels — before we were
well clear of Camden Town it began to rain and so it
continued to do until we had passed Golders Green —
it was so slight however that we were very little incom-
-moded — it cleared up and before we reached the
        road
Edgware ˄ near the 7 mile stone it was very fine
we had many fine views but after we had passed

3. Place to Mrs Place, 24 August 1811 (Add. Mss. 35,143, f. 201v).

4. Westminster Hustings, 1818, by I. R. Cruikshank (from *The Poll Book, for . . . Westminster*, 1818).

The Rump Chronicle.

No. 3.   COVENT GARDEN, MONDAY.   [MARCH 1.

In the Press, and speedily will be published,

A TREATISE on HOBBY-HORSES; with a Chapter on HOBBY-ASSES. Illustrated with a View of the Hustings at Covent-garden.

"But oh! but oh! the hobby-horse is forgot."

SHAKESPEARE.

WE are authorised by honest TOM CLARKE, of St. George's, to state, that though he did appear on the hustings with Mr. Hobhouse, he is not the Mr. Clarke who was sent to Mr. Lamb's Committee-Room as a spy.

THEATRE, COVENT GARDEN.

THIS EVENING will be presented the Play of the CON-STANT COUPLE, and the Farce of HOB in the WELL.

Actors as usual.

DINNER EXTRAORDINARY, CHARING CROSS.

Yesterday, Mr. Place entertained Sir Sly-go Bribett, Mr. Hob-goblin, Mr. Brookes, Mr. Clarke, and a numerous party of fashionables. The dinner was sumptuous, and the gin and beer excellent—we observed a large dish of cabbage near the host, and Mr. H. who seemed out of spirits, contrived, however, to make a hearty meal of his *own-words*. After the cloth was removed, the Chairman rose to propose a toast. It is unnecessary for me (said he) to enlarge on Mr. H.'s merits, as he has already done that *for himself* so often and at such great length on the hustings. I shall therefore simply propose the health of "The man who dares talk treason bareheaded in the worst of weather."

SONG.—Tantararara.

Mr. H. rose with evident affectation. He said the kind allusion made to him, and his sufferings on the hustings,

was deeply engraven on his heart.—True it was, the weather was against him; and his worthy friends, he feared, were very cold, but he begged to state that he did not quite despair. He had seen an advertisement that day from a new Candidate (cries of name, name). He would name him—it was Mr. John Ketch. That gentleman said, that he was a more radical reformer than he (Mr. H.) was. That was strange, for he thought no man could go further than himself; however, he begged to assure them, that there was no length which he could not now go to get in for Westminster, if they wished it; nay, he would even go to the devil, if they ordered him (shouts of bravo!) He held in his hand a most extraordinary placard of his opponent's committee. It was like all the rest of their assertions; he would not use harsh and ungentlemanlike expressions, but he must say, it was a d—d lie. This infamous placard stated, that he (Mr. H.) had had thoughts, during the late snow storm, of addressing them in a Welch wig—(groans)—He rose to repel that insinuation; nothing was ever further from his thoughts, for so much did he detest wigs, that he would stand (here Mr. H. looked at his notes for a quotation) "bareheaded, exposed to the pelting pitiless storm—poor Tom's a cold"—than trust his ears beneath a thing of so unconstitutional an appellation—(much applause). Mr. H. concluded an eloquent speech by declaring his horror at being called a toadstool by the Lying Chronicle.

The Chairman then gave " St. Giles's Pride, and Petty France's Glory—Sir Sly-go Bribett."

SONG.

" I wonder we havn't better company upon Tyburn tree."

Sir SLY-GO said, he felt it an honour that his name was now universally associated with St. Giles's. He hated

---

5. *Rump Chronicle*, no. 3, Whig mock newspaper issued during the Westminster Election, 1819 (Add. Mss. 27,841, pt. 3, f. 593).

PATRIOT
BURDETT's
AT OUR HEAD.

Tune—"*Scots who ha' wi' Wallace bled.*"

ELECTORS, by fair freedom led,
Electors, who no tyrants dread,
Patriot BURDETT's at our head,
      HOBHOUSE AND LIBERTY!

We will to all England show,
The sacred Rights of Man we know,
Our hearts with fervent ardour glow,
      We live but to be free!

See, by Whigs and Tories led,
LAMB presumptuous lifts his head,
There he stands—in Maxwell's stead!
      To crush our Liberty!

Silly LAMB!—for Freedom bright,
In our City deigns to light,
Though Corruption strives to blight'
      Our efforts to be free!

By our great and glorious cause,
By our late suspended laws,
By the Votes which Freedom draws,
      Still we shall be free!

Now the hypocrites we know,
The Whigs their Coalition show,
LAMB—HUNT—CASTLEREAGH and Co!
      Assail our liberty!

Pull away for
HOBHOUSE!

Tune——"*Hearts of Oak.*"

COME cheer up Electors, 'tis Liberty's call,
To vote for brave HOBHOUSE, your Country,
  and all;
'Tis for Freedom you struggle, for Freemen's
  great name;
For honour—for HOBHOUSE—for Westminster's Fame.

CHORUS.

Then for Hobhouse come vote, he's the man of
  your choice,
     And resolv'd, firmly stand,
     Now join hand in hand,
And shew you're not gull'd by a LAMB's silly voice

That red-headed wolf in sheeps clothing, believe
By delusion and art will still try to deceive,
He's a humbug Reformer, he's a Tory Whig bred,
And his promise is empty just like to his head.

   Chorus—Then bring up your votes for the
      Man of your Choice, &c.

Cheer up bold Electors, for HOBHOUSE make
  way,
He'll be true to your cause, and repel tyrant's
  sway;
He'll drag from their holes, and expose to your
  view,
The wretches who rob both the Country and you.

   Chorus—Then bring up your votes for the
      Man of your Choice, &c.

6. Election songs for Hobhouse, 1819 (Add. Mss. 27,841, pt. 3, f. 492v).

Give not thy strength unto women, nor thy ways to that which destroyeth kings.

Solomon.

7. Caricature of George IV by George Cruikshank (from *The Queen's Matrimonial Ladder*, by William Hone, 1820).

Gatcomb Park, Minchinhampton
9 [...] 1821

Dear Sir

I have gone through the whole of your M.S
with the greatest attention, and have great pleasure in saying
that in my humble judgment it is a complete and satisfactory
answer to all Mr. Godwins objections to the theory of Population
as explained by Mr. Malthus. I have no doubt but that
its publication will bring you great credit & fame, and
will be deemed a proof of your being possessed of a good
stock of industry and talents. I hope you will be able
to make such arrangements as that it may speedily
appear in print. To take off a little of the value of
my praise I must candidly confess that I am not very
familiar with calculations concerning births, marriages
& deaths, and therefore am entitled to be considered only in
the light of an ordinary reader, paying great attention
to the subject before him.

In looking over the paper of my notes, made during
the time I was reading your M.S, I observe that there

8. Ricardo to Place, 9 September 1821 (Seligman Collection,
Columbia University).

THE MARRIED OF BOTH SEXES.

IN the present state of society, a great number of persons are compelled to make an appearance, and to live in a stile, which consumes all their incomes, leaving nothing, or next to nothing, as a provision for their children. To such persons a great number of children, is a never fading source of discomfort and apprehension; of a state of bodily, mental, and pecuniary vexation and suffering, from which there is no escape. This state of things pervades, to a very great extent, that respectable class of society called genteel. To those whose incomes depend on some particular exertion, which cannot be remitted, these distressing circumstances are from various causes, greatly increased. To those who constitute the great mass of the community, whose daily bread is alone procured by daily labour, a large family is almost always the cause of ruin, both of parents and children; reducing the parents to cheerless, hopeless and irremediable poverty; depriving the children of those physical, moral, and mental helps which are necessary to enable them to live in comfort, and turning them out at an early age to prey upon the world, or to become the world's prey.

For these general reasons, cognizable by every body, it is of the greatest possible importance that married people should be informed of the methods used to prevent such tremendous evils.

If methods can be pointed out by which all the enjoyments of wedded life may be partaken of without the apprehension of TOO LARGE a family, and all its bitter consequences, he surely who points them out, must be a benefactor of mankind. Such at any rate are the motives which govern the writer of this address.

The means of prevention are simple, harmless, and might, but for false delicacy, have been communicated generally. They have long been practised in several parts of the Continent, and experience has proved, that the greatest possible benefits have resulted; the people in those parts, being in all respects better off, better instructed, more cheerful, and more independent, than those in other parts, where the practices have not prevailed to a sufficient extent.

The methods are two, of which the one to be first mentioned seems most likely to succeed in this country. It has been successfully resorted to by some of our most eminent physicians, and is confidently recommended by first rate Accoucheurs, in cases where pregnancy has been found injurious to the health of delicate women. It consists in a piece of sponge, about an inch square, being placed in the vagina previous to coition, and afterwards withdrawn by means of a double twisted thread, or bobbin, attached to it. No injurious consequences can in any way result from its use, neither does it diminish the enjoyment of either party. The sponge should, as a matter of preference, be used rather damp, and when convenient a little warm. It is almost superfluous to add, that there may be more pieces than one, and that they should be washed after being used.

The other method resorted to, when from carelessness or other causes the sponge is not at hand, is for the husband to withdraw, previous to emission, so that none of the semen may enter the vagina of his wife. But a little practice and care in the use of the sponge will render all other precautions unnecessary.

THE MARRIED OF BOTH SEXES.

IN
Genteel Life.

AMONG the many sufferings of married women, as mothers, there are two cases which command the utmost sympathy and commiseration.

The first arises from constitutional peculiarities, or weaknesses.

The second from mal-conformation of the bones of the Pelvis.

Besides these two cases, there is a third case applicable to both sexes: namely, the consequences of having more children than the income of the parents enables them to maintain and educate in a desirable manner.

The first named case produces miscarriages, and brings on a state of existence scarcely endurable. It has caused thousands of respectable women to linger on in pain and apprehension, till at length, death has put an end to their almost inconceivable sufferings.

The second case is always attended with immediate risk of life. Pregnancy never terminates without intense suffering, seldom without the death of the child, frequently with the death of the mother, and sometimes with the death of both mother and child.

The third case is by far the most common, and the most open to general observation. In the middle ranks, the most virtuous and praiseworthy efforts are perpetually made to keep up the respectability of the family; but a continual increase of children gradually yet certainly renders every effort to prevent degradation unavailing, it paralizes by rendering hopeless all exertion, and the family sinks into poverty and despair. Thus is engendered and perpetuated a hideous mass of misery.

The knowledge of what awaits them deters vast numbers of young men from marrying and causes them to spend the best portion of their lives in a state of debauchery, utterly incompatible with the honourable and honest feelings which should be the characteristic of young men. The treachery, duplicity, and hypocrisy, they use towards their friends and the unfortunate victims of their seductions, while they devote a large number of females to the most dreadful of all states which human beings can endure, extinguishes in them to a very great extent, all manly, upright notions; and qualifies them to as great an extent, for the commission of acts which but for these vile practices they would abhor, and thus to an enormous extent is the whole community injured.

Marriage in early life, is the only truly happy state, and if the evil consequences of too large a family did not deter them, all men would marry while young, and thus would many lamentable evils be removed from society.

A simple, effectual, and safe means of accomplishing these desirable results has long been known, and to a considerable extent practised in some places. But until lately has been but little known in this country. Accoucheurs of the first respectability and surgeons of great eminence have in some peculiar cases recommended it. Within the last two years, a more extensive knowledge of the process has prevailed and its practice has been more extensively adopted. It is now made public for the benefit of every body. A piece of soft sponge about the size of a small ball attached to a very narrow ribbon, and is slightly moistened (when convenient) is introduced previous to sexual intercourse, and is afterwards withdrawn, and thus by an easy, simple, cleanly and not indelicate method, no ways injurious to health, not only may much unhappiness and many miseries be prevented, but benefits to an incalculable amount be conferred on society.

9. 'To the Married of Both Sexes' (Place Coll., Set 61, part 2 of 1 vol., p. 43).

society, I have caused to be printed and have forwarded to you some bills, which however much they may revolt you on a first perusal, will I am sure on a serious consideration, be approved, and I hope be the means also of preventing much evil.[23]

If the case were really as bad as that, it is hard to see how man could ever have escaped from barbarism. Place was quite capable of stating his case rationally and moderately, but too often he undermined it by overstatement.

What the clergymen did with the leaflets Place cannot have known, but a letter and package of leaflets sent to Mrs Fildes, famous for her courage during the Peterloo Massacre, produced dramatic results. The letter was opened at her father-in-law's, and suspicion that she had agreed to distribute the leaflets led her to protest vigorously in order to show her innocence. When a complaint to the Attorney General produced no result, she wrote to Thomas Wooler of the *Black Dwarf,* who published the text of the leaflet with a condemnatory comment. Place must have been delighted at seeing practical instructions for birth control thus published. The controversy led to Wooler being sent the story about Owen importing the sponge from France, which Place had previously sent anonymously to another journal. The story was published in the *Black Dwarf,* and Place presumably then told his friend Wooler that he was the author. He persuaded Wooler to publish an anonymous essay in favour of birth control with an introduction by Place himself, and from October 1823 to January 1824 anonymous articles by John Stuart Mill and others defending contraception on Malthusian grounds alternated weekly with articles by Wooler attacking it.[24]

John Stuart Mill was closely involved in the campaign, even though he was only seventeen years old. At about this time he was arrested for throwing leaflets down in the areas of houses for servant girls to pick up. He was released without being charged, but efforts to hush the matter up were not entirely successful, and the humorous poet Tom Moore satirised the incident in *The Times*:

> There are two Mr M——'s, too, whom those that like reading
> Through all that's unreadable, call very clever; –
> And, whereas M—— Senior makes war on *good* breeding,
> M—— Junior makes war on all *breeding* whatever!

The experience had a profound influence on John Stuart Mill. For the rest of his life he continued to believe in the necessity of birth control, but he always repudiated it in public. After his death the incident was revived in an attempt to sabotage a proposed memorial to him in Westminster Abbey, and Gladstone withdrew his support as a result.

Not surprisingly, almost all the leading Utilitarians concealed their opinions on the subject. The cases of John Stuart Mill and Bentham are well known, that of Ricardo less so; writing to Place he approved of the passage which defended birth control in the *Illustrations and Proofs,* observing: 'You acknowledge, that to delay marriage, and to prevent too many being born, are the only efficient remedies for the evils which the poor suffer.' Writing to Malthus his tone was different: 'Place speaks of one of Owens preventives to an excessive population − he does not dwell upon it, but I have a little doubt whether it is right even to mention it.'[25]

It is unclear whether any large-scale propaganda got off the ground in London, but the scandal over Mill made this aspect of the compaign well known, and opponents claimed that tens of thousands of bills had been distributed, especially among the Spitalfields weavers.[26] Place's successful campaign against the Combination Laws brought him into contact with trade union leaders from all over the country, and he seized every opportunity to put forward his views. By the spring of 1824 his hopes of success were rising, and on 1 May he wrote triumphantly to Sir Francis Burdett that contraception 'will I have reason to believe be as speedily as extensively adopted. Should the physical check become general or even partial over even a fourth part of the population, all our wishes for the comfort and happiness, morally and politically of the people will be in a fair way to be accomplished.' But the circulation of propaganda was still extremely limited; in August William Longson, a leading Manchester cotton weaver, told Place that he doubted whether it was worth getting a letter on population printed, as he did not think he could get forty copies distributed. Soon afterwards, Place sent William Ellis an essay by Longson arguing that birth control was compatible with Christianity. Ellis was one of the group of young Utilitarians around John Stuart Mill, and Place urged Ellis to get the aid of Mill and another of the group, George Grote, to finance Longson setting up in business. In the event they helped him to set up a trade union among the cotton weavers around Manchester, with the aim of enabling him to spread birth control literature more widely.[27]

In 1825 the early birth-control campaign reached its peak. At this time the Government was seeking a partial reversal of the repeal of the Combination Laws in order to bring trade unions under tight control, and once again Place organised the campaign of resistance. For a time he acquired great influence over some northern and Scottish unionists, who distributed his contraception handbills in their own area. In March 1825 Martin Blackett, a Stockport trade unionist, asked him for 'a few of those bills on the method of Checking P——n', and the following month he wrote to say that some friends of his had resolved to reprint them for a more extensive circulation. At the same time Thomas Foster of the Manchester cotton spinners was telling Place: 'I have cautiously mentioned the population system, & find it received as it always has been by those to whom it is first communicated.' But two weeks later Foster and his ally David McWilliams promised to make 'a judicious use' of a small parcel of bills. In August John Tester, leader of the great Bradford woolcombers' strike, asked Place whether it was true that 'The paper upon anti-conception . . . emanated from Mr Mill, *Mr Place* &c, who in a political point of view consider it a matter of first rate importance. This sentence was in a letter received by a particular friend of mine from a person who has suffered much through daring to write and speak what he thinks.' By February 1826 he was a convert, writing to Place: 'Many thanks to you for the tale of Sadi &c – they are much better than the tales of the magi. Those which Farrar brought me, I have given away, inclosing in each a copy of "Advice to the Married &c".' Carlile said that thousands of the handbills had been circulated throughout the populous districts of the north.[28] In order to disseminate the arguments in favour of smaller families, Place made a summary of a lecture by the Scottish economist, M'Culloch, which defended high wages and argued that wages were controlled by the supply and demand for labour. Thousands were sold in various towns, including South Shields, Bradford, Aberdeen, Glasgow and Manchester.[29]

Place was still optimistic in January 1826, telling the working people in the *Trades' Newspaper* that the time was not far distant when they would no longer be misled into thinking that Malthus was their enemy. But his supporters faced great difficulties. In the same month a Keithley trade unionist told Place that advocating the population restriction plan in his town, where anyone known to question the existence of a divine providence was shunned like a pestilence, would be a dangerous and arduous task, though these things would not daunt the sincere friend of the human race. In April Peter M'Dougall of Glasgow told Place:

> The last parcel of tracts which I rec'd has astonished a great number of persons here the doctrine being so repugnant to the principles of our Scotch enthusiasts. Their arguments (in their own opinion) are infallible that God never permitted a Child to come into the world unless there were a sufficiency to maintain it. And with regard to the Address to the Married of both Sexes which I rec'd from you while in London great numbers who heard of it came and solicited a reading and their general opinion was that were it practical it would have the greatest tendency to produce immorality and they always inferred that it was contrary to the law of nature & of God.[30]

* * *

At the same time as the movement was growing, a backlash was gaining strength. This was partly Place's own fault. When he befriended Richard Carlile he set out to educate him in political economy and philosophy. He sent him a copy of *Illustrations and Proofs,* but at first Carlile rejected birth control, partly because he feared that it would undermine sexual morality. Place denied this on the basis of his own investigation into the behaviour of different classes: chastity was not preserved among the poorest, and among the higher classes it was preserved mainly from moral considerations, but delayed marriage encouraged men to indulge in seduction and debauchery.

I am for early marriages, but I am for rendering them provident, improvidence is folly as well in marriage as in everything else, and early marriages must in the present state of things be generally improvident, and that they should be so is a most lamentable circumstance, not to be able to marry is perhaps the greatest of all physical evils, or at least it is the most extensive.

Place appears to have been the first to have rejected delayed marriage in favour of an exclusive reliance on birth control, and so the originality of his views has been underestimated.

He also expressed his conviction that birth control would especially benefit women:

there are some first rate women as to intellect, married excellent delightful women as free from all sorts of superstition as mortal can be, and as well informed, as learned in all things as they can well be, who do not have more than two children, who have no fear of those two or either of them dying, and will therefore have no more. . . . Now only think of the breeding and the feeding children, as it regards the woman, and the loss and cost and the pain of losing them, and see what a mass of misery would be prevented by my proposal, and add to this the pleasure of seeing the number of children a woman might choose to have, healthy . . .

Speaking of those excellent women, to whom I have alluded, I will add that I know of no intercourse so truly exhilarating and charming as their company, and among such women unchaste thoughts have no place. I know no man of understanding who does not enjoy their company, most exquisitely, and most *holyly* if I may use the word.[31]

Elizabeth Place bore the last of her fifteen children in 1817, shortly before her 43rd birthday, and eighteen months before her husband learnt about the contraceptive sponge.

Carlile helped Place to distribute his handbills and allowed him to use his shop as a publishing 'drop', and by August 1824 he was coming to accept the Malthusian case. Place then broached the subject of free love: 'One thing may be worth your consideration, in a better state of society would it be desirable that the sexes should regard each other as brothers and sisters, on the contrary would it not be desirable that the sexual intercourse should be free. I think it would. But at any rate the better instructed and better provided for people as they would then be would decide that matter for themselves.'[32] This was an opinion which Place was very careful to keep secret, because he was aware that a connection between birth control and advocacy of sexual freedom would kill any chance of popular acceptance of contraception. He therefore insisted in his propaganda that birth control would reduce sexual licence by making it practicable for all to marry early, before they had become corrupted. He apparently saw free love as he saw Spencean socialism, something which would be dangerous in his own time but which he looked forward to in the future.

With these views, Place made a very serious mistake when he broached the subject of free love with Richard Carlile, who was not the man to keep any opinion to himself, however unpopular. Carlile was soon converted, and he saw it as a message valid not only for the future but for the present. Indeed it was the potential of birth control as a challenge to Christianity — putting procreation under the control of man rather than leaving it to God — and as a means to sexual liberation, which caught his imagination. In May 1825, in spite of Place's frantic efforts to dissuade him, he devoted an issue of his journal, the *Republican,* to an essay entitled 'What is Love?' Although he argued the Malthusian case and said that he was the last of a multitude of converts to it, he advocated birth control primarily as a means to free love without the danger of children. The essay was soon revised as a pamphlet called *Every Woman's Book, or What is Love?* This was several times reprinted, and Carlile claimed that 10,000 had been sold by April 1828, but potential converts on economic grounds were bound to have found their worst fears confirmed. Carlile's approving reference to a duchess who always carried a sponge with her to parties was calculated to associate the practice with upper-class licentiousness in the eyes of working people. Cobbett attacked the pamphlet fiercely, increasing its circulation, but inducing his followers to condemn it and helping to ensure that birth control and promiscuity became firmly linked in popular opinion. Carlile's shopmen were far more tactful in their support for birth control. In 1825–26 Place often visited them in Newgate prison, and William Campion and Richard Hassell put the social and economic case for contraception in the shopmen's *Newgate Monthly Magazine.* Place said of Hassell: 'He is a sedate, moral, excellent and very extraordinary young man and will probably rise to some eminence.' Unfortunately, he died in November 1826 at the age of twenty-six.[33]

A letter from William Smith of the *Bolton Chronicle* in March 1826 shows that Place was prepared to circulate Carlile's pamphlet. Smith thanked him for a parcel of them, and said that he had 'engaged a person (who travels through this county with *Sedition & Blasphemy*) to distribute them, I am happy to inform you that in the most poverty stricken districts, he has sold a large quantity of *"What is Love . . ."*.'[34] The reason for this change of tack may have been financial. Even before he lost two-thirds of his income in 1832, he could not have afforded to print handbills by the thousand, and his campaign of 1823–26 must have been financed by allies such as the younger Utilitarians. The circulation of handbills may have ceased because the hostility it aroused discouraged them from supporting it, but Place could hope to recover most of his expenses when he promoted the sale of a pamphlet.

He continued to take every opportunity in other ways to spread his message. His numerous articles and letters in newspapers were of greatly varying quality, ranging from plain and cogent argument to confused reasoning and simplistic exaggeration. Sometimes he would write as if the country was on the verge of ruin, but his considered view was that although on balance the standard of living was rising, an excessive supply of labour was holding down the wages of working people, and reducing certain groups, principally the agricultural labourers and cotton weavers, to starvation.[35] One unsolved puzzle about Place's campaign is why he was never prosecuted, and it is probable that Carlile's successful war against the blasphemy laws taught the Government that the only result would be to give publicity to the propaganda. But Place's role soon became notorious, and the *Dublin Evening Post,* demanding where M'Culloch stood, asked: 'Does he recommend physical means, like a certain philosophic Tailor in Westminster, who dispatched circulars that would disgust, we believe, the denizens of a brothel?' The editor of the *Trades' Newspaper,* Joseph Robertson, nursed a grudge over his defeat by Place in the LMI, and in August 1825 he called for public vengeance on advocates of birth control as 'the MUIRHEADS of the day' (a reference to a man convicted of an indecent assault on a youth).

In September Robertson referred to John Stuart Mill's arrest in the *Trades'*. After demanding to know whether Place was the author of a handbill, 'A Matrimonial Index to the Population Tables', a twopenny pamphlet, 'Marrying Made Harmless, a Dialogue between Frank and Sally, Two Servants out of Place', and 'To the Married of both Sexes', he went on:

> Was it the author of the *Illustrations and Proofs,* who employed certain young gentlemen (only think of employing *young* gentlemen on such a mission) to hand about at market time among the wives and daughters of mechanics and tradesmen, copies of one or other of the productions aforesaid, and which young gentlemen were, for their pains, dragged by an indignant crowd before a Magistrate, and held to bail, (though by some well understood manoeuvring, never brought to trial) for the misdemeanour?

Robertson described Place's system as 'prospectively murderous at least', and unnecessary because 'there can be no more mouths in the land, than Providence has, for some good purpose, sent there'.[36]

Robertson was involved in the even more vicious slander of Place in the *Bull Dog* in August and September 1826, written by William Haley, a former shopman of Carlile's. Haley had been imprisoned for selling blasphemous literature, but released early after recanting, and he was condemned by the shopmen's *Newgate Magazine* as a renegade, and by Carlile as 'little better than a thief'. Place ignored Haley's libels, and the *Bull Dog* died after four issues, but it is hardly surprising that few were prepared to incur the obloquy brought by an open advocacy of contraception. Place observed that no one would dare to declare openly in favour of birth control unless he had established a high moral character, in case he had atrocious propensities attributed to him. Even he feared the hostility of men like Robertson and Haley, and when Joseph Hume told Haley some years later that he had decided to refuse him assistance on Place's advice, Place complained to Hume about the use of his name, saying that 'you have unnecessarily irritated some of the most malignant of mankind'.[37]

*   *   *

The full extent of Place's campaign will never be known, since only fragmentary evidence survives. Supporters were naturally unwilling to put details on paper, and some of the evidence was almost certainly destroyed, since Place's papers were censored after his death.[38] In London there would have been little need for written communication, but it is, nevertheless, significant that all the claims of a large-scale circulation of handbills in the metropolis derive from opposition sources, whereas evidence from supporters relates almost exclusively to the north and Scotland. Carlile, in *Every Woman's Book,* only referred to circulation of the handbills in the north. It seems likely that the campaign started in the summer of 1823 in London with John Stuart Mill and his friends dropping bills in the areas of houses, and a limited circulation among the Spitalfields weavers. Mill's arrest in late 1823 or early 1824 probably killed the London effort, and then there seems to have been a lull until the campaign in the north got under way in mid-1824, reaching its peak in late 1825 and ending in early 1826.

By 1829 Place had lost his optimism of quick success, observing that only the people could do themselves permanent service, and they were not likely to use the means necessary. He nevertheless continued to seek converts to neo-Malthusianism for the rest of his life. In December 1831 the proprietor of the *Westminster Review,* Colonel Perronet Thompson, suspected the middle-class radicals, J.A. Roebuck and Erskine Perry, of wanting to use the journal to propagate what he called 'Place's nasty theory'.[39] In September 1832 William Ellis[40] helped Place to raise a subscription for the radical publisher, James Watson, to print the first English edition of the birth control tract *Moral Physiology* by Robert Dale Owen, a son of Robert Owen. Place thus launched Watson as the leading publisher of birth control works of the 1830s and 1840s.[41] Place often gave away copies of his own *Illustrations and Proofs,* and once *Moral Physiology* was published he at last had an unexceptionable book of practical instruction to send to potential converts.

Until the late 1820s Place rejected the orthodox Malthusian view that relief under the Poor Laws should be abolished, arguing that this would only reduce the people to the condition in Ireland, where there was no Poor Law and population increased even faster than in England: the only result of abolition would be to provoke the people to insurrection. He agreed that the poor law system had degraded the people: 'the question is how to destroy the mischievous system without further degradation − I have a sort of horror at any thing that tends that way − as likely to prevent for a very long period any amelioration, which I am sure can only arise from, a diminution of child getting, from conviction of its being the only remedy − and this cannot be taught to the people if they be more degraded, if once taught good bye for ever to the poor laws'.[42] The failure of his campaign led him to reconsider his views, and by 1827 he had become a supporter of the abolition of relief for the able-bodied. Although cruel, he concluded, it would prevent the destitute from breeding, and thus dragging down the mass of the working people to absolute poverty.[43] This was in accordance with his belief that opinions must be formed by reason, however unpleasant the conclusions, but it led him to forget what he had understood so well before, that if society allowed men to starve then it would pay for it in their violent rejection of the system, and any attempt to convince them of the justice of such a situation only hindered the acceptance of the case for birth control.

Thus after the introduction of the New Poor Law in 1834, which (in theory) abolished relief outside the workhouse for the able-bodied, the Malthusian reasons given to justify the hated system provided an additional reason for working people to reject neo-Malthusianism. In 1843 Lawrence Pitkethly, a leading Chartist who had a great respect for Place, told him that it was said that he was the concocter of the New Poor Law: 'if this is true, some fiend ten thousand times blacker than the King of hell has . . . mesmerised you'.[44] However, Place still had some successes. In 1837 he was delighted when speakers at Sunday conversations of the London Working Men's Association ably argued the case for Malthusianism, but the great majority of LWMA members were hostile to the theory. In 1840 he observed that he had converted many working men by reasoning with them, but that they were next to nothing compared with the mass.[45]

Place concluded that his campaign had been a failure. In 1841 he remarked that he knew 'a considerable number' who limited their families, but only two couples who were working people. Elsewhere he wrote that limitation

> is practised to a considerable extent among respectable people whose incomes are small, and to some extent up to those who have what may be called large incomes, these persons being unwilling that their children should be thrust down into a lower grade than that in which they have been brought up than which no desire can be more commendable, no practice more laudable.[46]

*   *   *

In 1843 Carlile wrote:

> From Francis Place . . . I have gleaned all the ideas that I have of political economy, and the all-surpassing physical or moral question of the regulation of the numbers of the people, by the means of providing them with the greatest possible amount of profitable employment and happiness. This question is the very first of social order, under the best form of government that can be devised. . . . It was he, not myself, who first gave me the epithet of *Atheist,* in my weekly publication, making it then a point of honour. I owe to him very much of my political direction. From Bentham, through Place, I was taught not to attempt the building of any system of my own, but to go on pulling down existing errors, every item of success in which is in fact so much good building.[47]

In the short run Place's conversion of Carlile to neo-Malthusianism proved unfortunate, but in the long run it ensured that advocacy of birth control became part of the political map. *Every Woman's Book* was soon published in the United States, and Robert Dale Owen was bitterly attacked for cautiously praising it. He wrote *Moral Physiology* in order to make his own views clear, and this was followed in 1832 by Charles Knowlton's birth control tract, *Fruits of Philosophy*. Both pamphlets were reprinted in Britain in the early 1830s, and they became the classic texts of the birth control movement for the next half-century in both countries. After 1830 the influence of Carlile on British freethought declined, and for the next thirty years it was primarily an offshoot of Owenism. Atheist printers such as James Watson kept *Moral Physiology* and *Fruits of Philosophy* in print, but most freethinkers preferred to avoid the subject.[48] Place's attempt to launch a national campaign of propaganda in favour of birth control had no successor until the trial of Bradlaugh and Besant in 1877.

It is now known that a rapid increase in population in sixteenth-century England was halted by a decline in the proportion of the population marrying, among other factors, in the seventeenth. Although Place recognised that the rate of marriage varied with the level of prosperity, he underestimated the practicability of Malthusian 'prudential restraint', partly because his personal observation was confined to the atypical circumstances of London, and partly because he was opposed to late marriage. Since he lived in an age when the population was growing faster than at any previous or subsequent period in English history, it was not unreasonable for him to conclude that the task of halting the rise was of overwhelming importance. He could not know that the unique conditions of the early nineteenth century for the first time allowed rapid population growth and a rise in the standard of living to take place at the same time, nor that the later nineteenth century would witness a decline in European birthrates just when the growth slowed down, even in areas where there had been no birth control propaganda. Whether the spread of birth control significantly influenced the size of the population in the late nineteenth century is uncertain, although it did produce a much earlier decline in the birthrate than a change in the pattern of marriage could have done. But birth control did greatly extend the area of freedom in daily life, and Place was *the* pioneer in its advocacy.[49]

10   The Decade of Achievement: the 1820s

Place's achievements in the 1820s were considerable. Apart from launching the birth control movement and playing an important role in the foundation of the London Mechanics' Institute, he brought about one major change in the law and several minor ones. The major one, the legalisation of trade unions, brought him a wide circle of friends and contacts among working-class leaders. His advice on tactics in disputes with employers and dealing with Parliament was eagerly sought, and for a short period he acquired great influence over some leading trade unionists, especially in the north-east. These successes were possible because the mid-1820s were the calm between the storms of George IV's attempt to divorce Queen Caroline and the Reform Bill agitation. Dissatisfaction among working people was at a relatively low ebb, and the Government was ready to concede piecemeal reforms, while at the same time working-class radicals were developing the ideas and organisation which were to reach fruition in the 1830s and 1840s.[1]

At the beginning of 1820 such tranquillity seemed extremely unlikely. The repressive Six Acts had crushed radical agitation, but also inevitably created great bitterness among working people. When the Prince Regent succeeded as George IV in January, he demanded that his Ministers institute divorce proceedings against his wife for adultery (a divorce then acquired an Act of Parliament), a demand which they were extremely reluctant to comply with. They realised that it would bring Queen Caroline enormous public sympathy, invite comparison with the King's own scandalous private life, and bring execration on the Ministers themselves. They hoped that she would stay out of England, but on 4 June she forced their hand by returning to England to an ecstatic popular welcome.

As a republican Place was reluctant at first to take the part of the Queen, especially since she received £40,000 a year, and 'I could have no respect for a receiver of the plunder of the people'.[2] But he knew that a violent controversy would undermine popular reverence for royalty, so when demands grew in Westminster for a public meeting to support the Queen, he threw his weight behind them. He drafted the address and resolutions for the meeting which was held on 4 July. Like other radicals he set to work to procure further meetings and addresses – an easy task in the prevailing atmosphere of excitement. He was greatly encouraged when the Government, under pressure from the King, decided to proceed with a divorce by introducing a parliamentary bill in the House of Lords. The Whigs threw their support behind the campaign for the Queen, and all through the summer there was a stream of processions and deputations to her. Radical journals gleefully seized on the chance to attack the King and his Ministers, who found themselves slandered by a flood of caricatures and lampoons.

When the bill was going through the Lords in the autumn, Place was in Brighton, and from there he sent essays to *The Traveller* and other newspapers picking holes in the evidence against the Queen and attacking the Attorney General as a fool and a rogue.[3] Place's vituperation was better than his logic. By this time he had probably realised that the Queen was guilty, although he refused to take her 'crime' seriously. He considered the King 'the most contemptible man that ever sat on the British Throne', whereas the Queen

> had been ill used by her husband, had left the country to him and his mistresses (what a comfortable name this for a set of ——), and all that could be said against her was that she kept a man, a fine handsome fellow, this was no concern of anybody's and if she liked to do so, it was a matter in which she ought to have been indulged without scandal, without reproach, while she could be no bad example at home.

The final qualification was inserted as an afterthought, a concession to the growing 'Victorian' morality. Meanwhile Place's colleagues were organising a grand Westminster meeting for the Queen. They were somewhat discomfited because he was unwell and unable to give his usual help, although he drafted the Address.[4]

The majority for the bill in the Lords dropped at each successive vote, and when it fell to nine on the third reading on 10 November the Government abandoned the divorce. However, agitation for the Queen to be given the full rights of her position continued into the new year. Place as usual stayed out of the limelight, but he was being consulted by the Queen's chief adviser, Alderman Wood, and helping to organise the agitation in Westminster. Public excitement gradually diminished as the Queen ceased making public appearances and accepted a government grant – a decision which was seen as a betrayal of her claim to receive the full rights of the King's consort. In August she died, and her funeral procession produced a last victory for the Queenites. The Government directed that her funeral cortège should skirt the capital, but Londoners wanted her body brought through the City so that they could pay their last respects to her, and immense crowds forced it to go through the centre by blocking all alternative routes.

The Queenite agitation was a traditional campaign of pressure in support of an aristocratic faction, after the more forward looking agitation of the late 1810s in support of popular rights. But the Whigs were drawn along behind instead of taking the lead as they had done in the past. The affair proved cathartic, allowing the radicals to avenge the defeat of 1819 in a campaign which did not threaten the system of government. Most of the leaders were motivated by dislike and contempt for the King rather than belief in the Queen's case, but the mass of her followers believed passionately in her innocence. As Thomas Hodgskin put it in a letter to Place:

> The ministers never did anything so beneficial to the country as putting the Queen on trial. It has roused up the sympathies of a million of persons who would never have signed an address or moved a hand for the sake of their own right. Their generosity is greater than their justice and they come forward zealously to support an injured Queen when they would never stir to resist the tax gatherer. There is something poetical and chivalrous and at the same time loyal in contending for a Queen and a woman, and she has united against our despots a host of men who would otherwise have gone inactive to their graves. . . . The sentiments of many of her answers to addresses are bolder than we ever could expect to come from a person near a throne, and have given the sanction of royal authority, which has so much weight with many people, to the most *radical* doctrines.[5]

The agitation produced a temporary reassertion of London's traditional but declining role as the chief centre of radicalism. The City of London took the lead, and the subsidiary campaign in Westminster was the last fruit of the important alliance between the reformist Westminster tradesmen and the upper-class radical leaders, before Burdett and Hobhouse moved over to the Whigs and the Westminster Committee went into decline. The Government found it impossible to suppress the flood of ribaldry and invective, and thus the attempt to impose strict controls on radical activity and publications under the Six Acts of 1819 was undermined. However Place gave the main credit for defeating censorship to Carlile's campaign, and in his view the Queen Caroline affair was important mainly because it caused a decline in respect for royalty and aristocracy. He said that he assigned the expectation of this result 'as the reason for my *interference* in favour of the Queen, as it was called'.[6]

*   *   *

In the eighteenth century many Acts were passed prohibiting combinations of workmen in specific trades, and when Place organised trade unions in the 1790s he followed the usual practice of disguising them as benefit societies in order to avoid prosecution. In 1799 and 1800 blanket laws were passed prohibiting combination, but employers generally preferred to prosecute under the common law of conspiracy, because the sentences could be much heavier.[7] The laws did not succeed in preventing trade unionism. In some trades, especially in London, employers and unions quietly cooperated to regulate wages and conditions, but it was always in the power of masters to use the law against the men, and this encouraged hatred and suspicion between the two sides. Unions were secretive organisations, bound together by oaths, and the dangers of taking the lead tended to put courageous rather than discreet men at the head.

Cases of persecution of workmen often aroused Place's ire. The sufferings of the cotton spinners led him to reflect that: 'The wonder is not that the men refrain from violence but that they not Burn all the factories and put the owners to death.' He stated that he decided to start working for the repeal of the Combination Laws in 1810, as a result of savage sentences passed on printers in dispute with *The Times*. In the same year he claimed that his evidence to a House of Commons committee frustrated an attempt by the master tailors to break their journeymen's powerful combination by an Act of Parliament. He showed great persistence in his campaign in spite of many discouragements, and believed that the repeal of the laws in 1824 was mainly due to his efforts, a claim accepted by the latest historian to examine the episode.[8]

Place started his campaign in 1814. Whenever there was a dispute or legal proceedings between workmen and their employers, he would write to the newspapers about it with the aim of advancing repeal. He wrote many letters to trade societies in London, and whenever he heard of a dispute outside the capital he wrote for information. At first he had little success: 'My means were small, my influence very narrow.' The upper and middle classes generally supported the laws and working men did not believe that repeal was possible. Too often deceived to trust anyone who was not well known to them, they were unwilling to furnish information which might be used against them, so few replied to his letters and hardly any gave the information which he wanted. He said that he understood them and was not offended; in this as in many other matters they had to be served in spite of themselves: 'I was not to be put from my purpose as I had seen strange things accomplished by perseverance, and I was resolved to persevere.'[9] Many provincial newspapers inserted his articles, but for some years his campaign produced no visible effect.

In 1818 he acquired an important ally in John Wade, a woolcomber who founded the weekly *Gorgon,* the first journal to carry extensive information based on trade union sources. Place, Bentham and Bickersteth lent Wade money, which was repaid, and Burdett also contributed. *The Gorgon* proved the turning-point in enabling Place to start building up trade union contacts. He sent copies of the paper to trade societies, and they were drawn into correspondence. He was able to get information on wages, prices, strikes and trade unionism which Wade worked up into articles. Place also supplied copies of *The Gorgon* to manufacturers, newspapers and MPs. The numbers sent to Joseph Hume proved crucial, persuading him to start on the collaboration with Place which was to secure the repeal of the laws. In June

1819 Hume brought in a parliamentary bill for repeal in order to get discussion on the subject, and by September Place was hoping for partial repeal in the following session. He was also pleased at increased support by the press. 'Only think of it', he boasted to Hobhouse, 'that I sitting in my Sky light as the sycophant Perry called it, have by taking advantage of circumstances induced the Chronicle and even the Times to set this matter on its right footing.'[10]

In the short term he was disappointed, but the cause of repeal continued to gain ground. According to the traditional view combination had been unnecessary because journeymen could secure fair treatment by appealing to magistrates under the Elizabethan Statute of Apprentices, but the dominance of *laissez-faire* opinion had long made this a dead letter, and after its formal repeal in 1814, the abandonment of restrictions on the right of workmen to combine seemed a natural corollary. Liberal Ministers such as Peel and Huskisson admitted that the laws inevitably operated unjustly, because they were supposed to prohibit combinations of masters as well as men, but the masters openly combined in defiance of the law. Repeal had the support of Cobbett as well as the *Morning Chronicle,* but Place's most influential supporter was the Edinburgh economist, John M'Culloch, the most effective popular exponent of Ricardianism. In October 1820 he sought information from Place through Thomas Hodgskin for an article on the laws in the *Edinburgh Review.* Publication was postponed for fear of harming the *Review's* upper-class circulation by espousing the cause of workmen, but articles by M'Culloch in the *Scotsman* newspaper influenced several provincial newspapers and increased discussion. By 1822 Place was becoming confident and Hume was sufficiently encouraged to announce his intention of bringing in a repeal bill. He told Place that many opposition MPs now supported repeal and Ministers had promised not to oppose a select committee to enquire into the laws. Meanwhile Place had managed to acquire useful contacts in northern industrial districts and he was getting articles published in a number of newspapers.[11]

However, Place again proved to have been overoptimistic. When Parliament met in February 1823, Hume canvassed support for a select committee, but he had little success. Then Gravenor Henson, the Nottingham lacemakers' leader, and George White, a House of Commons clerk, entered the scene with a plan to repeal the Combination Laws and erect instead an elaborate system of regulation, resembling twentieth-century legislation. They persuaded Peter Moore, a veteran Foxite MP, to introduce their bill. As a supporter of *laissez-faire,* Place naturally disapproved of the system, although he admitted that it was well drawn and that its authors were well intentioned. He pointed out that much of the system would be unworkable, although he was prepared to consider adapting the plan, and he exaggerated his differences with its authors in restrospect.[12] The bill had no chance of passing Parliament, but it proved useful in bringing new groups of workers into active support of repeal and making the subject more difficult to ignore. Place and Hume could now press straight repeal as the less extreme proposal.

From the late 1810s Place had constantly been urging working men to petition for repeal. He had had some success, but his limited contacts with London trade societies were shown when he had difficulty in contacting them for the LMI as late as September 1823. Moore had not pressed his bill that year, and for the 1824 session Place worked hard to secure as many petitions as possible, citing Hume's promise to bring the subject forward. In January he had a draft petition inserted in the *Black Dwarf,* and in the same month M'Culloch's *Edinburgh Review* article was at last published.[13] It had considerable influence on Members of Parliament. Place persuaded Hume to move for a select committee to examine not only the Combination Laws, but the laws prohibiting the emigration of artisans and restricting the export of machinery. However, when Hume asked William Huskisson, the President of the Board of Trade, whether the Government would agree to the committee, he persuaded Hume that it would be better to leave out the Combination Laws in case Moore made trouble. Thus it seemed that Place's successful efforts in building up the repeal campaign were to be wasted, but as usual he refused to be discouraged, and he wrote Hume two letters. The first, to be shown to Huskisson, pointed out that if the committee did not cover combinations then Moore would be free to bring forward his bill and thus appear a friend to the working people, while the majority of the House of Commons would appear their enemy because they voted down an impracticable measure, whereas if Moore were allowed to talk 'his nonsense' and was then voted down in committee he would be no threat. Place's second letter, a private one, pointed out that he could only explain Hume's change of mind to the petitioners by saying that he had broken his promise.[14] These arguments persuaded Hume and Huskisson, but at first Hume had difficulty in finding the 21 members he needed for the committee – when the proceedings were discovered to be 'amusing', the membership rose to 48. White and Henson were naturally angry at first at seeing their bill pushed aside, but they soon came round and cooperated with Place when they saw what he was about.

Place and Hume tried to ensure that no one would be able to accuse the committee of bias. Hume wrote a circular letter to the mayors of towns all over the country inviting evidence, which was published in the newspapers. No one who wanted to give evidence was excluded, and all MPs who wanted to sit on the committee were allowed to do so. These precautions did not stop the Government unfairly claiming the following year that the committee had been fixed. Of course, Place did ensure that the case for repeal was put over and the arguments against it answered. It was usual for interested parties who had the ear of members to attend committees in order to guide them in their questioning, and Place had done this in other committees, but on this occasion jealousy of outside interference and prejudice against him as a tailor and a radical led to his exclusion. Since Hume was too busy with other parliamentary matters to undertake the necessary preparatory work for himself, Place pre-examined the witnesses and made a summary of their evidence so that Hume would know what questions to ask. This led to accusations that Place had engaged in extraordinary and reprehensible manipulation of the committee, but he reasonably argued that his method was merely an expedient adopted because he was prevented from helping Hume in the usual way in the committee room.

By the end of the hearings the members and the Government were convinced by the case for repeal, but Place feared that arguments on points of detail might still prevent success, so he persuaded Hume to submit a short set of resolutions to the committee, instead of the usual report which would give more room for discussion. This tactic succeeded. A barrister was then employed to draw a parliamentary bill, and when Place did not like the result he quietly rewrote it without anyone noticing, although he later suffered some embarrassment when the barrister repudiated Place's compliments on his skill. As the bill passed through the Commons pains were taken to prevent its supporters from speaking, so as not to rouse up opposition. In spite of sniping from The Times,[15] the bill passed through both Houses almost unnoticed. It nearly fell at the last hurdle when Lord Lauderdale, a supporter of the bill, said that he would object to it on the ground that the evidence to the committee had not yet been printed by the Lords' printer, and it was beneath the House's dignity to rely on evidence printed by order of the Commons. If Lauderdale had said this in the Lords, Place observed, the bill would have been lost, but with great difficulty he was persuaded to hold his tongue and the bill passed into law.

The working-class witnesses to the committee had supported repeal mainly because they believed that the laws held down wages, a view which Place did not accept, and he had concealed his own opinions in order to avoid causing dissension.[16] Once the bill had passed, he called them together and explained his views to them, but the great majority rejected them. Parliament's apparent endorsement of the working-class belief that the law had unfairly held down wages coincided with a trade boom and rising prices in 1824 and early 1825, producing a wave of strikes and a number of outrages. Attempts by Hume and Place to damp down the agitation, warning that it would lead to a renewal of the Combination Laws, had only limited success. In early 1825 the London shipbuilders, who were involved in a bitter dispute with their employees, persuaded Peel and Huskisson of the need to reintroduce restrictions. Place was especially indignant because he thought that the men were wholly in the right in this case. After some equivocation, Ministers moved for a committee to examine the conduct of workmen and propose a new law. In contrast to the 1824 committee, the new one was intended to exclude all evidence unfavourable to the employers' case. The Ministers did not dare to keep Hume off the committee, but other supporters of repeal were excluded.

Place immediately gave up all other activity in order to devote his whole time to opposition. He wrote an able pamphlet, which was widely reprinted and circulated in industrial areas, refuting allegations against working men in Huskisson's speech in the House of Commons.[17] In 1824 trade unionists had been hesitant about coming forward to support a reform which they believed that Parliament would reject, but in 1825 they readily organised to prevent a reversal of victory. The London trade societies formed a committee which worked closely with Place to direct opposition by petitioning and sending witnesses to the parliamentary committee, and other towns such as Manchester formed their own committees. Place sent a steady stream of information, advice and exhortation to each centre of activity.

Ministers intended that the committee should only hear the masters' side of the case, but the terms of reference included investigating the conduct of workmen, and this gave an opening for trade unionists to claim the right to be heard, especially when their employers accused them of misconduct. The committee tried to make it impossible for workmen to reply by voting to keep the evidence secret, but Hume ignored the ruling and passed printed copies daily to Place, who would attempt to find out the men's side of each case, and to get representatives to London who would demand the right to defend themselves before the committee. In order to draw the House's attention to the committee's bias he instructed the delegates to crowd outside the committee room, loudly demanding the right to be heard and making it difficult for the members to get through. These tactics had some success. Hume was able to pressure the committee into hearing some of the accused men, although it refused to hear others, and it would not receive the evidence of workmen who merely wanted to testify that the Act was working well. Place stopped many towns from sending delegates because they had no chance of being heard.

The members of the committee retaliated by threatening to summon Place to answer for his conduct. Hume was alarmed, but Place thought that a summons would give him a chance to expose the committee's partiality in the eyes of the House. The worst that they could do was to commit him to prison for the rest of the parliamentary session, and he would be almost as comfortable in his own private cell as at home. He urged Hume to provoke the members, which he did, but unfortunately they backed down. The committee went on to produce an extremely biased report – for instance, it listed the petitions for amendment of the law but not those against.

Place never forgot that his overall purpose was to prevent the renewal of oppressive laws against combinations, and since Ministers had committed themselves to amending the law, he aimed to wear them down until they made their bill innocuous, rather than attempting to secure the defeat of the bill in the House. He had the great advantage that the bill which the shipbuilders had sold to the Government was quite impracticable, since its provision that a combination would only be legal if a magistrate agreed to be its treasurer would have hit charitable and Bible societies. Once the committee had reported, the next stage was to put pressure on the Attorney General, Copley. Hated for his support of repressive measures but also widely respected, Copley had been asked to draft the Government's bill, but he was easily persuaded to refuse when Hume showed him that he would be drafting nonsense. These tactics worked and the bill finally produced recognised the rights of unions to agitate and strike over wages and hours. Place said that the bill was even put into Hume's hands for amendment, although Ministers knew that this really meant amendment by Place, and although Place's amendments were altered in turn, this was carefully done by Copley.

When the bill was debated in the Commons Hume was supported by Burdett and Hobhouse, and all three men were insulted by ministerial speakers. On one occasion when Place was in the gallery, Canning told Burdett that he did not understand the matter and had to talk as he did because he was under surveillance. Place's role came under frequent attack in the House, and Hume admitted and justified the help he had received from him. 'I confess I thought myself a tolerably sturdy fellow', Place observed, 'but Mr Hume's sturdiness, had on this occasion my most unqualified admiration. I am certain, no man but himself could have been found, who would have behaved with such unshaken firmness, and so successfully have replied to a host of opponents.' Place attended the Report Stage with the French economist J.P. Say, who was so embarrassed at the insulting allusions to Place that he persuaded him to withdraw.[18]

Place's main objection to the amended bill was that it removed the provision in the 1824 Act which made trade unions immune from the common law principle that combinations in restraint of trade were illegal (which was never used against combinations of employers). The bill did legalise combinations to defend wages and hours, but if workmen struck over grievances outside this area, they might be open to an indictment for conspiracy under common law. When the bill went to the House of Lords Place wrote to a number of peers asking them to take up this aspect, and he persuaded Lord Rosslyn to propose an amendment after sending him delegations of shipwrights and weavers to explain the need for unions to negotiate conditions as well as wages and hours. Rosslyn withdrew his amendment after Lord Chancellor Eldon gave an assurance that the common law could not be used to evade repeal. Thus, Place observed, everything possible was done, and in his view the rights of trade unions had not been significantly eroded, although he would not have taken the chance that a man might be indicted for conspiracy at common law. In 1840 he wrote that no such case had occurred.

In theory the 1825 Act severely limited trade union rights, not only by the reintroduction of common law, but by the insertion of a vague clause against 'molesting' and 'obstructing'. However, in practice the Act made very little difference until the 1850s. In the 1830s and 1840s, leading trade unionists were rarely prosecuted, and major strikes were won or lost without the intervention of the law. Rank-and-file unionists did suffer considerable persecution at the hands of local magistrates, but this was usually by the use of laws which had not been affected by the 1824 or 1825 Combination Acts. Prosecutions were generally brought under the master and servant law, which made it a criminal offence for a workman to break a contract with his employer, and thus allowed him to be sent to prison if he left work unfinished when he struck. Workmen also suffered by the willingness of some magistrates to believe allegations of violence and intimidation on weak evidence against unionists. In the 1850s and 1860s judges increasingly interpreted the common law illegality of combinations to harass trade unions, and successful campaigns were waged to secure legislation to protect trade union rights.[19]

Place's efforts received a rare and very welcome acknowledgement, as he told Ebenezer Elliot of Sheffield in 1834:

> To the honour of the working men of Sheffield, they without giving me the least notice of their intention sent me a case of Knives and Forks; which, excepting a silver cup and cover sent to me by the seamen of the Tyne and Wear; I prize above anything in my possession. Such a case of Knives and Forks as I had never seen such a case as every man to whom I have shown them says he never saw. They are now exactly in the condition in which I received them, in that condition they will go to my eldest son whose names are the same as mine, and I hope to the eldest of my grandchildren who shall bear the same name. You will be at no loss to estimate the value I set on the good opinion of the men who subscribed their money for the present, although it would be hypocrisy in me to pretend to think I did not deserve it.[20]

The arrival of delegates from all over the country to testify to the 1825 committee greatly increased contacts between trade unionists, and led to discussions about methods of securing closer cooperation in the long term. The London trades committee, formed to coordinate the unions' defence before the parliamentary committee, became the basis of these efforts, and by May 1825 two rival groups of delegates were planning to publish a newspaper for artisans. The *Journeyman, and Artizans' London and Provincial Chronicle* commenced publication on 5 June, but the leading delegates supported the other project for a paper owned by trade societies. Place appears to have agreed with them, and at first they were disposed to rely on his advice on finance and the choice of editor. He recommended Edward Baines Junior, son of the proprietor and editor of the respected *Leeds Mercury*. This was probably a mistake since Baines must have seemed too much of a gentleman for a committee of artisans to control, and too likely to be wedded to views on economics which they rejected. Then another rival entered the scene, Place's enemy Joseph Robertson, who was still sniping at the London Mechanics' Institute and Place personally in the *Mechanics' Magazine*. Robertson put forward his own project for a mechanics' newspaper, and the delegates decided to meet the threat by merging with him and appointing him editor, against Place's violent opposition. Their *Trades' Newspaper* commenced publication on 12 July, and Place's provincial admirers were exasperated and confused to find both the *Trades'* and the *Journeyman* claiming his support.

Place kept a promise to receive and pass on money for the *Trades'*, but he transferred his support to the *Journeyman,* and urged his correspondents in North and South Shields, Sunderland, Glasgow, Sheffield, Birmingham and other places to push its circulation. At last he had a platform for addressing working people and he was a frequent contributor. The *Journeyman* proved popular with Place's provincial correspondents, but inefficient distribution lost many sales, and its circulation was probably still rising when it ceased publication in September.[21]

The *Trades' Newspaper* seems to have been even more inefficiently managed, but its control by a committee of trade union leaders gave it the active support of a circle of able and energetic men and allowed it to survive. Although Robertson used the paper for vitriolic attacks on Place over birth control in August and September, Place started writing for it in October when the *Journeyman*'s collapse deprived him of an outlet. By the end of the year Robertson was in severe financial difficulties, and he misappropriated contributions passed to him for the striking Bradford woolcombers. When he was committed to the King's Bench for debt in early 1826, the committee again ignored Place's recommendation for the editorship, but the disappearance of Robertson allowed cooperation to be resumed, and Place's diary shows that the new editor frequently called to consult him. Some of Place's articles helped to sell the paper, and on one occasion the editor asked permission to advertise an article by Place on mechanics' institutes as containing some account of his life, which he thought would sell an extra thousand copies. Place's constant contact with publicity seekers had given him an obsessive aversion to self-advertisement, and he refused.

Although Place was a frequent contributor to the *Trades'*, the general tone of the paper naturally reflected the views of artisans. Some committee members sympathised with Robertson's criticisms of the LMI, and Place was told that they had destroyed his article on mechanics' institutes, but it was found lying in the street in Blackfriars Road. The *Trades'* was always in trouble because of inefficient management, and in July 1826 Place lent the committee £20 to avert a rebellion among its printers. In June 1827 Place arranged a merger with another paper as the *Trades' Free Press,* and in December the paper was sold. It was important as the first newspaper run by and for trade unions, and for encouraging the growing cooperation and exchange of information among them.[22]

*   *   *

Place's aim remained constant over the decade of his campaign against the Combination Laws, but his views on the effect of the laws changed drastically. At the beginning he had held the artisans' view that the laws succeeded in 'taking from the workman his fair share of the produce of the earth',[23] but Ricardo convinced him that the general level of wages was determined solely by the ratio between the supply of labour and the amount of employment available. He still believed that the Combination Laws reduced wages and trade unions raised them in specific cases, but he no longer thought that they affected the total amount paid out in wages in the long run. His ambiguous use of language has led to a misconception about his views on trade unionism. He opposed what he called trade unions, that is large-scale unions of workers in a number of trades, which in his view invariably adopted impracticable objectives, but he strongly supported trade clubs, combinations of workers in each trade to defend their wages and conditions. He claimed that wages in trades which had been unable to combine were only one third of the amount in those which had trade clubs, and commenting on evidence in favour of the Combination Laws to the 1824 committee by a Glasgow cotton master, he observed: 'Spinners would soon be as ill paid as weavers if the[y] did not combine.'

He was grossly overoptimistic about the effect of the repeal of the Combination Laws, believing that it was the power of the masters to prosecute combinations which allowed them to act oppressively – once the laws were abolished masters and men would agree by negotiation, only temporary combinations would be necessary, and strikes would be rare.[24] In a letter to Burdett in June 1825, he even implied that combinations were superfluous,[25] but his view at this time was influenced by his optimism that a rapid adoption of birth control would create a shortage of labour and give workers the advantage over employers. He always strongly suported trade unionism in practice, and soon returned to defending it in principle once his hopes of an early adoption of birth control declined and he saw that repeal of the Combination Laws had not persuaded employers to stop oppressing their work people.

He was always ready to give advice and help to trade clubs. For example, in August 1826 the linen drapers' shopmen asked him to organise them, and he drew up an address and rules for them and took the chair at their opening meeting. In the same year the Birmingham silverplaters sent a delegate to London to seek assistance in a strike. He came to Place, who gave him an introduction to the London trade societies. Place also helped working men defend their interests in Parliament, and in 1827 he worked with the seamen's unions in an unsuccessful attempt to abolish the press gang. Although he was always outspoken in stating his own views, he treated working men as equals. He was aware that he needed to do so if he was to gain their trust.[26]

One field where he was not so helpful was factory legislation. Ricardo had reinforced Place's Godwinian scepticism about the ability of governments to bring about positive improvement by legislation, making him an opponent of attempts to improve the lot of workers by factory legislation, except where children were involved. In 1830 he told Hume:

> No restrictive laws should exist. Every one should be at liberty to make his own bargain in the best way he can. I cannot however but lament that the tendency of this freedom is against the interest of the workman and in favour of his employer.
>
> Whatever any man who employs a large number of workpeople proposes as a regulation is sure to be something for his own advantage and for the disadvantage of the workpeople. . . .
>
> I would if there were no alternative, rather be hanged here in London, than be compelled to live in one of our large manufacturing towns. This being so, I cannot but lament the impossibility, I fear it is so, of any law being efficient between masters and men which shall have the effect of assuring to the working man and woman the fulfilment of their contracts. They had better however be robbed than defrauded, without the 'humbug' of 'protecting' laws, than with them, and therefore it is upon the whole better to repeal all the acts relative to their contracts and payment of wages than to suffer them to remain.

Place did not foresee that the development of the factory inspectorate would provide an effective means of enforcing protective legislation, but he was proved right in his belief that it was futile to attempt to protect workers in declining industries such as cotton weaving by setting minimum wages.[27]

By the early 1820s the failure of such projects as the Chrestomathic School had made him highly cynical about the good intentions of the middle classes. 'Pray take a retrospect of the last 30 years', he urged the editor of the *Labourers' Friend* in 1823, 'and see if you can any reasonable ground of hope that the *'Middle Classes'* will concur in any measure which may tend to improve the condition of the labouring classes, be assured that you will find no ground for any such hope.'[28] In the political field he regarded the middle and working classes as natural allies against the aristocracy, because they both stood to benefit from a pure *laissez-faire* system with the removal of all abuses and restrictions on trade. But in the relations between masters and men he saw them as inevitable enemies, and he scorned any appeals by the men to the humanity of the masters. The fact that he saw opposite relationships between the classes as necessary in the political and economic fields created a contradiction which he never managed to solve, since it was impossible in practice that the different classes would act as allies politically when they regarded each other as enemies in their daily lives.

Place set out his views in a letter to John Doherty, the Manchester cotton spinners' leader, in April 1829. Doherty had written to say that the spinners were on the verge of a protracted strike against a large reduction in wages. He enclosed their address, and expressed the fear that the masters were applying for a renewal of the Combination Laws. Place was able to reassure him on this point. Ministers, he observed

> are *now* too well informed to believe that the general welfare of the country can be promoted by monopolies and restrictions, and would not lend themselves to any

project for interfering between the masters and their men. I am glad that you wrote to me, and you may depend upon it, I will carefully attend to your suggestions.

I . . . was sorry tho' not at all surprised to find so much misery had been inflicted, and that so much more impended over the head of the working people in the Cotton Manufacture. It is to be expected that people so distressed and so generally ill used, should impute all the evils they endure to the conduct of their employers, and should speak of them generally as cold blooded tyrants towards those who are dependent on them. True enough and lamentable enough it is, that generally speaking they are regardless of the very miserable condition of their work people, but this is the inevitable consequence of their situation. You ejaculate – 'Of what materials are these men made.' I reply of none differing in the least from the workmen themselves. Few are the persons who follow Trade or Manufacture from their love to either, the only reason why either are promoted, is the love of gain, and this is enough to make them what they are. It operates in precisely the same way upon the workmen when they become employers, and the very men who have suffered the most from what they call wilful merciless oppression, generally in a few years after they become masters, are as wilfully merciless as they whom they formerly complained of.

A really humane man will not be a practical cotton manufacturer, very few such men will embark capital in such concerns, the scenes of wretchedness which in the one case he would be compelled to witness, and those in the other case which he could not avoid hearing of, the images these would raise in his imagination, would be continually present, and make him unhappy. To avoid this painful state he would quit the employment. Thus it is, as in our Slave Colonies, men who remain in them become inured to cruelty, till it ceases to affect them, while they who are more humane quit them.

A large portion of the printed Address is worse than useless, in as much as it is an appeal to the humanity of the masters, against their interest. . . . Depend upon it the working people never will, as they never have, obtained any thing by such appeals. The struggle is a struggle of strength and 'the weakest must go to the wall'. Whatever the people either gain or even retain, is gained or retained, and must always be gained or retained by power.

Working people, he complained, see that the price of bread is regulated by the state of the harvest, not by the will of the bakers, but they will not see that their own wages are determined by the supply and demand for labour, not by the will of the masters.

Unfortunately, there has always been too many hands in the Cotton Manufacture, and the consequence has been a gradual 'tho not a regular reduction of wages, and this will continue until it shall become utterly impossible to reduce wages any lower, and the whole of the working people in this manufacture are brought into a state of most abject and pitiable misery. Is there then no remedy? Yes, one, and only one, ceasing to produce hands faster than there is a demand for hands. There is no other. . . . Government can do nothing for you, neither can the public do anything which will permanently relieve you, you must help yourselves, or remain helpless . . .

You will see by the printed table sent with this letter, that during the war there was a constant struggle in London, as there was in some other places, on the part of the workmen to raise their wages to a corresponding height with the advanced and advancing prices of necessaries. This was the case in every trade which required skilled labour. You will see that they were unable fully to accomplish their purpose.

But there has been, this curious and satisfactory result, of their efforts, that during the last ten years, journeymen in London have been better paid than they ever before were in any preceding ten years, necessaries having fallen more in price than wages have fallen, but then, in London the several trades have societies similar to what you call *'unions'*, and they have flourished for many years. Each man pays a weekly contribution, and in many trades when the business is slack, they who cannot find employment are maintained by the club, each man receiving about 8/- a week, and sometimes a larger sum. This plan never has been followed by the Cottoners, and cannot now be adopted with any chance of success. In all the London trades there are periods in almost *every* year when the whole number of hands is insufficient to perform the work required, and this is the cause of their wages remaining high as they are. But the Cottoners are always in excess, . . . and consequently no times when they can successfully make a stand, and thus it is that they are continually depressed and more and more broken down, and this must continue so long as the number of hands exceeds the demand for hands. Nothing seems to me to be more absurd than attributing low wages to what is called the *Grinding System,* the same desire to reduce wages has existed in all times in all places, and in every trade and manufacture, and would be put in practice in every trade as it is amongst the Cottoners, did the matter depend upon the will of the masters.[29]

Place's logic was as brutal as it was impeccable, and it is not surprising that the cotton workers refused to accept it.

                              *   *   *

Apart from combinations, the 1824 select committee had also examined the laws prohibiting the emigration of artisans and restricting the export of machinery. These laws aimed to prevent foreigners gaining the knowledge and equipment to compete with Britain industrially, but the ban on emigration was unenforceable, because artisans only had to claim to be unskilled workmen to evade it. Its main effect was to discourage emigrants from returning home because they feared prosecution, and repeal was agreed without difficulty. Allowing the export of machinery was a very different matter. As a believer in complete free trade, Place opposed any restrictions on exports, and the leading engineers, including Place's old friend from the LCS, Alexander Galloway, cooperated closely with him to try to secure repeal. But Hume found that there was no chance of getting Parliament to accept a measure which appeared designed to give away Britain's industrial lead, and he was forced to accept a compromise under which the Government privately agreed to exercise its discretion to grant licences in all cases not likely to cause controversy.

In the 1820s Place was regarded as a prime authority on getting things done in Parliament. In 1824 he secured the repeal of restrictions on butchers under the Cutting and Flaying Act, and as a result the tanners came to him the following year for help. He learnt from his usual ministerial contact, William Holmes, a Treasury Whip, that the Government was willing to abolish the prohibitions on tanners being curriers and vice versa, provided that the duty on leather could still be collected equally easily, but the tanners could not devise any way of achieving this, so the matter was dropped. Place's expertise, and his ability to point out faults in proposed legislation and work out practicable remedies, enabled him to influence even Peel. Place would write detailed comments on Home Office proposals for reforming the criminal law, which were shown to Peel by Holmes and other members, and which often resulted in changes of detail. Place worked even more closely with opposition members. In January 1828 Brougham told him that he was planning to propose a parliamentary commission to enquire into the state of the law, with the aim of totally abolishing common law. Place was violently opposed to common law, which in his view rested on the judges' perversion of medieval statutes. To abolish it, he declared, Brougham could command his time to any extent.[30]

With Place's aid, Hume had become the leading parliamentary advocate of economy and detector of waste and corruption – principally the appointment of government supporters to sinecure offices. Place's desire to cut down the scope of government led him to pay great attention to its finances, and in the late 1810s and the early 1820s he devoted considerable effort to unravelling government accounts in cooperation with Ricardo and Hume. Place claimed that as a result of his studies he perhaps knew more than anyone else out of office, but he was unable to construct an accurate balance sheet because no two published accounts agreed. Hume pressed the question in the House of Commons, against the fierce opposition of Ministers, who, Place said,

> made it a constant practice to deprecate Mr Hume's exertions, to impugn his motives, to charge him with blunders which were their own, and to convert any error he committed, into a sort of crime committed by him, whilst their partisans within the house and their retainers without, represented him as a man so incorrect and vague as not at all to be relied upon.

In 1822 Hume secured a Select Committee on simplifying the public accounts, and Place devoted his time to helping him, much to the anger of some members of the committee. Place said that the usual notice on commitee proceedings that they were not to be shown to outsiders was made even stronger, with the aim of putting non-ministerial members at a disadvantage compared with ministerial ones who could consult the clerks. Hume countered the sniping by asking Place to come to the committee room, and then publicly handing him the proceedings and asking him to read them and advise him. 'No more was at that time heard', Place observed, 'of the Tailor at Charing Cross to whom "some members went for their daily lessons" &c &c.' An improved form was adopted for the accounts.[31]

Place's great triumph in this field was over the Sinking Fund. This was a scheme introduced by Pitt, under which money from borrowing and taxes was used to purchase government stock. The Fund was supposed to grow by compound interest until it equalled the national debt and would then be used to pay it off. Place pointed out that it would have been far better to have used any excess of income to buy out and cancel stocks; the Sinking Fund involved unnecessary administrative costs and borrowing money at a high rate in order to purchase stocks which paid a lower one.

In 1812 he started to campaign against the Fund, but at first he only brought ridicule on himself, and no paper would insert a paragraph on the subject if the editor knew that it came from him. In 1813 Robert Hamilton's well-regarded *Inquiry concerning the Public Debt* attacked the Fund, and citing this Place was able to get many short essays published under fictitious names. In December 1816 the *Morning Chronicle* published an article over his initials which argued that the Fund was a fraud. His case was not clearly put, but it started a debate on the subject, and a number of writers attacked it as a burden, although rejecting his view that the very concept of a sinking fund was nonsense. A further letter from him in the *Chronicle* in January 1817 put his case ably, but soon afterwards one by the Earl of Lauderdale dismissed the opinions of 'New Light F.P.', and this closed the *Chronicle* to him since allowing a reply would have put him on a level with the Earl.

By this time Ricardo was consulting Place in his efforts to unravel the mysteries of government accounts, and at the end of the year he told Place that his friend Pascoe Grenfell, an MP and authority on finance, was publishing a defence of the Fund. Place sent Grenfell a reply through Ricardo but, Place said bitterly, 'this Copper Manufacturing gentleman, who was remarkably proud, could not take any notice of a tailor'. Place then sent the reply to Perry, the editor of the *Morning Chronicle,* who published it out of enmity to Grenfell. This article produced a much greater effect than Place's earlier efforts, many influential men were introduced to him and several MPs were converted. In 1819 Ricardo became a Member of Parliament, and Place immediately tried to persuade him to take up the subject in the House of Commons, but Ricardo declined because he was not yet clear about it − Place complained that Ricardo's ideas developed so slowly that he died before he could perfect them. Ricardo asked Place to comment on his *Encyclopaedia Britannica* article on the Sinking Fund, but he rejected Place's view that the concept of a sinking fund was nonsense.

During the late 1810s and the 1820s Place and others seized every opportunity to attack the Fund. A well-argued article of his, 'The Mystery of the Sinking Fund Explained', in the *Traveller* in 1821, produced such a demand for the paper that copies could not be supplied, and thousands of copies of his essay were printed as a pamphlet and given away. The *Traveller* sent a copy to each banking house, and to Place's delight several principals asked for extra copies. But he was disappointed by the debate on the Budget in the House of Commons in 1822, when 'the gabble of members on this occasion respecting the Sinking Fund was enough to make a Dog Sick, and to drive anyone to despair who was not fully imbued with the notion that "Truth is great and will prevail".' Ricardo, Hume and others were gradually moving towards a complete condemnation of the Fund in the House, and the leading economic Ministers had become convinced that it was useless. But it was still protected by the great authority of Pitt, and many people regarded it as the only guarantee that the national debt would eventually be abolished and government finances restored to solvency, so Ministers were unwilling to attack it for fear of damaging the Government's credit. Finally, in May 1829 the Sinking Fund was quietly abolished, to Place's great delight. In his old age he added a note to his account of his efforts: 'To my son Francis Place. I not only may be considered the first person who set the people on to the consideration of this question . . . but I killed it and buried even the name.'[32] The snobbery which hindered his efforts illustrates why his hatred of the aristocracy was so strong.

Place also came to be recognised as an authority on the laws which restricted press freedom. In the 1820s the battle for freedom of the press centred on the libel law.[33] In 1822 he wrote a series of articles in the *British Luminary* urging the abolition of the crime of libel, which were reprinted as a pamphlet by Leigh Hunt's brother, John.[34] The definition of libel at that time made the truth or falsity of the statement complained of irrelevant, and this in itself was enough to condemn the law in Place's view. He thought that the law of defamation, under which someone who was slandered could sue for damages, was the only law on the subject which ought to exist. Carlile led the fight against the libel law in the 1820s, and he succeeded in wearing down his prosecutors and enlarging the area of freedom of speech, but he did not secure any change in the law, and in 1832 Place helped a man who was charged by the Duke of Cumberland with criminal libel over the Sellis affair (see p. 77), because he thought that any proceedings under this law ought to be opposed.

The newspaper stamp received less attention during the 1820s. The cheap radical press of the 1810s had been killed by one of the Six Acts of 1819, which made journals of comment liable to the stamp duty of 4*d,* and Place constantly urged his parliamentary acquaintance to move for the repeal of the Acts, but he had little success. In late 1826 or early 1827 he did succeed in securing Brougham's promise through James Mill to move for the repeal of the extension of the stamp to journals of comment, but when Canning came to power with Whig support in April 1827, Brougham decided not to bring the motion. Persistent as ever, Place persuaded Hume to take the matter up, and at first Brougham supported him, but early in May Brougham changed his mind and the Whigs started pressing Hume to drop his motion in order to avoid embarrassing the Government. Sir Robert Wilson, a Whig MP, succeeded in persuading Hume not to proceed, so Place wrote an article for the *Trades' Newspaper* which cited Hume as an example of how well-meaning Members were operated on to make them infirm of purpose. Hume reacted by deciding to persist with his motion, and 'that sneaking hound Sir Bobby

Wilson' — as Place called him — accused Hume in the House of Commons of breaking his promise. The Whigs made one further effort by suggesting that Hume's motion should only apply to small publications and not newspapers, but Hume showed unusual presence of mind in replying that he would agree if the Government would support the motion. He thus robbed the Whigs of an excuse for opposing him. When he brought his motion on 31 May the Whigs tried to get the House counted out, but the anti-government section of the Tories helped Hume make a quorum, presumably in order to embarrass the Whigs. When the government whip sent for the Whig MPs to make a large majority they were not to be found, and this annoyed him so much that he threatened to resign. The story illustrates why Place, who disliked 'shuffling' above all, hated the Whigs more than the Tories.[35]

His contacts with MPs frequently caused him great frustration. All too often they would drop projects after persuading him to do the necessary preparatory work, and he would resolve to have nothing more to do with politicians. But the memory of his successes would draw him back, and if an MP such as Hobhouse complained of difficulties he was quick to tell him that it was a politician's duty to do his best whatever the difficulties, and that he had seen too many things done which were said to be impossible to respect a man who was unable to perform impossibilities. In the late 1820s he was less active because he was spending much of his time with Mrs Chatterley at Brompton, but on their marriage in 1830 he 'reconciled myself to my old way of consuming time'. In the same year his allies in the House failed to oppose the increase of the bail required of editors against a libel charge, provoking him to comment:

> These things sometimes vex me and almost make me resolve to cut my parliamentary acquaintance and this I certainly should do, were it not that the matters I have accomplished encourage me to hope I shall still be successful. It was only after 6 years of continued exertion in a great many ways that I at length induced Mr Hume to procure a committee which led to the repeal of the laws against Combinations of Workmen, and the act which forbade Artizans leaving the country — it was only after long continued efforts that the exportation of Machinery was brought to the state it now is, it was in defiance of the opinion of the Speaker and the Attorney General that I procured the repeal of the Cutting and Flaying act, and it was only after efforts continued during 7 years that I at length was the means of a committee sitting on the conduct of the Commissioners of Hackney Coaches which will probably put an end to the abuses and to the absurd laws which incommode that business and inconvenience the public. If I did not console myself with these and similar results I should abandon all such efforts, shut out my political *friends,* and betake myself to more agreeable pursuits.

Place did succeed in getting the law on hackney coaches reformed, although his part in it (briefing Hume what to do) was carefully concealed to avoid arousing the jealousy of the parliamentary committee concerned. He attributed his final success partly to Spring Rice, the secretary to the Treasury, picking up a copy of his brief which an MP had mislaid in the committee room, and adopting his suggestions.[36]

11   The Reform Bill

In the mid-1820s interest in parliamentary reform was at a low ebb.[1] However, the concession of Catholic emancipation in 1829 by the Duke of Wellington's extreme Tory Government showed that the old system was not immutable, and at the end of the decade agitation revived. The Duke's determination to resist further concessions led many to conclude that parliamentary reform was a prerequisite to progress, and the formation of the Birmingham Political Union to campaign for parliamentary reform in January 1830 led to many similar societies in other towns. A depression in trade and the 'Swing' disturbances (attempts in southern agricultural areas to intimidate farmers into increasing wages by riots and arson) encouraged a belief that the country faced ruin without major reforms. The Whigs responded to the changed public mood by coming out strongly for reform. At first, Place played little part in the campaign. The history of Whig equivocation over parliamentary reform had convinced him that they would not support any radical proposals until the mood of the country became overwhelming. In his view this required united support by the middle classes, who were not yet ready to join in agitation on a large scale.

The number of contested seats in the General Election in the summer of 1830 was not above average, but the Government did badly where there were contests. The reformers and the Whigs were further encouraged by the French Revolution of July 1830, and Place said that the working people were particularly influenced by newspaper coverage which compared the courage of the Parisians favourably with that of Londoners.[2] Working-class reformers started a campaign against the 4*d* newspaper stamp by launching unstamped newspapers illegally. Desire of Londoners to prove their courage, economic distress, the rising tide for reform and the unpopularity of Peel's new police combined to produce increasing riotousness in the capital in the autumn.

Place wrote that the new police were as yet very ignorant of their duty, frequently officious or inattentive. They gave great offence by blocking the pavement outside the houses of rich people when they gave parties, thus forcing pedestrians into the road where they risked injury from carriages. Hatred of the police was encouraged by the unstamped press (the 'taxes on knowledge', as he never tired of pointing out, prevented publications on the other side), and the police commissioners were somewhat overawed by the general feeling against them. Traditionally, radicals emphasised liberty at the expense of law and order, but like other Benthamites Place believed that a weak police only encouraged riots and lawlessness which gave the Government an excuse for repression, and he decided to instruct the police how to carry out their duties. He set out first to prevent the King from going in procession on 9 November to visit the Lord Mayor. Place was convinced that this would lead to serious riots, and he urged cancellation on all the influential men he knew. He persuaded a police superintendent called Thomas to warn against the plan, and officials from three government departments called on him to discuss the matter. After receiving similar information from the Lord Mayor, the Government became so alarmed that it not only cancelled the procession but fortified the Tower. Place considered the cancellation a great triumph, claiming that it was the first time that the Government had openly changed its plans out of fear of the people, and was thus 'the First Step in the British Revolution'.[3]

Thomas then brought some police sergeants to him for advice, and he urged them to teach their men to act politely to people who were not disorderly. He also advised them not to molest rioters until they were attacked, and then to retreat to where they could get support. If they were followed, they should spread across the street and charge, thrashing the mob soundly but taking no one into custody. Thomas took Place's advice when a large crowd gathered in the City on the day of the cancelled procession, 9 November. The mob pulled down part of a hoarding in Chancery Lane to make staves and marched through Temple Bar, shouting as usual 'down with the Police'! Thomas and his men retreated to their station in Catherine Street, followed by the rioters, and then the police formed across the Strand and charged. The mob instantly fled and the police chased them back to Temple Bar, hitting them but not seriously injuring them. After this there was an end to rioting, a result which in Place's view proved that there was no danger from mobs unless people were cowardly, and that the Government's fondness for calling in soldiers was unnecessary. The episode led one historian to credit Place with being the inventor of the baton charge.[4]

Parliamentary reform had become so popular by the autumn of 1830 that an unequivocal declaration against it by the Duke of Wellington on 2 November had weakened the Tory Government, and the cancellation of the procession a week later made it look ridiculous. As a result, the Whigs looked like taking office at a time when they were committed to parliamentary reform. But Place was not hopeful. Commenting on a speech by Brougham, he wrote: 'As for his or any other plan being adopted, no man not actually mad can expect it there will be no reform till the whole thing goes altogether.'

The shuffling Whigs, he said, would be no better than the Duke in office, and without reform no Whig would be tolerated as Prime Minister for twelve months by the King or people. He did not want the Government driven out too soon, preferring that the Whigs should have time to commit themselves more thoroughly to reform first.[5] But not surprisingly they did not see the matter his way, and they kept up the pressure until Wellington was outvoted over the Civil List on 15 November and resigned.

Contradicting his contemptuous assessment of the Whigs, Place admitted that their new Government was the best that could be formed – he thought that it was a patchwork since wise statesmen were rarest among those from whom an administration was chosen, but this was inevitable until the great majority were wise enough to be judicious legislators themselves, which he could not conceive. Although he remained a supporter of universal suffrage, he was becoming far more sceptical about the extent of the benefits it would bring. The Whigs soon alienated him by prosecuting Richard Carlile for a defence of the Swing rioters which Place believed that the Wellington Government would have ignored.[6] With an administration in power committed to parliamentary reform, the movement in the country grew rapidly, and the skill and perseverance of the people, Place observed, astounded and palsied the opposition. Many people sought his help in arranging meetings and drafting petitions. He gave it freely in order to put pressure on the Government and educate the people on the virtues of reform. At this time he considered Thomas Attwood, founder of the Birmingham Political Union, as 'the most influential man in England', but he held him in considerable suspicion. Attwood had launched his campaign in the hope that a reformed parliament would adopt his unorthodox views on currency, and Place, without questioning the sincerity of his views, believed that he was partly motivated by the hope of profiting personally from the change which he advocated.[7]

During the winter Place concentrated his attention on the rural Swing disturbances. The more he studied them the less he could see a solution, believing that they were due to poverty caused by excessive population. When George Lamb, the Home Secretary's brother, came to ask him to write addresses to persuade the labourers to stop firing ricks, he refused on the ground that there was no chance that they would listen to such advice at a time when their tactics were securing higher wages. At the urging of James Mill, Joseph Hume and others, he set out his views in his *Essay on the State of the Country in respect to the Condition and Conduct of the Husbandry Labourers,* which was printed in February 1831 after being circulated among leading economists and Benthamites. His conclusions, which he said were sanctioned by 'all those wise and learned men to whom I consider it my pleasure as well as an honour to be able to call my friends', were remarkably alarmist, warning that a social and economic collapse was likely as a result of the rural agitation. The Swing disturbances contributed to the belief that revolution was possible if the Reform Bill was not passed, but Place and other radicals laid little emphasis on them as they saw no solution which a reformed parliament could adopt.[8]

*   *   *

Place still believed that extensive parliamentary reform would not be passed until the system of government collapsed, and he shared the general amazement at the extent of the Reform Bill outlined by Lord John Russell in the House of Commons on 1 March 1831. The rotten boroughs were to lose 168 MPs, additional Members were allocated to the counties and unrepresented boroughs, and the boroughs were to have a uniform £10 householder franchise. Place was as delighted as he was surprised. He believed that the Tories could have held power for many years by making concessions gracefully, and using the steadily growing revenues to lower taxes without reducing corruption. The Duke's indiscreet declaration had let the Whigs in, he thought, and they took advantage by calling on the people to support them in promoting parliamentary reform, thus producing a general and intense demand for it, which forced them to keep their promises. However, his analysis was unfair to the Whigs, since the Government had decided on an extensive reform soon after they took office. The Whigs believed that reform was necessary to prevent revolution and restore the confidence of the people in the system of government.[9]

Place said that any description could but feebly describe the excitement of the people after Russell's announcement. Many people came to urge him to call a public meeting in Westminster, and since no one else would take the lead he did. The resolutions he prepared called for shorter parliaments and the secret ballot. This was not because he was dissatisfied at their omission from the bill — he described the reasons given by Russell for leaving them out as unnecessary, because so much had been given that no one could demand more — but on the principle that you should always demand more than you can hope to get so that there is something to be cavilled at and given up. He was furious when Hobhouse, displaying the usual Whig trickery, accepted his resolutions at the preparatory meeting and then successfully opposed them at the public one, on the ground that they would destroy unanimity.[10]

Place decided that he could no longer keep to his determination not to go out of his house on political matters — in such an emergency it was the duty of every man to help in any way he could. The part of each ordinary man would be small, he observed somewhat disingenuously, but the services of an immense number would be needed if Ministers were to be enabled to carry the bill.[11] On 6 March he was approached by Erskine Perry, the radical son of the former editor of the *Morning Chronicle,* on behalf of a group of young gentleman radicals who proposed a society to point out suitable parliamentary candidates. Parliament would be dissolved when the bill was defeated or passed, so an early General Election was likely, and Place welcomed the suggestion. He and other leading radicals had often been approached in the past by local groups of reformers looking for candidates, but they had usually been unable to help because few radicals were able and willing to afford the heavy costs of a contest. He decided to concentrate his efforts on the Parliamentary Candidates Society (PCS), although at first he tried to stay in the background.

From the beginning the PCS ran into trouble. Perry's friends took fright at an attack on parliamentary adventurers in the draft address which Place drew up. Such abuse of respectable Members of Parliament would be considered ungentlemanly. Perry's friends withdrew, but many people told Place that they would join if he took a share in the management, so he decided to take the le d. He and Perry summoned a meeting on 14 March. Twenty-one attended, including John Stuart Mill, Thomas Hobhouse, half-brother of the MP, John Arthur Roebuck, who was to be Place's main parliamentary ally in the 1830s, Edwin Chadwick, who was to gain fame as a Poor Law and sanitary reformer, and two radical military men, Colonels Leslie Grove Jones and Perronet Thompson. Place's draft was watered down, almost provoking him to withdraw.

He railed against the 'mean pitiful miserable notions' of his colleagues, 'their timidity, their fears of giving offence', which palsied them. It was not so with the Tories, who persuaded themselves that anything they wanted to do was genteel. In the 'vile conspiracy' called the Constitutional Association, which had tried to suppress the radical press by prosecution in the early 1820s: 'They did not palter like shuffling whigs, and the mongrel breed of half whig whig half reformers, . . . no absurd notions of shabby gentility restrained them, they had no fear of being looked upon as ungenteel, none of being discountenanced by Holland House people, and Brooks's club people, like the poor half and half people with whom it was necessary I should associate.' These men

> might if they were honest to themselves, bold persevering and energetic, lead all who are classed below them, a large proportion of those in stations of life analogous to their own, and induce many who range above them to take part with them. The working classes, who are of little importance in any useful political proceeding unless countenanced by those called their betters. . . . The shopkeeping race, and such as they, who are among the most despicable people in the nation in a public point of view . . .

But, he said, 'the curse of gentility' was on the gentlemen radicals.[12]

He was convinced that a mild address would make the society appear so milk-and-water that it would attract no support. The main battle turned on the decision to examine and publicise the public conduct of MPs, which had been added to objects of the society. The decision was upheld in spite of the fears of some members that it would be considered ungentlemanly, although Colonel Thompson resigned, and then the society began to gain strength.

Joseph Hume had agreed to join the general committee, but he found the hostility of the House of Commons too great to bear, and on 28 March he resigned from the society. Colonel Thompson followed him by publicly announcing his resignation, and they were followed by a stream of other secessions.

The Reform Bill passed its second reading with a majority of only one, and a General Election was called on 21 April after a defeat on the committee stage. By then the society had abandoned its original purpose of finding reform candidates, and delegations approaching it were referred to the Treasury. Instead, the PCS concentrated on supplying details of the votes and speeches of anti-reform MPs to their constituency opponents, aided by the collection of information which Hume privately offered on the conduct of MPs. Although it incurred great hostility in London, the PCS proved popular with provincial reformers, and by 28 April it had published accounts of the conduct of 22 anti-reform MPs, and sent out details of many more on the promise of publication in local newspapers. Thousands of copies of pamphlets on Kent and Dorset MPs were distributed, and John Marshall wrote from Leeds promising £20 for the PCS in gratitude for the information he had received. The result of the election was a landslide for the reformers. Although the PCS was greatly harmed by secessions, the intense hostility of MPs to its strategy suggests that it was one which they greatly feared. By starting to campaign soon after the bill was introduced, the PCS encouraged reformers to start preparing for the battle well before the election was called, and it made it far more difficult for anti-reform MPs to conceal their opinions.[13]

* * *

After the General Election, the country was quiet while the second Reform Bill passed through the House of Commons, but agitation revived in September 1831 with the prospect of a battle in the Lords. The bill's rejection there by a majority of 41 on Saturday 8 October was greeted by riots in Derby and Nottingham, but at first reaction in London was muted; the reformers could not agree what to do and they were uncertain of working class support. Over the next few days excitement built up and Tory bankers were worried by a run on gold. The following Monday a great meeting was held in Regents Park, organised by the parish vestry reformers of Marylebone, and an attendance of 80,000 was claimed. Place remarked that the resolutions and one of the speeches seemed extreme, but they were really 'commendable as quietly letting down the exacerbation without impairing the disposition to use physical force should it become necessary to employ it'. By Tuesday, some reformers were becoming disturbed at evidence that Ministers intended a long prorogation of Parliament, which would give time to negotiate a compromise. Place wrote to Sir John Hobhouse (he had become a baronet on the death of his father) complaining that Ministers' conduct was discouraging

the people's ardour, and warning that continued doubt about the
Government's intentions would produce a financial panic, which would lead
to a collapse in trade and a breakdown of government.[14]

The following day (Wednesday the 12th) a great procession was staged to
the King's Levée in support of the bill. It was organised by two unknown
journeymen, John Powell and Thomas Bowyer, with Place's encouragement
and introductions from him to the leaders of the vestry reform movement in a
number of parishes. The journeymen encountered considerable difficulties
because the parishes did not cooperate with each other and their leaders were
jealous of interference, but Powell and Bowyer succeeded by keeping in the
background and allowing the leaders to take the credit. Powell claimed its size
at 70,000, the *Morning Chronicle* at 300,000.[15] As Place mingled with the
procession his hopes rose, and he became convinced that the working people
would stand by the bill.

In the evening he met Erskine Perry and three others at the Crown and
Anchor Tavern to plan a metropolitan political union on the Birmingham
model, but they were soon called to another room in the tavern, where over
100 parish delegates had assembled. These were veterans of the campaign
against the select vestries, and they had now taken the lead over agitation for
the Reform Bill in London, but Place found that they had no idea what to do,
and that they were content to trust the Government's intentions. Several of his
allies became so disgusted at the delegates' indecision that they decided to
leave, and to prevent this Place addressed the meeting himself, even though he
was only there as a spectator. He warned them that the Government was
planning a compromise, quoting passages from Ministers' speeches in proof
of his allegation. The mood of the meeting changed completely, and George
Rogers, one of the more extreme Westminster reformers, moved that Place
draw up a Memorial to the Prime Minister, Earl Grey. The proposal was
carried with shouts of applause, and Place immediately complied. The
Memorial expressed astonishment at reports that it was intended to prorogue
Parliament until after Christmas, and warned that unless there was the
shortest possible prorogation and the bill was again introduced, there would
inevitably be a violent revolution. At the suggestion of a radical surgeon, John
Constantine Carpue, the meeting agreed that the Memorial should be
presented immediately, so a delegation of seventeen parish delegates,
including Place, arrived in Downing Street at 10.45 at night. They were
admitted, but they got little satisfaction from Grey, who emphasised how
tired Ministers were, the time that would be needed to draw up a new bill, and
the absurdity of proposing a measure which could not be carried. Hobhouse,
who strongly disapproved of the deputation, said that some of them looked so
disreputable that a friend of his stood in front of one man so that Grey would
not see him.

However, after the procession on 12 October public excitement rapidly
declined. Replying on the 14th to Place's warning of a financial panic,

Hobhouse was justifiably sceptical. On Sunday the 16th Place wrote to the radical banker, George Grote:

'Look on this picture and on this.' What a change in one short week. Last Sunday we feared, and had cause to fear, that the working people would not take part with the middle classes. You lamented this was hurt at it deplored it as a great misfortune. They however soon demonstrated their feelings and proved that they were ready at any risk and at any sacrifice to stand by us, and then what did we do? We abandoned them, deserted, betrayed them, and shall have betrayed them again before 3 more days have passed over our heads betray them again, for we shall all of us before that time be well acquainted with the new facts,
1. That no peer will be created
2. That Parliament will be prorogued for a very long period
3. That such a bill as the Lords will please accept, will be promised to be brought in, 'a conciliatory bill'.
And we − yes we, the dastardly − talking − swaggering − dogs will sneak away with our tails between our legs. Why did we desire to have a demonstration made by the working people? For what purpose but to influence ministers to make a very short prorogation, to induce them to recommend and the King to attend to their recommendation to make as many peers as should secure the passing of the bill. And now, − now that the people have made the demonstration, made it too in a mighty way, far beyond, not only any expectation which the most sanguine could form, but even beyond our wishes, we abandon them, and give up every one of the things we so ardently desired their support to enable us to demand, thus showing ourselves, as some at least among them have described us enemies. Instead of telling them that with their cooperation we will command compliance, that aid which only last sunday seemed so desirable, we now scorn their proffered aid, despise the wholesome terror their assistance would have produced, and declare to the very ministers who have flung back our wishes in our teeth, that we have the fullest confidence in their wisdom and integrity to do, even that which they themselves tell us they do not intend to do. . . . The Tories are exulting over us boasting of reaction, and can we blame them? Time, gaining of time was their surest means of defeating us, and truly wonderful it was that the patience of the people and their confidence in ministers held out as it did, still more wonderful it was that so much excitement could be produced after so long a period. It reached its crisis on wednesday, and has passed without producing any consequences dangerous to the enemy, any good effect upon ministers, any use to the nation, and now it is rapidly declining, in a few days it may settle down among the working classes and to a great extent among the middle classes into sulkiness. It will recreate the subsiding distrust of the working classes for the middle classes . . . . the middle classes plodding quietly at money getting and showing themselves off in their half genteel half vulgar frippery will no longer give themselves any trouble towards the support of an administration, which has − bewildered themselves and misled the nation. . . . It seems to me unreasonable to expect the people will again be excited as they have been by the promises of the present administration . . . . the Tories are shrewd and brave . . . . any out of the way occurrence may blow up the Government all at once. A thousand enormous evils may happen before the people have been made familiar with expectations of important changes, without producing any serious or permanent effect any one of which may operate extensively and permanently when the people have been made familiar with expectations of great changes, and this is now our present state.

On the 19th, Place rather defensively told Burdett that his warning to Grey of an immediate panic had been justified in the public mood at the time, and warned that if the Government was not vigorous then public apathy might give victory to the Tories. [16]

Meanwhile the delegation to Grey was causing a growing public sensation. Place had publicly announced that it had been ascertained that Parliament was to be prorogued until after Christmas and a more conciliatory bill introduced, and Grey disputed his claims in the House of Lords. Place replied in a letter published in the *Morning Chronicle* on 19 October, which contradicted Grey's account. Colonel Torrens, a moderate radical MP, then called on Place to say that Grey was offended at his letter. He convinced Torrens that there was no cause for offence, but would not agree to Torrens' suggestion that he should go and see Grey, as he never called on great men. Cobbett added fuel to the fire by complaining that Place had been dilatory in not letting out the full story until a week after the delegation, so that the people had been misled into giving the Government their confidence. Place replied that Cobbett was right, but that the delay was the fault of the leader of the delegation, who should have sent the Memorial to the press. [17]

*   *   *

In his Reform Bill narrative, Place observed that the weeks following the rejection of the bill by the Lords were a disagreeable period, due to conflicting opinions among the people and a discouraging attitude by Ministers to agitation in their support. He claimed that the midnight delegation to Grey, as it became known, was of more importance than it was given credit for. It caused a great sensation, and this with numerous meetings, a growth of political unions and riots, convinced Ministers that a compromise involved risks which could not be justified. This seems on the face of it unlikely, since it was in the days following the delegation that he was complaining about growing apathy, but if the reaction was delayed until his controversy with Cobbett the following week then it becomes more plausible. [18]

An even more important result of the delegation to Grey, in Place's view, was that it encouraged the parish reformers to continue their efforts instead of relying on the Government, and thus provided the impetus for the formation of the National Political Union. The need for a union in London on the Birmingham model to organise support for reform had long been felt, but two attempts in 1830 had failed. In October 1831 the need became increasingly urgent because of the growing influence of the intransigent National Union of the Working Classes (NUWC), which rejected the bill as a measure to exclude the working people from power, and thus cast doubt on claims of united support for it. The meeting of parish delegates on 12 October had adjourned to the 14th, and when they reassembled, Erskine Perry proposed the formation of a comprehensive union of all classes. This was adopted, but at first Place would only help with advice. Perry and his friend Major Beauclerk had taken the lead in trying to organise agitation in the metropolis since the rejection of the bill by the Lords, but they had faltered over the Parliamentary Candidates Society, and Place did not want to become a member and commit himself to go on if others withdrew in the face of the inevitable problems which would arise.[19]

The first great difficulty was to find a chairman. It was taken for granted that a 'great man' was needed to get the union off the ground, but there was no obvious choice.[20] The three men preferred were Joseph Hume, Henry Warburton and George Grote, all three close friends and allies of Place. Hume was liable to be frightened by the disapproval of his friends and parliamentary colleagues. Warburton was a respected radical MP, and he was important to Place because his friendship with Lord Althorp, the Chancellor of the Exchequer and Leader of the House of Commons, ensured that Place was kept well informed about the Government's thinking and intentions, but he was also cautious. Place said of him: 'I can hardly tell you how much I esteem him, and yet his old batchelor sort of prudence, spite of his enlarged views, and accurate reasoning makes a droll thing of him sometimes.'[21] Grote was a leading banker and a Benthamite radical, but even Place admitted that it would be undesirable for him to sacrifice his influence with the bankers and merchants of the City by being too outspoken. They all refused to become chairman of the NPU, and Hobhouse disapproved of unions, leaving Burdett, who agreed and then had second thoughts.

He wanted a union solely to support the Ministers and the bill, but Place tried to persuade him that this would not do − if the NPU was to attract working men away from the NUWC, it must have aims wide enough to attract them. On 26 October, he wrote gloomily to James Mill that he had persuaded Burdett to agree to altering the declaration, but not enough. The union ought to have 100,000 members, and it might if it were properly conducted, but he was not hopeful. However when he wrote to George Grote on the same day, he was in more cheerful mood, saying that he was 'all but overwhelmed with people, all asking what can be done, all more or less cast down, all entertaining the notion however, that nothing can be so useful as keeping ministers up to the mark. Until lately every one was for keeping the enemy down, now every one is for keeping the ministry up, pushing them forward.' He advised people to join the proposed general union and form local ones, and he hoped that the general union would make 'a great splash'.[22]

Burdett proposed a public meeting to establish the union on 31 October, but at a private meeting on 27 October there was a long and stormy dispute over the aims of the union. Although the Rotundanists (as the members of the NUWC were known from the name of their meeting hall) were not present, it was only with great difficulty that universal suffrage and annual parliaments, which would have severely limited middle-class support for the NPU, were excluded. The first aim was finally agreed as : 'To obtain a full, free and effectual representation of the middle and working classes in the commons house of Parliament', but this incurred Burdett's disapproval, because he said that there were no classes and it was absurd. Perry nevertheless put Burdett's name to a handbill for the public meeting with the disputed words, relying on his permission to use his name, only to hear that he wanted the meeting put off. Burdett accepted the situation when he heard that his name had already been published as chairman, but relations between him and the union were always difficult.

As usual, a preparatory meeting was held just before the public one. The Rotundanists had already planned a public meeting on 7 November with the radical surgeon Thomas Wakley in the chair, and they regarded the NPU one as an attempt to spike their guns. As it was known that the Rotundanists would oppose the NPU organisers, they were called in to ask what they intended. Place had been voted into the chair as the meeting was bound to be stormy. The Rotundanists claimed that their union was better than the new one, which would be governed by the aristocracy and shopocracy to keep the working people in slavery. They demanded that the union commit itself to universal suffrage, which the managers refused to agree to. Place succeeded in frightening Wakley into withdrawing his consent to act as chairman at the NUWC public meeting by arguing that it was intended to cause a riot.[23] The Rotundanists then threatened to disrupt the formation of the NPU by violence, but Thomas Murphy, another key ally of theirs, did not approve of their tactics. Since Wakley and Murphy were their two best orators, they were disposed for a compromise.

The audience for the public meeting was so large that it was adjourned from the Crown and Anchor Tavern to Lincoln's Inn Fields, and Place feared that with half the crowd unable to hear what was going on a universal suffrage amendment would be carried. After considerable uproar and confusion some of the NPU managers agreed a compromise with the Rotundanist leaders, under which a motion that half of the council of the union should be working-class was accepted in return for the withdrawal of the universal suffrage amendment. Place disapproved because he knew that the middle classes would be deterred from joining, but he returned to the Crown and Anchor to start enrolling members. When no one turned up, he decided that the union was a failure and went home.

But for once he had been less persistent than his associates, some of whom came along to the tavern soon afterwards and formed a committee. Several Rotundanists present were included, on the principle that they could do less damage there than they would opposing from the outside. The next day Place and his friends spent all day at the tavern enrolling members, and 300-400 working men joined. Any man who looked respectable was then questioned to find out whether he was a Rotundanist. If he was not, he was invited into the committee room, and asked to name sober and discreet men who had the confidence of their fellow workmen, who might be invited to join the union with a view to their election to the council. Place remarked that almost all seemed to know and dislike the Rotundanists, and readily cooperated in pointing out suitable men. Several of Place's colleagues came in, and were promptly despatched to question the employers and neighbours of the men named to enquire about their character. Soon the NPU leaders had enough such men to provide a slate which would attract working-class support, and the Rotundanists lost further ground when they abandoned their meeting of 7 November in the face of a Government Proclamation prohibiting it.[24] Both sides were attempting to 'pack' the NPU, but whereas working-class supporters of the Reform Bill joined in considerable numbers, the NUWC leaders were unable to persuade many rank-and-file Rotundanists to pay the one shilling NPU subscription.

At a committee meeting of the NPU held on 2 November, Place took the chair. All members had a right to attend as spectators, and the room was crowded to overflowing. The Rotundanists almost caused a riot, and according to Place, disgust at their conduct was so great that they were left in no position to do any harm. Although socialist views were gaining ground among working people, many still welcomed the Reform Bill as a step forward, and were alienated by the violence of the Rotundanists. At a general meeting on 10 November, Thomas Murphy approvingly described how the working-class members of the council had been chosen – although not that the purpose had been to exclude the Rotundanists. The managers secured a majority for their list, and an attempt to add Rotundanist candidates including Henry Hunt was defeated. When the membership grew too large to fit in one room, the leaders encouraged the formation of branch unions, ignoring the law which prohibited political organisations from having branches. But they soon grew more cautious, and instructed NPU delegates sent to help set up new unions to withdraw just before they were formally inaugurated – now as separate unions instead of NPU branches – and handbills urging the formation of branches were destroyed.[25]

Although the decision that half of the council should be working-class alienated many middle-class supporters of the bill, it must have aided Place and his allies in achieving one of their main aims, gaining the allegiance of the majority of working men from the NUWC, especially since the NPU leaders were forced to seek out working men who had the confidence of their fellows as members of the council. It was shown, Place argued,

by the conduct of the working men who joined the National Political Union; and the numbers who joined the many other metropolitan unions; that they the better sort of such men though very generally, to some extent, entertaining the no property doctrine were not misled to an extent either to cause them to place the least dependence in the rogues or to believe that the union was not intended to promote their interests.

It was most fully demonstrated that they were willing to cooperate with those called their betters and to place sufficient reliance in them. This was a disposition which should have been taken advantage of and turned to good account. It should have met with *general* approbation and encouragement instead of which it was very partially acknowledged.

Those among their *betters* who were flourishing men, money getters and money lovers for its own sake, and the sake of the most ridiculous importance, are very selfish, and though generally in some silly particular profuse are remarkably mean, much more so than are the working people among their own class. The pride and ignorance of these people their false notions of dignity arising from absurd displays of contemptible importance, from what they persuade themselves is acting like the richer classes of society, in the haughty airs they give themselves and the contumely with which they treat those who are dependent on them, are great impediments to the rapid improvement of this class. Yet even by these people as a body these absurdities are carried to a much smaller extent than they were since I can remember, and by a much relatively smaller number of persons. On these people the conduct of the Rotunda men had produced a very bad effect. They were very generally desirous that ministers should be supported their opponents subdued and the Reform Bill be carried, but under their circumstances they could not consent to operate in common fellowship with the working people even to save the bill. They were ready to associate with great men, if great men would come among them, they were willing enough to level downwards but not at all willing to level upwards. They therefore kept aloof from the National Political Union and those of them who joined it at its commencement left it. Numbers of the better informed however even in this class joined it, as did also a great number of respectable well informed men who were not engaged in business.

In the first quarter 5000–6000 joined the NPU, which combined a middle-class radical leadership with a working-class membership. The result was to make it easy for Place and his allies to control the union, and their dominance was seldom successfully challenged. What opposition there was came from the more extreme members, and Place and his allies could meet this by accepting strongly-worded resolutions and petitions without acceding to any steps they considered dangerous. If the NPU had succeeded in recruiting wider middle-class support, the leaders would probably have found it impossible to satisfy both the timid and extreme, and the union might have been more divided and less effective. The Westminster reformers formed a rival 'respectable' union, but it collapsed within a month.[26]

* * *

The foundation of the NPU coincided with the worst riots of the Reform Bill period. Sir Charles Wetherell had said in Parliament that in such towns as Bristol, the £10 householders were paupers, and that it was beneath the dignity of a Member of Parliament 'to solicit votes in the *lazaretto*'. These and similar remarks so angered the reformers that when he visited Bristol in his capacity as Recorder on 29 October, they demonstrated against him, and the demonstration developed into riots which left twelve dead and 94 wounded. Place attributed the riots to the incompetence and cowardice of the authorities, and modern historians have come to the same conclusion, but at the time they caused great fear and harmed the NUWC.[27]

The riots also encouraged demands for a National Guard of householders, and on 18 November the Birmingham Political Union published an illegal plan to organise on military lines. The Government persuaded the union to drop the plan through Place's friend Joseph Parkes, a Birmingham solicitor. Place disapproved of the idea of a National Guard. He realised that no government could concede so much power, and the proposal aroused the resentment of working-class people who saw it as a middle-class organisation to suppress them. The Birmingham plan overcame this objection by including working-class members, but such a combined guard would not have been practicable in London where class hostility was greater. Place stated that the NPU did not even discuss the idea. The Government attempted to follow up its victory by publishing a Royal Proclamation against political unions, but a Proclamation could not go beyond existing law, and Place promptly replied with an NPU handbill which showed that all unions apart from the Birmingham one under its new plan were legal. He thus helped to prevent a decline in the unions, and greatly annoyed the King and those members of the Government who thought that the Proclamation would suppress them.[28]

*　　*　　*

In November Grey started negotiations with the Tory waverers in order to discover what concessions might secure a majority in the Lords, but Place had succeeded in reducing the Cabinet's room for manoeuvre by his use of the parish delegation. On 13 November, Althorp told Grey that it was doubtful whether Parliament should meet before Christmas, but he went on to say that:

> Brougham is eager for it; he says that in consequence of the false report of what passed at the interview you had with Mr Carpell [sic] and his party [the meeting with the parish delegates] the public have indissolubly connected the meeting after Christmas with the material alteration in the measure itself, and that if they find that Place was right when he said he inferred from what you said that Parliament would not meet till after Christmas, they will believe he was right also in his inference that great alterations were to be made in the bill.

For these reasons Althorp favoured an early meeting, although he would have preferred postponement otherwise. Grey hoped that delay would give time for the unions' fervour to cool. On 16 November Lord Wharncliffe, one of the leaders of the waverers, had an interview with Grey, but three days later the Cabinet agreed to recall Parliament on 6 December against his opposition. According to Lord Holland's account:

> the state of the country, the pressing representation of all our friends, the dread of the unions made us all shrink from the responsibility of leaving the Country in its present state for another month without a Parliament. We felt, whether with reference to measures for suppressing, or diverting or legalising the Unions, or to the rapid progress of reform as the sole cure of the propensity to form them, that an immediate session of Parliament was, in spite of inconveniences, by far the safest course. This view of the subject was much confirmed by Lord Melbourne's report of the state of the publick mind and his somewhat reluctant but decided opinion that it would be aggravated very materially by a postponement of the meeting.

Lord Palmerston, the Foreign Secretary, was disgusted. 'Were you aware yesterday', he asked Melbourne,

> when you turned the scale in favour of meeting in a fortnight, what has been the nature of the communications between Wharncliffe and Grey? . . . I am convinced that if time had been allowed for this negotiation it would have succeeded, and that by some modification in the bill, which from what Wharncliffe said need not have been great, we could not only have improved the measure, but have insured a majority in the House of Lords for that and all other purposes *before* Parliament had met. How this is now to be done I hardly see.

Wellington indignantly claimed that Parliament was recalled because 'the unions and the press insisted upon it, and they could not be resisted. . . . Who ever heard of assembling Parliament and having nothing for them to do? Nobody, but the mob and Mr Place the tailor!'[29] The negotiations collapsed at the end of November.

The third Reform Bill introduced on 12 December contained no important concessions to the Tories, and agitation then largely ceased. Place thought that the bill was improved on the whole, but it strengthened one clause which, in his view, would severely reduce the borough franchise and reopen the way to corruption. This was the 27th clause, which disqualified anyone who did not pay rates and taxes when they were due. Place knew from his long experience of election management that this would disqualify the great majority of electors, and a petition against the clause was agreed by the NPU at his instigation, with words which would cause a row in Parliament in order to get newspaper coverage. In this he succeeded, but few reformers could be persuaded to master the complex legal questions involved, and he was unable to rouse any concern over the matter.[30]

*   *   *

The last fortnight of December was a critical period for the NPU. Public excitement had died and no funds were coming in. Erskine Perry and Daniel Wakefield, a son of Place's old friend, kept it alive by raising money to open a reading-room for members. A show of activity in the council also helped – a motion on banking partnerships proved controversial and led to a lively discussion. On 26 January 1832, according to Hobhouse, Place said that there had been little real public feeling the previous October, and that even now the NPU and the Birmingham PU were just moonshine. But this must be treated as hyperbole since the NPU was then holding weekly council meetings with thirty present, plus spectators. On 2 February the NPU held a rowdy general meeting. Burdett caused uproar by refusing to put a petition critical of Ministers to a vote, and then walked out. Place had opposed what he considered unnecessary objectionable expressions in it, and in the end it was referred back to the council for amendment. Two weeks later, a ballot was held to choose the first elected council, with 36 working-class members and 36 non-working-class. The NUWC candidates were almost all defeated, and Place was elected in eleventh position among the non-working-class candidates – his relatively low position no doubt reflected both his aversion to publicity and his reputation for rudeness.[31] The council took a moderate line on the punishment of the rioters in Bristol and Nottingham. They agreed that if any people deserved the death penalty then the rioters did, but they nevertheless agreed to petition against the sentences on the ground that they disapproved of capital punishment.

Activity by the council served the dual purpose of keeping the NPU going until the bill returned to the Lords, and giving an opportunity for the political education of working men so dear to Place's heart. NPU tracts were printed under his supervision, paid for by subscriptions. An attempt to bring political economy before the council was abandoned for fear of causing dissension, but Place scored a triumph with a motion on the Anatomy Bill, which made bodies available for dissection. He had first taken an interest in the problem in 1826 or 1827, when a medical bookseller called Highley had sought his help in finding a body in connection with a forthcoming book. At that time it was almost impossible to obtain bodies legally, and Place drew up a petition for an alteration in the law, which Highley pressed on his timid medical acquaintance. Prejudice against dissection, which was considered sacrilegious, was so strong that doctors and surgeons were unwilling to sign the petition at first, but they did so after an eminent surgeon took it up, and in 1828 Warburton unsuccessfully attempted to get an Anatomy Bill through Parliament. The Burke and Hare cases made the subject a matter of public controversy, and in 1832 Warburton tried again. Place decided to attempt to get a petition for the bill from the NPU, but he faced great hostility from the working-class audience at the council, and opposition from several leading members, including Wakley, the editor of *The Lancet*. Place succeeded in swaying the audience, and after discussion over three successive weeks a petition in favour was agreed. Aided by support from Sir Robert Peel, the bill became law.[32]

*   *   *

In March 1832 excitement grew once again as the date approached for the return of the bill to the Lords. Place wrote that the reformers feared that the Cabinet were relying too much on the waverers, and would be deceived; the NPU led the way in reviving agitation by circulating an address headed 'Crisis', which was inserted in newspapers all over the Kingdom. This, he said, greatly excited apprehension and feelings against the Lords. Press coverage was critical for the unions, because correspondence between political societies was illegal. Place wrote that until May 1832 there was little communication around the country save by newspapers, and he thought that this was more effective than correspondence would have been.[33] At an NPU council meeting on 21 March, with 300 spectators, there was fierce controversy over whether to petition the Lords. The prevailing desire among the audience was to provoke the aristocracy to violence rather than to petition, but the 'rational' party, as Place described himself and his allies, argued that a petition could go far enough to satisfy the most ultra, provided that the wording was 'respectful' enough to satisfy the forms of the Lords, and that it would be useful propaganda. A petition which threatened the refusal of taxes was agreed and widely circulated − it was even praised by Cobbett. Place remarked that he did good service supporting the bill in his *Register,* and would have been of all but infinite use but for the narrow selfishness which cut him off from others and deprived him of information. The people were in a painful state of suspense, Place observed, which partly paralysed them. They were unwilling to distrust Grey, but could not understand why he did not create peers. Business slackened and there was a general vague notion of impending mischief. However Place and his allies did not want an early creation of peers, which a majority of the Cabinet were prepared to support at one time or another, arguing that the peers would have to submit if the people did their duty, and if they did not do their duty then they were in no condition to benefit from the Reform Bill.[34]

One of the demands of the Tory waverers was a reduction in the representation of the metropolis, even though it was greatly under-represented under the bill's provisions. Place supplied the Cabinet Minister Lord Durham with statistics through Colonel Leslie Grove Jones to defend London's case, although he told Jones that he would be willing to give up the new metropolitan boroughs if there was no other way to save the bill.[35]

With the support of the waverers, there was a majority of nine on the second reading on 14 April, but it was clear that the bill was likely to be mutilated in committee. A delay of two weeks before the committee stage gave time for the people to organise which, Place said, they did to an amazing extent, seeing a prospect of success if they did their duty. Many meetings were held, and opinion grew that the choice was between the bill and a revolution, with a revolution no longer dreaded. Thus in Place's view the NPU had to proceed cautiously but be ready to act manfully, and resolutions by George Rogers threatening the Government were referred to the Business Committee. An NPU petition which was hardly less extreme warned the Lords that if the bill was mutilated, the ultimate consequence would be the extinction of the privileged orders.

On 2 May Joseph Parkes sent Place a desperate appeal for financial help to keep the Birmingham Political Union going. In his reply on 3 May, he assured Parkes that he was 'working like a devil in a mud wall' to raise money and observed: 'You as well as I know the securities we and others can easily take to prevent, *reaction*.' He managed to get £50 each from Grote and Warburton. It does not seem to have occurred to him to wonder whether the appeal suggested some weakening in the stronghold of reform agitation.[36]

Place said that when the committee stage started on 7 May, excitement was wound up to its highest pitch yet. Business was widely neglected because men felt that they could only attend to the fate of the bill, which would decide whether they would continue their occupations or enter another state. The Government suffered an immediate defeat on a procedural motion, and the Tories hastily announced their acceptance of the abolition of the 113 seats in Schedule A (which contained the constituencies with the smallest electorates), in the hope that this would prevent agitation and stop the Ministry making peers or resigning.[37] But the gesture had no effect because hardly anyone would trust the Tories to support an effective Reform Bill, and the next day the Government asked the King for full power to make peers, offering their resignation as the alternative.

The NPU called a meeting of Westminster inhabitants at the Crown and Anchor in the evening, and many were unable to get in. An address to the King was agreed which asked him to save the country from anarchy by creating peers. Several leading members of the NPU claimed at the meeting that they had refused to pay taxes until the bill was passed. On the same day, the union deputed Major Revell to chair a meeting of the Bethnal Green Union, the first open breach of the law by the NPU. Thereafter the council met nightly until the end of the crisis. On 9 May it became known that the King had refused to make peers and had accepted the Government's resignation, and on the 10th, London was placarded as never before with bills calling for meetings of unions, parishes and trades. In the evening the NPU held a general meeting; an immense crowd gathered in the square outside the NPU office and hundreds were unable to get in or join the union. The meeting voted confidence in the Whig ministry, and agreed to petition the House of Commons to withhold supplies from a Tory Government. It also voted to call a public meeting on Hampstead Heath in conjunction with other unions, much to the embarrassment of the council, which could hardly set it aside but dared not carry it out. Such cooperation between unions was illegal, but this did not worry them in such an emergency. What did concern Place and his allies was the fear that in such a location half a million would have attended, and it would have been impossible to engage the attention of them all, so the 'mischievously disposed' could have held their own meetings and caused riots. This might have caused a reaction in favour of the Tories, so the council put off a decision on a Hampstead Heath meeting from day to day, until the crisis was over.[38]

On Friday the 11th, delegates from Birmingham and other towns met in Place's library to concert opposition if the Duke of Wellington succeeded in forming a Government. According to Place's account, they agreed that Birmingham was the place to raise the standard of revolt. Plans were further refined at a meeting the following day, Saturday the 12th, at a tavern in Covent Garden at noon attended by the delegates and leading Londoners. The leaders of the NPU were then in communication with influential middle-class men in nearly all the large towns and many other places, all of whom agreed to barricade their towns and await proceedings in London if the Duke formed a Government. In the capital the plan was to avoid a fight but keep the bulk of the army close to the capital by demonstrations. The reformers calculated that a stoppage of trade and refusal of paper money would lead to unemployment and halt supplies of food, and thus produce outrages which the army would be unable to prevent, bringing a Tory Government down within a week. For the present there was no Government in existence, so the radicals believed that they could plan resistance in comparative safety; they thought that the Duke probably had spies among them, but if he had arrested respectable men for High Treason it would have caused an insurrection, and they hoped that knowledge of their plans would help to deter him from attempting to form a Government. However, they greatly overestimated his interest in their proceedings.

In the afternoon the delegates came again to Place, excited at confirmation that the King had ordered the Duke of Wellington to form an administration. They agreed that as soon as he took office all the delegates apart from three from the most important towns should return home to put the people in opposition to the Duke. 'It was quite certain', Place believed, 'that the bulk of the people would rise *en masse* at the call of the Unions, and the deputies now in London and other Cities.' Newspaper reports of a run on gold suggested that a financial panic might provide a bloodless means of preventing the Duke taking power, and the delegates were puzzling over how to encourage the run when someone suggested a placard. Parkes started to write one out, and Place saw the words 'we must stop the Duke', which struck him as saying nearly all that needed to be said. He took a sheet of paper and wrote:

TO STOP THE
DUKE
GO FOR
GOLD

Everyone immediately said that no more words were needed, money was put on the table and within four hours billstickers were at work all over London. Men were engaged to distribute bills in taverns and shops, wherever people would engage to put them up, and parcels were sent to other towns. Place's bill was only one of many urging resistance to the Duke, and every site was covered.[39]

The Tories were having great difficulties in forming a Government. The King had insisted that the new Government must pass an extensive Reform Bill, and Wellington and other leading Tory Lords had in any case accepted this on 7 May. Peel had suffered so much abuse by reneging on his opposition to Catholic emancipation that he was unwilling to be seen to 'rat' again, so he refused to serve. Two leading Tories in the Commons, Alexander Baring and the Speaker, Charles Manners-Sutton, refused to serve under the Duke because of his record as an opponent of all reform, so the Tories were forced to fall back on Manners-Sutton as their candidate for Prime Minister. Their position looked extremely weak, with the City thoroughly frightened and urging Grey's return, but on Sunday 13 May the Whigs surprisingly agreed to accept a Tory Government pledged to reform, and on Monday Peel advised Manners-Sutton to accept the premiership.

On the same day, Monday the 14th, an attendance of 80,000 was claimed at a meeting of the parishes of Marylebone, St Pancras and Paddington in Regents Park, at which Colonel Leslie Grove Jones said that he was ready to lead the people against the army. According to Place, this was an experiment to determine how easily soldiers could be brought to London and kept there. It proved successful since the whole metropolitan police was organised and soldiers were brought in.[40] Numerous public meetings all over the country showed a great state of excitement. There were constant calls for a refusal of taxes if the Duke of Wellington took power, and frequent references to the fates of Charles I and Louis XVI.[41] Determination to resist a Tory Government led the radicals increasingly to ignore the law, often without realising that they were doing so.

In the evening the proposed Government faced the House of Commons. The hostility it encountered was so great, even from some leading Tories, that Manners-Sutton never declared himself. His chief spokesman, Alexander Baring, caved in and called for Grey's return. Wellington had known for some days that Rothschild was only preventing a fall in government stocks with great difficulty, and the next day, Tuesday the 15th, he resigned his commission and the King recalled Grey. Place exultingly told George Grote, who had disowned the 'Go for Gold' placard in the *Standard* for fear that it would alienate the bankers:

> We may now sing 'Glory to God in the highest' the bill is won, won too without the help of the City Life and Fortune men. It will now be the peoples bill and Lord Grey the peoples minister. . . . Here is the conclusive answer to your note of yesterday, containing your, what? − Oh! arguments against Go For Gold showing that it was no go at all, just as an early copy of the Standard was brought to me containing your letter to the Editor, came a great man, who seeing the placard Go for Gold on my table, pointed to it and said in a tone of admiration, 'that's the settler, that has finished it'. . . . 'Go for Gold & Stop the Duke' is my motto.

The 'great man' was Sir John Hobhouse, who had been appointed the Secretary at War in February. Out of coined gold of £3-4 million held by the Bank of England, £1.6 million had been withdrawn over a week to ten days, and a reduction in the reserves of £2 million in total was only prevented by withholding the April dividend. On 15 May, Lord Holland noted in his diary that the announcement of Grey's return had 'suspended the frightful demand of gold'.[42]

However, there were still further alarms. Grey demanded that Wellington guarantee that he would no longer oppose the bill, but in the Lords on Thursday the 17th the Duke instead issued an uncompromising denunciation. Ministers then had to decide whether to insist on the power to make peers, and early on Friday the 18th Hobhouse asked Place for his assessment of the position, to read to a Cabinet meeting at noon. Place said of his reply: 'In quiet times . . . the letter might have been thought treasonable, but on the day it was written the memorable 18 May 1832 when all were ready and willing not only to write treasonably but to act treasonably, there was nothing very remarkable, much less extraordinary in my sending such a letter to his Majesty's Secretary at War.'

18 May 1832

Dear Sir John

I am again becoming anxious, you promised to come and tell me what was going on, in case of any peculiar difficulty, or any hitch – or any thing conclusive. I have not however seen you, and spite of my desire to believe that *all* may go right I cannot satisfy myself that *any thing* is going right.

Last night at the National Political Union I had much of difficulty in appeasing many members of the council. The persons who assembled in the Great Room and in the passages were gloomy and sulky. This mornings newspapers will make things worse. The moment it was known Earl Grey had been sent for, the *Demand for Gold* ceased. No more placards were posted, and all seemed to be going on well at once. Proof positive this of the cool courage and admirable discipline of the people. We cannot however go on thus *beyond to day*. If doubt remain until tomorrow, alarm will commence again and panic will follow. No effort to *STOP THE DUKE — BY GOING FOR GOLD* was made beyond a mere demonstration and you saw the consequence. What can be done in this way has now been clearly ascertained and if new efforts must be made they will not be made in vain. Lists containing the names addresses &c of persons in every part of the country likely to be useful have been made. The name of every man who has at any public meeting showed himself friendly to reform has been registered. Addresses and proclamations to the people have been sketched, and printed copies will, if need be, be sent to every such person all over the kingdom – means have been devised to placard towns and villages, to circulate hand bills and assemble the people. So many men of known character, civil and *military* have entered heartily into the scheme, that their names when published will produce great effect in every desirable way. If the Duke come into power now, we shall be unable, longer to 'hold to the laws' – break them we must, be the consequences whatever they may, we know that all must join with us, to save their property, no matter what, may be their private opinions. Towns will be barricaded – new municipal arrangements will be formed by the inhabitants and the first town which is barricaded, shuts up all the banks. *GO FOR GOLD* it is said will produce dreadful evils, – we know it will, but it will prevent other evils being added to them. It will *STOP THE DUKE*. Let the Duke take office as premier and we shall have a commotion in the nature of a civil war, with money at our command. If we obtain money he cannot get it. If it be but once dispersed, he cannot collect it. If we have money we shall have the power to feed and lead the people, and in less than five days we shall have the soldiers with us. Here then is a picture not by any means over drawn – not too highly coloured, no, not even filled up. Look at it, it is worthy the serious contemplation of every man. Think too upon the results. Think too of the consequences to the public creditor – to the Church – the King – the Aristocracy

– think of the coming republic. Think of the certain destruction of those from whom opposition may be apprehended, and you will at once discover how all depends on Earl Grey being restored or not being restored to office. You will see the fearful necessity there is for prompt proceedings to *compel* the King to request his services, and to enable him to possess sufficient means to accomplish his purposes. Keep him up for Gods sake. Let us have one man worthy of a statue in every town and village, and let us have through him and his colleagues (we can have it in no other way) peace among ourselves, safety comfort and prosperity.

If I am to meet the people at the great meeting tomorrow night, in Leicester Square, with doubts, all but infinite mischief may follow.

If the meeting at the London Tavern on Monday is to take place whilst doubt remains – all may be ended. *GO FOR GOLD* may then settle the matter at once.

Yours truly
Francis Place

Ironically this letter may have helped to reassure the Cabinet that the situation was not as desperate as they thought. Several Ministers attended the Cabinet meeting at noon convinced that only an immediate creation of peers would meet the situation, but after hearing many letters and reports, they decided that a power to create would be sufficient. It is noteworthy that even in this emergency Place did not urge an immediate creation, and his reference to a meeting on Monday implied that time had not run out.[43] At 3 p.m. Hume came to Place with a message from Hobhouse that everything was going wrong and the people must look to themselves. Place and his allies then agreed that if the Duke was appointed premier, Birmingham would be barricaded and other towns would follow its lead. The families of as many Tory Lords as possible would be seized and carried into the towns as hostages. In London nothing would be done at first beyond pursuing the run on gold, this alone being expected to cause such chaos as to bring down the Government. But these plans became irrelevant when it became known that evening that the King had finally given Grey the power to make peers, and the crisis was over. The Tories stayed away from the House of Lords, and the bill passed its remaining stages without further trouble.[44]

On 7 June 1832, the English Reform Bill received the Royal Assent. In July the Scottish Reform Bill was passed, and finally in August the Irish one. Fifty-six rotten boroughs returning 111 members lost representation, thirty small boroughs lost one of their two representatives, and one borough lost two of its four members. Sixty-five extra seats were awarded to the counties, twenty-two large towns and newly created London metropolitan districts each gained two representatives, and twenty-one smaller towns one. The borough franchise was standardised on a yearly rental of £10. In the counties the franchise was granted to forty shilling freeholders, £50 tenants, £10 long leaseholders and £50 medium leaseholders.

*   *   *

The question of whether there would have been a revolution if the bill had

failed has long exercised historians. The major modern study of the passage of
the bill, Michael Brock's *The Great Reform Act,* concluded that there would
have been a rising if Wellington had come to power in May 1832, but other
historians have increasingly moved to the view that there was no real danger.[45]
Place believed that the people would have accepted a lesser reform at the
beginning, but would not once the bill had been introduced in the House of
Commons in March 1831.[46] The key periods were those following the House
of Lords' rejection of the second Reform Bill in October 1831 and the third in
May 1832. The earlier period appears to have been more dangerous, since it
was marked by major riots, and in retrospect Place had no doubts. He said
that the working people wanted revolution and destruction of the aristocracy;
those above them would not countenance this, but the state of alarm was such
that there could easily have been a panic, a run on gold and a stoppage of
business, which would have thrown the working people out of employment
and stopped food coming into towns; in these circumstances only the political
unions would have been able to keep order, and power would have devolved
on them. If the Tories had come to power, the unions would have risen. These
and similar circumstances, he argued, were the ones which produced
unexpected revolutions.[47] But he admitted that up to May 1832 he had
doubted the courage and judgement of the people; it was the 'Days of May'
which showed that the Duke would have been resisted in his view. The
argument is dubious because in the autumn of 1831 the danger was that the
Whigs would compromise, and the people did not prove their willingness to
resist this in May 1832. Probably the most reasonable verdict is expressed in
his letter to Grote (see p. 185), where he warned of the danger of a Tory victory
if the reformers relaxed, but also argued that when expectations had been
roused an 'out of the way occurrence' might blow up the Government.[48]

The state of high excitement and the tone of threatening confidence which
the reformers adopted in May 1832 contrasts strongly with the mood of doubt
in the previous autumn.[49] The rapid growth of tension in May made all
previous calculations about the balance of strength between reformers and
anti-reformers irrelevant — even Place had been ready to give up the new
metropolitan seats in April, but after Grey's resignation he would have
regarded such a concession as inconceivable. The reformers' claim to have
had military men ready to take command has been questioned. Place wrote
that he was in contact with thirteen, all of the rank of major or above, and
there were a number of military men among his close allies. The only one he
named was Colonel George de Lacy Evans, who went on to command an
Auxiliary Legion which fought on the Constitutional side in the Spanish civil
war in the late 1830s. Other possible commanders among Place's
acquaintance were Colonel Leslie Grove Jones, who offered to lead the
people against the army at the open air meeting on 14 May; Major William
Aubrey Beauclerk, one of the more extreme leaders of the NPU; Major Henry
Revell, who was deputed to a local political union in the first open defiance of

the law by the union; Colonel Perronet Thompson, who favoured the formation of a 'corps of Yeomanry infantry' to defend the bill in November 1831; and Colonel Robert Torrens, who threatened the House of Lords with abolition in a speech in September 1831.[50]

It has been argued that the strategy of Place and his allies was hardly designed to win a full-scale war with the army, but this ignores the fact that they were relying on producing a financial panic and breakdown. It has also been argued that the radicals did not complete their plan until too late, since they were still finalising it when the possibility of a Wellington Government had disappeared. But it was only natural that they should carry on refining details so long as there was time to do so − this does not mean that they could not have moved effectively if a Tory Government had been formed earlier. In any case, their strategy did not depend on carrying through an elaborate plan. Although the army was not as weak as they believed, it was much too weak to cope with a large-scale outbreak; with competent military leaders and the populace on their side the radicals would not have found it difficult to stave off defeat long enough to bring about an economic collapse. 'Go for Gold' had the subsidiary aim of ensuring that if a Tory Government were formed, paper money would be worthless and gold would be in the hands of the reformers, who would thus be able to buy the loyalty of the soldiers whom Ministers would be unable to pay. The strongest evidence for the credibility of Place's claims is that the run on gold did reduce the Bank's holding of gold coin by half, even though the run was confined to London, Wellington never succeeded in forming a Government, and he gave up the attempt only two days after Place started distribution of his placard, so that a full-scale campaign against gold did not have time to get under way. Most of the drain took place before the placard was circulated, and the radicals aimed to build on the incipient panic and trade recession which already existed.

However it is doubtful whether Birmingham would have taken the lead as the radicals expected. Place was not well informed about the Birmingham Political Union, which was a more moderate body than he realised. The lack of communication between radicals in different towns before the 'Days of May' meant that London reformers' image of the union was the one which it presented through newspaper reports of its proceedings. It seems likely that the Birmingham delegates in London during the crisis were infected by the atmosphere of excitement, and made promises which they would have been unable or unwilling to carry out. Place himself cast doubt on their determination when he complained that the city had not carried out their promises to join the run on gold.[51] The campaign planned in London would probably have been successful in bringing down a Wellington Government, but the evidence does not suggest that a situation existed in which revolution was possible. The question of whether the radicals would have opposed a Tory Government led by Manners-Sutton and pledged to reform is one that Place did not answer, although his account suggests that they would have refused to believe in the sincerity of the pledge, and would have gone ahead with resistance.

The question of the degree of influence which Place and other extra-parliamentary radicals had on the passage of the bill is also controversial. He was not as extreme as is often thought. In October 1831, he supported an immediate creation of peers, but in the spring of 1832 he opposed it – because he did not want such a revolutionary step when he was confident that the bill could be carried without it. His opposition to a National Guard and his willingness to give up the new metropolitan seats also suggest relative moderation, and even his famous letter to Hobhouse of 18 May 1832 was hardly extreme at a time when the King was being threatened with the fate of Charles I and Louis XVI in public speeches. To Ministers and MPs Place was an expert although biased witness on the state of popular opinion. His role was that of a communicator, coordinator and organiser. He was in contact with the Rotundanists and kept a close watch on their activities and publications. Together with Parkes he was a key link between the Government and the movement in the country, and his contacts and reputation as the leading Westminster reformer were also important.[52]

His role in the passage of the bill was most critical in October and November 1831. He played a key part in the foundation of the NPU, which was important because the lack of a London union cast doubt on the unions' claim to speak for the nation, and because its establishment encouraged a growth of political unions. Even more important was his use of the delegation to Grey to alert the reformers to the fact that the Government was attempting to negotiate a compromise, thus not only helping to revive agitation but making any delay in the recall of Parliament appear evidence of his claims. Postponement might have given time for an agreement with the waverers, and even if the negotiations had failed, recall after Christmas would have given time for agitation to decline, making a watered-down bill more likely.

The NPU was not as influential as the Birmingham Political Union. In a city which had so many disparate loyalties and channels of agitation as London, the NPU could not hope to unite the reformers as the Birmingham one did, and legal difficulties made matters worse by prohibiting it from forming branches. The organisers of the procession on 12 October 1831 had to be careful to stay in the background and let the parish leaders take the credit in order to get their cooperation,[53] and when the NPU called a Westminster public meeting in May 1832 the chairman felt obliged to explain why the union had taken such a liberty. Class hostility was also greater than in Birmingham, although it was not such a problem as in Manchester or Leeds. But the NPU did capture the initiative from opponents of the bill in the NUWC, which was especially important in London where the Tories were constantly on the lookout for any evidence of a reaction which they could cite in Parliament – few things gave them more pleasure than Henry Hunt's claims that the working people were indifferent to the bill.

On occasion the NPU could give the lead to reformers in other parts of the country, as when it urged the need for a revival of agitation with its 'Crisis' address when the bill returned to the Lords in March 1832. Place attached great importance to the role of the political unions in providing a safe channel for agitation, and thus preventing outrages, but in London the NPU seems to have shared this role with the other metropolitan unions, Westminster public meetings and the parish reform associations.[54] The NPU concentrated on propaganda and political education through the press and the publication of tracts. The jealousies among London reformers may have been a factor in the failure of the NPU to call open air public meetings, although the main reason seems to have been fear of Rotundanist disruption.

Place claimed that May 1832 was the one time when the NPU was more important than the Birmingham PU, but his assessment appears to be based on his belief that the run on gold, which never got under way in Birmingham, prevented the formation of a Tory Government. He overestimated the Tories' chances of success and their willingness to use force. He had a great respect for their courage, and he failed to realise the extent to which they had already conceded defeat. The King made the passage of an extensive reform a condition of the formation of a Tory Government, but even before this the leading Tories had announced their acceptance of the abolition of the 113 seats in Schedule A of the bill. The Duke's attempt to form a Government was in difficulties from the start, because the diehards thought that he was selling out, and the moderates thought that if the bill was to be passed then the Whigs should carry it. But Place relied for his information on the Whigs, who did not realise the weakness of the Tories' position. His main informant was Hobhouse, who was especially pessimistic. On 15 May he told Place not to be too sure of Grey's return, and as late as the 17th he believed that a Tory Government would be formed.[55]

Wellington had been too preoccupied with his attempt to form a Government to take much notice of the radicals' campaign, but it had some effect even on him. After the failure of his proposed Government in the House of Commons on 14 May, it was proposed to make another attempt, but the Duke declined, saying that 'the King had better send for Lord Grey at once. He will have to do it at last; and it is not right to keep the country in agitation during the interval.'[56] Its effect on the Whigs can be seen by contrasting two statements by Hobhouse. After the Second Reading victory on 14 April he told Melbourne that 'they ought not to be pertinacious about the clauses in Committee, for let the Lords mutilate the Bill as they pleased, it would still be ten times more radical than Lord Brougham's scheme in 1830'. On 16 May he told the leading Tory Alexander Baring that even a little modification 'was rendered difficult, if not impossible, by the events of last week; for the Political Unions were now raised to an importance which rendered their immediate suppression almost impossible. Baring seemed to agree with me.' The 'Days of May' were important because they made amendments to the bill, which even Place had been prepared to accept until then, impossible.[57]

There is no serious evidence to support Place's belief that his 'Go for Gold' placard prevented the formation of a Tory Government. He overestimated its importance because he was misled by Hobhouse's remark on 15 May that the placard had 'finished it', and by a dubious story he heard from a government source that it was a warning from the Bank of England about the state of gold which finally persuaded the King to give Grey power to make peers.[58] If the Tories had succeeded in forming a Government, Place's role in coordinating resistance would have been very important, but as it turned out his contribution was less critical. He played an important part in preserving in London the image of determination without disorder which so impressed the Whigs. His efficient organisation ensured the rapid circulation of the 'Go for Gold' placard, and this was far more important than the fact that he hit on the words used.

Place's part in the passage of the Reform Bill was much greater than he claimed in his Reform Bill narrative, but it was smaller than he clearly believed.

                              *   *   *

Once the initial euphoria following the introduction of the bill in March 1831 had worn off, Place realised that it was intended to preserve aristocratic control, although his view of how the Government achieved this intention was eccentric. He thought that two clauses were critical. One was the clause which required early payment of rates to qualify borough voters, and although he was correct in believing that the Government intended it to limit the democratic effect of the bill, he was unable to rally opposition until it was too late. The other was the Chandos clause, which enfranchised tenants in the counties who were wholly in the power of their landlords. Place had seen too much of the servility of Westminster tradesmen to their aristocratic customers to be in favour of extending the franchise to dependent voters without the secrecy of the ballot to protect them; he even defended the restriction of the franchise in the Irish counties under the Catholic Emancipation Bill. He warned that the Chandos clause would eventually allow the Tories to gain control of the counties, but to his fury it was passed with radical support against government opposition. In the circumstances, his charge that Ministers accepted the defeat because they were pleased to damage the bill carried his predilection for conspiracy theories about Whig motives to the point of absurdity.[59]

On 20 May 1832 he wrote that even a year ago the people were essentially loyal to the King, Bishops, Lords and Commons, now much of the absurd loyalty had been destroyed for ever. Replying in July to a vote of thanks from the Huddersfield Political Union for a present of books, he wrote: 'The Reform Bills will be of little value in themselves, except that they will be the commencement of the practicable mode of breaking up the old rotten system,

& for this they are invaluable. It is the insertion of the wedge and if we do not do our best to drive it home, we and we only shall be to blame for the evils which may remain . . .' He urged petitions by the hundred for shorter parliaments and the secret ballot.[60]

Place suspended his usual complaints about the dishonesty of the daily press during the Reform Bill period, and since the press generally reflected public opinion, this suggests that it was the one period when public opinion reflected his views. He confirmed this by writing that many political matters were better understood during the Reform Bill period than before or after it.[61] His hopefulness that the 'wedge' could be quickly driven home, and that attitudes had radically changed as a result of the victory, soon disappeared. Comments he wrote in 1838 show the characteristic mixture of fierce antagonism and caution in his outlook:

> Government in this country is a perpetual cheat, a fraudulent game at factitious honours, and real emoluments, for the purpose of enabling a comparatively small number of persons to be ridiculously great, substantially powerful, and to provide extravagantly for certain families at the expense of the people, and against their interests in many ways. It is a continual practice of pompous meanness founded on the absurd reverence the people have long been taught to pay to the aristocracy.
>
> This reverence is however declining – declining but slowly because the people gain wisdom but slowly, and it is probably a happy circumstance that it does not decline more rapidly as it might then exceed the rate at which knowledge advances and produce serious mischief.

Those who had an interest in maintaining corruption, he argued, were supported by the 'apers of gentility' and 'the great manufacturers, whose continued practice [is] of treating the common people with unspeakable contempt and are consequently with but few exceptions ready to support any measure of the government which has a tendency to exalt the rich and depress every other class'.[62]

His attitude to the Whigs was highly ambivalent. He believed that fundamentally they aimed to defend the interests of the aristocracy against those of the rest of society. He never tired of quoting Grey's remark that he would stand by his order, and he was frequently angered by their policies in office. On the other hand he was often able to work with individual MPs, his differences with the Whigs over the Reform Bill were mostly on tactics rather than principle, and he had a respect for some Whig leaders, especially Brougham, Durham and Althorp.

He had much in common with the Whigs. Both believed that change towards a democratic form of government was inevitable in the long run, and that wise ministers would make concessions in time rather than allow a dangerous degree of resentment to build up. Both were cautious about moving towards democracy too quickly, but whereas Place considered the development something to be welcomed and worked for, they often considered it as an undesirable trend to be resisted when this could safely be done. At times he would present himself as a friend of Ministers, as in August 1832, when he told Lord Melbourne's secretary, Tom Young, that 'I, and all the men with whom I acted, were desirous they should stand well with the people'. His verdict on Grey, that he made a mistake in conceding so much in the bill because it was bound to destroy his order in the long run, cannot be accepted. Destruction in the sense Place meant, the end of the aristocracy's privileges, was inevitable, and Grey played a critical role in making sure that it occurred without physical destruction. Place was generally unfair to the Whigs, a result of their tricks and equivocations and his own hostility to the upper classes.[63]

*   *   *

After the bill had passed Place was finally able to raise alarm over the ratepaying clause, by showing that it drastically reduced the borough electorates. In Westminster the electorate should have been 17,738, but only 2946 had paid their rates by the qualifying date, including 1500 in St Martins, where a dispute was going on and a small rate had been levied for emergencies. Articles by Place in the *Morning Chronicle* produced parish protest meetings, and radical MPs were finally pressured into making a row in Parliament. Urged to call on Lord Althorp to explain the matter, he declined, his aversion to waiting on 'great men' being even stronger than his desire to see the clause altered. As usual, when he was worrying the Home Office, Tom Young called and tried to pacify him. Place urged a short session of Parliament to push through an amending bill, but this was politically impossible immediately after the passage of the Reform Bill, so the Government equivocated and quietly instructed the overseers to evade the law and add enough names to the list of electors to make the size of the electorate respectable.

Place could not discover the principle on which the extra electors in Westminster had been chosen. Under the provisions of the Act, existing scot and lot voters kept their votes even if they did not qualify for the £10 franchise. This should not have applied to Westminster, because no houses were rated under £10, yet the electoral list included scot and lot voters. Place concluded that these were favoured voters who had not paid their rates by the qualifying date, and that the choice was biased against the independent-minded small tradesmen who were not dependent on aristocratic customers. In 1843 the law was altered to allow three months for payment, and in 1849 this was extended to six months.[64]

*   *   *

Once the bill was safe the NPU concentrated on the forthcoming General Election. Several candidates sought its endorsement, and sometimes the question of which candidate to endorse was a matter of debate. Pledges were widely demanded, and the Benthamites became worried that these were often too detailed. John Stuart Mill and W.J. Fox wrote articles against excessively detailed pledges, and Place wrote an NPU tract in the same vein. After a complaint from Blackburn to the NPU about a candidate who was treating the voters with food and drink, a warning against treating was circulated to the new boroughs. Joseph Hume urged Place to use his influence to form subcommittees in every part of the country to prepare against opposition – advice which Place was unlikely to carry out even if it were practicable, in view of his reluctance to interfere in electoral politics except in an emergency.[65]

In spite of all his arguments with Ministers, Place was on good terms with them at this time. In June he sought through Hobhouse the endorsement by Lord Althorp of William Hutt, a candidate for Hull. Althorp declined because he was already committed to another candidate, but he told Hobhouse: 'I am very sorry I cannot comply with Mr Place's request. I should have been most happy to do so if I could because he is one of those men on whose recommendation one can safely depend, and it would have given me great pleasure to have done what he wished from my own private feelings of respect for his character and conduct.' In the event, Hutt's rival did not stand, Althorp gave his recommendation and Hutt was elected. In August Place helped with Althorp's election campaign in Tower Hamlets.[66]

Towards the end of the year the NPU went into decline. Place tried to resign from the council, but he was persuaded to let his name remain in case his example damaged the union. Early in 1833 the Government brought in the Irish Coercion Bill, which partly suspended habeas corpus and introduced martial law in disturbed districts in Ireland. Anger at the measure sparked a revival of the NPU, and a crowded general meeting was held on 2 March, but the decline soon resumed. On 12 June Place and his allies tried to secure the dissolution of the union. They were outvoted, but their opponents soon gave up the attempt to keep it going, and Place joined in paying off the debts in order to ensure a respectable end.[67]

12   The Reformed Parliament

The good relations between Place and the Whigs following the passage of the Reform Bill did not last long. By August 1832 Place was angry about Whig equivocation over the ratepaying clause, and trouble was brewing between Burdett and Hobhouse on the one hand, and Hume and Place on the other. Hobhouse's brother Henry stood for Bath in the General Election, and when he declared his belief that the Reform Bill should be a 'final measure', the Bath reformers applied to Hume and Place for another candidate. They recommended Roebuck, and Hume went down to Bath to support him, incurring the bitter resentment of Burdett and Sir John Hobhouse. Sir John charged Roebuck with being irreligious, and Roebuck asked Place for damaging information on the Hobhouse set, such as evidence of Sir John's irreligion. Roebuck was greatly wounded at Place's reply, which presumably condemned retaliating in kind, but the Hobhouse tactics did not prevent Roebuck from winning the seat.[1]

During the campaign Sir John had threatened to oppose Hume's return for Middlesex, provoking suggestions that Hume should be put up against him in Westminster. Place blocked the movement as long as he could. Burdett and Hobhouse had moved into the mainstream of the Whig Party, but they were useful ministerial contacts, and he retained a considerable regard for them. He regarded Burdett as high and lazy, but he did not question his integrity. Even when Burdett denounced what he had accepted a few days earlier, Place took for granted that the explanation lay in his bad memory.[2] Burdett's services to reform in its darkest days made him invulnerable to challenge in Westminster however much he neglected his duties. Hobhouse on the other hand was vulnerable. Many reformers, although not Place, had objected to his accepting government office, and he had offended some constituents by his offhand manner towards them and his neglect of constituency business. Place considered him a shuffler and lazy, but talented, kind-hearted and well-meaning.[3] In his occasional bursts of energy he had done good work in Parliament in the fields of factory and local government reform.

In the autumn, electors from every parish but one came to Place to urge that

Hume should be put forward; a proposal that Place should stand himself he rejected out of hand. The suggestion that Hume should stand in Westminster never came to anything, because his Middlesex seat proved to be safe, but the controversy started a movement against Hobhouse. On 15 November, Colonel Evans, the radical MP for Rye, told Place that he would stand in Westminster. Place tried to discourage him by warning him of the costs he would incur, and thought he had succeeded. He also unsuccessfully urged Hume to seek a reconciliation with Burdett.[4] But Evans was not to be dissuaded, and he offered the Westminster reformers £500 towards the cost of an election.

Place was bound to support the radical against the Whig if he was not to repudiate his political principles, and Evans had earned his gratitude by taking up the ratepaying clause when no other MP would do so. Even so, Place made one final effort to save Hobhouse by suggesting that he should be asked to pledge himself to support four causes which he had supported in the past – the secret ballot, shorter parliaments, repeal of the taxes on knowledge, and repeal of indirect taxes. At a meeting of electors on Saturday 17 November, at which Place was not present (now that the crisis was over he had returned to his decision not to leave his house on political business), it was decided provisionally to run Evans if Hobhouse refused to agree to the four pledges. The next day a delegation called on Hobhouse, but he was by now convinced that he would be opposed whatever he did, and he rejected the demand on the ground that he disapproved of pledges on principle. Evans' candidature was announced, and Place finally committed himself to supporting it. Told by Colonel Jones that the Whigs were accusing him of having plotted to oust Hobhouse, Place gave him copies of his correspondence to disprove the charge, observing: 'you have become the keeper not of my conscience, but of my *reputation*! of which by the by, every man who really deserves to have any, has more than he deserves. . . . You in your new office, may say and do as you please, and this is I think, a very strong mark of my all important confidence, and of your sublime discretion.'[5]

At a meeting of the supporters of Burdett and Hobhouse on Monday 19 November, according to the *Morning Chronicle,* the chairman said that he was sorry to see Colonel Evans 'acting a part for some one whom they all knew, and who lived not far from Charing Cross. There were so many men looked up to him, that he actually treated them as his servants.' Another speaker 'believed that if Sir John Hobhouse had submitted to dictation, and would have remained a mere tool in the hands of Mr Place, of Charing Cross, they would never have heard of this opposition'. The *Chronicle* commented: 'Several observations were made respecting Mr Place, which, at the request of the Chairman, who pronounced them disorderly, we omit.' A week later, Hobhouse denounced the demand for pledges as a ruse by Place to pave the way to oppose him, and Place defended himself in *A Letter to the Electors of Westminster,* accusing Hobhouse of charging him with a trick knowing it to be untrue. Statements by Hobhouse during the 1819 election defending pledges were printed on slips and distributed in thousands.[6]

Place had refused to manage the election, observing that there were many intelligent men younger than him, who should spend time, bear the loss, and incur odium as he had done. An organisation was set up in accordance with his advice, but for once it failed to work. This was due to Evans, who decided not to have any canvassing, which he considered unnecessary. His supporters were confident, but Place warned him that he would lose – he said that the body of electors were so ignorant that many would vote for the man they were canvassed for, considering it a compliment. He cited the example of a man who worked hard canvassing for ten days, and then complained that he had not been canvassed himself. In the event Evans' defeat was so heavy – 3517 to 1173 – that it seems unlikely that canvassing could have saved him. In an NPU report, Place said that the claim that pledges were useless had been generally rejected, and he cited Westminster as the most disgraceful exception.[7] The result was probably also influenced by the biased selection of the list of eligible electors.

In March 1833 Hobhouse moved to the Irish Office. Electoral law of the time required him to resign his seat and contest a by-election; Evans offered himself as a candidate, but Hobhouse was elected unopposed. He had pledged to support the abolition of the window tax, and when the Government decided against it, he resigned his office and seat and stood in another by-election in May. This time a Tory stood as well as Evans, and with the anti-radical vote split, Evans won by 2027 to 1875 for Hobhouse and 738 for the Tory.[8] Evans proved even less satisfactory to Place than Hobhouse. He was a poor parliamentary speaker, and the following year he destroyed Place's trust in him by making public a confidential warning that Hobhouse might be put forward again.[9]

By this time Place had moved to Brompton, so he was no longer a Westminster elector. In 1833 the supporters of Evans formed the Westminster Reform Society to support household suffrage, triennial elections and the ballot, and the Westminster Committee thus finally became a formal constituency association. The Westminster reformers had become far more moderate since the late 1810s, and as always Place's relations with them were uneasy, but they continued to come to him when they were in difficulties, and he remained a force behind the scenes. In the 1835 General Election Burdett and Evans easily defeated a Tory candidate, but soon afterwards Evans went to Spain to lead the British Legion in a civil war, and since Burdett was inactive Westminster was effectively unrepresented. The leading electors asked Place to direct them in the next election, but once again he refused to do more than advise. With Evans not expected to return in time for the next General Election, Colonel Perronet Thompson sought Place's support in Westminster in September 1836. Thompson was one of the few middle-class reformers to become more radical after the Reform Bill, and by this time he was close to

Place, who readily agreed to help him. Place secured the approval of the Westminster men, and when the aristocratic radical Sir William Molesworth also sought his support, he tried to divert him to Marylebone. Neither proposal came to anything. Evans returned to England a war hero just in time to stand in the General Election of July 1837, and Molesworth was elected for Leeds.

Earlier in the year, Burdett had moved over to the Tories, and John Temple Leader, the radical MP for Bridgwater, offered to resign and stand in Westminster if Burdett would seek the approval of the electors for his change of party. Burdett accepted the challenge, and during the by-election in May Place made one of his very rare public speeches in support of Leader, although he emphasised his continued respect for Burdett. The result was a narrow victory for Burdett. Place complained that the Duchess of St Albans commanded tradesmen to vote for Burdett, and a liberal MP took away his custom from Francis Place Junior because he voted for Leader.[10] At the General Election Burdett retreated to Wiltshire, and Leader and Evans defeated a Tory candidate.

In the late 1830s the relationship of uneasy cooperation between Place and the Westminster reformers continued. In November 1837 they asked him to draw up resolutions for a public meeting for parliamentary reform, but the declaration for manhood suffrage in his draft proved too strong for them, and vague resolutions in favour of extension of suffrage were used instead. A key issue for the radicals in the late 1830s was support for the democratic movement in Canada, which supported the elected assemblies of Upper and Lower Canada against the governors appointed by the British Government. In 1837, Canadian democrats rose in rebellion, and the Whig Government suppressed the rebels by force, against the opposition of the radicals. In January 1838, the Westminster reformers asked for Place's help with resolutions for a public meeting on Canada. Again his draft proved too strong, but he nevertheless agreed to conduct the meeting as the managers were 'all abroad'. Evans he now regarded as a 'Renegade'.[11] The Tory victory in the General Election of 1841 cost Evans his seat, but he recovered it in a by-election in 1846. Westminster continued to be regarded as a Mecca for aspiring radical MPs, and in 1865 John Stuart Mill was greatly flattered to be invited to stand; he represented the constituency from 1865 to 1868.

Place's relations with Hobhouse and Burdett in the late 1830s and early 1840s were distant but not unfriendly. Place sometimes appealed to Hobhouse for help on humanitarian issues such as the treatment of imprisoned Chartists, and he would readily agree. Both baronets would respond when he appealed for help for their old Westminster supporters who had fallen on hard times, and in 1840 Burdett gave the Westminster Literary, Scientific and Mechanics Institute £50 on being given a note of recommendation from Place.[12]

From the late 1810s Place had been regarded by many as virtually having the power to choose the MPs for Westminster, but in practice the reformers had little choice in the selection of their candidates, which was generally determined by the circumstances at the time. Place was almost always dissatisfied with the MPs, but he saw the importance of the elections in the example Westminster set to the rest of the country of electors in an important constituency carrying the seats in defiance of the Whigs and Tories, so he would throw his considerable influence behind the parliamentary reformer who had the best chance of being elected. By the 1830s the importance of Westminster had declined, but the continued success of the reformers in defying the power of the 'factions' nevertheless provided an example and encouragement to radicals in other seats.

*   *   *

Both before and after the Reform Bill, Place was involved in the campaign against the 'taxes on knowledge', of which the most important was the 4*d* stamp on newspapers. In the 1820s the stamp had taken second place to the libel law as a political issue, but in the autumn of 1830 two working-class radicals, William Carpenter and Henry Hetherington, started the 'war of the unstamped' by launching unstamped journals. The stamp became the key issue for working-class radicals in the 1830s, and in 1833–36 Place concentrated his energies principally on the campaign to repeal it. Many unstamped journals were published and hundreds of publishers and vendors were imprisoned, while middle-class radicals fought a parallel campaign for abolition through petitions and delegations to Ministers.[13]

In 1830 several leading Whigs promised to support repeal, but they changed their minds when they came to power in November. Place pursued the matter through Hume, but in January 1831 Hume was himself persuaded by Ministers that it had to be delayed on financial grounds. Furious, Place wrote *A Letter to a Minister of State,* Poulett Thompson, who had promised before the fall of the Wellington Government that he would bring in a motion on the stamp, but dropped the matter on becoming a Minister. In his *Letter* Place outlined the case against the stamp, and argued that a postage charge would bring in more revenue (stamped newspapers travelled free of postage). Hume was sufficiently impressed to send a printer to Place, who was thus able to send fifty copies of the *Letter* to the newly formed Society for Promoting the Repeal of the Taxes on Knowledge. They voted to pay the printing costs. Place soon became worried by signs that leading members of the Society were ready to support a compromise on a penny stamp. He always insisted that a penny would be worse than fourpence, because the change would be accompanied by a tightening of the law which would eliminate unstamped newspapers, the only ones which the poor could afford to buy. This phase of the agitation came to an end in June, when he advised Hume and Warburton not to seek an interview with the Chancellor of the Exchequer until the Reform Bill had passed.[14]

The National Political Union had the repeal of the taxes on knowledge among its objects when it was formed in October 1831, and it cooperated with the parliamentary champion of repeal, E.L. Bulwer. When he brought the subject before the House in June 1832, Place offered to write notes on the debate for an NPU pamphlet. This was agreed, and 5000 copies were printed. The following month the union petitioned against the conduct of the Stamp Commissioners, who prosecuted unstamped journals which they disliked and ignored those they approved. Repeal was included among the pledges from parliamentary candidates recommended by the NPU, although at this time Place put the measure second in importance to the ballot. In January 1833 the leading Benthamite radicals planned a Society for the Diffusion of Political and Moral Knowledge, but when they heard that the stamp would soon be repealed, they decided to wait until they could publish their proposed magazine without fear of prosecution. Place had considered being editor, but he would not have edited an unstamped journal because of the damage to his family if he was prosecuted.[15] The stamp was not repealed, and Bulwer yielded to the advice of Grote and other radicals to postpone his motion until the next session in view of flagging public interest, a decision which Place condemned. He continued to urge repeal constantly in correspondence, and by January 1834 he was describing it in a letter to Tom Young as 'the old subject'. He said that repeal was the most important measure which Ministers could carry through, because it would allow correct doctrine to be preached on wages and profits, and thus put an end to the ferment among working people in favour of trade unions for impossible objectives.[16] In spite of his boasted hardheadedness, he was prone to claim grossly exaggerated benefits for projects which had proved abortive.

The appointment of a Select Committee on the libel law in the summer of 1834 gave an opportunity for propaganda against the stamp, and Place set Erskine Perry to find everything in the Statute Book on the newspaper stamp and small publications, in order to testify to the Committee. Lord Chancellor Brougham comprehensively condemned the stamp in his evidence, and Place optimistically claimed that after such a denunciation the Act must be repealed. 10,000 copies of Brougham's evidence were printed on a subscription from Hume and other MPs. Brougham was believed to want repeal in order to ruin *The Times,* with which he had quarrelled, and Place had commented that the ruin of *The Times* would be a public good. The paper replied by warning its enemies that they were under its surveillance, and Place retaliated by sending copies of Brougham's evidence to every *Times* journalist. (The paper got its revenge by describing his evidence to the Education Committee of 1835 as 'miserable and vulgar twaddle'.)[17]

The Benthamite radicals were seen at their weakest in their constant plans to launch new journals and newspapers. They were at a disadvantage in competing with the working-class radicals, because they had too much to lose to flout the law openly with an unstamped journal and risk imprisonment and financial ruin. An even more important factor in their failure was that the finance and organisation to give a good chance of success were never provided, so the few journals that were launched had short and troubled lives. One problem was the amount of money required – Place insisted that a minimum of £20,000 would be needed to rescue the *Constitutional* daily newspaper in 1836. This required the cooperation of wealthy radicals, but none was willing to put up money unless it would take his own line. Hume thought Place's managerial talents necessary to save the *Constitutional,* but he was unwilling to put up his share of £5000 for the intransigent paper Place would have made it. Place was often reluctant to join in plans for journals because he was jealous of his reputation for giving sound advice on money matters, but he was liable to be drawn in by his indefatigable and indiscreet ally of the late 1830s, the American Dr James Roberts Black.[18]

The one moderate success was Roebuck's *Pamphlets for the People.* The only unstamped journal published by a leading Benthamite, it was issued weekly from June 1835 under the fiction that each number was a separate pamphlet, but was patently illegal. Place was among the leading contributors, and the *Pamphlets* were well written and intransigent. Roebuck expected the financial aid of wealthy radicals, but he went ahead without securing their support first, and the *Pamphlets'* extreme tone alienated many potential allies. Even Place was unwilling to defend Roebuck's predilection for personal abuse. Although the *Pamphlets* reached a circulation of 10,000 at their peak in the summer of 1835, they had built up a debt of £150 by January 1836, and Place appealed to Hume for help. Hume was the chief fund-raiser among radical MPs, but he declared himself unable to help, because Roebuck had shown himself unwilling to make any concession to the views of those whose support he sought; George Grote had disowned the *Pamphlets* 'on the ground that he could not identify himself with Mr Roebuck's ultra and startling reforms'. The *Pamphlets* ceased publication the following month.[19]

In April 1835 Dr Black, under Place's direction, had started to organise an informal agitation against the stamp, with clerical help from Place's working-class radical contacts. Again, Hume shocked him by suggesting that the campaign should be delayed until they knew what the Government planned. Place angrily pointed out that they had relaxed on receiving a government promise in 1833, and the result was that Ministers were able to justify inaction on the ground of the lack of public feeling. It would not be his fault if they could ever make the same excuse again. Hume once again responded to the goad, turning up unexpectedly to join a delegation on 8 May to Spring Rice, the new Chancellor of the Exchequer, and giving Rice the impression that the propaganda was under his direction. The delegation was headed by Birkbeck. He had been persuaded to come forward by Brougham, who told him: 'The country is *up* on the subject. I have seen F. Place on this, who feels all you and I do and has been working like a horse for it.' A correspondence was opened with 3000 people across the country, and it was successful in raising petitions and meetings against the stamp. But even more important was the growing respectability and success of the unstamped press, which was undermining the circulation of the stamped newspapers. This provoked them to start pressing for a penny stamp, which would cut their prices and force up the cost of the hitherto unstamped press to a price few of their readers would be able to pay. By May 1835 Place had extended his efforts to cooperating with the unstamped, even helping the radical journalist, John Cleave, to edit his paper from prison. At the same time, Place complained that working men would not subscribe for his propaganda, ignoring the fact that their money and energies were absorbed by the unstamped.[20]

At a Crown and Anchor meeting early in August, the leading parliamentary radicals declared that nothing short of abolition would be acceptable, but in a parliamentary debate later in the month they inexplicably reversed themselves and declared for a penny stamp, thus undermining the whole campaign of the last five years. Place was justifiably bitter at their betrayal, and he condemned their inconsistency in an article in Roebuck's *Pamphlets*. He threw himself into a desperate attempt to avert the looming prospect of a penny stamp. In January 1836, the most able organiser among the London radicals, William Lovett, agreed to a request for further help and expressed his pleasure at Place's renewed efforts in the 'Holy Cause'. The *Radical* newspaper provided him with a platform against the stamp, and he became joint treasurer with Birkbeck of a committee to pay fines levied on Hetherington and Cleave, two of the leading martyrs of the unstamped war, thus emphasising the willingness of middle-class radicals to endorse the illegal unstamped. In April Dr Black formed the 'Association of Working Men to Procure a Cheap and Honest Press', composed mainly of ex-NUWC members who had moderated their views and started cooperating with middle-class radicals. But it only had time to publish one address before the stamp was reduced to a penny in the summer. Only Thompson and Wakley among the supporters of the campaign stood out for total repeal, apart from Roebuck who was ill. As a last throw in August, Place appealed for help from Hobhouse, now a Cabinet Minister, 'almost as a prayer', but it is unlikely that he responded.[21]

In a letter published in the *London Dispatch* in December, Place praised Hetherington and Cleave as brave men who were well known to him – he honoured them for their conduct. In his view, it was really the unstamped which had forced the Government to move to a penny stamp; when the Government replied to appeals to reason with persecution, the people had a duty to break bad laws in order to save themselves from despotism. The comment shows that he did not oppose breaking the law on principle. Rumours that Peel would declare for repeal led to delegations of working men to him, and Place said that if he came out for repeal he would 'shout at the top of my voice for the Tories'. But the rumours turned out to be false, thus saving Place from a terrible dilemma. Place blamed the betrayal of the parliamentary radicals over the stamp for the rise of physical force Chartism, a view which has some validity. The penny stamp caused great bitterness among working-class radicals, and it opened the way to the unchallenged domination of Feargus O'Connor's extreme *Northern Star,* since only a large circulation newspaper could hope to survive. Cleave's paper had sold 40,000 unstamped, but stamped it could not pay its expenses.

In 1849 the Newspaper Stamp Abolition Committee was formed at Place's suggestion, and he became the Treasurer. This became the Association for the Repeal of the Taxes on Knowledge in 1851, which organised the final and successful campaign against the taxes. The stamp was abolished in 1855, the year after Place's death, and the aims of the Association were completely realised in 1869, when the last of the taxes on newspapers was abolished.[22]

*   *   *

In 1832 Place's chance to get into Parliament finally arrived. Apart from Westminster, he was invited to stand in two other constituencies, in one of which he believed that he could have been elected without personal expense. But the opportunity had come too late. He concluded that even if he were elected free of charge, the unavoidable costs of carrying out the duties of an MP properly would be at least £500 a year, and since his income had been reduced to £400, he had to decline the offer. Place's case was not uncommon, so there was the usual shortage of good radical candidates. Even in Westminster the claim that no contribution would be required from the candidate had become a sham, although the amount required was around £500, rather than the £4000 or more needed in most constituencies. In spite of these difficulties there was a large accession of radicals into Parliament, but in Place's view many bad men were elected and the result was a retrogradation of government.[23] However, even those men that he most respected proved, apart from Roebuck, far too moderate and indecisive to satisfy him.[24]

The advent of a Whig Government dependent on radical support created a dilemma which the radicals never succeeded in solving. The Whigs had always supported an extensive Reform Bill on the basis that it was needed to settle the question and prevent further controversy; they expected the gratitude of the reformers for their sacrifices, without being willing to make major concessions to radical demands. The radicals had seen the bill as unsatisfactory, but deserving support as inserting the wedge which would lead on to the destruction of the old corrupt system. They were torn between the desire to put pressure on the Whigs to bring in further parliamentary reform and the fear of letting the Tories back in, especially since the Whigs did bring in important reforms in such fields as the Poor Law and municipal government.

In this conflict Place was always on the side of the intransigents. He had realised very early that the Reform Bill would not destroy aristocratic power, and like other radicals he made his first priority the removal of its defects, although he soon found that any attempt to keep up a large-scale agitation was doomed to failure. Single-handedly, he made the clause requiring early payment of rates as a qualification for voting into a major issue. Other changes such as the introduction of the secret ballot he saw as long term, but he constantly urged the radicals to campaign in and out of Parliament to build up a strong body of public opinion in favour of further reforms.

Place had particular reason to be more hostile to the Whigs than other middle-class radicals, because it was on issues affecting the working classes that the Government was most unwilling to move, and these were his overriding concern. He complained that the Whigs had no energy except against the working people.[25] He wanted the parliamentary radicals to gain the confidence of the working classes, but most of them had little contact with working people and little interest in the issues which most affected them. Mrs Grote expressed Place's attitude when she said that the consequences of a break in the Whig–radical alliance would be disastrous, but that these would be preferable to declaring to the people that they had no champions. Yet she was unenthusiastic about the campaign against the taxes on knowledge, and her husband referred to it contemptuously as Place's 'hobby'.[26] Place had difficulty in finding radical MPs who were willing to work in the parliamentary committees on drunkenness and trade unions, to defend working people against upper-class slander. These failings of the parliamentary radicals, and their pusillanimity in dealing with the Whigs, encouraged the sense of betrayal and growing class hostility which marked working-class attitudes during the 1830s.

Yet even Place wavered between insisting that he aimed to drive the Whigs on, not push them out, and treating the two 'factions' as indistinguishable. The radicals' electoral decline in the 1830s did not take him by surprise. He had foreseen that the defects in the Reform Acts would eventually allow the Tories to gain a majority because of the scope they gave for corruption and the creation of dependent copyhold voters in the counties. In 1836 he was setting the Tory victory presciently at the election after next. He also warned that radical electors would become indifferent if their representatives came to be seen as indistinguishable from the Whigs. But he was forced on to the defensive by evidence that criticism of the Government by parliamentary radicals was unpopular with the middle classes, and had to confess that the strong line he advocated would be unpopular at first, claiming that it would soon rally the people and show that they had not really retrograded.[27] His optimism was contradicted by the bitterness he expressed at the selfishness and class-consciousness of the middle classes, and he confessed that he was inclined to be overoptimistic. He shared the common radical delusion that the old party system would quickly break up, and that the Whigs would split between the Tories and the reformers.

On the other side, moderates such as Joseph Parkes insisted that a Whig–radical alliance was the only game on the cards, and complained that the radicals risked letting the Tories in by failing to give the Government wholehearted support. In retrospect it seems unlikely that either line could have prevented a decline in support for the radicals in the almost inevitable reaction which followed 1832. The alliance Place wanted between the Benthamites and the working-class radicals could hardly have survived the emergence of the New Poor Law and factory reform as key issues in the late 1830s, but it would have mitigated the class bitterness of the 1840s.

*   *   *

Place's parliamentary influence had always depended to a great degree on living near to Parliament, so when he moved to Brompton in 1833 his career as the master parliamentary manipulator came to an end. His colleagues would sometimes complain about the difficulty of finding him – they might catch him at the Exchequer Coffee House, but they were not sure when he would be in if they went to Brompton. Place welcomed this, since it made it easier for him to escape to the more congenial occupation of writing. Ever since 1808 he had constantly been trying to withdraw from politics, and as constantly been drawn back in as his political associates put forward projects he felt himself bound to help with. His removal to Brompton and his bitter dissatisfaction with the parliamentary radicals made withdrawal easier, but even so he was often drawn back when radicals like Sir William Molesworth or a liberal Whig such as Lord Durham made moves which seemed promising, and he remained a leading figure in radical politics.

The decline in his parliamentary role was not only due to his move and his dissatisfaction with the radical MPs. The liberal Tory Governments of the mid-1820s had given considerable scope for backbench MPs to introduce reforms; in the 1830s, Whig Governments depended on radical support, a situation which paradoxically reduced the scope for Place's legislative manoeuvring, since the Government was far less relaxed about accepting independent initiatives, and the radicals were never willing to carry defiance to the point where they risked letting the Tories in. More fundamentally, Place's scope for parliamentary manoeuvre was doomed to decline, because the growing expertise and professionalism of the Civil Service was eroding the legislative role of independent MPs. So during the 1830s Place concentrated more and more on working with extra-parliamentary pressure groups in order to mould public opinion, and thus to move Parliament from the outside.

But it was only at the end of the decade that he became completely disillusioned about the usefulness of working with MPs. In the mid-1830s he continued to work closely with, and sometimes against, parliamentary committees. When Hume supported a proposal to charge for parliamentary papers in 1836, he complained that his old ally had helped to destroy his occupation – he could not afford to buy them and he would no longer be able to give reliable advice to MPs.[28]

In 1834 he bitterly attacked the Select Committee on Drunkenness, dominated by the 'Saints' (Evangelicals), who in his view aimed to slander 'the people whom they in their arrogance call *"lower orders"* and *"lower classes"'*, and to introduce impracticable and undesirable legislative controls. The active members of the committee, he said, were mostly men who 'desire that this gay earth should be made as gloomy as the dungeons of the Inquisition, and the people as ignorant and as docile as sheep'. His first step on its appointment was to point out well-informed witnesses, but his suggestions were ignored, because his witnesses would have testified to the decline in drunkenness among London artisans, whereas the committee wanted to show that drunkenness was increasing in order to make a case for legislative controls. Place peppered his copy of the evidence to the committee with comments such as 'This Mr Arnold is a *tricky* − saint', 'Music. That horror of Saints', and 'A lie − a wicked lie'. (The last comment was on evidence that almost all tailors spent two or three days a week drinking.) He replied by publishing an essay he had written in 1829, which argued that the manners and morals of the working people were improving.[29]

The incident illustrates both the way that nineteenth-century parliamentary enquiries were manipulated to produce the evidence that the committee members wanted, and Place's eighteenth-century scepticism that legislative controls could ever produce social improvement: 'I do not approve of Government doing much or any thing for [the working people] in the active way either of teaching or recreation, beyond promoting places of public resort, opening museums &c since individuals cannot do these things.' His attitude was influenced by his Godwinian hostility to state control, and by his conviction that any real social improvement must come from changes in the individual. 'Temperance people', he wrote, 'begin at the wrong end, and instead of endeavouring to make a man have a higher notion of his own respectability and moral consequence, endeavour to make him humble − a canter − a coward, and a grovelling slave. . . . I am averse from all attempts to make people sober by coercion, they must be sober from conviction or not at all, coercion has all along made them drunkards.'[30] His conversion to publicly funded education the following year showed that he was not as doctrinaire as he gave the impression of being. The episode also showed his ability and limitations as a social statistician. More sophisticated and conscientious than the parliamentary committee in his analysis, he was nevertheless unable to show that drunkenness had declined, because of the paucity of the statistics available.[31] He found even worse problems in another area, being unable to find any useful information on the changes in prices and wages over time.[32]

He also tried to apply his skills as a social researcher to the problem of juvenile delinquency. This had been taken up by William Allen and his colleagues in the Lancasterian schools movement in the 1810s, and they found 12,000 destitute boys in London. They sought Place's help in founding a society to suppress juvenile deliquency, but he refused because his own research had convinced him that attempts at reform were doomed to failure.

A young thief or prostitute might behave well for a time, but would relapse in a time of adversity. The only solution in his view was to send the children to the colonies as apprentices, where they would be cut off from their old associates. In 1829 Henry Wilson sought his help with another scheme to reform delinquents. At first Place refused, but he was impressed by Wilson's success with vagrants under his care at West Ham Abbey, and when Wilson accepted that emigration was the best solution for the boys after they had been reformed, Place gave him his support. In 1832 Place's recommendation secured important supporters, including John Smith, a liberal MP, Burdett and Hobhouse, but Wilson was opposed by the Society for the Suppression of Juvenile Vagrancy. Subscriptions for Wilson collected through Place were even passed to the Society. When Place protested, the Society insisted on appointing him arbitrator on the disposal of the money. In 1835 Place secured the support of Lord Brougham, who wrote to the Home Secretary recommending Wilson's plan, but it was successfully opposed by the Society.[33]

*   *   *

Place's relationship with Joseph Hume exemplified the difficulties he faced in the 1830s. Hume's slowness and his proneness to verbal gaffes sometimes made him a laughing stock, but his persistence in seeking economies in government during the 1820s made him the leader of the reformers in the eyes of radical electors. Even Mrs Grote described him in 1835 as 'our leader', although in the view of many, her own husband would have been the best candidate for this role but for his diffidence. Place maintained that Hume was 'by far the most useful man of our time', and he remained a key parliamentary ally, but during the 1830s they moved further and further apart, and by 1837 he was saying that only Hume's past services prevented him breaking with him. Hume had earned his laurels by his doggedness under attack, but Place complained that he was far too liable to give way when treated with kindness by the Whigs. Place would relate their contemptuous remarks to him in order to stiffen his resolve, but in the 1830s the tactic proved less successful. Place would too often convert him to his own point of view, only to find him changing his mind in response to pressure from others. Place also thought that he tried to tackle more subjects than he could pursue effectively, and unsuccessfully urged him to specialise in the taxes on knowledge and the ratepaying clause of the Reform Act.[34]

Place's chief political ally during the 1830s was John Arthur Roebuck. He had many of Place's virtues and faults in more extreme form, and their opinions were very similar. Indeed Place once told a correspondent to regard a reply from him as from Roebuck as well, because they had so many views in common, and Roebuck addressed a letter to 'My Dear Father Place'. Place thought that Roebuck was much the best of the Benthamite MPs, but he complained that he was rash and hasty, and that he had a vexatious spirit. This seems an ironic comment coming from Place, but it is impossible to imagine him involving himself in a duel with a newspaper editor because he made unjustifiable allegations, as Roebuck did. Place wrote that Roebuck was 'singularly impatient of advice, but still he takes it well from me'. Roebuck had worked closely with Place in the Parliamentary Candidates Society and the National Political Union, and his election for Bath in 1832 owed much to Place's support. His extreme invective earned him the parliamentary sobriquet of 'tear 'em', and he was prepared at times to go further than Place in his opposition to the Whigs. Place was constantly urging liberal MPs to oppose the Government on specific issues, but as Roebuck angrily told him in 1836, 'all you prudent politicians went half mad', when he proposed to threaten separation from the Whigs. In his reply, Place said: 'Vanity apart, or vanity indulged, I care not which, but I do believe that were I in the house you and I could − aye − and would do much of what ought to be done, though we should be both bitterly hated, dispised we could not be, but the hatred even would not last beyond a session or two.' In 1838 Mrs Grote described Roebuck as 'the only sound Radical qualified to head a vigorous move'.[35]

Another parliamentary ally of Place was Benjamin Hawes. He was a moderate, and Warburton urged Place to show him up as a sham reformer when he stood for Lambeth in 1832, but Place respected him for his efforts to remove abuses such as imprisonment for debt. In 1835 Hawes took up the reform of the City of London police at Place's instigation. Hawes complained that he received little parliamentary support for his campaign, but promised to carry on the fight until Place cried hold. Hawes was described as Place's protégé by one of his correspondents, but this reflected Hawes' respectful attitude rather than a close political alignment. Place did not berate him as he did closer political allies, probably because Hawes did not make promises which he did not keep.[36]

The fall of the Whigs in November 1834 did not persuade Place that his hard line was wrong − in his view the subservience of the radicals had made the people quiescent, and thus helped the Tories to manoeuvre for power without fearing public wrath. But the reality of a Tory Government did jolt him into supporting moves for cooperation between the opposition groups: the Whigs, radicals and Irish. He advised radical election committees during the General Election of January 1835, and afterwards Henry Warburton consulted him about the tactics for cooperation in the new Parliament. Place supported proposals for the opposition parties to back a Whig challenge for the Speakership and a moderate amendment to the Address in reply to the King's Speech. Hobhouse suggested an amendment in favour of the ballot and triennial elections (this was when he was rumoured to be aiming to return to Westminster), but Place angrily objected that there was no chance of united opposition support for these reforms. He was delighted when the Whig candidate was elected Speaker and the amendment to the Address was passed,[37] but as usual he quickly became disillusioned after the Whigs returned to power in April.

In May 1835 he asked Joseph Parkes, who was then the Secretary of the Municipal Corporations Commission, for government funds to circulate an essay supporting the forthcoming Municipal Corporations Bill. Parkes replied asking him to edit a temporary newspaper to be called the *Corporation Reformer* to meet the expected opposition. Place agreed, provided that his essay could be the prospectus, which was accepted, and over 70,000 were circulated. It was well written, and Place exulted in the circulation of a 'goodly mass of republican notions', but the expected opposition in the Commons did not materialise, with the result that few took an interest in the bill, and only five numbers of the newspaper were published. In a private letter, Parkes called it 'a temporary paper some slaves of mine have set up which I overlook'.[38]

When the bill went to the Lords it was mutilated, and Place persuaded the leading radical MPs to reject the Government's revisions to the Lords' draft as inadequate. But the radicals gave way when the Government threatened to resign unless they supported the amended bill. Place's objection was not to the substance of the amended bill, but to the retention of an insulting preamble which the Lords had introduced. He thought that this provided an opportunity to provoke a conflict between the two Houses which would rouse the people, show which House was master, and revive support for a reforming Whig Government. Even if the Whigs had refused to play, the radicals would have shown that they were not a mere adjunct of the Government and raised themselves in public opinion. But he wavered between arguing that the Whigs would not have carried out their threat to resign, and declaring that the Government was so bad that its survival was not desirable: it seems likely that his judgement was unbalanced by the fact that he had persuaded the radical MPs to take his line only to see them break their promise.[39]

He was strongly opposed by Parkes, who nevertheless kept his respect by answering back vigorously to his complaints, instead of agreeing with him and then changing his mind as the radical MPs did. Place was so isolated on the issue that he became quite defensive, denying Parkes's assumption that he wanted to oust Ministers:

My intention was to rouse people to their support so as to compel them to march in a much straighter path than they would choose for themselves.

I endeavour to take large views and if I am not mistaken I sometimes succeed, . . . and altho' I have at times been thought rash and condemned for my rashness by some of my intelligent friends, because as they thought I injured my utility, I am of opinion that so far from this having been the case I have upon the whole increased my utility. I took none of the chances of being debauched or controlled, as all men who take a mild course are; they lose a large portion of their utility and are unconscious of their loss, since no one can tell how useful he might have become in time had he gone on doggedly observing and acting for himself.

In estimating my conduct you should always remember the very narrow scope of action my circumstances have permitted.[40]

He was convinced that the radical MPs could not hope to maintain their position, let alone advance, unless they tried to rouse the people.

In the summer of 1836 Place cut his contacts with radical MPs, disillusioned by their failure to make a stand against the penny stamp on newspapers. But he did not succeed in maintaining his isolation for long. In the autumn he was drawn back by discussions over a radical daily newspaper and manoeuvring over a possible successor to Evans in Westminster. At the end of the year his optimism was raised by hard-line public letters by Sir William Molesworth. Place even agreed to be a steward at a Whig-radical Middlesex dinner in order to support uncompromising radical speakers – a remarkable decision in view of his aversion to public dinners – but he withdrew when he discovered that Roebuck and Molseworth had not been invited. The other reformist MPs did go, but they were humiliated when the Whig leaders did not turn up.[41]

On 31 January 1837 Roebuck fiercely attacked the Whigs in a House of Commons speech on the Address, again raising the spirits of Place, who launched a subscription to reprint it. The result was disappointing, most radicals feeling that Roebuck had gone too far. Replying to Place's appeal, John Stuart Mill urged that 'those who did such great things for the Stamp Question would set about doing the same thing for the Ballot'. Place retorted that the stamp agitation had cost only £110 for two years work, yet he was £20 out of pocket. In answer to a further letter from Mill enclosing £5 and urging him not to hibernate, Place described the fluctuating state of his mind. He had sent out 200 notes and over 2000 circulars to raise money for the stamp agitation, and his applications had been so neglected and the replies when he asked in conversation so insulting that he could only bring himself to apply to fourteen people for the subscription for printing Roebuck's speech. A committee had started to work for the repeal of the corn laws, but they refused to help with the ballot or the stamp.

> How lamentable it is my dear John Mill, that so many useful movements should all depend upon one man. Were I living at Charing Cross, these and other desirable things might be done, but I am out of the way and no one will take my place. . . . When I was *compelled* to remove there was an end to all useful public proceedings, until Dr Black undertook to do what no Englishman would do, and he worked the stamp duty without the assistance of one Westminster man.

Place went on to say that the people were supine, the House of Commons reformers had made them so. Foreseeing it, he urged a stand on the Municipal Reform Bill, and promises were made, but not one was kept. He had tried again with the Irish Municipal Reform Bill in 1836 and failed, and since then he had gone to work on his own with much more satisfaction than for a long time. Molesworth had roused him again with his correspondence, and Roebuck's speech was all but invaluable – if Molesworth seconded him then Colonel Thompson would fall in. They might become the people's men and raise their hopes that they were not forgotten. Then he might become active

again, but he did not want to worry himself working with men who were
infirm of purpose. Mill called the letter 'a memorial of the spiritless, heartless
imbecility of the English radicals'. He meant 'to fling it in the teeth of some of
them'.

To Place's surprise, at a meeting of the Radical Club (a dining club formed
by Place and his friends when the NPU collapsed) he succeeded in persuading
the Westminster men to hold a public meeting on the ballot. But their plans
were upset by Hume's mismanagement of a project for a memorial to the
Scottish martyrs of 1793 (see pp. 22-3 above). Hume equivocated on the
question of whether the martyrs were supporters of universal suffrage, and
thus roused the suspicions of the working-class radicals. As a result, the future
Chartist leader, Feargus O'Connor, and the London Working Men's
Association joined hands to disrupt a public meeting for the memorial in
February 1837, and the Westminster men hastily abandoned their meeting for
the ballot, fearing similar disruption. It was an early example of what was to
become a standard Chartist tactic.[42]

Place's hopes for a strong move by the reformist MPs were not realised.
The radicals were split on how far to go in opposing the Whigs, and in Place's
view Molesworth abandoned Roebuck.[43] In the General Election in the
summer of 1837, for the first time he refused to give any help to the reformers,
and he was not displeased when most lost their seats. Hume, he said, lost
Middlesex because he hooked on to his Whig colleague in order to save the
expense of organisation, and was betrayed as he deserved. Place told Mrs
Grote that none of them had acted well in the last two sessions, apart from
Roebuck in the last one only. They had assisted the Whigs to push back the
people, and could not bring them on when they needed their votes. It would
have been better if all the reformers had been defeated, then the Whigs would
not have made headway against the Tories and the value of the reformers
would have been seen. If they had done their duty, the result would have been
the merging of the Whigs and reformers, but the event had only been delayed,
and they would live to see it. He turned out to be overoptimistic, since the
Victorian Liberal Party did not emerge until the 1860s.[44] Once again he
decided to give up working with every MP but Hume, whose dereliction he
forgave on account of his past services.

In July 1837 Colonel Jones told Place: 'Though you are an Arch Daemon of
Mischief yet, there is sufficient of *humanity* about you to do *good at times* –
and in such great quantities as to be a redeeming quality for all your
Devilism.'[45] He asked for Place's help in drawing up parliamentary reform
proposals for Lord Durham, who was then regarded as a possible radical
leader. Place agreed, but he broke off the correspondence when it became
clear that Durham did not intend to break with the Whigs. Then Place did the
same with Lord Brougham, who was not too snobbish to deal with him
directly. Brougham suggested a ratepayer suffrage, with the addition of a
voluntary election rate of one shilling a year for non-ratepayers, which would

give a vote to every man who wanted it. This plan was to provide Place with a 'respectable' version of universal suffrage in the 1840s. He also helped Brougham to prepare a successful attack on the Government's Canada policy in the House of Lords.[46]

The introduction of penny postage in 1839 was the last major reform which Place was closely involved in at the parliamentary stage. As early as 1834 he had advocated a penny post on letters all over the country, instead of the existing system of charging according to distance, and he considered Warburton's Select Committee Report on the subject of February 1839 'the most statesmanlike I have ever seen', although he regretted that the Select Committee had recommended a 2d post. In March he supplied the chairman of the committee, Robert Wallace, with a plan for getting the support of the press, and urged the committee to stick to a penny, warning that 2d might be opposed by working people as a Whig trick. He pointed out the parallel with the stamp on newspapers, urging that a difference of a penny was very important for working people, and that Cleave's newspaper and the *Satirist* had been ruined by the penny stamp duty. At a dinner of members of the committee who supported a low rate, he helped to persuade them to work for a penny only. The weakness of the Melbourne Government allowed the measure to pass rapidly, and Place said: 'I may claim the merit of having been the indirect but certain cause of the bill being passed in the last session, by suggesting the plan for working it out', and assisting those who worked for it, although he said that his efforts were small compared with those of several other men.[47]

His last attempt to interfere in party politics was in May 1839, when leading radical MPs sought his advice on the terms to be demanded for supporting a Whig Government, and he wrote a paper for a meeting at Molesworth's. He urged the radicals to demand that the leading points of parliamentary reform must become open questions and the ratepaying clause be repealed as the price for support of the Whigs. The radicals once again failed to make a stand, and the only minor concession was to make the ballot an open question.[48]

13 Chartism

The increase in class hostility in the 1830s created the conditions for the growth of a large-scale working-class political movement. Although the NUWC and its allies had opposed the Reform Bill, they were bitterly disappointed at the unwillingness of middle-class men to work with them for manhood suffrage once the bill had been won. Place saw faults on both sides. Some working-class leaders had destroyed the sympathy of the other classes by vilifying them, and by the propagation of anti-property ideas. On the other hand, the insulting treatment of working people by the middle and upper classes had discouraged the working-class radicals from being reasonable. 'My long experience and continued intercourse with people in all ranks and conditions', he observed,

> satisfy me that with few exceptions, all above the merest workman are enemies to the improvement of the *'lower orders'*. Sure I am that people who have property are what they always were desirous that the working people should be kept as poor and as ignorant as it is possible to keep them. The working people as a body have always by them been considered as beings scarcely worthy of attention except as mere machines, instruments to be employed for their convenience, to work and to fight, to be worn out, or killed off, for their advantage.

In 1840 William Lovett told Place that when the 'ignorance and folly' of the working classes were referred to as obstacles, 'the extreme selfishness and cupidity of the middle classes *should not be forgotten*'. Place replied:

> Your description however of the middle class is unfortunately too true, true in all particulars but one, they are not − such intentional − such pernicious enemies of the *common* people, as the aristocracy, ever have been, are and ever will be so long as they have the power of the state in their hands, but even they, *en masse,* are not malicious, they consider themselves too high the people too low, to permit malignity to prevail generally and continually. Whatever the middle class people are that too the working class people are, whatever apparent difference there is arises solely from difference of position, the working people, being of the two, the most intolerant.

Elsewhere he observed that 'step by step, all look with contempt on those beneath them in the true "spirit of Despotism" in the aristocratic country'.[1] The complaint by working men that the middle classes led them on when they needed their help, and then abandoned them when the victory was won, was justified in his view.

In the aftermath of the Reform Bill the NUWC gained strength, and like the NPU it benefited from the hostility aroused by the Irish Coercion Bill in early 1833, but soon afterwards it went into decline. According to Place many working men believed that the working-class unions did not go far enough, and so did not join or soon left; this kept the unions too small to be important and was the reason for the failure of the NUWC. The last major public meeting of the NUWC, at Cold Bath Fields in May, was violently broken up by the police and a policeman killed. Place welcomed the verdict of justifiable homicide given by a coroner's jury — he hoped the people would never submit to such wanton attack without resistance. Commenting on the order given by one of the Police Commissioners, Colonel Rowan, that the police were not to strike unless they were resisted, Place said:'Any man at all acquainted with the conduct of constables of either the old or the new Police force would consider this an order to attack whom they pleased in any manner they pleased, and Coln Rowan so intended it to be understood — "resisted" — a police man is resisted if another man does not get out of his way faster than his staff can go.'[2] The comment shows the depth of his disillusionment since he had supported and advised the police in 1830.

*   *   *

As working men lost faith in political action they turned to trade unionism. Robert Owen had never believed in political action, and when his attempt to regenerate society by establishing socialist communities failed in the 1820s, he turned to worker cooperatives and trade unions as an alternative. In 1833–34 Owenite propaganda for a general trade union received an enthusiastic response from working people. Although Place regarded trade clubs as an essential bulwark against the degradation of the working people, he had nothing but contempt for this type of trade unionism. He accepted that the working people could achieve general objectives such as an eight-hour day for twelve hours' work if they held together, but he argued that it would be equally easy to achieve representative government, and they were no more likely to hold together for the one purpose than the other. He was convinced that attempting such overambitious schemes only weakened the working people, and cited the case of the powerful trade society of the London tailors who were, in his word, 'Owen-ized', and whose extremism provoked a reaction from their employers which broke the society and reduced the tailors from being among the best-paid journeymen to the poorest of sweated labour. The working people would subscribe for grandiose plans, he complained, but they would not give money for practical objects.

In 1834 *The Poor Man's Advocate and Scourge of Tyrants* of Manchester extolled the conduct of six young women who had been blacklisted from working in the local cotton mills, but it did not offer a collection from the working people for them — Place told the editor that this was 'the empty praise, not the solid pudding'. A farthing a fortnight from each would have kept all six in comfort and had more effect on the cruel masters than 'a whole Advocate of thanks'. In 1832 four men were arrested at a public meeting in Manchester. Place urged the leaders to raise a subscription to support them, but this was not done, and he commented: 'The fact is this, the working people are as a rope of sand, they have little regard for one another and yet they complain continually that those in other ranks disregard them.'[3]

Place admired the writer Harriet Martineau, and he was always ready to supply information for her popular books on economics. In 1834, he told her about the long struggle of the Bradford woolcombers in 1825–26:

> I had much intercourse with some of the leaders in the Great Bradford Strike and they were all of them honest men. I saw at once and soon convinced these men that they could not succeed, but the body of workmen could not be convinced and for a long time no one of the leaders dared tell them, as a body, that they must submit. There is I assure you in a vast many cases much less leading by the nose than is imagined, though there are cases in which the working people have been led by sad rascals. I have now before me a list of 114 delegates from trade societies whom I at various times have seen and conversed with, and I am sure there are not ten bad men among them. Delegates are appointed and sent on Missions in great ignorance of the world and of all sound principles. They scarcely ever accomplish the purpose for which they are appointed and therefore disappoint those who send them; others are then appointed the same consequences follow, and thus the matter goes on perpetually. There is an error, which is very widely spread namely that strikes are mere matters of course, but it would be found on examination that the same men who have failed once can seldom be induced to strike again, or at least to become leaders or promoters of a second strike for a long time, which is generally accomplished by the younger hands who have grown up since the last great strike, and thus it is that from every seven to ten years there is a fresh ebullition. Masters are quite as much to blame as men and more especially the small and middle masters who are very often the cause of mischief . . .
>
> There needs however resistance on the part of the workmen to attempts to reduce their wages even when they have no chance of preventing the reduction, as it impedes their fall, and prevents the badly disposed masters reducing wages continually and rapidly and bringing the people to Mud Cabins — Potatoes and salt. This is however only one evil to some extent counteracting another evil, and this will continue to be the case, until hands are proportioned to labour, mouths to food, and notions of comfort and decent respectability are greatly increased.[4]

In 1833, the rise of the movement for an eight-hour day alarmed the Government, and in November Joseph Parkes wrote to Place urging him to write a pamphlet explaining the law on combinations and giving advice to working men, to be paid for by the Government. Place declined, because he did not believe that Ministers would approve the pamphlet he would write, which would be fair to workmen as well as masters. He foresaw that the movement would collapse if left alone, and in March 1834 its central Manchester Committee was nearly moribund when the barbarous sentence of seven years' transportation on the 'Tolpuddle Martyrs' for taking illegal oaths led to a revival. In London, the recently formed Grand National Consolidated Trades' Union proposed a general strike and procession in protest, but Place urged that the general strike proposal was absurd since not one in twenty would join in. In accordance with his advice it was agreed that a petition should be carried in procession to Lord Melbourne, but not more than six should present it in order to comply with the law. Place and others counted the procession on 21 April at 42,000.

He then wrote four 'Essays for the People',[5] which condemned 'trade unionism', and eloquently defended the working people, trade clubs and strikes:

> Trade clubs have been beyond all comparison the most highly useful arrangements ever devised for the advantage of the working people, mentally, morally and physically . . .
> Persuade the working people to abandon their trade club, persuade them to be satisfied with a lower rate of real wages, and they will speedily become a debased, hideous mass of misery vice and violence, happily this never can be accomplished the skilled workmen will become *better and better informed* will associate for mutual protection will improve their condition, and will assist to improve that of nearly the whole of the community.[6]

In the fourth essay he compared the working men's unions favourably with the 'trade unions' of the landowners, which produced the Corn Laws, and of the barristers. Parkes promised publication of the first essay, but, as Place expected, the promise was not kept.

He maintained his contacts with the leading London working men, some of whom used to come to his house on Sunday mornings to seek advice and exchange information. A letter from Colonel Jones in 1837 shows that radical working men called on Place daily. Jones told Place that he was unwilling to call on him because he had a horror of those he might meet there. Place received everyone, and employed anyone he thought could help him. Jones would only call when he would not meet the men he called 'the "Tory Radicals" the *Malignants*'. Place poured scorn on an old soldier displaying 'the tact of an exquisite'. Many of those Jones condemned were instruments of good to themselves and others because of the easy intercourse they had with Place, and as useful men they bore comparison with those Jones esteemed. In 1834 the London block coopers presented Place with a model of a brewhouse butt for his help during a recent strike: through Hume, he had stopped the Admiralty from supplying workmen in place of the strikers. In the same year delegates came to London from the cotton spinners, and Place persuaded two of them to go to Rouen to inspect the mills there. The men came back satisfied that the mills were too poor to represent any threat, and that import controls were unnecessary. The £20 which Place had lent them was repaid.[7]

In 1835 Place was asked to get an address from the Manchester cotton spinners and factory workers reprinted in Roebuck's *Pamphlets*. He complied, adding a long commentary of his own. He urged working men that the appeal to religion and humanity in their address was a broken reed − the weavers had the power already to help themselves if they were united and wise, but no canting and threatening would help them. If avarice had ground them down, why had this not happened in other trades? Because they had been wise enough to combine when they were rich and prevent an increase in hands. Machinery could not be blamed for the problems of the cotton industry, because almost within living memory there had been only 40,000 hands, now there were 1.2 million,[8] and if there were only one million wages would be good. He disliked rich men who pinched down working men to make even more wealth, but this was no concern of the working men, who could help themselves by refusing to work too many hours. A short-time bill would not and ought not be passed by Parliament, which should not interfere with manufacturers carrying on their business as they saw fit (except concerning children). He had never seen inside a cotton factory, although he had read and heard much of them. A cotton mill was more abhorrent than he could find words to describe, and he would not submit to see such misery. Place had an appeal for the cotton weavers in a 1799 newspaper reprinted as a handbill in order to show that the belief in a weavers' golden age was a myth.[9]

His methods are further shown by his correspondence with John Fowler of Sheffield, who wrote in 1836 to ask for advice on forming a union of journeyman steel converters and steel refiners. Place readily agreed, and sent back a list of nine questions on the organisation of the trade. On receiving the answers he gave his advice, urging them not to attempt to keep strangers out of the trade, as it only led to jealousy with other working men and an influx of new hands. If all trades were to succeed in restricting the supply of labour, he claimed, it would lead to a war on their own children. Members should establish a committee, refuse to work with non-members, and pay six shillings a week to unemployed members unless they could get more another way or they received parish or charity aid. No eating, drinking or smoking should be allowed in meetings, which should not be held in a public house. The arrangements should be as little obnoxious as possible to the masters, and the club should help the masters when they could do so without hurting the workmen, even if the masters' conduct was bad. They should remember that the only power they had was to withdraw their labour. Clubs were good, he said, firstly because they made the members better acquainted and increased mutual respect, and secondly because the master was equal at least to all the men together, and while wages were regulated by the supply and demand for labour, a club could delay a wage-cut and sometimes prevent it.[10] It is not difficult to imagine the conflicting emotions Place must have aroused by his mixture of hectoring and practical help.

In February 1838 he once again took the initiative in organising the defence of trade unions against a parliamentary committee, this time one set up as a result of a proposal by the Irish Catholic leader, Daniel O'Connell, who wanted to expose violence and intimidation by Dublin unions. Place's first move was to publish a letter complaining that the inquiry ought to be into the conduct of the masters as well as the men; as a result the Government took the matter out of O'Connell's hands and moved for a committee in the terms Place had suggested. He was unwilling to undertake the day-to-day organisation of the defence as he had in 1824 and 1825, but he wrote letters to Working Men's Associations and trade unions around the country urging them to raise money, send up petitions and be prepared to send delegates to London to testify to the committee. He urged the London Working Men's Association to take the lead, but a committee of London trades was already forming independently. The committee appointed William Lovett secretary and George White parliamentary counsel on Place's recommendation.

The working men's efforts often failed to satisfy him, as he would point out in the most peremptory terms. Told by the London trades committee that a vote of thanks had been passed for his efforts, he replied telling them to stop wasting time. His admonitions could be effective. John Doherty wrote to him on behalf of the Manchester spinners: 'As usual, when we want anything for the working people, we must apply to you.' He asked for £10 to £12 to make enquiries to meet allegations made in the committee. In reply, Place fiercely berated the spinners for neglecting to raise the money and declared that no one would supply funds if they failed to do their duty: 'Let them, either become more manly, or never more complain of anything which may befal them since they so cowardly and meanly succumb to the enemy.' His letter shamed them into joining the Manchester Combination Committee and increasing their delegates to London from one to three. The parliamentary enquiry was abandoned without producing a report, in Place's view because the men's determination to answer slanders against them had made the committee's work unpleasant and dull. He continued to act as an adviser to working men into the 1840s. In 1839 he urged Lovett to recall the London Trades Committee in order to meet slanders on working men, and in 1842 he said that he was intensely occupied with delegations of working men on matters concerning them.[11]

*   *   *

The London Working Men's Association was formed by Dr James Black of Kentucky in 1836. In early 1834 he had set out to organise working men into small groups for educational self-improvement, but until he met Place in about August he had little success. Place encouraged him and introduced him to the Sunday discussions with leading working men. In 1835 Black agreed to organise the campaign against the newspaper stamp, and to seek the help of working men with the clerical work, as something good in itself and a way of gaining their confidence.

In the spring of 1836 one of these men, Anthony Morton, a journeyman carpenter, planned to form societies for mutual instruction, and he asked for Place's advice on the best plan. Place replied through Black, recommending as usual the class plan used by the LCS, with Godwin as the key text, but Black did not pass the letter to Morton until mid-June, and by then events had moved on.[12] Black had formed the Association of Working Men to Procure a Cheap and Honest Press in April, and when the stamp was reduced to a penny in May, he proposed that the Association become an educational society. Meetings were held at his home, and what emerged was a political society, the London Working Men's Association.[13] The founding of the LWMA was one result of a gradual moderation of the views of the former NUWC leaders in the mid-1830s, which made it possible for Place to work with them increasingly closely. Many had dropped their former Owenite views, but more important was their willingness to abandon the rhetoric of class hatred.

The membership of the London Working Men's Association was always small, deliberately because admission was dependent on recommendation and balloting, but it quickly gained a high reputation because it included many of the leading London working men, and because it issued well written addresses which attracted attention. Place considered an address on education drafted by Lovett 'of surpassing excellence', and Hume ordered 500 of them to enclose with every letter he sent for the next three months. Although the LWMA was formed by Black with Place's assistance, the rules were drawn to ensure that control lay in the hands of working men; middle-class allies could only be honorary members, and could not have a say in the Association's affairs. Place was careful to point out that its unsuccessful rival, the more extreme Universal Suffrage Club, was led by gentlemen. In the autumn of 1836 lectures to the Association by Colonel Thompson on free trade raised interest among members, and Place took advantage of this to urge that regular discussions should be held, in the hope of converting the members to Malthusianism and orthodox political economy. These were held every Sunday morning from January to June 1837, and Place claimed that four members outlined the case for Malthusianism better than Malthus or Ricardo could have done in the same space of time. 'The members of this association were the intractable people last year, they are the tractable people now', he boasted to Mrs Grote in November, 'thanks to the Sunday morning conversations, and some other circumstances.' He was sure that he could not employ his time better than in helping them. But Malthusian converts were a small minority. The autumn of 1837 saw successful tours by LWMA missionaries to the north, midlands and west to form provincial WMAs. Place approved of this, and boasted that over 100 WMAs had been formed (sometimes the number went up to 250), but he disapproved of later tours on which physical force was advocated.[14]

At the beginning of 1837 Place and others had been working on a proposed pamphlet, the 'State of the Representation of the People in Parliament'. Two men were working full-time, and Place helped. He complained that he could not raise the money to publish it, but the research probably provided the basis of the LWMA's pamphlet, 'The Rotten House of Commons', which made the Association's name nationally.[15] In February, the Association followed this up with a successful public meeting in Westminster, which approved the full radical programme of parliamentary reform, including votes for women. The LWMA also began to work with radical MPs. In the same month it voted an address to Roebuck for attacking the Whigs in the House of Commons. In April the LWMA held a public meeting on the Canadian situation at the suggestion of Sir William Molesworth, and he and three other MPs attended. On 31 May, thirteen radical MPs attended a meeting with members of the LWMA, and as a result six MPs and six LWMA members were appointed a committee to draw up a parliamentary bill for what were to become known as the six points of the Charter: manhood suffrage (full universal suffrage was abandoned as too controversial), annual elections, the secret ballot, equalisation of electorates, the payment of MPs, and the abolition of property qualification for membership. But the MPs did not keep their promise to help draw up a bill, and since the members of the LWMA lacked the legal expertise to draft it, they deputed William Lovett to ask Place for help. He agreed, provided that Lovett set out the points to be covered and the members were willing to abandon other controversial topics such as their opposition to the New Poor Law, and concentrate on working for the Charter. The LWMA agreed to the terms, and Place drew the outline of a bill for the six points which was published as the Charter in May 1838.

Place praised the LWMA for keeping to the terms they agreed with him, observing:

> The so called liberal members of the house of commons who had assisted to procure the reform bill in 1832 and had led the multitude to expect many important changes favourable to their class abandoned them. . . . The middle classes had subsided into a state of quiescence and abject submission in which the parliament did its utmost to keep them and the working classes were left wholly to themselves, and to some extent under the guidance of Leaders some of whom have been shown to be equally ignorant and dishonest, yet the more rational portion of the working men who had become prominent as propagators and supporters of Working mens and Radical associations conducted themselves with more steadiness and effect than any considerable number of such men had ever, of themselves, heretofore done.

But he thought that the working people owed much to the middle classes which they were not willing to acknowledge: 'To them they owe Infant, and Lancasterian and Sunday schools, and these together with the stimulus they have given to a vast number of working people to educate their children to an extent heretofore unknown are the great causes of the movements of the people on their own account, when left to themselves as they have been since the passing of the reform bills in 1832.'[16]

In the autumn of 1838, the Radical Club set up a committee to examine the Charter. The Club had been formed in 1833, when Place and his friends had resigned from the NPU. They had agreed to meet occasionally, and thus prevent the friendships and alliances formed in the NPU from breaking up. A quarterly dining club was formed, with membership chosen by ballot. By the late 1830s the Radical Club included MPs, Westminster men, other middle-class radicals and LWMA members. The atmosphere was sufficiently congenial to overcome Place's aversion to large dinners. When he missed one meeting, the members delighted him by suggesting that they should meet nearer his home. He replied that he cared little for the opinion of the world, but much for that of the good men who knew him, for these were his world; to meet them in the same spirit he would attend in future without putting them to the inconvenience of altering the place of meeting. By the late 1830s the Club provided a centre for London middle-class radicals to keep in touch, coordinate their activities, and reach out towards the working-class radicals of the LWMA. The committee set up to examine the Charter included Place, Hume and Colonel Thompson. It suggested some alterations of detail which were agreed by the LWMA, and Lovett and Place produced a revised edition which was published in September.[17]

The Charter rapidly became the Bible of reformers all over the country, but it was adopted in conjunction with a national petition launched by a revived Birmingham Political Union. Place disapproved of the petition because it hinted at the unorthodox views on currency of the Birmingham men, and also because he thought that many separate petitions were a more effective way of keeping parliamentary reform before Parliament and the public than a single mass petition. Another proposal of the Birmingham men was for a General Convention to represent the people and press the national petition on Parliament. According to his later account, Place opposed this, but a letter he wrote in September 1838 shows that he then approved of it. The LWMA selected him and Roebuck as two of the eight delegates to the Convention for London. He declined on the ground that it would take too much time and that they ought to choose a man who was younger and lived nearer central London, but he unsuccessfully urged Roebuck to accept. Place was successful in urging that the delegates should be elected at public meetings rather than by societies, in order to keep within the law. The *Morning Chronicle* and the *Sun* urged Corn Law supporters to disrupt the formal Westminster public meeting on 17 September to choose the London delegates by proposing a motion on the Corn Laws, but at the request of the LWMA leaders Place persuaded the newspapers to repudiate the idea, as he never tired of reminding the Chartists when they later disrupted corn law meetings. The LWMA had no difficulty in controlling the Westminster meeting of 12,000 against the more extreme London Democratic Association, and its eight nominees as Convention delegates were elected. Place indignantly condemned the exclusion of Westminster electors from the platform against all precedent – his attachment to the traditions of local democracy was one of the few things which could lead him into contradicting his general contempt for tradition.[18]

As the Convention approached, Place's attitude to it became more hostile, leading to a break in relations with his Chartist contacts, but shortly after it opened on 5 February 1839 his friends among the delegates started coming to him again. Writing to Lovett on 13 February, he described the Convention's address as bad, but the rules good. He hoped that the delegates would persevere and encourage the people to persevere when they encountered disappointment. The Convention nevertheless saw the end of the close alliance of 1835–38 between Place and the LWMA leaders.[19] London was moderate and apathetic at this time, as the delegates discovered to their dismay. The middle-class Birmingham men soon dropped out when they discovered that the Convention would not endorse their ideas on currency, and control fell into the hands of proponents of class warfare. These were mainly from the north, which was the heartland of Chartist strength. Their leader was Feargus O'Connor, and his popularity in the north gave him a dominance of the movement which continued until it declined in the late 1840s. Here Chartism had been largely built on the campaign against the New Poor Law, and Place's support for the reform became an increasingly important barrier between him and the Chartists. He was as well informed about the situation in the north as it was possible to be from reading and conversation (better than most LWMA members, who did not read the provincial newspapers in their library), but his lack of personal experience of conditions there and his support for the New Poor Law led him to underestimate the pressure of bitterness, and to exaggerate the importance of the Birmingham men's role in diverting the Chartists from the WMAs to the Convention and proposals for the use of physical force. The consequence, in his view, was a move based on wrong foundations, leading to 'a further division between the middle and working classes, which may never be reconciled'. This was an untypically pessimistic comment; he was generally more hopeful about the long term.[20]

The apathy of London persuaded the Convention to move to Birmingham, where it could expect public support, on 13 May. The Birmingham magistrates brought in London police to put down Chartist public meetings in the Bull Ring, and their violent tactics brought a condemnation from the Convention of the police as a 'bloody and unconstitutional force'. The declaration was signed by Lovett as secretary to the Convention, and in July he was sentenced to a year in gaol for libel, together with John Collins, the leading Birmingham Chartist who had accompanied him to the printer. Place was greatly attached to Lovett, and he complained bitterly when Lovett was

abused by more extreme Chartists: 'Lovett's views are large only in
particulars', Place told Richard Moore, one of the LWMA delegates to the
Convention, 'but he is ever honest in them all. . . . It should ever be
remembered that of all the working men he has attempted more for his class
than any one else. That his course has ever been one as seriously honourable as
is possible and that it has been as straight as honourable.' The conditions in
which the men were held led to fears for their lives, so for the next year Place
devoted much of his time to securing an amelioration. His efforts produced
some improvement and a better diet, and he believed that he was responsible
for saving Lovett's life. He also raised money for Lovett through the Radical
Club and the LWMA, and tried to clear him of debt over the *Charter*
newspaper. Lovett had accepted legal responsibility for its debts, and he and
Place were bitter about misconduct by the managing committee during his
imprisonment which left him liable for heavy sums. Place and two of his
friends each lent £5 to help wind up the newspaper, and when the money was
not repaid he complained to the committee: 'In almost every case where
money has been concerned I have been ill treated and cheated by working
men, and it vexes me much . . . to find, that in this respect, at least, they differ
from all other men in being utterly dishonest.' This must be regarded as his
usual rhetoric, since the great majority of his loans to trade clubs were
repaid.[21]

Place hoped to take advantage of Lovett's enforced inactivity to convert
him to political economy and Malthusianism, and at first Lovett agreed to
read the books Place sent him, but he was soon diverted into writing a book on
his own plan for a national network of Chartist schools. When Lovett sent the
manuscript to Place for his opinion, Place pointed out that Lovett would
never be able to raise the money to carry out such a scheme, also objecting that
it was a plan for centralism and dogmatism. The charge of dogmatism might
have been raised against Place himself, since he thought that political
economy and Malthusianism should be taught in schools. But in his view they
were proven scientific facts, whereas Chartism was a dogma, albeit one he
approved. However he told Lovett that as he never tried to force his opinion
on anyone he would take the manuscript to James Watson to get it printed,
and would not state his own opinion of it. Later he helped Lovett to amend the
plan to make it legal, and proofread the book and saw it through the press
while Lovett recuperated in Cornwall after his release. In his autobiography
Lovett was rather ungrateful for Place's help, accusing him (although not by
name) of delaying publication.[22] Initially, Lovett had considerable success in
winning the support of middle-class radicals and Chartists for his project, but
most of his Chartist supporters recanted after O'Connor condemned the
plan, and it failed to get wide Chartist support.

The summer of 1839 saw the Convention decline into impotence amid
defections and quarrels, and many arrests of Chartists. In an atmosphere of
plots and with an attempted rising in Monmouth in November, some 500

Chartists were arrested over the next year. Place had a reputation for helping political prisoners – in 1837 a radical newspaper declared that many unjustly condemned men owed their life and liberty to him[23] – so he was flooded with appeals for aid. He devoted most of his time and effort to trying to help them, and his contacts with the Government and MPs brought some success, raising his prestige among the Chartists. Once again he was forced to abandon his decision not to work with Members of Parliament, who were at first uncooperative owing to the hostility the Chartists' tactics had aroused, but worked hard once the number of arrests created sympathy. His efforts were sometimes impeded by Chartist threats of vengeance if sentences on prisoners were not remitted, which made Ministers less inclined to leniency in case this was attributed to fear.

Place devoted considerable effort to preventing the execution of the men convicted of involvement in the Monmouth rising, and he believed that he was responsible for getting the death sentences commuted, although in fact the recommendation of the trial judge was the deciding factor. In this case the main argument Place used was based on opposition to the death penalty, since he did not believe that the rebels' conduct could be defended. Sometimes he would cooperate in tactics he disapproved of. In January 1842, John Collins asked him to get a memorial for the leader of the rebellion presented to Queen Victoria; Place dismissed it as futile, but he told Collins that he would attempt to comply with the wishes of the memorialists: 'I hold myself bound to do whatever any body of working people may require of me, which is at all proper to be done, whether it accords with my own opinions or not.' Place also thought that he was responsible for securing remission of the death sentence on rioters in the Birmingham Bull Ring. He complained bitterly about the inadequacy of the Chartists' subscriptions for prisoners' families, contrasting them with the support of the LCS for prisoners' families, and condemning especially the failure of the Convention to support Lovett's and Collins' dependants when they had been arrested carrying out its orders. His diatribes had some effect. Lawrence Pitkethly, a leading Huddersfield Chartist, responded to one by promising his aid, and he became Place's main ally in trying to help the Chartist prisoners, while Richard Moore of the LWMA replied to a letter in similar vein by acknowledging its justice and thanking him for his note as a stimulant. Place's efforts were not confined to purely political offences, and with the help of Brougham he was able to secure the early release of five Glasgow cotton spinners accused of conspiracy.[24]

Place had become close to the families of some LWMA leaders, and Lovett's wife constantly consulted him about her husband's welfare. He also became closely acquainted with the family of another former NUWC leader, John Cleave, who was a supporter of birth control and atheist propaganda. Place admired his courage, but he wrote to Lovett that Cleave's conduct to his wife and daughters was too atrocious to be written about – apparently a reference to Cleave introducing a mistress into his home. Place even objected to Cleave's signature to the Address of Lovett's National Association on the ground that in a paper teaching morality it raised doubts of its sincerity. But he was still ready to recommend Cleave to the Scottish *Chartist Circular* as a London agent. Significantly, the *Circular* promptly accepted his suggestion although it had ignored a direct offer from Cleave. When Cleave's wife went to her daughter's confinement, she wrote to inform Place, in case he should think she had stayed away from him disrespectfully. The daughter was married to Henry Vincent, the best orator of the LWMA, who had been imprisoned for advocating physical force during a propaganda tour of the West Country.[25]

Place also made great efforts to help Vincent, with the help of a Tory MP who had taken part in his prosecution and formed a good opinion of his character. They were able to secure an amelioration in Vincent's conditions, and Place succeeded in converting Vincent to Malthusianism by correspondence and sending him books. However, Place said that he was unable to help him financially; he had begged so much on behalf of Lovett that 'impudent beggar as I am, I cannot again for some time to come carry on my avocation'. Vincent disappointed him when he came out of gaol, returning to the role of travelling agitator against Place's advice that he should settle down and make some money before going back into politics. But Vincent became much more moderate, becoming a supporter of the middle-class Complete Suffrage Union and making temperance a main feature of his propaganda. He made several attempts to get into Parliament, encouraged by Roebuck and Colonel Thompson. The latter told Place that as 'the lawyer of the clan' he must settle whether Vincent could stand for Parliament without the property qualification to be an MP. Place's response to Vincent's appeals for help was to demand evidence that he had a realistic chance of success.[26]

O'Connor's dominance made Lovett and Vincent peripheral figures in the Chartist movement. The main dispute was between the supporters and opponents of physical force. The lines were far from clear, since the dispute was essentially one over tactics rather than principle. The question was whether force had any chance of success and whether threats could achieve anything. All the disputants tended to waver in their line, torn between the impracticability of using force successfully and the impossibility of persuading Parliament to introduce universal suffrage except under the shadow of fear. Place himself was not opposed in principle — he remarked that force or the threat of force had generally been at the bottom of great changes in government. Neither of them, he urged Lovett, wanted a revolution brought about by 'our vices', and 'we are by no means in condition to bring about a revolution by our virtues'. Yet they wanted a revolution: 'Our Government is still what it has all along been an Aristocratical conspiracy against the people'. In his view the crime of the physical force Chartists was to advocate the use of force when it was certain to fail, and could only set back the cause of universal suffrage; many years of education would be necessary before the working people would understand and support democracy with sufficient determination and unity to enforce their demands. Intelligence had almost always proceeded from the middle classes downwards, although he hoped that the progress which had been made would soon put the best of the working classes in a position to teach many of their 'betters', then 'the only useful the only honest influence, that of intellect upon intellect will carry the Charter triumphantly'. He feared that if the six points were obtained too soon, the result would be half a century of confusion.

His insistence on the necessity for cooperation with the middle classes before success would be possible showed a scepticism about the ability of the working people alone to enforce their claims which was proved correct, but it also concealed an unspoken assumption that working people would have to abandon their widespread hostility to property and capitalism before they would be fit for the suffrage.[27] He often said that it was best for necessary changes to be delayed, because the later they took place the readier the people would be, and the less likely a convulsion. What was needed was quiet educational propaganda in order to bring forward the day when the people would be ready for representative government, and he had nothing but contempt for agitators who gained popularity by encouraging the delusion that success could be quickly and easily achieved.

But in a different mood he was realistic enough to recognise that his prescription was impossible. Sometimes he would argue that activities he disapproved of such as Owenism and the Convention were valuable in teaching people to think for themselves, and in the introduction to his narrative of Chartism in 1838, he wrote:

It should be remembered that every attempt to reform any old institution has necessarily been made by enthusiastic, but not well informed men, who saw but a small portion of the impediments which made their present success impossible. Such men are always and necessarily ignorant of the best means of progressing towards the accomplishment of their purpose at a distant time, and can seldom be persuaded that the time for their accomplishment is distant. Few indeed, such men, would interfere at all unless they imagined the change they desired was at hand. They may be considered as pioneers who by their labours and sacrifices smooth the way for those who are to follow them. Never without such persons to move forward, and never but through their errors and misfortunes, would mankind have emerged from barbarism.

It was argued that change should be sought only by patient use of reason, but he thought that it was unlikely that any great reform would ever be achieved in this way. 'Mankind seems destined to proceed through faults, and crimes to whatever may be their bettered condition hereafter, no other road seems open to them.' Yet Place immediately contradicted this realism by claiming that the rapid progress of the WMAs, which was expected to induce the middle classes to join in pressing for reform, was halted by the absurd conduct of the Birmingham men.[28] In his attitude to Chartism he wavered between realism and bitterness at the unexpected diversion of the WMA movement which he and Black had done so much to foster.

He was very aware of the desperation felt in the north:

> Great allowances should be made for men who have never been taught to reason on causes and consequences. The principal cause of action in such men is the hope of being able to better their condition by increasing their real wages and securing constant employment. It is this hope which sustains vast numbers and prevents them from becoming altogether reckless, as some among them in whom this hope is extinguished are continually becoming. Others and these by far the largest number having toiled on for years will sink into that state when by *ordinary* means all chance of bettering their condition by increase of wages [has gone,] will continue their toil their energies being concentrated, so far as regards their employment in preventing the decrease of wages. To men circumstanced as these two descriptions are the hope of benefit from political associations is very alluring, and the only matter for surprize is that they do not proceed with more of outrage . . .

Many workers, he continued, in poverty all their lives, live among others better off, and they conclude that the difference is due to bad laws and avaricious employers; escape is paramount and however cheerful at times they scarcely ever cease to feel anguish at their condition. They will eagerly seize on the most absurd scheme and hold on to it long after it has failed.[29]

                    *   *   *

By July 1840 Place was able to boast that he was clear of all political associations except the anti-corn law campaign, and he intended to remain so unless some really important national matter came up. His role in the Metropolitan Anti-Corn Law Association (MACLA) followed the usual pattern, with initial resistance to becoming involved, pressure from his friends, and full commitment once he was drawn in. Yet he was not as committed to free trade as his associates. When Henry Vincent was converted to Malthusianism, he pointed out to Place that according to the theory the campaign against the Corn Laws was pointless, since any improvement in the condition of the working people by a reduction in the price of bread would soon be cancelled out by a commensurate increase in population. Place admitted that he agreed, and that he did not accept the case of his colleagues in the campaign; free trade would do some good, but he supported it mainly because abolition would be a heavy blow against the power of the aristocracy.[30]

In the 1820s many letters and articles by Place against the Corn Laws had been published in the press, and he had secured petitions against it from working men, but there had been no large scale agitation. The London Anti-Corn Law Association had been founded in December 1836, and it had carried on a considerable correspondence, but by the end of 1839 it was at a low ebb.[31] In January 1840 the Manchester based Anti-Corn Law League deputed Sidney Smith to attempt to revive the London agitation. He arranged a meeting to found a new London society, and Warburton agreed to chair it provided Place would attend and manage the business. Place attended very reluctantly – he did not like to appear to desert Warburton because he 'acted magnificently in respect to Penny Postage'. At the meeting Place was named as a member of the committee of MACLA, and then his organising instinct took charge. He picked out men to stay after the meeting to put the society into business-like shape, and he proposed that each member should draw up a plan for the society to organise the metropolis, with the inevitable result that he was left to do it himself. On 4 March he told one of the leaders of the League, Richard Cobden, that he had been working from 7 a.m. to midnight each day getting the society off the ground, and he described the difficulties of organising London, the large distances and many different interests and trades, which prevented any community feeling. MACLA got off to a good start, and by May it was boasting of 92 lectures given, 215,000 tracts distributed and 705 petitions with 201,040 signatures. In June Place told Lovett optimistically that the stage of a do-nothing Government and middle class was drawing to a close with the growth of anti-Corn Law proceedings.[32]

But London's apathy proved too great a barrier for even Place's organisational talents to overcome. By September he was telling Cobden that their plans to organise the metropolis had been abandoned due to lack of money, and Cobden said that his letter was 'very much like a dying speech and confession'. Place had included in the MACLA rules a provision that the Association could not entertain any subject other than the Corn Laws, which he believed saved it from being destroyed by controversy. But the Chartists opposed the campaign against the Corn Laws as a diversion from the cause of parliamentary reform, and the rule could not prevent them from wrecking MACLA public meetings. 1840 was a low point in Chartism, but Place complained that 150 to 200 Chartists went round London anti-Corn Law meetings and made brawls – he could have put it down, but he was unwilling to go to places like Hackney at 11 p.m. He was then 69 years old. Their conduct at a MACLA public meeting in March 1841 convinced him that if the Chartists were not restrained by the police and soldiers they would repeat the worst scenes of the French Revolution. The Association was forced to restrict entry to the adjourned meeting to ticket-holders.

On the other side, he fought to keep the Association independent of the Anti-Corn Law League. In September he told a fellow member of the business committee that his 'obstreperous' conduct at a meeting had been intentional, because he found that Sidney Smith was manoeuvring to make them subservient to the League – if the League decided not to address the Queen, that was no reason why MACLA should not. In November he was disturbed to discover that Joseph Sturge, a leading Quaker member of the League, was demanding a parliamentary motion for a bill to repeal the Corn Laws. This was inadvisable, in his view, because the people were not yet in a condition to

back it up; Sturge should have been the last man to put it forward, since he had
been one of the prudent and patient anti-slavery campaigners, whose triumph
was so grand that it should serve as a caution and rule of conduct. Hearing
that Sturge and his friends were threatening to withhold large contributions
unless the motion was made, he reluctantly decided to go to a League meeting
in Manchester, although he had just recovered from bronchitis and feared a
relapse. He succeeded in persuading Sturge, and suffered from severe
bronchitis for a month afterwards. In August 1842 he was involved in an
archetypal dispute, when a member complained that an Address published by
the Association was too long, and Place claimed that it would be read if it was
three times the length. He devoted most of his time to the Association until he
was disabled by a stroke on 3 November 1844.[33]

*   *   *

At the beginning of 1840 Place and Black attempted to revive the LWMA, but
they failed. 'The men think our proposal will not do', Place observed, 'it will
move too slowly for them'.[34] In the 1840s he had little contact with the
mainstream Chartists organised in the O'Connerite National Charter
Association, although he was occasionally consulted on legal points. But the
help of middle-class radicals for Chartist prisoners, in which Place played
such a prominent part, helped to keep open the possibility of cooperation with
the moderate Lovett wing. Place tried to realise this with the Metropolitan
Parliamentary Reform Association in 1842, the last organisation in which he
played a major role. He continued to regard parliamentary reform as the
primary political objective.

Urged by Warburton and other reformers to cooperate in forming a new
society in April 1840, he argued that the time was not ripe since the gap
between middle- and working-class reformers was too wide, and it was better
to build on the unexpected success in getting working-class support for anti-
Corn Law petitions. In January 1841 he contemplated a fresh attempt to unite
middle- and working-class reformers in a society to support the Charter,
encouraged by a successful conference between Chartists and middle-class
reformers at Leeds. But Hume aroused the suspicions of Lovett and his
friends by trying to get their backing for his own household suffrage plan, and
Place's attempt fizzled out.[35] He continued to encourage good relations
between working- and middle-class reformers. In April 1841 he passed on to
Collins complimentary comments from Colonel Thompson about the
'Chartist Church' run by Arthur O'Neill and Collins, and urged them to stop
abusing the middle classes: 'If I were to quarrel with and call every man a
rogue who does what I dislike I should call both you and O'Neill rogues
instead of doing as I do respect you both very highly even for those things
which I think are errors.'[36]

On 31 January 1842 the Radical Club set up a 'Committee of Agitation for
the People's Charter'. Over the next month there were discussions on a plan of

reform, and leading members, including Place, Hume, Roebuck, Molesworth and Leader, agreed to support the six points, with the exception of triennial elections and Brougham's voluntary election rate. Place was unable to attend committee meetings, because he was confined to his house by bronchitis, but he wrote an essay for the committee. They greatly admired it, especially his exposition of the three stages of reform. The first was the Reform Bill, which had not reduced the power of the aristocracy, but had damaged its prestige. The second would be the repeal of the Corn Laws, which would be a much greater blow to the aristocracy's prestige and also affect its purse. The third would be manhood suffrage, which would lead to the destruction of the power of the aristocracy. The time for this had not yet come, since the case for it was not generally admitted in the way that the injustice of taxing the nation's food for the benefit of a few was, but it was time to start agitating in order to teach the mass of the nation the case for it.[37] On 7 March his paper was read at a meeting of the Radical Club, and it was agreed to adopt the reform plan and set up a separate association to agitate for it. The result was the Metropolitan Parliamentary Reform Association (MPRA), which was launched in May after some delay caused by Place's bronchitis.[38]

Place intended the MPRA to support the Chartist programme while avoiding the terms 'Chartist' and 'Universal Suffrage', which would frighten off the middle classes because they were used by men who advocated vengeance on the middle classes and the abolition of property. Joseph Sturge had launched the Birmingham Complete Suffrage Union on this basis in January. A successful London public meeting was held with Sturge and Lovett in February, and soon there were over fifty Complete Suffrage Associations. The National Complete Suffrage Union was formed at a conference with the moderate Chartists at Birmingham in April, providing further encouragement. Place corresponded with Sturge, warning him of the ways in which his Union breached the law.

A disappointment was the failure of Colonel Thompson to join in forming the MPRA. He would have been a valuable acquisition because he was respected by the Chartists – in 1840 Place had told him that he believed that he was the only anti-Corn Law supporter the out-and-out democrats would listen to. Thompson refused to join because of Hume's involvement – the two men had quarrelled in 1838. Place tried hard to persuade Thompson, and on 2 April he told Place: 'The friendliness of your letter of yesterday is such that if I had been taken at the moment of reading it, I must have thrown myself into your hands, to do anything you preferred to recommend.' But he went on to reiterate his objections. On 8 April he replied to a further letter: 'Your letters have always so much calmness and good reasoning, that they carry me away captive for a time, and afterwards I find myself turning round.'[39]

Ironically, Hume himself dropped out before the MPRA was formally inaugurated after a quarrel with Place. Early in April the committee agreed to print Place's paper as a private address to raise funds, and Hume infuriated him by intercepting it on the way to the printer and altering it. The changes were trivial, but Place complained that Hume had overridden the committee, and he corrected the proof before printing proceeded. Samuel Harrison, one of the members of the committee, agreed that Hume had done wrong, declaring that in the committee they were all equal, and he would not be treated as a nonentity by anyone. But he urged Place not to disturb himself by any serious quarrel with Hume, assuring Place that in the committee 'there is no one who will not entirely defer to your opinion as to what is to be done with the way of doing it'. The trivial incident brought an end to the relationship with Hume which had survived many serious differences over thirty years. Hume did not formally withdraw his support, but he ignored all requests to pay a donation he had promised. The MPRA was the first and last organisation in which Place was completely dominant. The leading figures were all close allies of his: Samuel Harrison, described by Place as 'one of the most considerate and honest hearted men I have ever known',[40] and his most faithful admirer in later life; Peter A. Taylor, more independent-minded but with very similar views to Place, and Dr Black, his close ally since 1834 and agent for Leader in Westminster. Typically, the only check to Place had come when the committee had objected to a long historical introduction on Major Cartwright and the London Corresponding Society in his draft address. Place had promptly produced a revised version in accordance with the committee's instructions, but the cuts had been restored when Hume took his side on the issue.

The MPRA was launched successfully with Warburton as chairman on 20 May. Ten MPs were included on the General Committee, but Henry Hetherington was the only well known Chartist to join.[41] The Association aimed, as Place put it, not to form a numerous society in the first instance, but to put others in the way of doing so, and to publish accounts of their activities in a cheap weekly stamped paper. In effect, Place aimed to repeat the role played by the LWMA in 1837–38, using the prestige of the capital to encourage provincial agitation rather than attempting the far more difficult task of rousing London. In the summer of 1842 this was an easy role to play, and the Association received an enthusiastic response from provincial reformers, many of whom reported their efforts to form local associations. But an attempt to launch an MPRA daily newspaper failed,[42] and a plan to hold lectures in London was deferred until Roebuck's advice could be sought on its legality. His verdict was favourable, but by the time the MPRA was ready to proceed in August major riots and strikes, aimed at preventing wage-cuts, had broken out in the north. The Chartists unsuccessfully attempted to divert the strikes to political aims, frightening off moderate reformers and effectively killing the MPRA. The first quarterly meeting of the General Committee was cancelled because of the Plug Riots – so-called because roving bands of strikers drew the plugs of factory boilers to enforce a general strike – and the secretary Dr Black struggled on almost unaided. On 21 September he reported that three public meetings, seven 'conversational' ones and three lectures had been held over the past month. Most of the meetings were with Chartists, whose prejudices, he claimed, were yielding. The last committee meeting was held in October. Two MPRA delegates attended a further conference between the National Complete Suffrage Union and the Chartists in December, but this broke down when Lovett very reluctantly took O'Connor's side against Sturge, because of the NCSU's arrogance in drawing up an unacceptable plan without consulting him.[43] In March 1843 Place attempted to wind up the MPRA, and as usual he was defeated on this point, the members voting to keep it formally alive in the hope that it could be revived in better times. The MPRA had promised to play a useful role as an auxiliary to the NCSU until it was destroyed by the Plug Riots, but it was always vulnerable due to the apathy of London reformers, and because of its own success in attracting prestigious men who were easily frightened into wrecking the Association by withdrawing their support.

*   *   *

In spite of his financial losses, the 1830s and early 1840s seem to have been a happy period in Place's life. His own children had not provided him with much companionship, but he now received some compensation from his daughter Annie's family. He was fascinated with the new railways, and in the late 1830s he often used to explore them with Annie's engineer sons, sometimes being turned off for trespassing. At this time he had two sons in Calcutta, one in the United States and one at home. In 1842 Place said that his present wife had from nearly the beginning been 'hail fellow' with all his children, but at about this time the marriage started to go wrong. Her son by her first marriage turned out, according to Place, 'a finished rascal of the meanest sort', and the debts which she incurred on his behalf brought Place to the verge of ruin. On 3 November 1844 he suffered a stroke which left him unable to read and write for considerable periods, and he must then have been in her power to some extent. By 1848 his losses had become so great that he offered to sell his books to Joseph Parkes, and in 1851 the Places separated and he went to live with Annie.[44]

Many years later Francis Place Junior described his father's later years as 'a terrible finale':

Mr Place's connection with the woman he took for 2nd wife was the only really false step that can be laid to his charge. It was a terrible falling off from his former rigidly virtuous life – a bad example to his family and the numerous young politicians that crowded around him for teaching and wordly wisdom. It is inconceivable how he could have made so false a step and belied all the moral teachings of which he was a living illustration. An ordinary unknown man might in obscurity have been guilty of so much laxity and the world none the worse for it, but in FP's case it was an outrage upon the class he lived in, indeed upon all society. It brought its consequences upon him in the wildness of his younger sons, in the anguish it caused his deploring and well disposed daughters, in the diabolical conduct (his own term) of the woman and in the utter desolation it brought upon him . . .

My two sisters and myself now aged people are all that are left of his once numerous family – we are all I am happy to say in easy circumstances to the attainment of which we cannot but feel we owe much to his generous conduct & his glorious example during our mother's life, and great was our consternation and grief when the noble edifice of his fine character became a wrick.[45]

The comment reflects the bitterness of Place's last years – and the rigid outlook of the Victorian moralist who censored his father's papers.

Place bore his troubles with stoical courage, and he devoted his time to cutting out and arranging newspaper articles, often while talking to people who came to him for advice. During respites he would resume his political activities, and in June 1846 he told Richard Cobden that he was 'choke full of public matters'. In late 1848 he was consulted by Cobden and the radical corn merchant, Sir Joshua Walmsley, about a plan to form a Great Parliamentary Reform League. He was asked to draw up an address for the new society, and did so. On his advice Walmsley did not approach Hume, Place saying that he had a great respect for him, but he had always been unqualified to assist in concocting a scheme for reform under difficult circumstances. In January 1849 Place summoned a meeting to form the new society, but Cobden rapidly cooled to the idea of raising parliamentary reform because he found that at public meetings even working men were more interested in reducing taxation, and the new body was called the Metropolitan Financial Reform Association. By February Place was too ill to play any further part, but the organisation went through various changes of name and gained strength until it became the National Reform Association in January 1850. By 1852 it had conducted a large-scale agitation for parliamentary reform, but it failed to raise enthusiasm outside the working classes.[46]

In the 1840s Place continued to advise trade unionists and radical politicians, and in 1844–45 he helped the journeyman coopers to secure the repeal of the duty on staves. According to George Jacob Holyoake, the leading secularist of the 1840s: 'In Mr Place's time, young insurgent politicians of any capacity went to him. He instructed them, he counselled them – I well know how wisely; in danger, he found them means of defence, and made known their peril to those who might protect them.' Place was an adviser when William Ellis established his secular schools in 1846, and he supported Holyoake's application for a post of teacher, but it was blocked by Lovett on account of Holyoake's heresy conviction. Lovett remembered Place as a 'clear-headed and warm-hearted old gentleman'.

The contradictions in Place's outlook remained to the end. On New Year's Day 1846 he wrote that the people were now better informed and disposed, especially since 1840. Looking forward to the abolition of the Corn Laws, he declared: 'There is reason to hope and symptoms which should lead us to expect that wisdom will guide our rulers and happy times be the consequence thereof.' But writing to Holyoake in 1849 he was at his most misanthropic, referring to the 'beasts of prey called mankind; for such they have ever been since they have had existence, and such as they must remain for an indefinite time, if not for ever. Their ever being anything else is with me a forlorn hope, while yet, as I can do no better, I continue in my course of life to act as if I really had a strong hope of immense improvement for the good of all.' Writing to Grote a year later he was again in optimistic mood, declaring that he hoped to live yet to see completely free trade, a vast improvement in knowledge including political economy, improved law and many of the working classes exercising the suffrage under the ballot.[47] He died in the night of 31 December 1853 and 1 January 1854 at the age of 82, and most of his hopes were realised within twenty years of his death.

14 Conclusion

Censorship of Place's papers means that some aspects of his career will never be fully known, especially his role in the birth control and secularist movements, and some important papers have been lost, notably the bulk of his correspondence with John Stuart Mill, while most of James Mill's letters survive only in summaries by Francis Place Junior. Some episodes are only referred to in passing remarks, such as his opposition to the passage of the Corn Laws in 1814–15. On the other hand, Place had a passion for recording his activities, and he made every effort to ensure that the results of his researches would be available to posterity. He thought that the British Museum was the proper place for his volumes on the working people.[1] The immense quantity of his surviving papers allows a very full account to be given of his life.

Place's writings have to be used with caution. As he warned Lovett in 1840, the same correctness was not to be expected in his letters as in a book revised for the press.[2] He always wrote what he believed at the time, but inevitably he wrote as an actor in events, giving his own point of view. The introductions to his narratives were generally balanced, but when he became involved in the story his vivid memory and strong passions often made him relive his emotions at the time. This gave his narratives immediacy, but it sometimes made it impossible for him to stand back and give a balanced judgement. This was a principal cause of his tendency to hyperbole, and he would comment on actions he disapproved of as if he were judging the whole character of the actor. Thus he sometimes criticised the conduct of Burdett as if he held him wholly in contempt, but elsewhere he would give a very different opinion of him in equal sincerity. His rhetorical condemnation is far more quotable – and quoted by historians – than the praise or balanced judgements he gave elsewhere. He has sometimes been accused of never having a good word to say for anybody, but a long list could be given of people of whom he had the highest opinion.[3]

In retrospect he tended to remember the times when he had predicted what had occurred, not the occasions when he had expected a different outcome, thus giving the impression of prescience which some historians find irritating. He sometimes made errors of detail, especially on dates, and his estimates of numbers could be grossly inflated. But his standard of accuracy was very high overall, and he made great efforts to get his facts right. The collections of minutes and documents of the organisations he was involved in are an important source for historians, and he also obtained first-hand accounts of other movements and events which concerned the working people, such as William Lovett's narrative of the NUWC and information on the Bristol riots of 1831. He took every opportunity to increase and update his knowledge of the working people, and his passion for long walks allowed him to remain well informed on conditions in London until his health failed.[4]

Place's humourless literal-mindedness could be irritating, but it often allowed him to cut through rhetoric and cant, and expose inconsistencies. Although he was not an original thinker, he often succeeded in seeing further than his contemporaries − especially in the analysis of legislation − by his insistence on following through the results of logical reasoning to their conclusion and his single-minded persistence. He sometimes found the conclusions he arrived at hard to bear, such as his view that free trade would produce no improvement in living standards in the long run, and he would have to counter the temptation to relapse into despair by contemplating the improvements which he had seen and telling himself that despair was futile.

Place has been accused of exaggerating his own importance, but cases where he did so are rare. One reason for the charge is that historians have sometimes claimed more for him than he claimed for himself, and their successors have wrongly assumed that these assessments reflected his own claims. He did claim the main credit for the repeal of the Combination Laws and a large share in the establishment of the LMI, and these claims are generally accepted. He did not say that his role in Westminster elections was important − although he occasionally implied it − probably because he knew that he was generally credited with even greater power than he had. One reason for the belief that he exaggerated his importance is the concentration on his own role in his narratives, but these were all to varying degrees autobiographical. He intended to write histories of the LCS and Westminster politics, but these works were never written, and the narratives which survive are memoirs. Thus when he inserted an address for a Middlesex meeting into his account of Westminster politics, he felt it necessary to explain that he had included it because he and Richter had drafted it. Even in his account of the Reform Bill, he said in his introduction that many would probably write histories of its passage, and that it was his intention to record aspects of the agitation which might otherwise be lost. Since he expected his account to be one source among many, his concentration on his own role cannot be considered evidence that he was trying to exaggerate his own importance. Thomas Hodgskin quoted him as saying that a man must have a number of projects on hand to achieve anything, but in writing it is rather the case that he attempted so much that most of his projects were not completed. The fact that it was the autobiographical works which he did finish doubtless reflected his self-confessed vanity. Mrs Grote said that she could never have worked so hard and allowed others to take the credit for what she had done in public as he so often did,[5] and his care in recording his achievements for posterity suggests that he only reined in an ambition for public admiration at considerable psychic cost. Unconscious resentment of the reputation of men who deserved it far less than himself may have been one cause of his overcritical attitude.

The two key factors in his outlook were his passionate sympathy for working people and his equally passionate resentment of the contempt he suffered as a tailor. Even his Benthamite friends were capable of treating him snobbishly, and when Samuel Harrison read Place's autobiography, he was surprised and distressed to discover that John Stuart Mill had displayed this attitude. The incident he was commenting on was later censored.[6] This prejudice could provoke Place to be offensive in his behaviour, sometimes unwittingly. Colonel Leslie Grove Jones in a letter introducing a Whig MP urged him: 'In *your conversation* with him I beg you to sit [illegible word] in your chair and not to play Dictator *marching* about your room.' Lord Durham wrote: 'Francis Place is a superior man, but why will he always wear a coat of bristles when he is in company with those who, by the accident of station, are his superiors in society? He is equal to them in reality, and yet he seems to think himself always called upon to evince his sturdy independence and his contempt for artificial distinctions.' The comment shows the blindness the aristocracy could display to the resentment their arrogance and contempt aroused.

The Chartist newspaper proprietor, A.H. Beaumont, gave the other side of the coin when he said that Place was 'the only tradesman I ever saw in the presence of a lord who had not on such occasions a curve in his back'. 'Judge the prejudices of this country', Place said to Gustave D'Eichtal in 1828.

> I really have many friends and many very influential people regard me with respect and affection; nevertheless, you will never see me dining with them. If they were to invite me, it would be a burden on them. If I were to decide to leave this house and take a pleasant country villa, my origins would soon be forgotten. But as long as I am a tradesman I cannot be counted a gentleman. I was consulted about the establishment of a political economy club; I gave my advice, my plan; never have my best friends, who themselves are members, talked about my joining.

He could rarely comment so dispassionately on the snobbery he suffered.[7]

The fact that he could never hope to be accepted by polite society helped to ensure that he would never lose his loyalty to the working people. As he observed in 1825: 'My being a *tailor* has been eminently serviceable to me by keeping my political acquaintances in their places and me in mine, preventing too close an intimacy which would inevitably have destroyed my utility, be its value whatever it may.' On the rare occasions that he received social invitations from upper-class men, he would refuse, because he knew that he would have to accept the role of the 'humble friend', thus jeopardising his claim to independence and equality, and reducing his political influence.

The problem was worst in London, and if he visited friends such as Bentham and Mill in the country, he would be accepted by their other guests as an equal. When he stayed with Bentham in Somerset in 1817, Bentham felt it necessary, in inviting Sir Samuel Romilly to stay, to warn him about Place's presence. Sir Samuel did not object, and his daughter took Place for a gentleman and MP. In the 1830s he used to visit friends such as the Grotes and Colonel Perronet Thompson. Unlike Place the parliamentary Benthamites were acceptable to polite society, but like him they stood to some degree outside the class system.[8]

The snobbery Place suffered, and the conspiracy theory of government which he shared with Bentham and James Mill, predisposed him to see the aristocracy as the enemy. He observed that historical events 'are but too generally represented as the results of deep laid and well conducted schemes, carried on by long sighted men, when . . . they who originated them had no suspicion, much less any intention of producing the results which followed them'. It was a point which he was liable to forget when he discussed the motives of the Whigs and Tories. However, his belief that the first task of a radical was to undermine aristocratic power did reflect contemporary realities. Recent historical studies have confirmed his view that power remained concentrated in aristocratic hands in the early nineteenth century, especially in the south of England, in one case in a field where Place failed to see it. It is ironic that he regarded the New Poor Law as a rational Benthamite reform, but it has recently been shown that it was designed and operated as an instrument to maintain the control of the landowning classes over the poor.[9]

Place's temper caused fewer problems with working men. Although he would criticise them freely, he would treat them as equals, and when the Chartists took offence, it was at his opinions not his manner. He often observed that men who thought for themselves were bound to differ, and that he was ready to change his opinion if he was shown that he was wrong — as he did over public education and the Poor Laws. He claimed that he did not quarrel over differences of opinion, a statement that is largely true. He was on good terms with many men he profoundly disagreed with: such as Robert Owen; Joshua Scholefield, Attwood's fellow MP for Birmingham and a supporter of his unorthodox currency theory; John Fielden, the factory reformer and disciple of Cobbett; and the Tory radical, Richard Oastler. Oastler 'is an odd fellow', Place told John Sadler in 1835, 'but so is every man who thinks for himself — you are odd — and so people say I am. Oastler calls himself a Tory, and in some matters he and I differ very widely, but he does much to serve the working people in the way he thinks best, and we have a sort of a bargain between us, that we will continue to disagree without quarrelling. I indeed never quarrel with anyone. They who are enemies to the working people I avoid, and they who are friends to them I court to a continuance of their exertions.' The claim that he never quarrelled with anyone reflected aspiration rather than reality, but Burdett and Colonel Jones even managed to renege on radicalism without earning his contempt, because he did not suspect their motives. His ire was aroused by behaviour he considered dishonest or cowardly, and the standard of honesty he demanded was almost obsessively high. In 1841 a Poor Law official urged him to try to disrupt an anti-Poor Law meeting arranged by the owner of *The Times* by telling the Chartists how badly he had treated his employees, and Place cited the proposal as an example of how official life debases a man's sense of honesty. He even claimed that Grey and Althorp must have been insincere when they praised the Corporation of London, because it was 'the most corrupt body on the face of the earth' — by which he meant that it spent large sums on entertainment.[10] The dishonesty accepted as normal among politicians was constantly drawing his passionate denunciation. He also attached the greatest importance to courage, and men such as John Gale Jones and Cobbett earned his contempt by displaying cowardice at crucial moments in their careers. Place was too aware of his own limitations of temper and intellect to consider himself superior to the human race, but few could hope to live up to his standards. Because he learned his ideas about honesty through books and lectures rather than as part of his upbringing, he could be rigid and intolerant in his judgements. But with all his faults he was never petty-minded, and if his standards were unreasonably high, they were ones he lived up to himself, and they brought their reward in the general acknowledgement of his integrity, even by political opponents.

He found a purpose in life in his allegiance to the working people, telling Lovett: 'You know that it is only for the working class that I have any especial sympathy, because they need sympathy more than either of the other classes, and that I would neither stir hand nor foot to promote any public matter whatever which did not tend to their advantage.'[11] He was far less dogmatic and consistent than he appeared. His loyalty to the working people conflicted with his opposition to government interference with private property. Sometimes he would argue that factory legislation was wrong in principle because men always ought to be free to make their own bargains, and interference by the legislature in the way that manufacturers ran their businesses would set a precedent which would eventually lead to ruinous controls; at other times he would express deep regret that it was impossible, in his view, to design legislation which would effectively control the excessive power of masters over their employees. In retrospect, he dismissed Moore's bill, which set up complex controls in place of the Combination Laws, in the most contemptuous terms, but his first reaction was to attempt to amend it to make it practicable, and when he opposed minimum wage legislation for the cotton weavers, he offered to support them if they could devise a practicable plan.

He opposed Owenism because he thought that it would require a uniformity of thinking which was impossible and undesirable, since mediocrity was incompatible with happiness, and because competition was a necessary spur to improvement.[12] He regarded any interference in property in the society of his own day as dangerous, but he looked forward to a Spencean system of public ownership of land in the future. This was probably more acceptable to him than expropriation of capitalist property because the principal sufferers would have been the aristocracy. However he frequently expressed intense bitterness at the conduct of large manufacturers towards their employees, and a strong dislike of the money-making mentality. His belief that competition was necessary to improvement, and that Owenism would lead to an undesirable uniformity, suggest that he was an opponent of socialism, but he disapproved of large disparities of wealth. 'There can, I think, be no doubt at all that civil communities will in time be differently and better organised than they are now', he observed in 1836, but he did not think that this would be possible while an excess of labour continued, and he confined himself to present circumstances.[13] Some historians consider Place backward and narrow-minded because he contemptuously dismissed the socialist schemes of the 1820s and 1830s, but his contempt was directed at claims that the success of socialism would be easy and certain. What form of society Place looked forward to in the long run is not known, because he was wary of recording fanciful hopes, for fear of being regarded as an advocate of them in his own time – just as he concealed his belief that sexual relations should and would eventually be free.

The contradictions in Place's outlook emerge again and again. He successfully opposed Thomas Hodgskin's being allowed to lecture on political economy at the LMI because of his socialist views, and he often complained bitterly about journals which 'misled' the people by preaching wrong doctrine, but he was always totally opposed to censorship, and in his view the only answer to the arguments of misleading writers was to refute them. He considered Hodgskin's lectures at the LMI an exception because the venue appeared to give 'official' sanction to a theory which he considered dangerous and scientifically unsound. He often emphasised in his writings for the press that he laid no claim to infallibility – with the aim of persuading his readers to accept that they too might be wrong and should consider his arguments. He was sometimes far too ready to dismiss anyone who rejected 'correct' doctrine as foolish or dishonest, but at other times he would show toleration and respect for those who differed from him, and he showed that he was genuinely prepared to change his mind if convincing arguments were put against his view. His fears of the result of an excessive growth of population sometimes led him to write as if the working people were heading rapidly towards starvation, but more typical is his comment to George Grote in 1839: 'Upon the whole the working people of Great Britain and especially the skilled labourers have been *"better off"* since the peace in 1815 than they ever were before in this country.'[14] His sometimes misanthropic view of human nature contradicted his belief in progress, and optimism or pessimism were uppermost in his outlook depending on his mood. In spite of his reputation for hardheadedness, he confessed that he was inclined to be overoptimistic, and he sometimes expressed grossly inflated expectations for the good which he expected his projects to effect – especially if they had never got off the ground.

The belief of radicals that the system would never reform itself led to contradictions in their thinking. Sometimes it could be a justification for quietism, and Place occasionally used this excuse, but he was too temperamentally active and energetic to be tempted for long, and even when he did refuse to join a project, he would always change his mind if he saw a real prospect that it would do any good. The belief did create a tension between his Godwinian preference for gradual change and his belief that only a collapse of the system would produce any real improvement. This contradiction can be seen in his willingness to contemplate revolution at times of emergency and his contempt for people who claimed that revolution could succeed, his unrealistic belief that representative government would 'spring out of the chaos' of a collapse of government, and the great importance he attached to political education in order to make his expectation less unrealistic.

The contradictions in Place's outlook are also seen in his attitude to women. He gave his daughters as good an education as possible, and expected them to earn their own living as governesses before marriage. He encouraged Harriet Martineau with fulsome praise for her educational and economic writings, and he almost certainly supported female suffrage, since he once cited a friend's support of it as proof of his political integrity.[15] He also fiercely criticised the double standards applied to men and women on sex. On the other hand, his attitude always remained basically traditional, believing that women's education should train them to be good wives and mothers, and that their employment opportunities should be secondary to that. Arguing that trade clubs should prevent women being employed in skilled trades in order to prevent an erosion of wages, he does not seem to have considered the position of women who did not have – or did not wish to have – a man to support them.

The most remarkable feature of his character was his willingness to forgive offences against himself. When Mrs Grote read Place's autobiography, she criticised Place's decision to forgive Richard Wild, his business partner who tried to ruin him, and told him that 'your *image*, Roebuck would never have committed this folly'. Place defended his decision, saying that eighteen years was too long to hold a grudge, but he agreed that his 'image' would have refused to pardon Wild. When Samuel Harrison read Place's papers on the Sellis affair (including some which have not survived) he remarked that no man but Place would have connected himself with public matters again after the way he had been treated.[16]

Place's extraordinary determination, his refusal to be put off by setbacks or diverted to minor objects, allowed him to achieve important results in a number of fields. His principal achievements were the founding of the birth control movement and the legalisation of trade unions. He played a key role in the 1807 Westminster election victory by persuading the reformers to put forward Burdett after his duel with Paull, and his organising genius and tactical sense were important factors in keeping the constituency under radical control in spite of the splits and apathy which afflicted the Westminster Committee. This success was crucial in reviving the radical movement over the decade after 1807. He also played an important part in a number of legislative reforms such as the repeal of the apprenticeship provisions of the Statute of Apprentices, the abolition of the Sinking Fund, and the introduction of penny postage. His diligence in the educational field bore fruit in the foundation of the London Mechanics' Institute in 1823, which launched the nineteenth-century movement for adult education for working men and helped to pave the way for the establishment of London University. His role in the Reform Bill agitation was important, but less important than he believed, because he was wrong in thinking that the radicals prevented the Duke of Wellington coming to power in May 1832. Indeed, he seems to have played a more important role in preventing a compromise in the autumn of 1831.

From the 1820s to the 1840s he was an important adviser for working men seeking to organise trade unions, secure legislative changes to remove grievances, and launch political and educational projects. In the 1830s society was widely seen as becoming separated into hostile classes, and Place was valued as one of the few remaining links between the two sides. To Government Ministers and middle-class politicians he was a man of 'sound' views who had some chance of being listened to by working people, and to the working people he was one of the very few people who had both the power and the will to help them. Both sides overestimated his influence on the other. The foundation of the LWMA owed much to the moderation of views of the former NUWC leaders and their willingness to work with middle-class radicals, which Place encouraged by the aid and advice he gave them and his determined support of the campaign against the taxes on knowledge. In drafting the Charter he made use of his expertise on election law and organisation, but it was the six points rather than the document which mattered to Chartists. In an age when elections were managed by solicitors on behalf of candidates, his pioneering of popular election organisation was not widely followed up until party organisations emerged in the 1870s.[17] Apart from birth control, Place was seldom an initiator, rather a man with an unrivalled skill and pertinacity in making a reality of other men's ideas.

In 1832 Place justly claimed: 'I have never ceased to be the friend of the working people. I have spent more time in their service than *any* man living, and I have done them more service than *any* man living.'[18]

Notes

CHAPTER 2

1. M.D. George, *London Life in the Eighteenth Century* (rev. edn, 1966), pp. 264–5; Publications of the Harleian Society, *Registers,* vol. XV (1889), 2 October 1746, p. 69.
2. Quoted in J.S. Burn, *The Fleet Registers . . .* (1833), p. 99.
3. Register of Baptisms for the Parish of St Ann Westminster, Middlesex, 25 October 1747; Libels and Allegations, London Diocesan Consistory Court, DL/C/180, 11 May 1785; Burn, *op. cit.,* pp. 99–100.
4. Registers of baptisms for the parishes of St Martins in the Fields and St Clement Danes; verse quoted in George, *op. cit.,* p. 93.
5. *The Autobiography of Francis Place (1771–1854),* ed. with an intro. and notes by Mary Thale (hereafter *Autobiography*), pp. 26–7.
6. Ibid., pp. 20, 34.
7. Ibid., pp. 61–2; Add. Mss. 36,625, f. 21v.
8. *Autobiography,* p. 21.
9. Ibid., p. 70.
10. Ibid., p. 47n.
11. Ibid., pp. 43, 44, 46.
12. Ibid., pp. 55–6; Add. Mss. 27,820, f. 127v.
13. *Autobiography,* p. 71.
14. Ibid., pp. 71–2.
15. Ibid., pp. 74–5, 77.
16. Add. Mss. 27,831, f. 208. The passage following the quotation has been censored.
17. *Autobiography,* pp. 76–7, 81.
18. Libels and Allegations, *op. cit.*
19. *Autobiography,* p. 93.
20. Ibid., p. 96.
21. Add. Mss. 27,825, ff. 270–3. Place's comments refer to the illegal practice of 'insuring'. Tickets in the State Lottery were expensive, and people who could not afford them would 'insure' small sums – gambling on which numbers would be drawn. Cf. circular letter from the Duke of Portland to the Magistrates of Police Offices, 10 February 1797, HO 65/1. In 1826 all lotteries were suppressed in Britain.
22. *Autobiography,* pp. 99–100.
23. Ibid., pp. 101, 109, 106.

24. Ibid., pp. 110–1.
25. Ibid., p. 114.
26. Ibid., pp. 115–6.
27. Ibid., pp. 119–20.
28. Ibid., p. 123; F. Place, *Improvement of the Working Class. Drunkenness – Education*. (1834), pp. 14–5 and note; Add. Mss. 27,822, f. 50; Report of the Select Committee on Artizans and Machinery, 1824, p. 46.

CHAPTER 3

1. On the parliamentary reform movement before 1790, see G. Rudé, *Wilkes and Liberty. A Social Study of 1763 to 1774* (1962); I.R. Christie, *Wilkes, Wyvill and Reform: The Parliamentary Reform Movement in British Politics 1760–1785* (1962); J. Cannon, *Parliamentary Reform 1640–1832* (1973).
2. T. Paine, *Rights of Man*, ed. H. Collins (1969), p. 148. The most recent and authoritative account of radicalism in the 1790s is A. Goodwin, *The Friends of Liberty: The English Democratic Movement in the Age of the French Revolution* (1979). See also M. Thale (ed.), *Selections from the Papers of the London Corresponding Society 1792–1799* (1983) (hereafter *LCS Papers*); E.P. Thompson, *The Making of the English Working Class* (rev. edn, 1968); and on the later 1790s, J.A. Hone, *For the Cause of Truth: Radicalism in London 1796–1821* (1982).
3. On the organisation of the LCS, see *LCS Papers*, pp. xxiii–xxix.
4. Add. Mss. 27,808, f. 175; *Address of the London Corresponding Society to the other Societies of Great Britain, united for obtaining a Reform in Parliament*, 29 November 1792, pp. 6–8.
5. The LCS admitted this, and said that if their example was followed by the whole nation, then it need not fear invasion by Frenchmen, Hessians or Hanoverians (*An Account of the Seizure of Citizen Thomas Hardy*, c. July 1794, p. 6).
6. Add. Mss. 27,817, ff. 138–73.
7. Add. Mss. 27,813, f. 114v (General Committee, 27 August 1795, Place in the chair. A member was accused of not being a good citizen, because he had been a Loyal Briton. 'Citn Place said he had once being [sic] a Loyal Briton, but he did not think himself any the worse for it . . .'); E.C. Black, *The Association: British Extraparliamentary Political Organisation, 1769–1793* (1963), p. 272.
8. Add. Mss. 27,808, f. 3. A description of the Chalk Farm meeting of the LCS in April is sometimes attributed to Place, but it is from Hardy's manuscript history of the society in Add. Mss. 27,814, ff. 74–6.
9. Add. Mss. 27,808, ff. 56–8, 12. The first draft is in Add. Mss. 27,808, ff. 2–117 (some sections have been crossed through when they were copied); the second forms part of the published *Autobiography*.
10. *Autobiography*, p. 132.
11. The Friends of Liberty, *A Letter . . . to the Members of the London Corresponding Society*, 6 April 1795 (Nuffield College); *The Correspondence of the London Corresponding Society* (1795), pp. 18–9, 23–6 (Nuffield College).
12. Add. Mss. 27,808, f. 26; LCS, *Addresses and Regulations*, May 1792 (Nuffield College). Place stated that the report was printed as *The Report of the Committee of the Constitution of the London Corresponding Society*. Both this and a *Revised Report* were printed before the arrests of May 1794 (General Committee report, 26 June 1794 (Groves), TS 11/965/3510A (2); W.A.L. Seaman, 'British Democratic Societies in the Period of the French Revolution', London University

PhD thesis, 1954, pp. 56–7, 89–90).

13. *Correspondence of the LCS,* pp. 19–22.

14. *Autobiography,* p. 131; Add. Mss. 27,808, f. 10; *Correspondence of the LCS,* p. 22.

15. *Correspondence of the LCS*, pp. 3–7; Add. Mss. 27,813, ff. 50, 73.

16. Add. Mss. 27,808, f. 27v (the words 'which tended much to embarrass many persons' are crossed through. In the second draft Place condemned the public meetings held at this time and said that he had opposed them); Add. Mss. 27,813, ff. 54, 121v.

17. Minutes for the first half of the year have not survived.

18. Add. Mss. 27,808, ff. 28v, 29; Add. Mss. 27,813, f. 125. Place stated that he was also elected to the Executive Committee, which is not confirmed by surviving minutes, but few survive outside July to September 1795; on 6 August he refused to stand for the EC on the ground that it was not in his power to attend (Add. Mss. 27,813, f. 100v).

19. Press cutting, Place Coll., Set 37, p. 57; Add. Mss. 27,808, f. 37; Add. Mss. 27,813, f. 128.

20. Add. Mss. 27,808, f. 38. His own division voted 4-0 against the meeting (PC 1/23/A38).

21. On 20 August his division put forward a proposal, defeated in a referendum, for the General Committee to meet twice a week (Add. Mss. 27,813, ff. 112v, 124v).

22. Thompson, *op. cit.,* pp. 152-3; Gwyn A. Williams, *Artisans and Sans-Culottes* (1968), p. 99.

23. *The History of Two Acts . . .* (1796), p. 100; Add. Mss. 27,808, f. 39.

24. Add. Mss. 27,808, ff. 46, 50, 54–5, 58–9.

25. Ibid., f. 65.

26. Ibid., f. 56.

27. Ibid., ff. 67, 70. Place probably ceased to be chairman of the General Committee on 4 February 1796, when John Oxlade was elected to the post (PC 1/23/A38).

28. Add. Mss. 27,808, f. 71v; Add. Mss. 27,815, f. 35; PC 1/23/A38.

29. Add. Mss. 27,808, ff. 71–2.

30. Ibid., ff. 75–6; PC 1/23/A38.

31. *Autobiography,* p. 153.

32. The latter charge was later answered to the delegates' satisfaction (*LCS Papers,* p. 390).

33. Place stayed in office after Ashley's resignation on 29 December, but by 13 February 1797 James Powell had replaced him (PC 1/23/A38; PC 1/41/A138).

34. Add. Mss. 27,808, f. 79. The words 'and as both . . . Birmingham' are crossed through.

35. TS 11/837/2832.

36. *Autobiography,* pp. 159–72; TS 11/978/3561.

37. W.H. Reid, *The Rise and Dissolution of the Infidel Societies in this Metropolis* (1800), pp. 5–9; PC 1/23/A38; *Correspondence of the LCS,* p. 71.

38. Place said that he moved there in the spring, but the pamphlet referred to on p. 32 above, published in October, gives his address as Back of St Clements, the slum he lived in immediately after his marriage.

39. *Autobiography,* p. 143.

40. Ibid., pp. 155–6.

41. Add. Mss. 27,808, ff. 83v, 85.

42. Archives du Ministère des Affaires Etrangères, Paris, Corr. Pol. Angl., vol. 53, ff. 159–62 and vol. 592, ff. 172–4, quoted in Seaman *op. cit.,* pp. 270–7.

43. Add. Mss. 27,808, f. 91. On the Irish dimension see M. Elliott, *Partners in Revolution: The United Irishmen and France* (1982).

44. Add. Mss. 27,808, f. 91. In 1823 Benjamin Binns sent Place information from the United States for his projected history of that country – and offered to bring documents to London if Place would pay for his journey (Binns to Place, Philadelphia, 25 May 1823, Add. Mss. 27,858, ff. 127–8).
45. Add. Mss. 27,808, ff. 91–2.
46. R. Hodgson, *Proceedings of the General Committee of the London Corresponding Society . . . on the 5th, 12th and 19th April 1798* (Newgate, 1798).
47. Hone, *op. cit.,* pp. 120–1.
48. *Autobiography,* pp. 180–3; Richard Ford's summary of a statement by Powell, early April 1798, HO 42/42; *LCS Papers,* pp. 436–7.
49. 230 members were reported present in their divisions on 29 March 1798 (PC/1/41/A138); 'Address of the London Corresponding Society to the British Nation', 14 June 1798 (Nuffield College); spy reports in PC/1/42/A144, PC/43/A153.
50. Although Place appears to redefine republicanism here, he made clear elsewhere that he wanted the abolition of the monarchy (Add. Mss. 27,849, f. 88).
51. Add. Mss. 27,808, ff. 113–14; *Autobiography,* p. 197.
52. Galloway to Place, 9 August 1829, Add. Mss. 37,950, f. 32v.
53. On revolutionary activity in the late 1790s see Goodwin, Thompson, Elliott and Hone, *op. cit.,* and R. Wells, *Insurrection: The British Experience 1795–1803* (1983).
54. Powell's LCS minutes were accurate, as comparison with the version in the Place papers shows, but his other reports were less reliable. In his report to Ford in early April (in HO 42/42) he claimed that Ashley sent the LCS a treasonable letter through his wife, which is inconceivable in view of the circumstances of Ashley's flight, and stated that the society had sent John Bone and Dr Robert Watson to Portsmouth in May 1797 to confer with the naval mutineers, although he must have known this was untrue because he was present at a General Committee meeting when Bone and Watson accused each other of doing so without LCS authority (*LCS Papers,* p. 397; Elliott, *op. cit.,* p. 149, n. 71). Powell was anxious to keep his lucrative employment as a spy, so he had a motive to embroider his reports (see two letters by Powell, 28 October 1796 and n.d. in PC 1/23/A38).
55. PC 1/41/A138; Elliott, *op. cit.,* pp. 149–50, 175–6; Hodgson, *op. cit.* Evans was intermittently secretary of the LCS in late 1797 and early 1798.
56. Out of the LCS members identified as involved in revolutionary activity in early 1798, the Binns brothers, John Bone, Thomas Stuckey and James Powell were not active in the society after late 1797. John Binns chaired a meeting of the Friends of Liberty on 6 November 1797 (PC 1/41/A138) and Place said that he was no longer a member of the LCS at the time of his arrest. Thomas Crossfield, an Irishman, chaired an Executive Committee meeting in January 1798 which issued an address on Ireland, but he was dropped from the EC as non-effective in March. The involvement of Alexander Galloway (an EC member) in the UE is doubtful, as it rests on Powell's deposition to Ford – in November 1797 Galloway presided over a meeting of his division which opposed an activist policy (*LCS Papers,* pp. 413–14).
57. Place to Wakefield, 21 November 1814, Add. Mss. 35,152, f. 108v.
58. Place to Thompson, 2 January 1841, Add. Mss. 35,151, f. 290.
59. Place to Rogers, 15 January 1832, Place Coll., Set 68, item 22; Add. Mss. 27,808, ff. 59–60.
60. Place to Thelwall, 5 November 1824, Add. Mss. 27,817, f. 118; *Autobiography,* p. 200.
61. Place to Morton, 2 April 1836, Add. Mss. 35,150, f. 117.
62. W. Godwin, *Enquiry Concerning Political Justice,* ed. I. Kramnick (1976), p. 197;

Place to Warburton, 5 May 1839, Add. Mss. 35,151, f. 166.
63. Place to Fraser, 21 November 1837, Add. Mss. 35,151, f. 38.
64. 'To the Parliament and People of Great Britain. An Explicit Declaration of the Principles and Views of the London Corresponding Society', 23 November 1795, Add. Mss. 27,815, f. 18.
65. Add. Mss. 27,808, ff. 141–330; Place to Whytoch, 28 October 1839, Add. Mss. 35,151, f. 185.
66. *Autobiography,* p. 143.
67. Add. Mss. 35,145, f. 29; E.W. Marrs (ed.), *The Letters of Charles and Mary Anne Lamb,* vol. 2 (1976), pp. 13–15, 70; Place to Brooks, 10 January 1813, Add. Mss. 35,144, f. 52; *Autobiography,* p. 188.
68. Add. Mss. 35,145, ff. 28–9.

CHAPTER 4

1. M. Jaeger, *Before Victoria: Changing Standards and Behaviour 1787–1837* (1956).
2. Add. Mss. 27,827, ff. 192–3; Add. Mss. 27,828, ff. 55–6, 68–70; *Autobiography,* p. 76; Add. Mss. 27,833, ff. 54–61.
3. Add. Mss. 35,144, ff. 181–5.
4. Mrs Grote to Place, 7 January 1836, Add. Mss. 35,144, f. 347; Place to Wade, 9 July 1833, Add. Mss. 35,149, f. 214.
5. *Autobiography,* p. 61; Place to Mill, 20 October 1817, Add. Mss. 35,153, f. 22.
6. *Autobiography,* pp. 232–3 (format and punctuation altered).
7. Add. Mss. 35,143, ff. 168, 174–279.
8. Place to Parkes, 8 November 1833, Add. Mss. 35,149, f. 236.
9. Hone to Place, 6 October 1824, Add. Mss. 37,949, ff. 144–5.
10. Place to Rogers, 15 January 1832, Place Coll., Set 68, item 22.
11. W. Godwin, *Enquiry Concerning Political Justice* (1st edn, 1793), p. 371.
12. *Autobiography,* pp. 137, 157.
13. Ibid., pp. 175, 176.
14. Ibid., p. 135.
15. Ibid., pp. 201–2; Place to Mrs Grote, 8 January 1836, Add. Mss. 35,144, ff. 355–6.
16. *Autobiography,* p. 205.
17. Ibid., pp. 216–17; G. Wallas, *The Life of Francis Place 1771–1854* (1898), p. 35.
18. Add. Mss. 27,849, f. 164; *Autobiography,* pp. 222–3.
19. Place to Mill, 18 January 1816 (reporting his analysis of his accounts), Add. Mss. 35,152, f. 196. In 1816 he expected profits £1000 lower due to the decline in trade (Place to Mill, 2 October 1816, f. 217).
20. Place to Carlile, 17 August 1822, Place Coll., Set 68, c. item 88; Mill to Place, 20 February 1818 (summary by Francis Place Junior), Add. Mss. 35,153, f. 42; Add. Mss. 27,804, f. 122; Place to Mrs Austin, 1 January 1829, Add. Mss. 37,949, f. 220; Place's diary, 14 and 19 August 1826, Add. Mss. 35,146, ff. 37, 38; B. Mazlish, *James and John Stuart Mill: Father and Son in the Nineteenth Century* (1975), p. 296.
21. Place to Miers, 7 March 1828, *Autobiography,* p. 256; Place to Mill, 20 July 1815, Mill to Place (summary by Francis Place Junior), 22 September 1816, Add. Mss. 35,152, ff. 140, 215.
22. Galloway to Place, 11 November 1824, Add. Mss. 27,817, f. 125.

23. Place to Miers, *op. cit.;* Place to Mill, n.d. [December 1816], Add. Mss. 35,152, f. 235.
24. *Autobiography,* p. 254; Place to Miers, *op. cit.,* p. 260.
25. L.G. Johnson, *General T. Perronet Thompson, 1783–1869: His Military, Literary and Political Campaigns* (1957), p. 226. On Mrs Chatterley see *Autobiography,* pp. 258, n. 1, 268–70 and *DNB* entry for William Simmonds Chatterley.
26. Place's diary, 16 September 1826, Add. Mss. 35,146, f. 47v; Add. Mss. 37,949, ff. 367, 371, 375; Place to Bulwer (later Lord Lytton), 5 February 1834, Add. Mss. 35,149, f. 273v. Place wrote two pamphlets concerning the theatre. *A New Way to Pay Old Debts* was printed in 1812 to oppose Sheridan's plan to rebuild the Drury Lane Play House as a fraud, but the distributors of the pamphlet were persuaded to suppress it (Add. Mss. 35,145, ff. 15–8). The other pamphlet opposed the monopoly licences held by the Drury Lane and Covent Garden Theatres (F. Place, *A Brief Examination of the Dramatic Patents* (1834), Add. Mss. 27,831, ff. 100–5).
27. Place to Mrs Grote, 8 January 1836, Add. Mss. 35,144, f. 349; *Northern Liberator,* 30 December 1837 (by A.H. Beaumont).

CHAPTER 5

1. W.E. Saxton gives a very full account of Westminster politics in 'The Political Importance of the Westminster Committee in the Early Nineteenth Century', Edinburgh University PhD thesis, 1957. Place's memoir of Westminster politics is in Add. Mss. 27,850. Add. Mss. 27,838 contains another account of the 1807 election and correspondence, pamphlets and newspaper cuttings. See also Hone, *op. cit.,* and A.M.S. Prochaska, 'Westminster Radicalism 1807–1832', Oxford University DPhil thesis, 1975. On eighteenth-century Westminster, see Saxton, *op. cit.,* chs. 1–3 and Add. Mss. 27,849.
2. On London radicalism during this period see Hone, *op. cit.,* pp. 117–46.
3. Add. Mss. 27,850, ff. 37–41.
4. Ibid., f. 6; *Cobbett's Weekly Political Register,* vol. 10, cols 193–8, 9 August 1806.
5. J.J. Sack, *The Grenvillites: Party Politics and Factionalism in the Age of Pitt and Liverpool* (1979), pp. 105–6.
6. Add. Mss. 27,850, ff. 19–22.
7. Ibid., ff. 23–7.
8. *Cobbett's Weekly Political Register,* vol. 33, col. 73, 17 January 1818.
9. Ibid., vol. 11, col. 204, 7 February 1807 and cols 370–1, 7 March 1807.
10. Add. Mss. 27,850, f. 47.
11. Ibid., ff. 49–50; Add. Mss. 27,838, ff. 92–5.
12. Add. Mss. 27,817, ff. 105–7; M.W. Patterson, *Sir Francis Burdett and his Times (1770–1844)* (1931), vol. 1, pp. 194–206; Hone, *op. cit.,* p. 159.
13. Add. Mss. 27,838, f. 18v.
14. Add. Mss. 27,850, ff. 68–9.
15. Ibid., f. 67.
16. Ibid., f. 78.
17. *Cobbett's Weekly Political Register,* vol. 11, cols 899–902, 16 May 1807; Add. Mss. 27,838, f. 20v.
18. Add. Mss. 27,850, ff. 75, 77.
19. Add. Mss. 27,838, f. 131.

20. Sheridan received 592 plumpers, shared 1527 with Burdett, 374 with Cochrane and 145 with Elliott; 1226 of his 2646 votes were cast in the last two days.
21. J. Horne Tooke, *A Warning to the Electors of Westminster* (1807), pp. 11–12.
22. Sack, *op. cit.,* p. 90.
23. Patterson, *op. cit.,* vol. 1, pp. 160–77, 187; Wells, *op. cit.,* pp. 240–6; Place to Mrs Grote, 13 May 1836, Add. Mss. 35,144, f. 366v.
24. [F. Place and J. Richter], *An Exposition of the Circumstances which gave rise to the Election of Sir F. Burdett, Bart. for the City of Westminster . . .* (1807), pp. 4–5.
25. Add. Mss. 27,850, f. 215.
26. Add. Mss. 27,850, f. 274. On Place's campaign against the High Bailiff see Add. Mss. 27,838, ff. 248–319. On 15 May 1827 Place gave evidence on the practice in Westminster elections to the House of Commons Select Committee on Election Polls for Cities and Boroughs, Report, pp. 9–15.
27. Add. Mss. 27,850, ff. 104, 91, 107; Hone, *op. cit.,* pp. 13–14, 361.
28. F.D. Cartwright, *The Life and Correspondence of Major John Cartwright* (1826), vol. 2, p. 298; Add. Mss. 27,850, ff. 108–9.
29. Add. Mss. 27,850, ff. 115–7.
30. On the O.P. Riots see Hone, *op. cit.,* pp. 183–5; Add. Mss. 35,145, ff. 2–6; Place Coll., Set 59.
31. Add. Mss. 35,145, f. 8.
32. Ibid., f. 13.
33. Add. Mss. 27,809, f. 17; Place to Cobbett, 21 September 1831, Place Coll., Set 21, p. 211; Place to Harrison, 2 May 1834, Add. Mss. 35,149, f. 291v. The case concerned the Deacles, a Hampshire gentry couple accused of leading a riot.
34. Add. Mss. 27,850, ff. 158–60.
35. Add. Mss. 36,627, f. 23v (Place's comment on Wilberforce's support for the repressive legislation of 1817).
36. Add. Mss. 27,850, f. 175.
37. Ibid., ff. 184–6.
38. Ibid., ff. 199–201; Add. Mss. 27,789, ff. 124–5; Patterson, *op. cit.,* vol, 1, pp. 263–70.
39. Add. Mss. 27,850, ff. 201–2.
40. Thompson, *op. cit.,* p. 511.
41. Add. Mss. 27,850, ff. 214, 218, 228.
42. Ibid., f. 231.
43. On the Sellis affair see Add. Mss. 27,851–2; Add. Mss. 35,144, ff. 2–94; F. Knight, *University Rebel: the Life of William Frend (1757–1841)* (1971), p. 255.
44. Add. Mss. 27,850, ff. 232, 235.
45. Knight, *op. cit.,* pp. 252–5; Hone, *op. cit.,* p. 191. Place had a high regard for Frend and Jones Burdett, neither of whom appears to have played any part in bringing the charge of spying against him.
46. Add. Mss. 27,850, ff. 239–41; *Memoirs of Henry Hunt esq. Written by himself* (1820), vol. 2, p. 423; L. Horner (ed.) *Memoirs and Correspondence of Francis Horner MP* (1843), vol. 2, p. 50.
47. Richter to Place, 19 September 1812, Place to Richter, 20 September, Add. Mss. 27,840, ff. 73–5. On the 1812 election see Add. Mss. 27,840, ff. 1–151.
48. [Place and Richter], *op. cit.,* p. 8.
49. Add. Mss. 27,840, ff. 55, 60, 94–6, 105; Hone, *op. cit.,* p. 215.
50. On the *Independent Whig* group, see A. Aspinall, *Politics and the Press c.1780–1850* (1949), pp. 310–11; I.J. Prothero, *Artisans and Politics in Early Nineteenth-Century London, John Gast and his Times* (1979), pp. 89–90; Add. Mss. 27,842, f. 255; Add. Mss. 35,152, f. 63.

51. For John King, see *Autobiography,* pp. 236–9, and for a contrasting view *The Reminiscences of Captain Gronow* (Folio Society edn, 1977), pp. 238–9.
52. Add. Mss. 35,144, f. 48.
53. Place to Brooks, 10 January 1813, Add. Mss. 35,144, f. 52.
54. Add. Mss. 27,850, ff. 266–74. Place's victory became irrelevant in contested elections when the Committee abandoned the practice of denying that their nominees were candidates from 1819, and in 1827 he estimated the unavoidable legal expenses in a contested election at £800, to be shared between the candidates (Add. Mss. 27,838, f. 1v).

CHAPTER 6

1. [Place] to [Mill], 30 October 1816, Add. Mss. 35,152, f. 225.
2. Add. Mss. 27,823, ff. 13–4, 19; G.J. Holyoake, *Sixty Years of an Agitator's Life* (3rd edn, 1893), vol. 1, p. 215. On the British and Foreign Schools Society see Add. Mss. 27,823, ff. 4–78 and Place Coll., Set 60.
3. Add. Mss. 27,823, ff. 31, 33, 43.
4. Ibid., f. 45.
5. Add. Mss. 35,147, f. 70; E. Wakefield, *An Account of Ireland, Statistical and Political* (1812).
6. 'Report from the Select Committee on the Education of the Lower Orders in the Metropolis', 1816, pp. 36–7, 40–3. On the WLLA see A.M.S. Prochaska, 'The Practice of Radicalism: Educational Reform in Westminster', in J. Stevenson (ed.), *London in the Age of Reform* (1977), pp. 102–16; Hone, *op. cit.,* pp. 239–45; Add. Mss. 27,823, ff. 80–118; Add. Mss. 35,152, ff. 54v–74; Place Coll., Set 60.
7. Fox to Place, 26 March 1814, Add. Mss. 35,152, f. 44v; Add. Mss. 27,823, f. 98.
8. Add. Mss. 27,823, ff. 96–7.
9. Wakefield to Place, 18 January 1814, Add. Mss. 35,152, f. 32.
10. Add. Mss. 27,823, f. 101.
11. Place to Mill, Place to WLLA, both 8 July 1814, Add. Mss. 35,152, ff. 56v, 58.
12. Memorandum, 19 July 1814, Add. Mss. 35,152, f. 69.
13. Mill to Place, 30 July 1814, Add. Mss. 37,949, ff. 18–19.
14. Report, pp. 267–9. Place also testified to the Education Committee of 1835, but he complained that his printed evidence was mangled (Minutes of Evidence, pp. 67–90, 30 June 1835; Add. Mss. 35,146, f. 138v).
15. Add. Mss. 27,823, f. 124.
16. On the Chrestomathic school see Add. Mss. 27,823, ff. 122–234; Place Coll., Set 60; Hone, *op. cit.,* pp. 244–5.
17. Place's account is in Add. Mss. 27,823, ff. 237–382; see also T. Kelly, *A History of Adult Education in Great Britain* (rev. edn, 1970), ch. 8; Prothero, *op. cit.,* pp. 191–203; Prochaska. 'Westminster Radicalism', *op. cit.,* ch. 5; E. Halévy, *Thomas Hodgskin* (trans. A.J. Taylor, 1956), pp. 84–91; C.W. New, *The Life of Henry Brougham to 1830* (1961), pp. 331–7.
18. On Birkbeck see T. Kelly, *George Birkbeck: Pioneer of Adult Education* (1957).
19. Place to Coates, 1 January 1834, Add. Mss. 35,149, f. 259v; Add. Mss. 35,154, f. 188.
20. Add. Mss. 35,146, ff. 6, 35, 78v, 91; Add. Mss. 27,823, ff. 292, 363–8; Add. Mss. 27,824, ff. 385–473; Add. Mss. 37,949, ff. 231, 236, 237; Place Coll., Set 57, p. 109.
21. Place to Mrs Grote, 13 May 1836, Add. Mss. 35,144, f. 366.

22. Add. Mss. 35,146, ff. 31–5. Place's account of the origin of London University is in Add. Mss. 27,823, ff. 385–419.
23. Add. Mss. 35,146, ff. 75v, 78; Add. Mss. 27,824, ff. 335–69; Add. Mss. 27,823, ff. 247–8 (the details of Brougham's tricks have been censored); Add. Mss. 27,789, ff. 260–1; Add. Mss. 27,824, ff. 361, 363–4.
24. Report from the Select Committee on Education in Ireland, 1835–36, pp. 201–96; Add. Mss. 27,819, ff. 13–17.

CHAPTER 7

1. B.M. Ratcliffe and W.H. Chaloner (trans. and eds.), *A French Sociologist looks at Britain: Gustave D'Eichtal and British society in 1828* (1977), pp. 54–5; 'Notes for the Use of the Hand Loom Weavers Inquiry', 1837, Add. Mss. 27,828, ff. 226–7. Place's identification of Henson as 'King Ludd' is not generally accepted by historians.
2. Place to Mill, 27 November 1814, Add. Mss. 35,152, f. 111. Place's views before 1814 are uncertain, because he did not start preserving his correspondence until then.
3. Mill to Place (summary by Francis Place Junior), Add. Mss. 35,152, f. 227.
4. Mill to Ricardo, 24 August 1817, P. Sraffa and M.H. Dobb (eds), *The Works and Correspondence of David Ricardo* (1951–1973), vol. 7, p. 183; Place's diary, 19 November 1826, 19 June 1827, Add. Mss. 35,146, ff. 58v, 91; Place to Harrison, 2 July 1834, Add. Mss. 35,149, f. 292; *Cobbett's Weekly Political Register,* vol. 34, col. 360, 12 December 1818.
5. Place helped to edit Bentham's *Book of Fallacies,* the *Plan of Parliamentary Reform,* and *Not Paul, but Jesus;* he also saw *Chrestomathia* through the press (Wallas, *op. cit.,* pp. 83–4).
6. R. Harrison, *Bentham* (1983), pp. 205, 258–9; P.H. Marshall, *William Godwin* (1984), ch. 7.
7. Add. Mss. 36,623, f. 90; Add. Mss. 35,145, ff. 19–25; Place to Mill, 8 September 1815, Add. Mss. 35,152, f. 167v; Hone, *op. cit.,* pp. 252–7.
8. Prothero, *op. cit.,* ch. 3; Hone, *op. cit.,* pp. 246–7.
9. Add. Mss. 27,809, f. 26.
10. Add. Mss. 27,825, f. 255; Add. Mss. 27,826, f. 192; Bennet to Place, n.d. [1816], Add. Mss. 37,949, ff. 29–30; Add. Mss. 36,623, f. 74v; Place to Hobhouse, 16 August 1819, Add. Mss. 27,837, f. 172; Add. Mss. 35,146, f. 52.
11. Place to Mill, 20 July 1815, Add. Mss. 35,152, ff. 141–2; Add. Mss. 35,145, ff. 71–8; Rose to Place, 13 July 1815, Add. Mss. 37,949, f. 32.
12. Place to Hodgskin, 30 May 1817, Add. Mss. 35,153, ff. 9–10; *Westminster Review,* vol. 8 (1827), pp. 253–303.
13. Add. Mss. 35,154, f. 195; Place to Hawes, 24 April 1839, Add. Mss. 35,151, f. 157v; *Northern Liberator,* 30 December 1837 (A.H. Beaumont); Place to Hume, 3 January 1837, Add. Mss. 35,150, f. 192v.
14. *Westminster Review,* vol. 6 (1826), pp. 158–201; Bowring to Place, 5 February 1829, Add. Mss. 37,949, f. 232; Place to Hume, 25 October 1829, Add. Mss. 35,145, f. 108; Place to Hume, 16 January 1837, Add. Mss. 35,150, f. 229.
15. Place to Thompson and Fearon, 24 December 1810, Add. Mss. 35,152, f. 3; Hone, *op. cit.,* pp. 330–9; Place to Harrison, 2 May 1834, Add. Mss. 35,149, ff. 283v–292; Ratcliffe and Chaloner, *op. cit.,* p. 46; Place to Fox, 5 November 1835, Add. Mss. 35,150, ff. 86–7.

16. J.H. Wiener, *Radicalism and Freethought in Nineteenth-Century Britain: The Life of Richard Carlile* (1983), pp. 95, 111; *Republican,* vol. 9, pp. 823–32, 25 June 1824; M.P. Mack, *Jeremy Bentham: An Odyssey of Ideas 1748–1792* (1962), p. 305.

17. Add. Mss. 35,144, f. 425.

18. A. Bain, *James Mill. A Biography* (1882), p. 163; Hodgskin to Place, n.d. [1820], Add. Mss. 35,153, f. 141. The loan to Mill was repaid, but it is uncertain whether the one to Hodgskin was.

19. Place to Mrs Austin, 1 January 1829, Add. Mss. 37,949, f. 220; Place to Hobhouse, 4 October 1818, Add. Mss. 36,457, f. 93.

20. Burdett to Place, 15 March 1832, Add. Mss. 37,950, f. 129; Patterson, *op. cit.,* vol. 2, pp. 565–9; Jones to Place, 5 December 1832, Add. Mss. 27,844, ff. 42–3; Place Coll., Set 41, item 173.

21. Add. Mss. 35,146, ff. 27v, 29v; Add. Mss. 35,151, ff. 81v–82, 148v–152.

22. Add. Mss. 35,145, ff. 30–69; D. Locke, *A Fantasy of Reason: The Life and Thought of William Godwin* (1980), pp. 233–41.

23. Place to Rogers, 11 January 1832, Place Coll., Set 68, c.item 22; *Autobiography,* pp. 240–4. On Place's understanding of economic theory see Ratcliffe and Chaloner, *op. cit.,* p. 49; D.J. Rowe, 'Francis Place and the Historian; *Historical Journal,* XVI (1973), pp. 55–6.

24. Place to Jones, 26 July 1837, Add. Mss. 35,150, f. 271; Add. Mss. 27,823, f. 61; Johnson, *op. cit.,* p. 227.

25. Ratcliffe and Chaloner, *op. cit.,* p. 49; Mrs Grote to Place, 18 April 1836, Add. Mss. 35,144, f. 364.

26. Place to Mrs Grote, 13 May 1836, Add. Mss. 35,144, f. 367v; Place to Lovett, 15 June 1840, Place Coll., Set 55, p. 589.

27. Add. Mss. 35,146, ff. 7–8.

28. Place to Mill, 10 December 1814, Mill to Place (summary by Francis Place Junior), 4 October 1815, Add. Mss. 35,152, ff. 123, 173; Place to Hodgskin, 8 September 1819, Add. Mss. 35,153, f. 73v; Add. Mss. 35,146, ff. 65–6.

29. Mill to Place (summary by Francis Place Junior), 26 August 1816; Place to Mill, 30 August 1816, Add. Mss. 35,152, ff. 206, 207.

30. Place to Ensor, 13 October 1816, Add. Mss. 35,152, f. 222; Place to Mrs Grote, 16 January 1837, Add. Mss. 27,816, f. 258.

31. Place to Hobhouse, 29 April 1819, Add. Mss. 27,837, f. 145v; Place to Mill, 18 January and 2 October 1816, Add. Mss. 35,152, ff. 195, 217. Place was commenting on James Gilchrist's *Philosophic Etymology, or Rational Grammar* (1816).

CHAPTER 8

1. *Edinburgh Review,* vol. 20. art. 8, July 1812, p. 140; W.A. Copinger, *The authorship of the first hundred numbers of the 'Edinburgh Review'* (1895), p. 23.

2. Add. Mss. 27,850, ff. 276–7. On the 1814 Westminster election see Add. Mss. 27,850, ff. 275–89; Add. Mss. 27,840, ff. 216–49; Add. Mss. 37,949, f. 18v; A. Aspinall, 'The Westminster Election of 1814', *English Historical Review,* XL (1925), pp. 562–9.

3. Add. Mss. 27,850, f. 281v.

4. Place's memoir of politics in 1815–17 is in Add. Mss. 27,809, ff. 5–126.

5. Ibid., f. 6.

6. Place to Cobden, 15 November 1841, Add. Mss. 35,151, f. 351v.
7. Add. Mss. 27,809, f. 8.
8. A. Aspinall, *Lord Brougham and the Whig Party* (1927), pp. 51–4; Place to Mill, 12 February and 29 August 1815, Add. Mss. 35,152, ff. 132v, 158v.
9. Add. Mss. 27,809, f. 14. The letter is quoted in Aspinall, *op. cit.,* p. 65.
10. Aspinall, *op. cit.,* p. 68.
11. Place to Mill, 2 August 1816, Add. Mss. 35,152, ff. 199–200.
12. Place to Mill, 30 August 1816, Add. Mss. 35,152, ff. 208–10; Add. Mss. 27,809, f. 20.
13. Add. Mss. 27,809, f. 33.
14. *Cobbett's Weekly Political Register,* vol. 32, cols 741–2, 13 September 1817.
15. *Hone's Reformists' Register,* cols 2–4, 39, 1 and 8 February 1817.
16. F.W. Hackwood, *William Hone: His Life and Times* (1912), p. 146.
17. W. Thomas, *The Philosophic Radicals: Nine Studies in Theory and Practice 1817–1841* (1979), pp. 41–3; Lord Broughton (John Cam Hobhouse), *Recollections of a Long Life,* ed. Lady Dorchester (1909), vol. 2, pp. 94, 113–14; Patterson, *op. cit.,* vol. 2, pp. 456–7, 462–4; Add. Mss. 36,623, f. 74v.
18. Add. Mss. 27,841, f. 132.
19. Place to Wooler (not sent), 5 June 1818, Add. Mss. 27,841, f. 115.
20. Add. Mss. 36,627, ff. 37–8; F.D. Cartwright, *op. cit.,* vol. 2, pp. 12–15; Burdett to Hobhouse, 22 May 1818, Add. Mss. 36,457, f. 31; R.E. Zegger, *John Cam Hobhouse: A Political Life 1819–1852* (1973), p. 57.
21. Add. Mss. 27,841, ff. 15–16; Add. Mss. 27,845, f. 7. Kinnaird had attended the 1812 anniversary dinner and may have been approached as a possible provincial candidate in that year, but he does not appear to have been active in Westminster politics between 1812 and 1818 (Saxton, *op. cit.,* ch. 7, p. 285; Add. Mss. 27,840, f. 111).
22. Brooks finally voted for Burdett and Kinnaird, but he did not formally join the campaign until the quarrel between Kinnaird's and Cartwright's supporters was settled. (Minute book in Add. Mss. 27,845 and *The Poll Book, for electing Two Representatives in Parliament for the City and Liberty of Westminster . . .* (1818), p. 134.)
23. M. Joyce, *My Friend H: John Cam Hobhouse, Baron Broughton of Broughton de Gyfford* (1948), p. 117; H. Brooks to Place, 9 June 1818, Miller to Place, 17 June 1818, Add. Mss. 27,841, ff. 154* and 253. Kinnaird had the active support of Hobhouse, Scrope Davies and James Mill; Hume wavered over whether to support Romilly.
24. Add. Mss. 27,841, f. 243.
25. Place to Hobhouse, 7 August 1819, Add. Mss. 27,837, ff. 166–7; [J.C. Hobhouse], *A Defence of the People in Reply to Lord Erskine's Two Defences of the Whigs* (1819), p. 107; Add. Mss. 36,623, f. 74v.
26. Quoted in Joyce, *op. cit.,* p. 118.
27. Add. Mss. 27,843, ff. 294–313. Brougham advised Place against action.
28. *Sherwin's Weekly Political Register,* 21 November 1818, Add. Mss. 27,842, f. 96; *Cobbett's Weekly Political Register,* 1818 and 1819, passim. For this episode see Add. Mss. 27,841, pt. 2.
29. Hobhouse to Byron, 16 July 1818, quoted in Joyce, *op. cit.,* p. 119.
30. Add. Mss. 36,457, ff. 19–20, 76–9; Add. Mss. 27,841, pt. 2, ff. 513–15, 578–82.
31. Add. Mss. 27,842, pt. 1, ff. 36, 43–4; Place to Ensor, n.d. [late January 1819], Add. Mss. 35,153, f. 115.
32. Miller to Place, 7 November 1818, Add. Mss. 27,842, pt. 1, f. 53.
33. Add. Mss. 27,842, pt. 1, ff. 39–42; Thomas, *op. cit.,* p. 71; Hobhouse to Place, 15

August 1819 and reply 16 August, Add. Mss. 27,837, ff. 170, 174.
34. Add. Mss. 27,842, pt. 1, f. 42v.
35. Hobhouse to B. Hobhouse, 18 May 1818, Add. Mss. 36,457, ff. 35–8.
36. Add. Mss. 27,842, f. 42. On Hobhouse's relations with the Whigs see Thomas, *op. cit.*, ch. 2.
37. Place to Ensor, n.d. [late January 1819], Add. Mss. 35,153, f. 115.
38. Zegger, *op. cit.*, p. 66; Ellice to Grey, 11 December 1818, quoted in Thomas *op. cit.*, p. 72; [Hobhouse], *A Defence of the People, op. cit.*, pp. 196–9; *Morning Chronicle,* 6 and 8 January 1819.
39. Add. Mss. 27,843, f. 391; J.G. Lambton to Lord Grey, 12 February 1819, quoted in Thomas, *op. cit.*, p. 79; Add. Mss. 27,847, ff. 82–9.
40. Thomas, *op. cit.*, pp. 79, 82.
41. *Cobbett's Weekly Political Register,* vol. 34, col. 363, 12 December 1818; Add. Mss. 27,842, pt. 2, ff. 284–93.
42. Quoted in Zegger, *op. cit.*, p. 71.
43. Add. Mss. 27,842, pt. 3, f. 605.
44. Add. Mss. 27,842; Place Coll., Set 20.
45. Hobhouse, *A Defence of the People, op. cit.*, p. 107; Add. Mss. 27,842, pt. 3, f. 607; Broughton, *op. cit.*, vol. 2, pp. 105–6; Place to Hobhouse, 17 March 1819, Add. Mss. 36,457, f. 260.
46. Memorandum, 1 June 1826, Add. Mss. 27,843, f. 391; [J.C. Hobhouse], *A Trifling Mistake in Lord Erskine's Recent Preface . . .* (1819), p. 33n.
47. An Elector of Westminster [Francis Place], *Reply to Lord Erskine* (1819), pp. 2–3, 8.
48. [Hobhouse], *A Trifling Mistake, op. cit.*, pp. 49–50; Place to Hobhouse, 29 October 1819, Add. Mss. 27,837, f. 188; Broughton, *op. cit.*, vol. 2, p. 116; Zegger, *op. cit.*, p. 77, n. 65.
49. Add. Mss. 36,623, f. 93; Hone to Place, 17 March 1820, Add. Mss. 27,843, f. 195.
50. Add. Mss. 27,789, f. 209v.
51. Burdett to Place, 24 November 1821, Add. Mss. 37,949, f. 101; Hobhouse to Place, 18 April 1822, Add. Mss. 27,837, f. 206v.
52. Place's diary, 7 December 1826, Add. Mss. 35,146, f. 69; Hobhouse to Place, 21 December 1827, Place to Jones, 5 November 1829, Add. Mss. 35,148, ff. 7–8, 36–7; Galloway to Place, 19 August 1829, Add. Mss. 37,950, ff. 39–40.
53. Place to Puller, 22 May 1822, Add. Mss. 27,843, f. 349.
54. Add. Mss. 35,146, f. 3.
55. R.G. Kirby and A.E. Musson, *The Voice of the People: John Doherty, 1798–1854. Trade Unionist, Radical and Factory Reformer* (1975), pp. 350–67; U.R.Q. Henriques, *Before the Welfare State: Social administration in early industrial Britain* (1979), pp. 70–3; Place Coll., Set 61, pt. 2 (of 1 vol.), p. 45; Add. Mss. 35,146, f. 101; Place to Pitkethly, 25 July 1832, Add. Mss. 35,149, f. 170v.
56. Add. Mss. 27,843, ff. 390–415.
57. Ibid., ff. 375–9. Hobhouse paid £308, including £200 which he had guaranteed for the action against the High Bailiff.
58. Broughton, *op. cit.*, vol. 3, pp. 262–3; Zegger, *op. cit.*, ch. 6.
59. Add. Mss. 27,789, ff. 73–115; Broughton, *op. cit.*, vol. 4, pp. 28–30.
60. Minutes of 1818 and 1819 elections, Add. Mss. 27,845 and 27,847, passim.
61. Bain, *James Mill, op. cit.*, p. 78n.

CHAPTER 9

1. It was reprinted in 1930 with an introduction and appendices by Norman Himes.
2. *Bull Dog*, 2, 9 and 16 September 1826, pp. 51, 86–7, 109–10.
3. *Black Dwarf*, vol. 11, pp. 499–500, 1 October 1823; Place's MS draft (to the editor of the *Labourer's Friend*), dated 5 August 1823, is in Place Coll., Set 68, c.item 115.
4. G.F. McCleary reprinted Owen's denial and reviewed the evidence in *The Malthusian Population Theory* (1953), pp. 88–92; he gave an open verdict.
5. N. Himes, *The Medical History of Contraception* (1936); J.Bentham, 'Situation and Relief of the Poor', *Annals of Agriculture and Other Useful Arts*, vol. 29 (1797), pp. 422–3; J.R. Poynter, *Society and Pauperism: English Ideas on Poor Relief, 1795–1834* (1969), pp. 123–5; W. Stark (ed.), *Jeremy Bentham's Economic Writings* (1952), vol. 1, pp. 272–3; J. Bentham, *The Theory of Legislation*, ed. C.K. Ogden (1931), Appendix, 'Bentham on Sex', pp. 473–97.
6. A. McLaren, *Birth Control in Nineteenth-Century England* (1978), ch. 1; P. Fryer, *The Birth Controllers* (1965), pp. 24–37; Place to Carlile, 17 August 1822, Place Coll., Set 68, c.item 88. The evidence of birth intervals suggests that abortion was not in wide use among married women in England at this time (E.A. Wrigley, 'The Growth of Population in Eighteenth-Century England: a Conundrum Resolved', *Past and Present*, No. 98 (1983), p. 131).
7. E. Halévy, *The Growth of Philosophic Radicalism* (trans. M. Morris, 1928), pp. 228–34; Poynter, *op. cit.*, pp. 40–3; T.R. Malthus, *An Essay on the Principle of Population* (1st edn, 1798), p. 154; P. James, *Population Malthus: His Life and Times* (1979), p. 61; W. Godwin, *Thoughts Occasioned by the Perusal of Dr Parr's Spital Sermon . . .* (1801), pp. 54–75; Bentham, *Theory of Legislation, op. cit.*, Appendix, esp. pp. 485–7; Place to Ensor, 18 January 1818, Add. Mss. 35,153, f. 40v.
8. Malthus, *op. cit.*, (5th edn, 1817), vol. 2, pp. 284–5; Ricardo to Malthus, 10 September 1821, Ricardo, *op. cit.*, vol. 9, p. 62; R. Owen, *The Life of Robert Owen written by himself* (1857), pp. 103–4, 111, 129; James, *op. cit.*, pp. 188, 376–7; Owen to Place, 24 June and 6 July 1814, 17 March 1818, Add. Mss. 37,949, ff. 14–16, 64–5; Add. Mss. 27,791, pt. 2, ff. 262–8; Ricardo, *op. cit.*, vol. 8, p. 153n.
9. *The Times*, 30 July 1817; *Supplement to the 4th, 5th and 6th editions of the Encyclopaedia Britannica* (1824), vol. 3 (preface dated February 1818), p. 261.
10. Place wrote that free love and uniform clothing for both sexes were secret parts of Owen's doctrine which were only imparted to trusted friends (Add. Mss. 27,791, pt. 2, f. 262). In 1835 Owen attacked the Church concept of marriage and advocated easy divorce: see R. Owen, *Lectures on the Marriages of the Priesthood of the Old Immoral World . . .* (4th edn, 1840); E. Royle, *Victorian Infidels: The origins of the British Secularist Movement 1791–1866* (1974), p. 62.
11. Some historians have suggested that there is evidence that Owen was interested in birth control in later life. The advertising of R.D. Owen's birth control tract, *Moral Physiology*, in *The Crisis*, a journal jointly edited by Robert and R.D. Owen, has been cited, but the book was only advertised after R.D. Owen had taken over the effective editorship (*The Crisis*, vol. 1, no. 35, 3 November 1832, p. 138).
12. Owen to Place, 17 March 1818, Add. Mss. 37,949, ff. 64–5.
13. Add. Mss. 35,149, ff. 229–30; Place to Mill, 17 October 1814, Add. Mss. 35,152, f. 94; Letters by 'P. Francis' in the *Sunday Review*, 1815, Place Coll., Set 7, vol. 1, pp. 18, 34, 40, 65; Place to Hodgson, 4 August 1814, Add. Mss. 35,152, f. 77;

Add. Mss. 27,809, f. 51v; *Hone's Reformists' Register,* 1 February 1817.

14. Place to Ricardo, 29 September 1817, Place Coll., Set 60; Pitkethly to Place, 30 May 1843, Place Coll., Set 56, vol. 22 (May–August 1843), p. 319.

15. Place to Ensor, 18 January 1818, Add. Mss. 35,153, ff. 40–1.

16. Marshall, *op. cit.,* pp. 347–8; Place to MacLaren, 25 November 1830, Place Coll., Set 62, p. 165.

17. Mill to Ricardo, 31 August 1821, Ricardo to Malthus, 10 September, Ricardo to Mill, 9 September, Ricardo, *op. cit.,* vol. 9, pp. 47, 61, 59; Ricardo to Place, 9 September 1821 and Place's comments, Seligman Collection, Columbia University.

18. *Quarterly Review,* vol. 26 (1821–22), pp. 148–68; *Edinburgh Review,* vol. 35 (1821), pp. 362–77; Longman Archives, University of Reading.

19. *Illustrations and Proofs,* pp. 165, 174–9.

20. Place Coll., Set 68, item 99 (Comment on 1817 edn, vol. 3, pp. 350–2).

21. *Illustrations and Proofs,* pp. 138, 154–6, 39.

22. See Illustration 9. There were two other versions of the handbill, addressed to the working people and those 'in Genteel Life'; the three bills are in Place Coll., Set 61, pt. 2 (of 1 vol.), pp. 41–3; they are reproduced and analysed in N.E. Himes, 'The Birth Control Handbills of 1823', *The Lancet,* vol. ccxiii, pp. 313–6, 6 August 1927; draft letters to clergymen in Place Coll., Set 68, items 95 and 119.

23. Ibid., item 119.

24. Longson to Place, 29 August 1824, Add. Mss. 27,801, f. 234; *Black Dwarf,* vol. 11 (1824), pp. 404 *et seq.* and vol. 12 (1825). Himes assumed that the articles which were not by Mill were written by Place, but this seems unlikely on grounds of style.

25. *The Times,* 21 February 1826; P. Schwartz, *The New Political Economy of J.S. Mill* (1972), pp. 245–56; Fryer, *op. cit.,* p. 95; Ricardo to Place, 9 September 1821, Ricardo, *op. cit.,* vol. 9, p. 55 and note; Ricardo to Malthus, 10 September 1821, p. 62; Ricardo also implied acceptance of the physical check in a letter to Hutches Trower, 25 September 1819, vol. 8, pp. 80–1.

26. E.g. *Cooper's John Bull,* 5 February 1826. G.J. Holyoake and J.A. Field cited statements in hostile sources (the latter claiming to quote Carlile) that the bills circulated among the Spitalfields weavers (Holyoake, *op. cit.,* vol. 1, p. 130; J.A. Field, 'The Early Propagandist Movement in English Population Theory', *Bulletin of the American Economic Association,* 4th series, vol. 1, no. 2 (1911), p. 217).

27. Place to Burdett, 1 May 1824, Add. Mss. 27,823, f. 338; Longson to Place, 29 August 1824, Add. Mss. 27,801, f. 234; 'Letter on Population and Wages . . .' by Longson, 15 September 1824, Place to Ellis, Longson to Place, both n.d. but c.September 1824, and note by Place on verso of latter, Place Coll., Set 68, c.item 104.

28. Blackett to Place, 5 March and 18 April 1825, Add. Mss. 27,803, ff. 268v and 273–4; Foster and McWilliams to Place, 31 March and 11 April 1826, ff. 308 and 272; Tester to Place, 27 August 1825 and 19 February 1826, ff. 349v and 411; 'What is Love?', *Republican,* vol. 11, p. 555.

29. Rippon to Place, 5 December 1825, Add. Mss. 27,803, f. 119; Tester to Place, 13 August 1825, f. 347v; Mowatson to Place, 19 July 1825, f. 478; Longson to Place, 6 August 1825, f. 321; M'Dougall to Place, 2 April 1826, f. 487v.

30. *Trades' Newspaper,* 29 January 1826, p. 449; Pillworth to Place, 28 January 1825 (error for 1826), Add. Mss. 27,803, pt. 2, f. 554; M'Dougall to Place, 2 April 1826, f. 487v.

31. Place to Carlile, 17 August 1822, Place Coll., Set 68, item 89. This letter is quoted at length in M. Stopes, *Contraception* (3rd edn, 1931), pp. 275–83.

32. Wiener, *op. cit.,* p. 126; Place to Carlile, 1 September 1824, Place Coll., Set 68,

item 91.

33. 'What is Love?' *op. cit.;* R. Carlile, *Every Woman's Book, or What is Love?* (4th edn, 1826) (in Goldsmith's Library) p. 38; 1838 edition (in the British Library), preface (dated April 1828); *Cobbett's Weekly Political Register,* vol. 54, cols 107–8, 9 April 1825; vol. 58, cols 131–41, 15 April 1826, col. 419, 13 May 1826; Wiener, *op. cit.,* p. 163; *Newgate Monthly Magazine,* vol. 2 (1825–26), pp. 97–104, 193–207; Place's diary, 2 June 1826, Add. Mss. 35,146, f. 26.

34. Smith to Place, 18 March 1826, Place Coll., Set 61, pt. 2 (of 1 vol.), p. 60.

35. *The Republican,* vol. 10, November 1824, pp. 581–8, 636–9; F. Place, 'Observations on Mr Ensor's Attack on the Political Economists', *Trades' Newspaper,* 18 June 1826, pp. 779–80; 'F.P.' to Editor of *Morning Chronicle,* 14 October 1824. See also Place to Doherty, 7 April 1829, Place Coll., Set 16, pt. 2, item 92; Place to Rogers, 15 January 1832, Place Coll., Set 68, c.item 22; F. Place, 'Mr Hanson's Speech Examined', April 1834, Add. Mss. 27,834, ff. 2–36; Place to Hume, 13 September 1838, Add. Mss. 35,151, f. 92.

36. *Dublin Evening Post,* 10 September 1825; *Trades' Newspaper,* 27 August and 11 September 1825, Place Coll., Set 61, pt. 2 (of 1 vol.), p. 52.

37. *Newgate Monthly Magazine,* vol. 2, 1 April 1826, p. 382; Add. Mss. 27,790, f. 175; Place to Hume, 19 January 1833, in the British Library copy of the *Bull Dog.*

38. *Autobiography,* pp. xxxi–xxxiii; for an example of censorship see Place to Hoare, 19 December 1839, Add. Mss. 35,144, ff. 428v–429.

39. Memorandum, 1829, Add. Mss. 35,146, f. 100; Johnson, *op. cit.,* p. 181. Roebuck was several times accused of being a supporter of birth control, but the charge was never proved (Schwartz, *op. cit.,* pp. 251–3). In a note to Place in 1831 he advocated delayed marriage and abolition of the poor laws (Add. Mss. 35,147, ff. 67–8).

40. William Ellis seems to have been the most active of the younger Utilitarians in the birth control campaign. As late as 1849, in his reply to congratulations from Place on his review of Mrs Gaskell's *Mary Barton,* he offered copies of the 'Causes of Poverty' and the 'Distressed Needlewoman' (Ellis to Place, 4 May 1849, Add. Mss. 35,151, f. 404).

41. Ellis to Place, 28 September 1832, Add. Mss. 37,949, f. 284; *The Crisis,* 27 October, 3 November and 8 December 1832, vol. 1, pp. 136, 140, 160. Watson's edition of *Moral Physiology* was followed almost immediately by one by Brooks.

42. *British Luminary,* 21 April 1822, Place Coll., Set 7, pt. 1, p. 116; ibid., 23 June, Set 19, p. 254; Comment 10 in 'Remarks upon Mr Ricardo's Observations', Place's comments on Ricardo to Place, 9 September 1821, Seligman Collection, Columbia University Library.

43. 'Observations', July 1827, Place Coll., Set 41, item 173; Place to Lovett, 18 October 1837, Place to Whytoch, 2 November 1839, Add. Mss. 35,151, ff. 21v–22, 185v–186.

44. Pitkethly to Place, 31 May 1843, Place Coll., Set 56, vol. 22 (May–August 1843), p. 319. There is no evidence that Place played a significant role over the New Poor Law.

45. Add. Mss. 27,835, f. 132; Place to Symons, 19 September 1840, Add. Mss. 35,151, f. 264v.

46. Place to Vincent, 21 January 1841, Place Coll., Set 56, vol. 11 (October 1840–February 1841); Place to Pitkethly, 25 May 1841, Add. Mss. 35,151, f. 341v. One working man who used birth control was William Hoare, a ladies' shoemaker and member of the London Working Men's Association who emigrated to New York and became an actor. He attributed his escape from poverty to the use of birth control, but he was so cautious that he only told Place that he was a 'practical Malthusian' after he had emigrated (Hoare to Place, 20

April 1839, Add. Mss. 27,835, ff. 146v–147; Place to Hoare, 19 December 1839, Add. Mss. 35,144, f. 428v).
47. *Christian Warrior,* 14 January 1843, p. 13.
48. Royle, *op. cit.,* pp. 142–3. The views of supporters and opponents of birth control in 1820–50 are discussed in McLaren, *op. cit.,* pt. 2.
49. Wrigley, *op. cit.;* E.A. Wrigley and R.S. Schofield, *The Population History of England 1541–1871. A Reconstruction.* (1981); J.A. Goldstone, 'The Demographic Revolution in England: a Re-Examination', *Population Studies,* vol. 40 (1986), pp. 5–33. On the later nineteenth century see M.S. Teitelbaum, *The British Fertility Decline: Demographic Transition in the Crucible of the Industrial Revolution* (1984).

CHAPTER 10

1. E. Royle and J. Walvin, *English Radicals and Reformers 1760–1848* (1982), ch. 8.
2. Place's diary, 19 January 1828, Add. Mss. 35,146, f. 95. On the Queen Caroline affair see: Prothero, *op. cit.,* ch. 7; J. Stevenson, 'The Queen Caroline Affair', in Stevenson, *op. cit.,* pp. 117–48; Place Coll., Sets 18, 71; Add. Mss. 57,841A and B; Add. Mss. 35,146, f. 95.
3. Drafts, 18 September 1820, Place Coll., Set 18, pt. 2, pp. 123–5.
4. Place Coll., Set 40, pt. 1, Introduction, 1 January 1846; Place's diary, 19 January 1828, Add. Mss. 35,146, f. 95; Place Coll., Set 18, pt. 2, pp. 157–69.
5. Hodgskin to Place, 17 October 1820, Add. Mss. 35,153, f. 178.
6. Add. Mss. 35,146, f. 95.
7. The term 'Combination Laws' was generally used to cover all laws against trade unionism, and it is used in this sense here.
8. Marginal comment on the evidence of the Stockport spinners to the 1824 Select Committee on Artizans and Machinery, Add. Mss. 27,801, f. 6v; Prothero, *op. cit.,* p. 172. Place's memoir of the repeal of the Combination Laws is in Add. Mss. 27,798.
9. Add. Mss. 27,798, f. 12.
10. Place to Hobhouse, n.d. [May 1819], Add. Mss. 36,457, f. 290; Place's diary, 25 June 1819, Add. Mss. 36,627, f. 39; Place to Hodgskin, 8 September 1819, Add. Mss. 35,153, f. 68v; Place to Hobhouse, 16 August 1819, Add. Mss. 27,837, f. 173.
11. Hodgskin to Place, October–November 1820, Add. Mss. 35,153, ff. 181v, 183–4; M'Culloch to Place, 28 November 1820, 4 March 1823, Add. Mss. 37,949, ff. 85, 127.
12. Prochaska, *op. cit.,* pp. 210–12; Add. Mss. 27,800, ff. 6–30.
13. *Black Dwarf,* vol. 12, pp. 59–60, 14 January 1824; *Edinburgh Review,* vol. 39 (1824), pp. 315–40.
14. Place to Hume (two letters), 7 February 1824, Add. Mss. 27,798, ff. 18–20. He told Hume that he had visited houses of call for the hatters, boot and shoe makers, smiths, carpenters, weavers and metal workers that day; tomorrow he would call on the bakers, plumbers, tailors, painters and glaziers. bricklayers and bookbinders.
15. *The Times,* 4 June 1824.
16. He set out his views frankly in his evidence to the Committee (First Report of the Select Committee on Artizans and Machinery, 1824, p. 48).
17. Add. Mss. 27,801, ff. 235–62; Add. Mss. 27,803, f. 323v; [F. Place], *Observations on Mr Huskisson's Speech on the Laws Relating to Combinations*

of Workmen (1825).

18. Add. Mss. 27,798, ff. 38–40. Place said that the newspaper reporters, who disliked Hume because his persistence prolonged the hours and session, gave the false impression that he had been defeated in debate by Ministers.

19. Add. Mss. 27,798, ff. 61–2; Add. Mss. 27,834, ff. 57–9; Royle and Walvin, *op. cit.,* p. 134; S. and B. Webb, *The History of Trade Unionism* (2nd edn, 1920), chs 2–4; Prothero, *op. cit.,* pp. 180–1; J.T. Ward and W.H. Fraser (eds), *Workers and Employers: Documents on Trade Unions and Industrial Relations in Britain since the Eighteenth Century* (1980), chs 2–3; J. Marlow, *The Tolpuddle Martyrs* (1971), pp. 58–9, 88–9; G. Abrahams, *Trade Unions and the Law* (1968), pp. 27–8.

20. Place to Elliott, 5 February 1834, Add. Mss. 35,149, f. 275.

21. Add. Mss. 27,803, ff. 79, 85, 100–1, 396–404, 470–1. On the *Trades' Newspaper,* see Prothero, *op. cit.,* ch. 10.

22. Tester to Place, 19 February 1826, Farrar to Place, 13 March 1826, Add. Mss. 27,803, ff. 410–1, 556–9; Place's diary, 20 April and 20 July 1826, Add. Mss. 35,146, ff. 14, 34v; *Trades' Free Press,* 26 August 1827; Place to Hume, n.d., Add. Mss. 35,148, f. 38.

23. 'Corn Laws' by P. Francis, *Sunday Review,* 2 March 1815, Place Coll., Set 7, vol. 1 (1814–40), p. 40.

24. [F. Place], *Observations, op. cit.;* Add. Mss. 27,801, f. 42.

25. Place to Burdett, 20 and 25 June 1825, Add. Mss. 27,798, ff. 57–8. It is sometimes unclear whether Place had in mind 'trade unions' or 'trade clubs' when he referred to combinations.

26. Add. Mss. 35,146, ff. 6v, 16, 75, 78; Add. Mss. 37,949, ff. 194–7; Add. Mss. 27,828, ff. 229–30. On Place's cooperation with trade unions see Prothero, *op. cit.*

27. Place to Hume, 7 January 1830, Add. Mss. 35,148, f. 40; Rowe, 'Francis Place and the Historian', *op. cit.,* p. 56.

28. 5 August 1823, Place Coll., Set 68, item 115.

29. Place to Doherty, 7 April 1829, Place Coll., Set 16, pt. 2, item 92.

30. Add. Mss. 35,146, ff. 4, 44v, 92v, 95v.

31. Add. Mss. 35,147, ff. 29–33.

32. Add. Mss. 35,147, ff. 9–40; Add. Mss. 27,836; Add. Mss. 35,153, ff. 1, 7v, 76; Ricardo, *op. cit.,* vol. 8, pp. 77, 105–6, 118–25. The Sinking Fund was revived in a different form later in the century.

33. W.H. Wickwar, *The Struggle for the Freedom of the Press 1819–1832* (1928).

34. [F. Place], *On the Law of Libel, with strictures on the self-styled 'Constitutional Association'* (1823). One of J.S. Mill's earliest published writings was a laudatory review of this pamphlet (Add. Mss. 35,144, f. 236).

35. Add. Mss. 36,628, ff. 41–2; Add. Mss. 35,146, ff. 87v–88v.

36. Add. Mss. 35,146, ff. 106, 110–1; Add. Mss. 35,148, ff. 80–92.

CHAPTER 11

1. A bill drawn up with Place's assistance in 1828 to transfer East Retford's representation to Birmingham was rejected by the Government (Add. Mss. 35,148, ff. 16–26; Cannon, *op. cit.,* pp. 188–9). On the Reform Bill see M. Brock, *The Great Reform Act* (1973); J.R.M. Butler, *The Passing of the Great Reform Bill* (1914); Cannon, *op. cit.;* J. Hamburger, *James Mill and the Art of Revolution* (1963); Prothero, *op. cit.,* ch. 14; A.D. Kriegel (ed.), *The Holland House Diaries*

1831–1840 (1977); A. Aspinall (ed.), *Three Early Nineteenth Century Diaries* (1952); Broughton, *op. cit.*, vol. 4. Place's account is in Add. Mss. 27,789–95.

2. Add. Mss. 36,628, ff. 51v–52; Add. Mss. 27,789, f. 164.

3. Add. Mss. 27,789, ff. 188–92.

4. Add. Mss. 27,789, ff. 182–92; Add. Mss. 36,628, ff. 57v–58; C. Reith, *The British Police and the Democratic Ideal* (1943), p. 72.

5. Add. Mss. 36,628, ff. 53–5; Place to Hobhouse, 8 November 1830, Add. Mss. 35,148, ff. 69–70.

6. Add. Mss. 35,149, ff. 12v–22; Add. Mss. 35,146, f. 130; Add. Mss. 27,789, ff. 202–3, 236–7.

7. Add. Mss. 27,789, f. 252; Add. Mss. 35,146, f. 126; Place to Hobhouse, 8 November 1830, Add. Mss. 35,148, f. 70; Place Coll., Set 16, vol. 2, p. 102; Add. Mss. 27,820, ff. 187–8.

8. Add. Mss. 27,789, ff. 207–19; Place to Beauclerk, 7 April 1831, Add. Mss. 35,149, f. 65; Add. Mss. 35,146, ff. 126–7; Add. Mss. 35,147, ff. 41–68. On 29 November 1830 Place told Hobhouse that revolution was inevitable due to the Swing riots (Broughton, *op. cit.*, vol. 4, p. 74).

9. Add. Mss. 27,789, ff. 256–60; Brock, *op. cit.*, pp. 136–53; Kriegel, *op. cit.*, pp. xxviii–xxx.

10. Add. Mss. 27,789, ff. 272–9; Add. Mss. 35,146, f. 133.

11. Add. Mss. 27,789, ff. 318–9.

12. Add. Mss. 27,789, ff. 335–8.

13. On the PCS see Add. Mss. 35,149, ff. 34–70; Add. Mss. 35,146, ff. 133–7; Add. Mss. 27,789, ff. 312–79; minutes and copies of pamphlets on Dorset, Kent and Bucks members are in Place Coll., Set 63.

14. Add. Mss. 27,790, ff. 16–7; Brock, *op. cit.*, p. 246; Place to Hobhouse, 11 October 1831, Add. Mss. 35,149, ff. 83v–84 and 88.

15. Accounts of the procession by Powell and Bowyer are in Add. Mss. 35,149, ff. 336–46.

16. Hobhouse to Place, 14 October 1831, Place to Grote, 16 October, Place to Burdett, 19 October, Add. Mss. 35,149, ff. 86–7, 98–9, 101–2.

17. Add. Mss. 27,790, ff. 54–87; Add. Mss. 35,149, ff. 113–4; *Cobbett's Political Register*, vol. 74 (1831), cols 193–205, 216–21, 268–9; Broughton, *op. cit.*, vol. 4, pp. 148–9.

18. Add. Mss. 27,790, ff. 97, 219–20; Add. Mss. 27,791, f. 9.

19. Add. Mss. 27,791, ff. 4–17.

20. On London's failure to produce leaders, see F. Sheppard, *London 1808–70: The Infernal Wen* (1971), p. 319 and Add. Mss. 27,789, f. 320.

21. Place to Hume, 16 February 1831, Add. Mss. 35,149, f. 29v.

22. Place to Grote, Place to Mill, 26 October 1831, Add. Mss. 35,149, ff. 120, 123; Broughton, *op. cit.*, vol. 4, pp. 146–7.

23. The handbill for the meeting declared: 'All property honestly acquired to be sacred and inviolate', and Benbow and other leading NUWC leaders openly urged that each man should come armed with a cosh (Add. Mss. 27,791, ff. 49–50).

24. Add. Mss. 27,791, ff. 47–72; see also W. Lovett, *Life and Struggles of William Lovett* (1876), pp. 74–7.

25. Add. Mss. 27,791, ff. 74–92.

26. Add. Mss. 27,791, ff. 89–90; Broughton, *op. cit.*, vol. 4, pp. 147, 152–3.

27. Add. Mss. 27,790, ff. 106–75; Add. Mss. 27,791, f. 95; *Parliamentary Debates*, vol. 4, col. 861, 6 July 1831; Hamburger, *op. cit.*, pp. 161–81.

28. Butler, *op. cit.*, pp. 316–7; Add. Mss. 27,789, f. 255; Place to Lovett, 4 June 1840, Place Coll., Set 55, pp. 575–6.

29. Butler, *op. cit.*, pp. 320–1; Kriegel, *op. cit.*, p. 82; Cannon, *op. cit.*, p. 226; A.R.

Wellesley (ed.), *Despatches, Correspondence and Memoranda of the Duke of Wellington* (vol. 8 of continuation series, 1880), pp. 157–8.

30. Add. Mss. 27,791, ff. 194–211.
31. Add. Mss. 27,791, ff. 121–46; Broughton, *op. cit.,* vol. 4, pp. 164–5.
32. Add. Mss. 27,828, ff. 261–337; Add. Mss. 27,796, f. 221v; Add. Mss. 35,146, f. 77v; Add. Mss. 35,150, ff. 275v–276. Place edited the NPU debates on the Anatomy Bill for an NPU tract.
33. Add. Mss. 27,795, f. 160.
34. Add. Mss. 27,792, ff. 15, 19–25, 41.
35. Place to Jones, 9 April 1832, Add. Mss. 27,792, ff. 45–51. Place's tables were printed as notes to Durham's speech in the House of Lords on 22 May 1832, *Parliamentary Debates,* vol. 12, cols 1233–46.
36. Add. Mss. 27,792, ff. 149–54, 307; Add. Mss. 35,150, f. 218v.
37. Aspinall (ed.), *op. cit.,* p. 239.
38. Add. Mss. 27,792, ff. 249, 256; Add. Mss. 27,793, ff. 123–4.
39. Add. Mss. 27,793, ff. 146–8, 180–2; Parkes to Place, 11 May 1832, Place Coll., Set 17, vol. 3, p. 177a.
40. Add. Mss. 27,793, ff. 140–1; *Morning Chronicle,* 15 May 1832.
41. See press cuttings in Add. Mss. 27,793 and 27,794.
42. Add. Mss. 27,794, ff. 84–5; Hamburger, *op. cit.,* p. 104; Kriegel, *op. cit.,* p. 180.
43. Add. Mss. 27,794, ff. 278–80; Kriegel, *op. cit.,* pp. 183–4.
44. Add. Mss. 27,794, ff. 282–3.
45. Brock, *op. cit.,* p. 309; Cannon, *op. cit.,,* pp. 238–40; N. Gash, *Aristocracy and People: Britain 1815–1865* (1979), pp. 6–7. In *James Mill and the Art of Revolution,* Joseph Hamburger argued that Place and his allies pretended to believe that the country was on the verge of revolution in order to trick the Whigs into passing the bill, but Hamburger's method was to contrast remarks on the state of the country made by reformers at different times, and these merely reflected the changing mood of the reformers as public excitement rose and fell. His use of evidence was sometimes misleading. For example, he cited Place's letter to Burdett of 19 October 1831 as an example of how his claims about the danger of revolution were conveyed to Ministers – because Burdett quoted the letter to Grey – yet elsewhere cited Place's complaint about public apathy in the same letter as evidence that the claims were fabricated (pp. 57, 125–6). Hamburger cited as evidence of Place's dishonesty his remark in 1836 that the bill might not have passed 'without . . . "crooked and disingenuous means" '. But the full quotation is 'without what you now call "crooked and disingenuous means" ' – by which Place meant his support for the defiance of the law by the unstamped press (p. 265 and note; [F. Place], *The Examiner and the Tax on Newspapers* (1836), p. 8, Place Coll., Set 70, item 423).
46. Add. Mss. 27,790, f. 330. Some historians have pointed out remarks Place made elsewhere denying that a revolution was possible, but these invariably refer to a purely working-class uprising.
47. Add. Mss. 27,790, ff. 97–100, 235, 243–4; Add. Mss. 27,791, ff. 18–22.
48. Add. Mss. 27,795, f. 28; Add. Mss. 35,149, ff. 98–9.
49. Hamburger (*op. cit.,* pp. 198–9) claimed that there was little public excitement in London in May 1832, but all evidence he cited came from Tories, who were constantly proclaiming a reaction against the bill and being disproved.
50. Add. Mss. 27,789, ff. 280, 418; Add. Mss. 27,790, f. 243v; Add. Mss. 27,791, f. 95; Add. Mss. 27,792, f. 256; *Morning Chronicle,* 15 May 1832; Add. Mss. 27,793, ff. 142, 202–3; Add. Mss. 35,149, ff. 151–2; Johnson, *op. cit.,* p. 175. On Evans see E.M. Spiers, *Radical General: Sir George de Lacy Evans 1787–1870* (1983).

51. C. Flick, *The Birmingham Political Union and the Movements for Reform in Britain 1830–1839* (1978); Add. Mss. 27,819, ff. 101–2.
52. Add. Mss. 27,789, f. 264; Add. Mss. 27,791, ff. 334, 344.
53. Add. Mss. 35,149, ff. 336–42.
54. D.J. Rowe, 'Class and Political Radicalism in London 1831–32', *Historical Journal*, XIII (1970), pp. 32–3; J. Brooke, *The Democrats of Marylebone* (1839), quoted in P. Hollis (ed.), *Class and Conflict in Nineteenth-Century England 1815–1850* (1973), pp. 150–1; Add. Mss. 27,790, ff. 8–15.
55. Aspinall (ed.), *op. cit.*, p. 239; Broughton, *op. cit.*, vol. 4, pp. 227, 231.
56. Broughton, *op. cit.*, vol. 4, p. 229 (quoting Alexander Baring).
57. Broughton, *op. cit.*, vol. 4, pp. 214, 229; see also Kriegel, *op. cit.*, pp. 178, 180.
58. Add. Mss. 27,794, ff. 287–8. Place quoted 'a confidential person of a cabinet minister', a phrase he used to refer to Thomas Young.
59. Add. Mss. 27,796, ff. 16–7; Add. Mss. 27,789, ff. 273–5; Add. Mss. 27,790, ff. 300–10; Brock, *op. cit.*, p. 265.
60. Add. Mss. 27,795, f. 28; Place to Pitkethly, 25 July 1832, Add. Mss. 35,149, f. 170.
61. Add. Mss. 27,789, f. 164.
62. Ibid., ff. 227–8.
63. Add. Mss. 27,796, ff. 105–6; Add. Mss. 27,790, ff. 211–6.
64. Add. Mss. 27,791, ff. 209–11; Add. Mss. 35,149, ff. 172–89; Add. Mss. 27,796, ff. 80–106, 164–5; Brock, *op. cit.*, p. 377; Add. Mss. 35,150, f. 26v.
65. Add. Mss. 27,796, ff. 52, 60, 135–57, 184; Hutt to Place, 6 September 1832, Add. Mss. 35,149, f. 160; Hume to Place, 24 August 1832, Add. Mss. 37,949, f. 267. Place approved of Mill's articles, but Roebuck attacked them as a repudiation of pledges (Thomas, *op. cit.*, pp. 215–16).
66. Althorp to Hobhouse, 17 June 1832, Add. Mss. 35,149, ff. 158–9; see also ff. 184 and 187; Add. Mss. 37,949, f. 260. In the event, Althorp did not go to the poll in Tower Hamlets.
67. Add. Mss. 27,796, ff. 206–54. The PCS and the NPU had a curiously similar history, although the extent of their success was very different. In each Erskine Perry provided the initial impetus, Place encouraged him but was unwilling to commit himself at first, then joining and playing a critical role in getting the organisation off the ground. In both, Place and his allies succeeded in maintaining control, and once each society had fulfilled its immediate purpose he urged winding it up, because he was convinced that any attempt to keep it going would be a failure; each time he was defeated over this and dropped out while others tried to keep it going, failing soon afterwards. Perry's contribution to the agitation deserves recognition.

CHAPTER 12

1. Add. Mss. 35,149, f. 195v; Add. Mss. 37,949, ff. 278–81. Place's letter does not survive.
2. Add. Mss. 27,791, ff. 116–7.
3. Place to Parkes, 17 July 1834, Add. Mss. 35,149, f. 310.
4. Hume to Place, 16 November 1832, Place Coll., Set 17, vol. 4, p. 211; Place to Parkes, 5 December 1834, Add. Mss. 35,149, f. 329.
5. Place to Jones, 19 November 1832, Add. Mss. 27,844, f. 30v.
6. *Morning Chronicle,* 20 November 1832; Add. Mss. 27,844, ff. 34–41, 59–60; Add. Mss. 35,149, f. 329.

7. Add. Mss. 27,796, pt. 2, f. 221.
8. On the Westminster elections 1832–33, see Add. Mss. 27,844, ff. 22–241.
9. Add. Mss. 35,149, ff. 328v–333.
10. Add. Mss. 35,150, ff. 140v–167, 266.
11. Add. Mss. 35,151, ff. 50, 78. See also ff. 113–124.
12. Place Coll., Set 55, pp. 55–60; Add. Mss. 27,824, f. 182.
13. On this campaign see P. Hollis, *The Pauper Press: a Study in Working-Class Radicalism of the 1830s* (1970), and J. Wiener, *The War of the Unstamped: the Movement to Repeal the British Newspaper Tax 1830–1836* (1969).
14. Add. Mss. 35,149, ff. 22v–32, 75v–76v; Add. 35,146, ff. 130–2; Place Coll., Set 70, p. 21.
15. Further attempts were made to launch the Society in 1834 and 1836, but it never got off the ground (Add. Mss. 35,154, ff. 161–84; Add. Mss. 35,150, ff. 38v, 171–5; Add. Mss. 27,835, f. 66; Add. Mss. 35,149, f. 307v).
16. Add. Mss. 27,796, ff. 33–4, 111–34; Add. Mss. 35,149, ff. 202, 269, 273v–274; Add. Mss. 35,154, ff. 137–60.
17. Add. Mss. 35,149, ff. 294–8, 307–13; *The Times,* 23 December 1835.
18. Add. Mss. 35,150, ff. 163–70.
19. Place Coll., Set 70, pp. 317–9; *Life and Letters of John Arthur Roebuck,* ed. R.E. Leader (1897), p. 77; Thomas, *op. cit.,* pp. 228–9.
20. Add. Mss. 35,146, f. 138; Add. Mss. 27,819, ff. 25–31; Add. Mss. 35,154, ff. 207–22; Add. Mss. 35,150, ff. 27, 35–8, 45–50, 114; J.G. Godard, *George Birkbeck, the Pioneer of Popular Education* (1884), p. 152.
21. Add. Mss. 35,150, ff. 67–72, 133–7, 189–90; Place Coll., Set 70, pp. 305–6, 423–4.
22. Place Coll., Set 70, pp. 601, 608; Place Coll., Set 48, vol. 1, pp. 463–74; Add. Mss. 35,151, f. 279; Prothero, *op. cit.,* p. 308; Royle, *op. cit.,* pp. 261–6.
23. Add. Mss. 27,796, ff. 178–9; Add. Mss. 27,844, f. 35v; see also Place to Hume, 11 March 1831, Add. Mss. 35,149, f. 34v.
24. On the role of the philosophic radicals (a term not used by Place), see Thomas, *op. cit.,* and J. Hamburger, *Intellectuals in Politics: John Stuart Mill and the Philosophic Radicals* (1965).
25. Place to Parkes, 21 April 1834, Add. Mss. 35,149, f. 281v.
26. Mrs Grote to Place, 26 May 1836, Add. Mss. 35,144, f. 374v; Place to Hume, 3 January 1837, Add. Mss. 35,150, f. 192; Place to Mrs Grote and reply, 8 and 12 November 1837, Add. Mss. 35,151, ff. 28–30.
27. Place to Hume, 30 July 1836, Add. Mss. 35,150, f. 133; Place to Baines, 4 January 1838, Add. Mss. 35,151, f. 57.
28. Place to Hume, 13 February 1836, Add. Mss. 35,150, f. 112.
29. Place to Turner, 19 October 1834, Add. Mss. 35,149, ff. 320–1; Add. Mss. 27,830, ff. 108, 110, 143v; F. Place, *Improvement of the Working People. Drunkenness – Education* (1834). He wrote another defence which was not published (Add. Mss. 27,829, ff. 72–148).
30. Place to Lovett, 21 November 1834, Add. Mss. 35,149, f. 328.
31. On this episode see B.H. Harrison, 'Two roads to social reform: Francis Place and the "Drunken Committee" of 1834', *Historical Journal,* XI (1968), pp. 272–300.
32. Place to Symons, 19 September 1840, Add. Mss. 35,151, f. 268.
33. Add. Mss. 37,950, ff. 42–3; Add. Mss. 35,149, ff. 134, 198–200, 203–9, 231–3; Add. Mss. 35,150, ff. 92–5.
34. Add. Mss. 35,149, ff. 29v, 312; Add. Mss. 35,150, ff. 36–8, 45, 47–9, 54, 282v; Add. Mss. 35,151, f. 15.
35. Add. Mss. 35,149, f. 139; Add. Mss. 35,150, ff. 90, 157–62; Add. Mss. 35,151, ff. 70v, 107; Place Coll., Set 70, p. 319. On Roebuck see Roebuck, *op. cit.,* and

Thomas, *op. cit.,* ch. 5.
36. On Hawes see Add. Mss. 37,950, ff. 27−9; Add. Mss. 35,154, f. 135; Add. Mss. 35,149, ff. 301v−304, 315; Add. Mss. 35,150, ff. 112v−113; Add. Mss. 35,151, ff. 157v−160; Place Coll., Set 52, p. 123; Set 55, pp. 130−40; Thomas, *op. cit.,* pp. 206−7, 297.
37. Add. Mss. 35,150, ff. 13v−26.
38. Add. Mss. 35,146, f. 138; Add. Mss. 35,150, ff. 45v−46v, 55−7, 62−79; Parkes to Tennyson, 20 March 1835, quoted in Thomas, *op. cit.,* p. 281n.
39. Add. Mss. 35,150, ff. 99−102, 128v; Add. Mss. 35,144, f. 357.
40. Place to Parkes, 3 January 1836, Add. Mss. 35,150, f. 102.
41. Add. Mss. 35,150, ff. 201, 206v−210, 229, 235.
42. Add. Mss. 35,150, ff. 237−42; Add. Mss. 27,816, ff. 284−6; F.E. Mineka (ed.), *The Earlier Letters of John Stuart Mill 1812−1848, Collected Works,* vol. 12 (1963), pp. 323−8 (Mill to Place, 13 February 1837, Add. Mss. 27,816, ff. 285−6 is not included, and letter 192 should be dated about 14 not 9 February). On the memorial to the Scotch martyrs see Add. Mss. 27,816.
43. Place to Parkes, 11 November 1837, Add. Mss. 35,151, f. 31.
44. Place to Roebuck, 10 September 1837, Add. Mss. 35,151, ff. 14v−15; Place to Mrs Grote, 23 August 1837, Add. Mss. 35,150, f. 282.
45. Jones to Place, 4 July 1837, Add. Mss. 35,150, f. 259.
46. Add. Mss. 35,150, ff. 273−7, 283−90, 294−5; Add. Mss. 35,151, ff. 14v, 45−6, 57v−60, 70, 152v−153.
47. Add. Mss. 35,149, f. 307; Add. Mss. 35,151, ff. 137v−41, 210v−219; Add. Mss. 37,949, ff. 396−7.
48. Add. Mss. 35, 151, ff. 168v, 171−2.

CHAPTER 13

1. Add. Mss. 27,797, pt. 2, f. 251; Place to Lovett, 21 November 1834, Add. Mss. 35,149, f. 328; Lovett to Place, 1 June 1840, and reply 4 June, Place Coll., Set 55, pp. 569, 573; 'Essays for the People', 1834, Add. Mss. 27,834, f. 44.
2. Add. Mss. 27,797, ff. 90v, 251−2.
3. Place to Longson, 28 May 1834, Place to Turner, 20 November 1834, Add. Mss. 35,149, ff. 293, 327; Add. Mss. 27,791, f. 369.
4. Place to Martineau, 31 March 1834, Add. Mss. 35,149, ff. 278−9.
5. Add. Mss. 35,149, ff. 235, 237v−238, 244v−249, 266v−268, 281; Add. Mss. 35,154, ff. 195−206; Prothero, *op. cit.,* pp. 302−3; 'Essays for the People', Add. Mss. 27,834, ff. 2−145.
6. Ibid., ff. 86, 106.
7. Jones to Place, 4 July 1837 and reply 7 July, Add. Mss. 35,150, ff. 264, 267; Add. Mss. 37,949, f. 327; Add. Mss. 27,819, f. 285.
8. This was an exaggeration (Ratcliffe and Chaloner, *op. cit.,* p. 48n).
9. 'Handloom Weavers and Factory Workers. A Letter to James Turner, Cotton Spinner, from Francis Place', *Pamphlets for the People* (1835), Add. Mss. 35,150, ff. 80−4; see also 118v, 121; Add. Mss. 35,151, f. 269.
10. Correspondence between Place and Fowler, 25 May to 6 June 1836, Place Coll., Set 53, sect. A, pp. 7−10.
11. Add. Mss. 35,151, ff. 104v−105, 160v−161; Place Coll., Set 52, pp. 290−441; Add. Mss. 27,810, f. 124; Kirby and Musson, *op. cit.,* pp. 309−10.
12. Place to Morton, 2 April 1836, Add. Mss. 35,150, ff. 116v−117; Morton to Place and reply, 14 June 1836, Place Coll., Set 32, pp. 223−5.

13. On the formation of the LWMA see Prothero, *op. cit.,* pp. 310–3.
14. Add. Mss. 27,819, ff. 32–42; Add. Mss. 35,150, ff. 210, 271; Place to Mrs Grote, 8 November 1837, Add. Mss. 35,151, f. 28; see also ff. 34–7, 101–2; Place Coll., Set 55, p. 551. On the Charter and London Chartism see Prothero, *op. cit.,* chs. 16 and 17; D.J. Rowe, 'The London Working Men's Association and the "People's Charter", *Past and Present,* No. 36 (1967), pp. 73–86; reply by Prothero and rejoinder by Rowe, No. 38, pp. 169–76; Rowe, 'The Failure of London Chartism', *Historical Journal,* XI (1968), pp. 472–87; D. Goodway, *London Chartism 1838–1848* (1982).
15. Add. Mss. 35,150, f. 192v; Add. Mss. 27,819, ff. 195–204.
16. Add. Mss. 27,820, ff. 4–5, 7.
17. Add. Mss. 27,796, pt. 2, ff. 292–6; Add. Mss. 35,151, ff. 85, 207; Add. Mss. 27,820, ff. 184–5.
18. Add. Mss. 27,835, ff. 117–9; Add. Mss. 27,820, ff. 200–1, 218–9; Add. Mss. 35,151, ff. 83–6, 90–2, 96v.
19. Add. Mss. 27,821, ff. 36v, 37v, 38v; Place to Lovett, 13 March 1839, Add. Mss. 35,151, ff. 146v, 148.
20. Add. Mss. 27,820, f. 137; Pitkethly to Place, 31 May 1843, Place Coll., Set 56, vol. 22 (May–August 1843), pp. 317–9; Add. Mss. 27,819, f. 116.
21. Add. Mss. 35,150, f. 224; Place to Moore, 14 April 1841, Add. Mss. 35,151, f. 322v; Place to Gotobed, 6 August 1840, Set 56, vol. 13 (January–April 1841), p. 14. On Place's efforts to help Lovett, see Place Coll., Set 55.
22. Place Coll., Set 55, pp. 332, 532–5, 709–10; Lovett, *op. cit.,* p. 236; Place Coll., Set 56, vol. 15 (September–December 1841), p. 189.
23. *Northern Liberator,* 30 December 1837. Place had helped to secure the release of the brother of the editor, A.H. Beaumont, from prison in Paris (Add. Mss. 27,819, ff. 218–9).
24. Place to Collins, 22 January 1842, Add. Mss. 35,151, f. 357v; Pitkethly to Place, 11 June 1840, Set 56, vol. 10 (May–September 1840), p. 130; Moore to Place, 20 October 1839, Place Coll., Set 55, pp. 121–3. On Place's efforts for political prisoners see Add. Mss. 37,949, ff. 408–13; Add. Mss. 35,151, ff. 161, 179, 195–207, 227–9, 255–62, 327–9, 338–40, 356–9; Place Coll., Set 55; Set 52, pp. 277–9; Set 53, sect. C; Set 56, vols for September 1839 to August 1841.
25. Place Coll., Set 55, p. 555; D. Large, 'William Lovett', in P. Hollis (ed.), *Pressure from Without in Early Victorian England* (1974), p. 107; Place Coll., Set 56, vol. 10 (May–September 1840), p. 343; Add. Mss. 35,151, ff. 360–1.
26. Place Coll., Set 56, vol. 11 (October 1840–February 1841), pt 2 (of 1 vol.); vol. 14 (May–August 1841), p. 204; Place to Gaskell, 29 February 1840, Add. Mss. 35,151, f. 229v; Place to Thompson, 21 August 1842, Add. Mss. 37,949, f. 437v.
27. Place to Gaskell, 1 March 1840, Add. Mss. 35,151, f. 230; Place to Lovett, 15 June 1840, Place Coll., Set 55, pp. 588, 593; Add. Mss. 27,810, f. 166.
28. Add. Mss. 27,820, ff. 5–6, 10.
29. Add. Mss. 27,819, ff. 8–9.
30. Place Coll., Set 56, vol. 11 (October 1840–February 1841), pt 2 (of 1 vol.), pp. 57–62.
31. Prothero, *op. cit.,* p. 219; Add. Mss. 35,147, f. 72.
32. Place to Thompson, 10 March 1840, Place to Cobden, 4 March 1840, Add. Mss. 35,151, ff. 234, 230v; Place to Lovett, 15 June 1840, Place Coll., Set 55, p. 591. On MACLA see Place Coll., Set 7; Add. Mss. 27,822, ff. 152–63; Add. Mss. 35,151, ff. 231–7, 271–6, 283–4, 323v, 348–52. In March 1840 MACLA published a pamphlet by Place, *Observations on a Pamphlet Relating to the Corn Laws . . . by the Rev. Thomas Farr,* Place Coll., Set 7, vol. 1 (1814–1840), between pp. 310–1.

33. Cobden to Place, 5 October 1840, Place to Collins, 2 March 1841, Place to Wilson, 8 September 1841, Add. Mss. 35,151, ff. 283, 323v, 348; Place Coll., Set 7, vol. 5 (March–September 1842), pp. 97–8.
34. Place to Taylor, 14 July 1840, Add. Mss. 35,151, f. 262v.
35. Add. Mss. 35,151, ff. 249–51, 297–314.
36. Place to Collins, c.14 April 1841, Add. Mss. 35,151, f. 326v.
37. Sidney Smith seized on the argument for giving corn law repeal priority, and published a long extract from the paper in the *Free Trader,* 2 April 1842, Add. Mss. 27,810, ff. 165–6.
38. On the MPRA see Add. Mss. 27 810.
39. Place to Thompson, 10 March 1840, Add. Mss. 35,151, f. 235; Thompson to Place, 2 and 8 April 1842, Add. Mss. 27,810, ff. 169, 190. The quarrel was over the Marylebone by-election, in which Hume backed William Ewart against Thompson as the radical candidate. According to Thompson, when he and his friends turned up to a meeting for Ewart, Hume persuaded them to leave by telling them that it was a private one, and then announced it as a public meeting to choose the radical candidate. Thompson was humiliated in the contest, receiving a derisory vote.
40. Harrison to Place, c.10 April 1842, Place to Thompson, 20 March 1843, Add. Mss. 35,151, ff. 115–6, 369; R.K. Huch, 'Francis Place and the Chartists: Promise and Disillusion', *The Historian,* vol. 45 (1983), p. 507; Add. Mss. 27,796, f. 292.
41. MPs included Roebuck, Hume, Leader, William Williams, Elphinstone, Bowring, Ewart, O'Connell; Chartists: George Huggett, Henry Mitchell, J.D. Stiles, Richard Cray.
42. Add. Mss. 27,817, f. 149.
43. A. Wilson, 'The Suffrage Movement', in Hollis, *Pressure from Without, op. cit.,* pp. 83–93.
44. Place to M.I. Brunel, 27 January 1839, Add. Mss. 35,151, f. 127v; Add. Mss. 35,144, f. 424; Parkes to Place, 10 November 1848, Add. Mss. 35,151, ff. 388–9.
45. Add. Mss. 35,144, ff. 130v–131.
46. Place to Cobden, 29 June 1846, Add. Mss. 35,151, f. 382v; Place Coll., Set 48, vol. 1; Wilson, in Hollis (ed.), *Pressure from Without, op. cit.,* pp. 94–8.
47. Place Coll., Set 51, pp. 225–43; Place Coll., Set 40, vol. 1, Introduction; Holyoake, *op. cit.,* vol. 1, pp. 216–8; Place to Grote, 28 February 1850, Add. Mss. 35,151, f. 408; Lovett, *op. cit.,* p. 164.

CHAPTER 14

1. Holyoake, *op. cit.,* vol. 1, p. 216; Add. Mss. 27,798, f. 4.
2. Place to Lovett, 15 June 1840, Place Coll., Set 55, p. 594.
3. E.g. Thomas Hardy, John Bone, Colonel Despard, William Frend, Philip Mallet, Lord Folkestone, Jones Burdett, John Miers, Thomas Evans Junior, Mrs Sarah Austin, Richard Hassell, Harriet Martineau, Mrs Harriet Grote, James Watson, Joshua Scholefield, Robert Dale Owen, Samuel Harrison, Peter Taylor, Richard Cobden.
4. See for example Place's evidence to the Select Committee on Education, 1835, Minutes of Evidence, pp. 67–90.
5. Mrs Grote to Place, 23 May 1836, Add. Mss. 35,144, f. 369v.
6. Harrison's notes on Place's autobiography, 1842, Add. Mss. 35,144, f. 393.

7. Jones to Place, 24 January 1833, Add. Mss. 35,149, f. 213v; S.J. Reid, *Life and Letters of the First Earl of Durham 1792–1840* (1906), vol. 1, pp. 346–7; *Northern Liberator*, 30 December 1837; Ratcliffe and Chaloner, *op. cit.*, p. 49.
8. *Autobiography*, p. 249; Thomas, *op. cit.*, pp. 36–7.
9. Add. Mss. 27,790, f. 34; A. Brundage, *The Making of the New Poor Law: The politics of inquiry, enactment and implementation, 1832–39* (1978).
10. Place to John Sadler, 31 October 1835, Place Coll., Set 52, p. 117; Set 56, vol. 13 (January–April 1841), p. 259; Add. Mss. 27,796, f. 55.
11. Place to Lovett, 15 June 1840, Place Coll., Set 55, pp. 591–2.
12. Place to Hoare, 19 December 1839, Add. Mss. 35,144, ff. 429v–430.
13. *Twopenny Dispatch*, 4 June 1836, Place Coll., Set 56, vol. 1 (1836–May 1838), p. 3.
14. Place to Grote, 9 March 1839, Add. Mss. 35,151, f. 145v.
15. Place to Martineau, 4 March 1834, Add. Mss. 35,149, ff. 275v, 278; Place to Lovett, 4 June 1840, Place Coll., Set 55, p. 572.
16. Add. Mss. 27,816, f. 258; Add. Mss. 35,144, ff. 347v, 357, 399.
17. C.R. Dod, *Electoral Facts from 1832 to 1853 Impartially Stated,* ed. H.J. Hanham (1972), Editor's Introduction.
18. Place to Rogers, 15 January 1832, Place Coll., Set 68, item 22.

Bibliography

Place of publication is London unless otherwise stated.

Abrahams, Gerald, *Trade Unions and the Law* (Cassell, 1968).

Aspinall, Arthur, *Lord Brougham and the Whig Party* (University of Manchester Press, Manchester, 1927).

—— *Politics and the Press c.1780–1850* (Home & Van Thal, 1949).

—— 'The Westminster Election of 1814', *English Historical Review,* XL (1925), pp. 562–9.

—— (ed.), *Three Early Nineteenth Century Diaries* (Williams & Norgate, 1952).

Bahmueller, Charles F., *The National Charity Company: Jeremy Bentham's silent revolution* (University of California Press, 1981).

Bailyn, Bernard, *The Ideological Origins of the American Revolution* (Belknap, Cambridge, Mass., 1967).

Bain, Alexander, *James Mill. A biography* (Longmans, 1882).

—— *John Stuart Mill. A criticism with personal recollections* (Longmans, 1882).

Bamford, Samuel, *Passages in the Life of a Radical,* ed. and intro. W.H. Chaloner (Frank Cass, 1967).

Banks, Joseph A., *Prosperity and Parenthood: family planning among the Victorian middle classes* (Routledge & Kegan Paul, 1954).

—— and Banks, Olive, *Feminism and Family Planning in Victorian England* (Liverpool University Press, Liverpool, 1964).

Belchem, John, *'Orator' Hunt: Henry Hunt and English working-class radicalism* (Clarendon Press, Oxford, 1985).

Bentham, Jeremy, 'Situation and Relief of the Poor', *Annals of Agriculture and Other Useful Arts,* vol. 29 (1797), pp. 393–426.

—— *Jeremy Bentham's Economic Writings,* ed. W. Stark, vol. 1 (Allen & Unwin, 1952).

—— *The Theory of Legislation,* ed. C.K. Ogden (Kegan Paul, 1931).

Best, G.F.A., 'The Religious Difficulties of National Education in England, 1800–1870', *Cambridge Historical Journal,* XII (1956) pp. 155–63.

Binns, John, *Recollections of the Life of John Binns* (The Author,

Philadelphia, 1854).

Black, Eugene C., *The Association: British extraparliamentary political organisation 1769–1793* (Harvard University Press, Cambridge, Mass., 1963).

Boner, Harold A., *Hungry Generations: the nineteenth century case against Malthusianism* (King's Crown Press, New York, 1955).

Brailsford, Henry N., *Shelley, Godwin and their Circle* (Williams & Norgate, 1913).

Branca, Patricia, *Silent Sisterhood: middle-class women in the Victorian home* (Croom Helm, 1975).

Briggs, Asa, 'The Background of the Parliamentary Reform Movement in Three English Cities 1830–32', *Cambridge Historical Journal,* X (1950), pp. 293–317.

—— *The Age of Improvement 1780–1867* (Longmans, 1959).

—— (ed.), *Chartist studies* (Macmillan, 1959).

—— and Saville, J. (eds), *Essays in Labour History in Memory of G.D.H. Cole* (Macmillan, 1960).

Brock, Michael, *The Great Reform Act* (Hutchinson, 1973).

Broughton, Lord, see J.C. Hobhouse.

Brown, Ford K., *The Life of William Godwin* (Dent, 1926).

Brown, Philip A., *The French Revolution in English history* (Allen and Unwin, 1923).

Brundage, Anthony, *The Making of the New Poor Law. The politics of inquiry, enactment and implementation, 1832–39* (Hutchinson, 1978).

Burke, Edmund, *Reflections on the Revolution in France,* ed. Conor Cruise O'Brien (Penguin, Harmondsworth, 1969).

Burn, John S., *The Fleet Registers . . .* (Rivingtons, 1833).

Burnett, Timothy A.J., *The Rise and Fall of a Regency Dandy: The life and times of Scrope Berdmore Davies* (John Murray, 1981).

Butler, James R.M., *The Passing of the Great Reform Bill* (Longmans, 1914).

Cannon, John A., *Parliamentary Reform 1640–1832* (Cambridge University Press, Cambridge, 1973).

Carlile, Richard, *Every Woman's Book, or What is Love?* (4th edn, 1826, unnumbered edn, 1838).

Cartwright, Frances D., *The Life and Correspondence of Major John Cartwright* (2 vols, Henry Colburn, 1826).

Cartwright, John, *Address . . . to the Electors of Westminster* (1818).

—— *Address to the Electors of Westminster* (1819).

Cestre, Charles, *John Thelwall* (Swan Sonnenschein, 1906).

Christie, Ian R., *Wilkes, Wyvill and Reform: The parliamentary reform movement in British politics 1760–1785* (Macmillan, 1962).

—— *Wars and Revolutions: Britain 1760–1815* (Edward Arnold, 1982).

Clapham, John H., *An Economic History of Modern Britain: the early railway age* (2nd edn, Cambridge University Press, Cambridge, 1930).

Clarke, Martin L., *George Grote. A biography* (University of

London, 1962).

Cobban, Alfred (ed.), *The Debate on the French Revolution 1789–1800* (Nicholas Kaye, 1950).

Cole, George D.H., *Life of William Cobbett* (Collins, 1924).

—— *Robert Owen* (Ernest Benn, 1925).

—— and Filson, A.W. (eds), *British Working Class Movements: select documents 1789–1875* (Macmillan, 1967).

—— and Postgate, R., *The Common People 1746–1938* (Methuen, 1938).

Collini, Stefan, Winch, Donald and Burrow, John, *That Noble Science of Politics. A study in nineteenth-century intellectual history* (Cambridge University Press, 1983).

Cook, Chris and Stevenson, John, *The Longman Handbook of Modern British History 1714–1980* (Longmans, 1983).

Copinger, Walter A., *The authorship of the first hundred numbers of the 'Edinburgh Review'* (Priory Press, Manchester, 1895).

Davis, Henry W.C., *The Age of Grey and Peel* (Clarendon Press, Oxford, 1929).

Derry, T.K., 'The Repeal of the Apprenticeship Clauses of the Statute of Apprentices', *Economic History Review,* III (1931–32), pp. 67–85.

Dickinson, Harry T., *Liberty and Property: political ideology in eighteenth-century Britain* (Weidenfeld & Nicolson, 1977).

Dinwiddy, J.R., ' "The Patriotic Linen Draper": Robert Waithman and the Revival of Radicalism in the City of London 1795–1818', *Bulletin of the Institute of Historical Research,* 46 (1973) pp. 72–94.

—— 'Bentham's Transition to Political Radicalism 1809–10', *Journal of the History of Ideas,* 36 (1975), pp. 683–700.

—— 'Christopher Wyvill and Reform, 1790–1820', York University *Borthwick Paper,* no. 39 (1971).

Dod, Charles R., *Electoral Facts from 1832 to 1853 Impartially Stated,* ed. and intro. H.J. Hanham (Harvester, Brighton, 1972).

Elliott, Marianne, *Partners in Revolution: The United Irishmen and France* (Yale University Press, 1982).

—— 'The "Despard Conspiracy" reconsidered', *Past and Present,* no. 75 (May 1977), pp. 46–61.

Emsley, Clive, 'The London "Insurrection" of December 1792: Fact, Fiction, or Fantasy?', *The Journal of British Studies,* XVII (1978), pp. 66–86.

—— *British Society and the French Wars, 1793–1815* (Macmillan, 1979).

Encyclopaedia Britannica, Supplement to the 4th, 5th and 6th editions (Constable, Edinburgh, 1824).

Epstein, James and Thompson, Dorothy (eds), *The Chartist Experience: studies in working-class radicalism and culture 1830–1860* (Macmillan, 1982).

Erskine, Thomas, *A Short Defence of the Whigs from the Imputations attempted to be cast upon them during the late Election for Westminster* (1819).

—— *A Letter . . . to 'An Elector of Westminster'* (1819).

Ervine, St John G., *Francis Place the Tailor of Charing Cross*, Fabian Tract no. 165 (The Fabian Society, 1912).

Eversley, David E.C., *Social Theories of Fertility and the Malthusian Debate* (Clarendon Press, Oxford, 1959).

Ferguson, H., 'The Birmingham Political Union and the Government 1831–32', *Victorian Studies*, 3 (1960), pp. 262–76.

Field, J.A., 'The Early Propagandist Movement in English Population Theory', *Bulletin of the American Economic Association*, 4th series, vol. 1, no. 2 (1911), pp. 207–36.

Finer, Samuel E., *The Life and Times of Sir Edwin Chadwick* (Methuen, 1952).

Flick, Carlos, *The Birmingham Political Union and the Movements for Reform in Britain 1830–1839* (Dawson, Folkestone, 1978).

Fraser, P., 'Public Petitioning and Parliament before 1832', *History* (1961), pp. 195–211.

The Friends of Liberty, *A Letter . . . to the Members of the London Corresponding Society*, 6 April 1795.

Fryer, Peter, *The Birth Controllers* (Secker & Warburg, 1965).

Garratt, Geoffrey T., *Lord Brougham* (Macmillan, 1935).

Gash, Norman, *Aristocracy and People: Britain 1815–1865* (Edward Arnold, 1979).

——— *Mr Secretary Peel: The Life of Sir Robert Peel to 1830* (Longmans, 1961).

George, Mary D., *London Life in the Eighteenth Century* (rev. edn, Penguin, Harmondsworth, 1966).

Glass, David V. (ed.), *Introduction to Malthus* (Watts, 1953).

Godard, John G., *George Birkbeck, the pioneer of popular education* (Bemrose, 1884).

Godwin, William, *Enquiry Concerning Political Justice* (1st edn, 1793; 3rd edn, 1798, ed. and intro. Isaac Kramnick, Penguin, Harmondsworth, 1976).

——— *Of Population. An enquiry concerning the power of increase in the numbers of mankind, being an answer to Mr Malthus's essay on that subject* (Longmans, 1820).

——— *Thoughts Occasioned by the Perusal of Dr Parr's Spital Sermon . . .* (Robinson, 1801).

Goldstone, J.A., 'The Demographic Revolution in England: a re-examination', *Population Studies*, vol. 40 (1986), pp. 5–33.

Goodway, David, *London Chartism 1838–1848* (Cambridge University Press, Cambridge, 1982).

Goodwin, Albert, *The Friends of Liberty: the English democratic movement in the age of the French Revolution* (Hutchinson, 1979).

Gordon, Linda, *Woman's Body, Woman's Right: a social history of birth control in America* (Penguin, Harmondsworth, 1977).

Grebenik, E., 'Origins of the birth control movement in Great Britain', *The Rationalist Annual for the Year 1961*, pp. 55–65.

Griffith, Grosvenor T., *Population Problems of the Age of Malthus* (2nd edn, Frank Cass, 1967).

Gronow, Captain Rees H., *The Reminiscences of Captain Gronow* (Folio Society edn, 1977).

Grylls, Rosalie G., *William Godwin and his World* (Odhams, 1953).

Hackwood, Frederick W., *William Hone: his life and times* (Fisher Unwin, 1912).

Halévy, Elie, *The Growth of Philosophic Radicalism,* trans. M. Morris (Faber & Gwyer, 1928).

—— A History of the English People in the Nineteenth Century, vol. 1, *England in 1815,* trans. E.I. Watkin and D.A. Barker; vol. 2, *The Liberal Awakening 1815–1830,* trans E.I. Watkin (2nd edns, Ernest Benn, 1949).

—— *Thomas Hodgskin,* trans. A.J. Taylor (Ernest Benn, 1956).

Hamburger, Joseph, *Intellectuals in Politics: John Stuart Mill and the philosophic radicals* (Yale University Press, 1965).

—— *James Mill and the Art of Revolution* (Yale University Press, 1963).

Hammond, John L. and Barbara, *The Town Labourer 1760–1832* (Longmans, 1917).

Hardy, Thomas, *Memoir of Thomas Hardy* (1832).

Harrison, B.H., 'Two Roads to Social Reform: Francis Place and the "Drunken Committee" of 1834', *Historical Journal,* XI (1968), pp. 272–300.

Harrison, Ross, *Bentham* (Routledge & Kegan Paul, 1983).

Hart, Herbert L.A., *Essays on Bentham: studies on jurisprudence and political theory* (Clarendon, Oxford, 1982).

Harvey, A.D., *Britain in the Early Nineteenth Century* (Batsford, 1978).

Henriques, Ursula R.Q., *Before the Welfare State: social administration in early industrial Britain* (Longmans, 1979).

Himes, Norman, 'The Birth Control Handbills of 1823', *The Lancet,* vol. ccxiii (6 August 1927), pp. 313–6.

—— 'Benjamin Franklin on Population: a re-examination with special reference to the influence of Franklin on Francis Place', *Economic History,* vol. iii (1934–7), pp. 388–98.

—— 'Jeremy Bentham and the Genesis of English Neo-Malthusianism', *Economic History,* vol. iii (1934–7), pp. 267–76.

—— 'John Stuart Mill's Attitude towards Neo-Malthusianism', *Economic History,* vol. i (1926–9), pp. 457–84.

—— *Medical History of Contraception* (Allen and Unwin, 1936).

—— 'The Place of John Stuart Mill and Robert Owen in the History of English Neo-Malthusianism', *Quarterly Journal of Economics,* vol. xlii, no. 4 (August 1928), pp. 627–40.

—— 'Robert Dale Owen, the Pioneer of American Neo-Malthusianism', *American Journal of Sociology,* vol. xxxv (1930), pp. 529–47.

History of Two Act . . . (1796).

Hobhouse, John C. (Lord Broughton), *Recollections of a Long Life,* ed. Lady Dorchester (6 vols, John Murray, 1909).

[–] *A Defence of the People in reply to Lord Erskine's Two Defences of the Whigs* (1819).

[–] *A Trifling Mistake in Lord Erskine's Recent Preface corrected . . .* (1819).

────── *Proceedings in the House of Commons, and in the Court of King's-Bench, relative to the author of the 'Trifling Mistake'* . . . (1820).

Hobsbawm, Eric, J., *The Age of Revolution: Europe 1789–1848* (Weidenfeld and Nicolson, 1962).

────── *Industry and Empire: an economic history of Britain since 1750* (Weidenfeld and Nicolson, 1968).

────── *Primitive Rebels (studies in archaic forms of social movement in the 19th and 20th centuries)* (Manchester University Press, Manchester, 1959).

────── 'The Social Functions of the Past: Some Questions', *Past and Present,* 55 (1972), pp. 3–17.

Hodgson, Richard, *Proceedings of the General Committee of the London Corresponding Society . . . on the 5th, 12th and 19th April 1798* (Newgate, 1798).

Hollis, Patricia, *The Pauper Press: a study in working-class radicalism of the 1830s* (Oxford University Press, 1970).

────── (ed.), *Class and Conflict in Nineteenth-Century England 1815–1850* (Routledge and Kegan Paul, 1973).

────── (ed.), *Pressure from without in Early Victorian England* (Edward Arnold, 1974).

Holyoake, George J., *Sixty Years of an Agitator's Life* (2 vols, 3rd edn, Unwin, 1893).

────── 'Mysterious Papers. An Unpublished Story of Facts', *The Present Day,* vol. 3 (1886), pp. 77–9.

Hone, J. Ann, *For the Cause of Truth: radicalism in London 1796–1821* (Clarendon Press, Oxford, 1982).

────── 'William Hone (1780–1842), publisher and bookseller: an approach to early nineteenth century London radicalism', *Historical Studies,* 16 (1974), pp. 55–70.

Hone, William, *The Every-Day Book* . . . (2 vols, William Hone, 1825).

Horner, Francis, *Memoirs and Correspondence of Francis Horner MP,* ed. L. Horner (2 vols, John Murray, 1843).

Hovell, Mark, *The Chartist Movement* (Victoria University, Manchester, 1918).

Howell, Thomas B. and T.J. (eds), *State Trials,* vols 24 and 26 (1818).

Huch, R.K., 'Francis Place and the Chartists: Promise and Disillusion', *The Historian,* vol. 45 (1983), pp. 497–512.

Hume, L.J., *Bentham and bureaucracy* (Cambridge University Press, Cambridge, 1981).

Hunt, Henry, *Memoirs of Henry Hunt esq. Written by himself* (2 vols, 1820).

Jaeger, Muriel, *Before Victoria: changing standards and behaviour 1787–1837* (Penguin, Harmondsworth, 1967).

James, Patricia, *Population Malthus: his life and times* (Routledge and Kegan Paul, 1979).

Jephson, Henry, *The Platform: its rise and progress* (2 vols, Macmillan, 1892).

Johnson, Leonard G., *General T. Perronet Thompson, 1783–1869:*

his military, literary and political campaigns (Allen and Unwin, 1957).

Jones, John Gale, *Sketch of a Political Tour Through Rochester, Chatham, Maidstone, Gravesend, &c.* (1796).

Joyce, Michael, *My Friend H: John Cam Hobhouse, Baron Broughton of Broughton de Gyfford* (John Murray, 1948).

Kelly, Thomas, *George Birkbeck: pioneer of adult education* (Liverpool University Press, Liverpool, 1957).

—— *A History of Adult Education in Great Britain* (rev. edn, Liverpool University Press, Liverpool, 1970).

—— *Radical Tailor: The Life and Work of Francis Place. Bicentenary Lecture at Birkbeck College* (Birkbeck College, 1972).

Kirby, Raymond G. and Musson, A.E., *The Voice of the People: John Doherty, 1798–1854, trade unionist, radical and factory reformer* (Manchester University Press, Manchester, 1975).

Knight, Frida, *University Rebel: the life of William Frend (1757–1841)* (Gollancz, 1971).

Knight, P., 'Women and Abortion in Victorian and Edwardian England', *History Workshop,* 4 (Autumn 1977), pp. 57–69.

Kriegel, Abraham D. (ed. and intro.), *The Holland House Diaries 1831–1840* (Routledge and Kegan Paul, 1977).

Langer, W.L., 'Origins of the Birth Control Movement in England in the early nineteenth century', *Journal of Interdisciplinary History,* vol. 5 (1975), pp. 669–86.

Linton, William J., *Memories* (Lawrence and Bullen, 1895).

—— *James Watson. A Memoir* (Heywood, Manchester, 1880).

Lloyd, Charles C., *Lord Cochrane* (Longmans, 1947).

Locke, Don, *A Fantasy of Reason: the life and thought of William Godwin* (Routledge and Kegan Paul, 1980).

London Corresponding Society, *An Account of the Seizure of Citizen Thomas Hardy* [c.July 1794].

—— *Address of the London Corresponding Society to the other Societies of Great Britain, united for obtaining a Reform in Parliament,* 29 November 1792.

—— *Addresses and Regulations,* May 1792.

—— *The Correspondence of the London Corresponding Society* (1795).

—— *Report of the Committee of Constitution of the London Corresponding Society* [early 1794].

—— *Revised Report of the Committee of Constitution of the London Corresponding Society* [early 1794].

—— *Selections from the Papers of the London Corresponding Society 1792–1799,* ed. and intro. Mary Thale (Cambridge University Press, Cambridge, 1983).

Lovett, William, *The Life and Struggles of William Lovett* (1876).

McCleary, George F., *The Malthusian Population Theory* (Faber and Faber, 1953).

Maccoby, Simon, *English Radicalism 1786–1832* (Allen and Unwin, 1955).

Mack, Mary P., *Jeremy Bentham: an odyssey of ideas 1748–1792* (Heinemann, 1962).

McLaren, Angus, *Birth control in Nineteenth-century England* (Croom Helm, 1978).

Main, J.M., 'Radical Westminster 1807–1820', *Historical Studies,* vol. 12 (1965–67), pp. 186–204.

Malthus, Thomas, *An Essay on the Principle of Population* (1st edn, 1798, 5th edn, 1817).

Marlow, Joyce, *The Tolpuddle Martyrs* (Andre Deutsch, 1971).

Marrs, Edwin W., (ed.), *The Letters of Charles and Mary Anne Lamb,* vol. 2 (Cornell University Press, 1976).

Marshall, Peter H., *William Godwin* (Yale University Press, 1984).

Mazlish, Bruce, *James and John Stuart Mill: father and son in the nineteenth century* (Hutchinson, 1975).

Micklewright, F.H.A., 'The Rise and Decline of English Neo-Malthusianism', *Population Studies,* vol. xv (1961), pp. 32–51.

Mill, John Stuart, *Autobiography* (Columbia University Press, New York, 1924).

—— *The Early Draft of John Stuart Mill's Autobiography,* ed. J. Stillinger (University of Illinois Press, Urbana, 1961).

—— *The Earlier Letters of John Stuart Mill 1812–1848,* ed. F.E. Mineka, *Collected Works,* vol. 12 (Routledge and Kegan Paul, 1963).

Miller, N.C., 'Major John Cartwright and the founding of the Hampden Club', *Historical Journal,* XVII (1974), pp. 615–19.

—— 'John Cartwright and radical parliamentary reform 1808–1819', *English Historical Review,* vol. LXXXIII (1968), pp. 705–28.

Mitchell, Austin, *The Whigs in Opposition 1815–1830* (Clarendon Press, Oxford, 1967).

Namier, Lewis, *The Structure of Politics at the Accession of George III* (2nd edn, Macmillan, 1957).

New, Chester W., *The Life of Henry Brougham to 1830* (Clarendon Press, Oxford, 1961).

Newbould, I.D.C., 'Whiggery and the Dilemma of Reform: Liberals, Radicals and the Melbourne Administration, 1835–1839', *Bulletin of the Institute of Historical Research,* vol. LIII (1980), pp. 229–41.

O'Gorman, Frank, *The Whig Party and the French Revolution* (Macmillan, 1967).

—— *The Rise of Party in England: the Rockingham Whigs 1760–1782* (Allen and Unwin, 1975).

Osborne, John, *John Cartwright* (Cambridge University Press, 1972).

Owen, Robert, *The Life of Robert Owen, written by himself* (1857).

—— *Lectures on the Marriages of the Priesthood of the Old Immoral World . . .* (4th edn, Hobson, Leeds, 1840).

Owen, Robert D., *Moral Physiology* (1st English edn, James Watson, 1832).

Packe, Michael St J., *The Life of John Stuart Mill* (Secker and Warburg, 1954).

Paine, Thomas, *Rights of Man,* ed. H. Collins, (Penguin, Harmondsworth, 1969).

Pares, Richard, *King George III and the Politicians* (Clarendon Press, Oxford, 1953).

Parssinen, T.M., 'The Revolutionary Party in London 1816–1820', *Bulletin of the Institute of Historical Research,* vol. xlv (1972), pp. 266–82.

—— 'Association, Convention and anti-Parliament in British Radical Politics 1771–1848', *English Historical Review,* 88 (1973), pp. 504–33.

Patterson, Melville W., *Sir Francis Burdett and His Times 1770–1844* (2 vols, Macmillan, 1931).

Peacock, A.E., 'The Successful Prosecution of the Factory Acts, 1833–55', *Economic History Review,* vol. 37 (1984), pp. 197–210.

Peel, J., 'Birth Control and the British Working Class Movement. A Bibliographical Review', *Bulletin of the Society for the Study of Labour History,* no. 7, Autumn 1963, pp. 16–22.

Petersen, William, *Malthus* (Heinemann, 1979).

Place, Francis, *The Autobiography of Francis Place,* ed. with an intro. and notes by Mary Thale (Cambridge University Press, Cambridge, 1972).

—— *A Brief Examination of the Dramatic Patents* (1834).

[——] *An Essay on the State of the Country in respect to the Condition and Conduct of the Husbandry Labourers and to the consequences likely to result therefrom* (1831).

[——] *The Examiner and the Tax on Newspapers* (Place Coll., Set 70, p. 423, 1836).

—— *Illustrations and Proofs of the Principle of Population* (Longmans, 1822), reprinted with an introduction and appendices by Norman Himes (Allen and Unwin, 1930).

—— *Improvement of the Working Class. Drunkenness – Education.* (1834)

[——] *A Letter to a Minister of State respecting Taxes on Knowledge* (1831).

—— *A Letter to the Electors of Westminster* (1832).

[——] *The Mystery of the Sinking Fund Explained . . .* (1821).

[——] *A New Way to Pay Old Debts: or observations on the reports made to the subscribers to the rebuilding of the Theatre Royal, Drury-Lane* (1812).

[——] *Observations on a Pamphlet Relating to the Corn Laws by the Rev. Thomas Farr* (1840) . . .

[——] *Observations on Mr Huskisson's Speech on the Laws Relating to Combinations of Workmen* (1825).

[——] *Observations on the volume just published entitled the 'Session of Parliament in 1825'* (1825).

[——] *On the Law of Libel; with strictures on the self-styled 'Constitutional Association'* (1823).

[——] (An Elector of Westminster), *Reply to Lord Erskine* (1819).

[——] *St Paul the Apostle, and William Campion: parallel between the cases of St Paul the Apostle and William Campion* (Carlile, 1824).

[——] *The Stamp Tax Bill* (Place Coll., Set 70, p. 424, 1836).

[—— and Hobhouse, J.C.], *An Authentic narrative of the events of the Westminster Election which commenced on Saturday, February 13th, and closed on Wednesday, March 3rd, 1819* (1819).

[—— and Richter, J.], *An Exposition of the Circumstances which gave rise to the Election of Sir Francis Burdett, Bart. for the City of Westminster* . . . (1807).

—— *London Radicalism 1830–1843. A Selection from the Papers of Francis Place,* ed. D.J. Rowe (London Record Society Publications, vol. 5, 1970).

Podmore, Frank, *Robert Owen: a biography* (2 vols, Hutchinson, 1906).

The Poll Book, for electing Two Representatives in Parliament for the City and Liberty of Westminster . . . (1818).

Poynter, John R., *Society and Pauperism: English ideas on poor relief 1795–1834* (Routledge and Kegan Paul, 1969).

Prochaska, A.M.S., 'Westminster Radicalism 1807–1832', Oxford University DPhil thesis, 1975.

Prothero, Iorwerth J., *Artisans and Politics in Early Nineteenth-century London: John Gast and his times* (Dawson, Folkestone, 1979).

—— 'Chartism in London', *Past and Present,* no. 44 (1969), pp. 76–105.

—— 'London Chartism and the Trades', *Economic History Review,* ser. 2, vol. 24 (1971), pp. 202–19.

—— Reply to Rowe's 'The London Working Men's Association and the People's Charter', *Past and Present,* no. 38 (1967), pp. 169–73.

Ratcliffe, Barrie M., and Chaloner, W.H., (trans and eds), *A French Sociologist looks at Britain: Gustave d'Eichtal and British society in 1828* (Manchester University Press, Manchester, 1977).

Reid, Stuart J., *Life and Letters of the First Earl of Durham 1792–1840* (2 vols, Longmans, 1906).

Reid, William H., *The Rise and Dissolution of the Infidel Societies in this Metropolis* (1800).

Reith, Charles, *The British Police and the Democratic Ideal* (Oxford University Press, 1943).

Ricardo, David, *The Works and Correspondence of David Ricardo,* ed. P. Sraffa and M.H. Dobb (11 vols, Cambridge University Press, Cambridge, 1951–73).

Robbins, Caroline, *The Eighteenth-Century Commonwealthsman* (Harvard University Press, Cambridge, Mass., 1959).

Roberts, Michael, *The Whig Party 1807–12* (Macmillan, 1939).

Robson, Robert (ed.), *Ideas and Institutions of Victorian Britain: essays in honour of George Kitson Clark* (Bell, 1967).

Roebuck, John A., *Life and Letters of John Arthur Roebuck,* ed. R.E. Leader (1897).

Rowe, D.J., 'Class and Political Radicalism in London 1831–32', *Historical Journal,* XIII (1970), pp. 31–47.

—— 'The Failure of London Chartism', *Historical Journal,* XI (1968), pp. 472–87.

—— 'Francis Place and the Historian', *Historical Journal,* XVI (1973), pp. 45–63.

—— 'The London Working Men's Association and the "People's Charter" ', *Past and Present,* no. 36 (1967), pp. 73–86; and rejoinder to

Prothero, no. 38, pp. 174–6.

Royle, Edward, *Victorian Infidels: The origins of the British secularist movement 1791–1866* (Manchester University Press, Manchester, 1974).

―――― and Walvin, J., *English Radicals and Reformers 1760–1848* (Harvester, Brighton, 1982).

Rudé, George, *Wilkes and Liberty. A social study of 1763 to 1774* (Clarendon Press, Oxford, 1962).

―――― *Hanoverian London 1714–1808* (Secker and Warburg, 1971).

Rudkin, Olive, *Thomas Spence and his Connections* (Allen and Unwin, 1927).

Sack, James J., *The Grenvillites: party politics and factionalism in the age of Pitt and Liverpool* (University of Illinois Press, 1979).

Saville, John (ed.), *Democracy and the Labour Movement* (Lawrence and Wishart, 1954).

Saxton, W.E., 'The Political Importance of the Westminster Committee of the Early Nineteenth Century', Edinburgh University PhD thesis, 1957.

Schwartz, Pedro, *The New Political Economy of J.S. Mill* (Weidenfeld and Nicolson, 1972).

Seaman, W.A.L., 'British Democratic Societies in the Period of the French Revolution', London University PhD thesis, 1954.

Sheppard, Francis, *London 1808–70: the infernal wen* (Secker and Warburg, 1971).

Shorter, E., 'Female emancipation, birth control and fertility in European history', *American Historical Review,* 78 (1973) pp. 605–40.

―――― *The Making of the Modern Family* (Collins, 1976).

Skultans, Vieda, *English Madness: ideas on insanity 1580–1890* (Routledge and Kegan Paul, 1979).

Spater, George, *William Cobbett: the poor man's friend* (2 vols, Cambridge University Press, Cambridge, 1982).

Spiers, Edward M., *Radical General: Sir George De Lacy Evans 1787–1870* (Manchester University Press, Manchester, 1983).

Steintrager, James, *Bentham* (Allen and Unwin, 1977).

Stephens, M.D. and Roderick, G.W., 'Science, the Working Classes and Mechanics' Institutes', *Annals of Science,* vol. 29 (1972), pp. 349–60.

Stevenson, John (ed.), *London in the Age of Reform* (Blackwell, Oxford, 1977).

Stopes, Marie, *Contraception* (3rd edn, Putnam, 1931).

Teitelbaum, Michael S., *The British Fertility Decline: demographic transition in the crucible of the industrial revolution* (Princeton University Press, Guildford, 1984).

Thomas, William, 'Francis Place and Working-Class History', *Historical Journal,* V (1962), pp. 61–70.

―――― *The Philosophic Radicals: nine studies in theory and practice, 1817–1841* (Clarendon Press, Oxford, 1979).

Thompson, Edward P., *The Making of the English Working Class* (rev. edn, Penguin, Harmondsworth, 1968).

Tooke, John Horne, *A Warning to the Electors of Westminster* (1807).

Veitch, George S., *The Genesis of Parliamentary Reform* (Constable,

1913).

Wallas, Graham, *The Life of Francis Place 1771–1854* (Longmans, 1898; rev. edn, Allen and Unwin, 1918).

Ward, John T., *Chartism* (Batsford, 1973).

—— and Fraser, W. Hamish (eds), *Workers and Employers: Documents on Trade Unions and Industrial Relations in Britain since the Eighteenth Century* (Macmillan, 1980).

Webb, Robert K., *The British Working-Class Reader 1790–1848; literary and social tensions* (Allen and Unwin, 1955).

—— *Modern England. From the eighteenth century to the present* (Longmans, 1969).

Webb, Sidney and Beatrice, *The History of Trade Unionism* (2nd edn, Longmans, 1920).

—— English Poor Law History, part 1, *The Old Poor Law,* Part 2, *The Last Hundred Years,* 2 vols (Longmans, 1929).

Wellesley, Arthur R. (ed.), *Despatches, Correspondence and Memoranda of the Duke of Wellington* (vol. 8 of continuation series, John Murray, 1880).

Wells, Roger, *Insurrection: the British experience 1795–1803* (Alan Sutton, Gloucester, 1983).

West, Julius, *A History of the Chartist Movement* (Constable, 1920).

Western, J.R., 'The Volunteer Movement as an Anti-Revolutionary Force 1793–1801', *English Historical Review,* 71 (1956), pp. 603–14.

Wickwar, William H., *The Struggle for the Freedom of the Press 1819–1832* (Allen and Unwin, 1928).

Wiener, Joel H., *Radicalism and Freethought in Nineteenth-century Britain: the life of Richard Carlile* (Greenwood, 1983).

—— *The War of the Unstamped: the movement to repeal the British newspaper tax 1830–1836* (Cornell University Press, 1969).

Williams, Gwyn A., *Artisans and Sans-Culottes, popular movements in France and Britain during the French Revolution* (Edward Arnold, 1968).

Williams, J.E., 'The British Standard of Living, 1750–1850', *Economic History Review,* series 2, vol. 19 (1966), pp. 581–9.

Woodcock, George, *William Godwin: a biographical study* (Porcupine, 1946).

Woodward, Ernest L., *The Age of Reform 1815–1870* (2nd edn, Clarendon Press, Oxford, 1962).

Wrigley, Edward A., 'The Growth of Population in Eighteenth-Century England: a Conundrum Resolved', *Past and Present,* No. 98 (1983), pp. 121–50.

—— 'Family Limitation in Pre-Industrial England', *Economic History Review,* series 2, vol. 19 (1966), pp. 82–109.

—— and Schofield, R.S., *The Population History of England 1541–1871. A reconstruction.* (Edward Arnold, 1981).

Zegger, Robert E., *John Cam Hobhouse: a political life 1819–1852* (University of Missouri Press, Columbia, 1973).

Ziegler, Philip, *Melbourne: a biography of William Lamb, 2nd Viscount Melbourne* (Collins, 1976).

Index

293